Praise for Jim Yardley's

BRAVE DRAGONS

"Remarkable. . . . *Brave Dragons* is about much more than basketball. It is about more than Weiss's adventures. It is a serious look at the deep divisions between American and Chinese cultures."
—*The Seattle Times*

"*Brave Dragons* is a winner—informative and conversational, occasionally funny and frequently suspenseful. . . . Yardley rewards readers with his close eye and felicitous prose. This book amounts to cultural catnip." —*The Plain Dealer*

"Exceptionally ambitious. . . . Yardley's observations of a country in transition are instructive, sometimes even poetic."
—*The Boston Globe*

"Entertaining, insightful, and extensively reported."
—*The New Republic*

"Yardley provides incisive accounts of basketball's history in China and of the NBA's desire to monetize its popularity there, alongside colorful portraits of the players and hangers-on."
—*The New Yorker*

"Entertaining. . . . Yardley presents basketball and young China's growing fascination with it as an apt, pacy metaphor for a China cautiously engaging with the West." —*Mint*

"*Brave Dragons* is thorough micro- and macro-history, capable of sucking in both the basketball-obsessed and the non-athletically inclined." —*The Onion*, A.V. Club (A–)

"Yardley strikes gold. . . . The Brave Dragons put together a decent season, and Yardley a memorable book."
—*Booklist*

"Unique. . . . Engaging. . . . A fantastically implausible, ultimately cautionary tale of how the Chinese and American ways often mix like oil and water."
—*Kirkus Reviews*

"Masterly. . . . *Brave Dragons* is a must-read for any hoops fans with a hankering to understand what is and isn't happening in China."
—*Slam*

"Entertaining, insightful, and extensively reported."
—*The New Republic*

"A reminder that U.S.–China relations is not always a government-to-government affair. . . . Jim Yardley does an amazing job of showing the compassion and humanity of each player on the Brave Dragons."
—*China Law and Policy*

JIM YARDLEY

BRAVE DRAGONS

Jim Yardley has worked as a journalist for *The New York Times* for the past fourteen years, including eight years as a foreign correspondent and bureau chief in China and India. His reportage on China's legal system won the 2006 Pulitzer Prize for International Reporting, which he shared with a colleague, Joseph Kahn. He has also won or shared numerous other awards, including the Overseas Press Club Award for best international environmental coverage and the Sigma Delta Chi Award for best foreign reporting from the Society of Professional Journalists. He lives in New Delhi with his wife, Theo, and their three children, Olivia, George, and Eddie.

BRAVE DRAGONS

BRAVE DRAGONS

A CHINESE BASKETBALL TEAM,

AN AMERICAN COACH, AND

TWO CULTURES CLASHING

山西中宇猛龙

JIM YARDLEY

VINTAGE BOOKS
A Division of Random House, Inc.
New York

FIRST VINTAGE BOOKS EDITION, JANUARY 2013

The Library of Congress has cataloged the Knopf edition as follows:
Yardley, Jim, [date]
Brave dragons : a Chinese basketball team,
an American coach, and two cultures clashing
Jim Yardley.—1st ed.
p. cm.
1. Shanxi Zhongyu Brave Dragons (Basketball team).
2. Basketball—China. 3. Social change—China.
4. Americans—China. I. Title.
GV885.52.S53Y37 2012
796.323'6409—dc23 201103514

Vintage ISBN: 978-0-307-47336-3

Author photograph © Ruth Fremson
Book design by Michael Collica
Map by Steven Shukow

Printed in the United States of America

FOR THEO

CONTENTS

CONTENTS

Teams in the Chinese Basketball Association usually have different English and Chinese names, which explains why the Shanxi Brave Dragons are more commonly known in China as the Shanxi Zhongyu. For the sake of this book, I've favored using the English names, when possible.

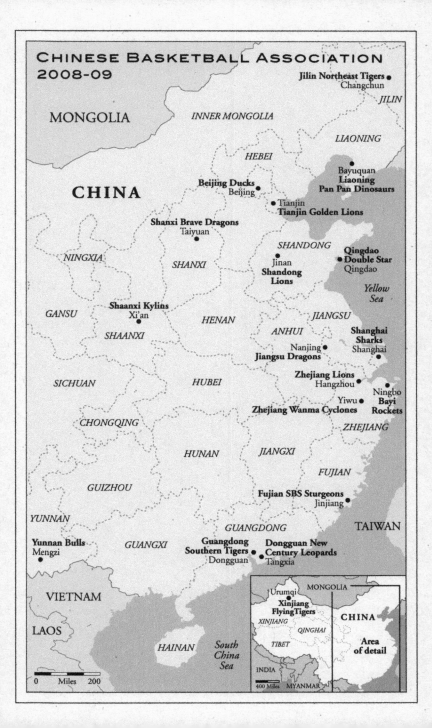

CHINESE BASKETBALL ASSOCIATION 2008-09

MONGOLIA

INNER MONGOLIA

Jilin Northeast Tigers •
Changchun

JILIN

LIAONING

HEBEI

CHINA

Beijing Ducks •
Beijing

Bayuquan •
**Liaoning
Pan Pan Dinosaurs**

• Tianjin
Tianjin Golden Lions

Shanxi Brave Dragons
Taiyuan •

SHANDONG

Jinan •
**Shandong
Lions**

**Qingdao
• Double Star**
Qingdao

*Yellow
Sea*

NINGXIA

SHANXI

GANSU

Shaanxi Kylins
Xi'an •

HENAN

JIANGSU

SHAANXI

ANHUI

Nanjing •
Jiangsu Dragons

**Shanghai
Sharks**
Shanghai •

SICHUAN

HUBEI

Zhejiang Lions
Hangzhou •

Ningbo •
Yiwu • **Bayi
Rockets**

CHONGQING

Zhejiang Wanma Cyclones

ZHEJIANG

HUNAN

JIANGXI

FUJIAN

GUIZHOU

Fujian SBS Sturgeons
Jinjiang •

YUNNAN

GUANGDONG

TAIWAN

Yunnan Bulls
Mengzi
•

GUANGXI

**Guangdong
Southern Tigers**
Dongguan •

**Dongguan New
Century Leopards**
Tangxia

VIETNAM

LAOS

HAINAN

*South
China
Sea*

0 Miles 200

Urumqi •
**Xinjiang
FlyingTigers**

MONGOLIA

XINJIANG

QINGHAI

CHINA

TIBET

**Area
of detail**

INDIA

400 Miles

MYANMAR

BRAVE DRAGONS

PROLOGUE
Summer 2008

Boss Wang's experiment was not working. From the moment he arrived in the mountains of western Oregon, he was displeased with what he saw on the court. He had sent his Chinese basketball team to America for a summer immersion program, figuring that since the best basketball was played in America, his players would improve there. So far, they were losing every game by 20 or 30 points against semipro teams on the West Coast. Boss Wang hated losing, truly *loathed* it, but the losing wasn't what most frustrated him now. What drove him crazy about his Chinese players was that they didn't play like Americans, no matter how hard he tried to alter their basketball DNA. In gathering up his team from central China and depositing them in the United States, Boss Wang thought the change in environment might help. But as he stood at the edge of the practice court, watching his Chinese coach run a scrimmage that seemed little different from a scrimmage in China, Boss Wang decided change was not happening fast enough.

Boss Wang was visiting the United States for the first time, having arrived in San Francisco after the eleven-hour flight from Beijing, and his son hoped he would spend a few weeks absorbing some American culture, maybe even drive cross-country. The son had hired a guide in Beijing who specialized in escorting Chinese bosses to America. The guide knew Chinese bosses liked to gamble in Vegas and tour the strip bars in L.A. The Statue of Liberty, the White House, and Disney World were perennials, too. He made the usual arrangements. But Boss Wang had little patience for any of that. He had a business deal to finalize back in China. He raced through six cities on both coasts in five days. In Portland, he bought a few pairs of $300 designer jeans. In Midtown Manhattan, he spent about $200,000 on jewelry. His biggest purchase was still pending. He was now convinced he needed to buy an American basketball coach.

Boss Wang was sixty-one, but looked younger, with tousled black hair that fell onto his forehead. He had a thick chest and thick hands, and his appearance was a little rough, unfinished. He didn't smile very often; he eyed most people as if they might take something from him. His son, Songyan, admitted that even now, as a grown man, he was still stopped cold by his father's glare, or by his father's voice when it splintered into sharp, angry edges. Boss Wang looked more like the son of a peasant farmer he was, rather than the steel baron he had become—one of the richest men in China. *Forbes* had estimated his wealth at roughly $260 million and ranked him as the country's 236th richest person, though gauging wealth with any precision is nearly impossible in China. What could indisputably be said was that money had showered down on China during the previous decade; it had sprinkled over hundreds of millions of people, enough to lift many of them out of aching poverty and push them, tentatively, into better lives. But for a smaller group, the money had poured down as if in a deluge, and this new Chinese class had become as fabulously wealthy as the most fabulously wealthy people in the world.

His team, the Shanxi Brave Dragons, had arrived in the United States a few weeks ahead of him. He had owned the Brave Dragons for several years but worried that he had inadequately immersed himself in the team. (His players and coaches felt quite the opposite.) Now he was selling his last steel mill in China in a merger, and given that entanglements had arisen about unpaid taxes, the deal resembled a shotgun marriage with the shotgun pointed at him. Still, he told friends the sale would be a relief. Now he could focus his energy and resources on basketball. The previous season, the Brave Dragons had won five games (two by forfeit) and lost 24, the worst record in the Chinese Basketball Association (CBA). What enraged Boss Wang as much as losing was how the team lost. Sometimes his players simply quit. "Basketball is a fight," he told me later. "You never quit. You never give up."

The Brave Dragons were based for the summer at the United States Basketball Academy, about forty-five miles outside Eugene, in the ridge-lines of the Cascades. It is a beautiful, isolated place, embroidered with fir trees and overlooking the McKenzie River. The academy was a boot camp for international teams looking for a crash course on the metaphysics of the American game, yet one where a foreign owner did not have to worry that his players would be distracted by anything other than basketball. When he arrived, Boss Wang was assigned the John Wooden Cabin. Filled with memorabilia from Wooden's coaching career at UCLA, the cabin was a tribute to one of America's most famous college coaches, the academy's holiest shrine. A special edition of Wooden's book about life and basketball, *Coach Wooden's Pyramid of Success,* rested on the coffee table like a Gideon's Bible.

Boss Wang had never heard of Wooden. What he knew of American basketball came from what he watched on state television in China, which meant the National Basketball Association. His admiration of the United States was mostly admiration of the NBA, and how NBA players played the game. He had skipped a visit to Los Angeles when he learned he could not attend a game of the hometown Lakers; in New York, he dedicated much of his day to visiting the trophy hall of the New York Knicks at Madison Square Garden. He watched almost every NBA game on China Central Television(CCTV), studying how the players moved up and down the floor, how the best guards glided toward the basket, as if they were running along a conveyor belt embedded in the court. He stared into his television set and saw movement, always movement, and he studied patterns and clues to whatever formula was making that movement possible. Yet when he tried to impart his knowledge to his team in China, barking out instructions and then waiting to see his vision realized, the result inevitably disappointed him. His players never moved the way the Americans did on television. They never seemed to get it right.

Among many of the general managers, players, and reporters who followed the Chinese Basketball Association, Boss Wang was regarded as just short of a madman, a meddler who had fired fifteen (or sixteen coaches?) since buying the team in 2002. He had fired a Korean coach, an Australian coach, and a dozen-plus Chinese coaches. He had been fined repeatedly for his outbursts during games, and although league officials appreciated his dedication to the sport (and the money he was willing to pour into it), they were probably relieved that his team was located far away from the media spotlight, in the city of Taiyuan, the capital of Shanxi Province, at the heart of the nation's polluted coal belt. The team was an embarrassment on the court, and Boss Wang was an embarrassment off it.

He hardly felt shamed. He had a sharply critical view of most Chinese coaches, considering them too stubborn, too close-minded, to embrace the concepts he saw in the NBA. He blamed them for lacking his passion, his love of the game. If his coaches hadn't been able to Americanize his players, he would just take the team to America. Yet now he realized that wasn't enough. In Oregon, he decided his latest Chinese coach was incapable of transplanting the NBA game onto a court in China. "He said no Chinese coach can understand his ideas," said the team's general manager.

The new CBA season would begin in four months, and Boss Wang knew that the league was conducting its own experiment this year. Officials were under pressure to produce better players and create a more exciting style of play, more like games in the NBA. Salary restrictions on foreign players and coaches were being lifted, which meant the richest teams could in principle hire the best talent available. Boss Wang decided that merely hiring an American head coach was not enough; he wanted to be the first Chinese owner to hire a former *NBA* head coach. He wanted a coach with a higher basketball consciousness, someone who understood the game the way he did.

It was 8 a.m. on June 12. A former NBA coach was losing consciousness on an operating table in a Seattle hospital. Bob Weiss was being sedated as the surgeons prepared to remove the cancer discovered in his body. In the waiting room, his wife, Tracy, was quietly terrified. It was a sunny morning in Seattle, and Tracy sat beside a big window filled with light, working on a needlepoint belt, trying to distract herself through the monotony of stitching, loop after loop after loop, until a hospital pager vibrated against her hip. Tracy called the nursing station. Her husband's operation had started. It was scheduled to last four hours.

Six months earlier a routine physical had determined that Bob Weiss had an elevated PSA count. A biopsy had brought more bad news: He had an aggressive, advanced stage of prostate cancer. Tracy interrogated the doctors and spent days conducting gloomy research on the Internet that had left her consumed with dread. She and Bob had married twenty-two years before, when she was barely out of college and he was coming off a broken marriage. He was an assistant coach for the Dallas Mavericks and seventeen years older. She was a teacher in Plano, a suburb of Dallas. They had shared a full, fun life. But now she suddenly, unexpectedly had to face the possibility her husband might soon die. The doctors hoped they could get all the cancer, but they were not certain what they would find. Tracy stared at the fine sunny Seattle day and returned to her stitching.

As a player in the NBA, Bob Weiss had known only minor health concerns. He had played for more than a decade, during the era of John Havlicek, Wilt Chamberlain, and Oscar Robertson, and was a rugged defender who teamed with Jerry Sloan on some tough Chicago Bulls teams. He was nicknamed "the Ironman" after his streak of 555 consecutive games; when he tore ligaments in the middle finger of his left hand, Weiss filed down the small cast so that he could continue to dribble and shoot. When his playing career ended, Weiss began a coaching career that lasted more than two decades. Bald, with oversized wire-rimmed glasses perched on his nose, Weiss was anti-glamour in a glamorized, hip-hop league. As a coach, his outfits were so mismatched that Tracy, appalled, began using color-coded sticky notes to coordinate his suits, shirts, and ties for road trips. Pat Riley and Phil Jackson were gurus. Bob Weiss was a regular guy.

It was now 9 a.m. Tracy was still stitching, glancing at the *Today* show, when her cell phone rang with a call from a friend, John MacLaren, who tried to ease her anxieties. The operation was the surgical equivalent of an arcade game wherein you use a joystick to try to retrieve a stuffed animal with a metal claw: The doctors were tapping buttons on a computer keyboard to manipulate a robotic arm performing the surgery. MacLaren teased that the doctors had probably run out of quarters for the operating machine. Tracy had to laugh.

Another old Seattle friend arrived in the waiting room. Bob and Tracy had lived in Seattle for fourteen years, raising two children in the city, an almost unimaginably long tenure in the vagabond NBA. Bob spent twelve of those years as an assistant coach for the Seattle SuperSonics and had accepted that he would likely retire as an assistant. He had arrived in Seattle after getting fired as head coach of the Los Angeles Clippers, which followed getting fired as head coach of the Atlanta Hawks, which followed getting fired as head coach of the San Antonio Spurs. He had a reputation as a smart tactical coach who was liked by his players, though perhaps liked too much, according to his critics, who considered his relaxed style a shortcoming. He had taken teams to the playoffs, but his head coaching jobs had usually been with second-rate teams. He had a sharp sense of humor, which made him popular with the beat writers stuck covering his teams. "We're going to be exciting," Weiss predicted of his 1992 Atlanta Hawks. "Of course, it was exciting when the *Titanic* went down." Beneath his wisecracks, though, Weiss always believed that he could have been a winner, given the right opportunity, even as he assumed his chances for another head coaching job were slim. Being an assistant in Seattle had kept him in the game and provided a nice life.

Then, quite unexpectedly, in 2006, the rising young Sonics coach, Nate McMillan, departed after a contract squabble and took the top job with the Portland Trail Blazers. Weiss, the lead assistant, became head coach. It would have made a heartwarming story, except Weiss was fired before midseason. Injuries and a lousy start had doomed him. Howard Schultz, founder of Starbucks, was an impatient owner who would soon sell the Sonics out of Seattle. During a road trip in the Midwest, Schultz ordered his general manager to replace Weiss with an assistant, leaving Weiss to return alone to Seattle, despondent and humiliated. The Seattle media rallied behind him, as did many of the fans, but Weiss spent weeks rarely leaving his house until one evening he and Tracy finally ventured out to visit a neighborhood bar called the Attic. The television was tuned in to the NCAA basketball tournament when the fired Sonics coach walked through the door.

"All these college kids stood up and gave Bob a standing ovation," Tracy said. He could show his face again.

For any fired coach, a guaranteed contract is better than a standing ovation, and Weiss had eighteen more months of paychecks. He kept busy as a television commentator in the Pacific Northwest while his youngest child, Grace, entered her final year of high school. By the time Grace graduated, his contract had expired. His son, Stuart, was already in college. The economy was falling apart, and tuition bills would be arriving. Weiss wanted to downsize but his house in a Seattle gated community wouldn't sell. He needed work. Tracy was inside a big, lonely house, fretting about an empty nest. She had always wanted to travel abroad. What about coaching overseas? Italy was beautiful. France might be romantic.

Bob Weiss had spent the first six decades of his life happily confined to the United States of America. The prospect of international travel so thoroughly unnerved him that he had never applied for a passport. He worried about terrorists, and he worried about silly things, like getting lost. When the Sonics played exhibition games in Germany, Weiss, then an assistant, volunteered to stay back and scout college players in Tracy's hometown of Memphis. Finally, after a friend invited them to France, and Tracy insisted on going, her nervous husband followed. France turned out to be quite nice. Later, when the Sonics traveled to Japan, Weiss went there, too. He began to think anew about the rest of the world. Coaching overseas might be fun, an adventure as well as a paycheck.

Weiss contacted Warren LeGarie, an agent known for placing American coaches and players with foreign teams.

"What about China?" LeGarie asked.

China was the future, LeGarie said. The NBA was getting into China, and getting in fast.

Weiss listened. France and Italy were not China. "That's not really what we were thinking about when we said 'abroad,' " he replied.

His cancer diagnosis interrupted his plans. Unlike Tracy, though, he did not bother researching prostate cancer or calculating his odds, figuring certain things were out of his control. Weeks before his surgery, China unexpectedly came calling again; Adidas invited him to coach at a basketball camp in Shanghai. What the hell, he figured. He stayed at the Shangri-la Hotel and enjoyed butler service in a room overlooking the Bund, the colonial-era district known as being where the East meets the West. Shanghai was spectacular and racing forward and he liked the Chinese kids in the camp. He returned to Seattle and soon entered the hospital.

It was now noon. Four hours were up. Tracy's imagination was spiraling downward into the mind's most fearful places. Why was it taking so long? The nurses never paged her with updates. Had something gone wrong? Finally, the doctor arrived: He thought he got all the cancer, but they would have to wait for more test results to be sure. Tracy shook with nerves and tears.

In early July, the results arrived. Weiss was cancer-free. He recuperated for a few weeks and took his family on a vacation to Oregon in late July. Alive and healthy, he still needed a job when the phone rang. Warren LeGarie was on the line.

Still looking for work?

Yes.

There's an opening in China. The job is technically as a consultant. The Chinese owner wants a former NBA coach to mentor his Chinese coach and players.

Where?

An industrial city. Taiyuan, or something like that. A bunch of young players, kids almost.

LeGarie lathered it on, talking in terms of legacy, of being the first former NBA head coach in China. "That can never be taken from you," he said. "Once you are the first at something, it is important."

The team wanted him in China within a week. Weiss asked how he would communicate. The team would provide an interpreter. Tracy was thrilled and already on her laptop researching a list of places to visit in China.

What the hell, Weiss figured.

He was curious about one more thing: the owner. Weiss had worked for some real characters in the NBA.

The owner is a big basketball fan. He is just crazy about the game, LeGarie said. And he really wants someone from the NBA.

It was August 10, a few minutes before tipoff. Henry Kissinger gazed down at the players around the basket. Warming up on the court was the greatest collection of basketball talent in the world, at least on one side of the court. The United States and China were about to play in the opening round of the basketball competition of the 2008 Beijing Olympics. The Americans, led by Kobe Bryant, LeBron James, and Dwyane Wade, would eventually win the gold medal. The Chinese had Yao Ming, the 7'6" center for the Houston Rockets, and a collection of players few people outside China had ever heard of. The game was expected to be a blowout, yet more than 100 million people, possibly more than 200 million, were watching on television, one of the largest audiences ever for a sporting event. In the stands, George W. Bush, in the final months of his presidency, sat not far from his father, former president George H. W. Bush. Television announcers were eagerly comparing the game with the Cold War showdowns between the United States and the Soviet Union. Geopolitical hype was good for business; NBC wanted to attract more viewers and the NBA regarded the Olympics as a worldwide demonstration project for its brand.

Yet it was not just hype. There was something else at play: At stake in the game, in the Olympics, was the same thing at stake in the world, the inexorable rise of China. No one expected China to win on this day (it lost, 101–70); the question was how fast it was gaining speed. The next morning, the Chinese sporting press was hardly disappointed; the game was close for a while, an indicator that China soon might compete at a higher level. The same principle was being applied to almost everything, whether military affairs, business, or science, and China had closed the gap in those areas much more quickly than in basketball. The relentlessness of the Chinese machine was a spectacle the rest of the world found both awesome and unnerving to behold.

Kissinger, of course, had been there at the beginning. In 1972, Kissinger escorted President Richard Nixon to Beijing after months of secret diplomacy between two countries that for decades had not formally recognized one another's existence. Nixon and Mao Zedong reopened the door between America and China in what, at the time, was classic Cold War politics. Yet, more profoundly, it was a bet on the future, a grand experiment: Despite differences in history, language, and political ideology, China and the United States both realized that they should, in their own self-interest as well as the best interests of the world, learn how to cooperate, how to get along. Superficially at least, that had been accomplished, except that the experiment was still in progress, and now that China had become a juggernaut, the experiment was changing in unexpected ways. That Kissinger was now staring down at a basketball game in China like some Cold War gargoyle only accentuated how much had changed since 1972, and how much had not.

Basketball, oddly enough, offered a timeline of the aspirations and anxieties of the relationship. Basketball had been introduced in both countries at almost the same time, as if a scientist had planted a pair of the same genetically engineered seeds in starkly different soils and produced starkly different fruits. When James Naismith invented the game in 1891, his sponsors at the Young Men's Christian Association immediately embraced it as a proselytizing tool. Within a few years of the game's creation, YMCA missionaries, carrying basketballs in their luggage, arrived in the port city of Tianjin. China's ancient imperial order was collapsing, and younger Chinese elites were grappling with an identity crisis, trying to reconcile the impotence of China's ancient civilization against the military and industrial ascendance of the West. The Y built gymnasiums, organized China's first national and international sports tournaments, and preached that basketball could help build stronger Chinese bodies and transform China into a proud, modern nation.

Mao's founding of the People's Republic of China in 1949 shattered the Y's ambitions and closed the door to the West. Mao introduced an atheistic, socialist state anchored in a disastrous cult of personality. He regarded "colonial" sports as bourgeois affectations but made an exception for basketball, the sport favored by his military. In the United States, meanwhile, basketball was emerging as the urban game, a stage for individuality and creativity, and by the 1960s and 1970s, Oscar Robertson, Bill Russell, Jerry West, and even Bob Weiss were creating a distinctive American brand of basketball that would keep evolving and one day give rise to Michael Jordan and the global game. In closed China, basketball evolved in a vacuum because China existed in a vacuum, and everything, including the game, existed to serve the state. Those who played did so in the name of the Communist Party, or as an escape from the drabness and desperation of daily life. One of them was Boss Wang.

The experiment launched by Nixon and Mao in 1972 began in earnest after Mao died in 1976. His successor, Deng Xiaoping, unleashed reforms that over the next three decades transformed the Chinese economy, while also loosening the state's once clenched grip on society. Young people could pierce their noses, dye their hair, or join punk rock bands. Or play basketball. By the opening of the Beijing Olympics, basketball had become the most popular sport in China, mostly because of the popularity of the NBA. Chinese youth were no longer partitioned from the outside world. Television programming expanded in China just as Michael Jordan was becoming the first global sports superstar and his sponsor, Nike, was becoming the first multinational corporation to grasp that sports could become a new global religion, and a very profitable one. If the YMCA had brought basketball to China to convert the heathens, the NBA and Nike now offered a different promise—inclusion in a hip new global order. Chinese youth were still grappling with an identity crisis, still trying to figure out how to be modern and Chinese, and Nike responded by saying Just Do It or Be Like Mike.

The problem was that China still wasn't very good at basketball, or at least not as good as it aspired to be, which, as with everything, meant being the best. Yao Ming's arrival in the NBA had rightly been treated as a geopolitical event and his success with the Rockets had injected new energy and global attention on the potential of Chinese basketball. Yet beyond Yao, China's basketball league was failing to develop talent on the court and failing even more off the court at running basketball as a business. The NBA thought it had a solution—itself. It already had a thriving business in China selling television rights and corporate branding partnerships and had recently formed a Chinese subsidiary, valued at more than $2 billion. The league's commissioner, David Stern, had decided he wanted an NBA league in China. The Olympics were his sampler; the NBA was helping to stage the basketball competition during the Games and had imported NBA cheerleaders, techno dance soundtracks, halftime trampoline teams, and even mascots so that Chinese fans could taste a version of the "NBA Experience."

Except that much had not changed in China. The Communist Party still dominated the government, outlawed any opposition parties, censored the press, and jailed dissidents. Basketball might seem unrelated to this authoritarian structure, but the Chinese Basketball Association was an expression of the government itself; the league was run by the government's sports ministry and the league's general secretary was appointed by the Communist Party. Whether he realized it or not, by declaring he wanted an NBA league in China, Stern was challenging the Communist Party. It would have been an untenable position, except the Chinese league was struggling to remain relevant. The same tensions coursing through Chinese society were coursing through Chinese basketball. Local governments or state-owned companies still controlled many teams, but Chinese entrepreneurs had started buying in and wanted more freedom to market their teams and develop talent as they saw fit. They wanted to disentangle the CBA from the government and operate as a purely commercial entity. As proof of their argument, the private teams were beginning to dominate the league, especially the top team from Guangdong Province, the region along the southern coast that once led China into the reform era.

The exception was the Shanxi Brave Dragons. Among the private teams, the Brave Dragons had only proved that bad management and bad players could transcend any system. This failure grated on Boss Wang, because he considered himself a reformer. He saw the NBA as an opportunity, not a threat, and he wanted to plumb its secrets. When his coaching search turned up Bob Weiss, even though the two men had never met or spoken, Boss Wang didn't hesitate. He believed Weiss could be the technology transfer he was looking for.

A Westerner living in Beijing and a lifelong basketball fan, I had spent five years observing what was changing in China, and what seemed impossible to change, and I thought that the partnership between Boss Wang and Bob Weiss would provide an object lesson in that distinction. Little did I know that basketball would help me understand China, and China's relationship with the United States, in ways I never imagined. In between Boss Wang and Coach Weiss would be a team of colorful, sometimes heartbreaking, oddballs from around China, and around the world, playing in a crazy, unpredictable season that carried them into stadiums in every corner of China, a season in which the games were as much about testing different cultures and about how well, or not, they could be blended together.

Weiss was supposed to take those two strains of basketball seeds that had grown so differently and try to commingle them in the same pot.

China had become the manufacturing colossus of the world, with factories that made televisions, cell phones, basketballs, and so much more. Making things had made China powerful again. But Boss Wang wanted to manufacture basketball players. And that would prove a very different challenge.

CHAPTER ONE

THE FOREIGN EXPERT

Walking out of baggage claim, pushing an overstuffed luggage cart, groggy and disoriented after the eleven-hour flight from Seattle, Bob Weiss was looking for someone named Joe. He had been anxious before taking off, having never heard of his Chinese carrier, Hainan Airlines, but the flight had been pleasant, the business class service attentive. He read a novel and dozed as the flight traced, in reverse, the migratory path of civilization: along the Alaskan coastline before turning left near the Bering Strait, flying over the chain of islands that anthropologists believe once formed a land bridge on which the first humans to reach North America walked over from Asia. Time itself spun forward at the International Dateline, and the airliner soon raced over Siberia, Mongolia, and Manchurian China before descending into the afternoon haze shrouding the ancient city of Beijing. Time had spun forward in Beijing, too: The opening ceremony of the Olympic Games was on Friday, two days off. Beijing was again the center of the world.

Weiss was looking forward to a few days in Beijing so that he could recover from the flight in a nice hotel, enjoy the Olympics, and get to know Boss Wang before they joined the team in Taiyuan. The two men had not met, and their language divide prevented them from speaking directly on the telephone, a situation that made the hiring odd, when compared to the vetting process in the NBA. Weiss wanted to make a good impression and brought a bottle of Kentucky bourbon as a gift. Weiss knew as much about China as the average American, which is to say not a great deal, so Tracy, the former schoolteacher, bought a load of books about the country, plumbed the Internet, and tutored Bob on what amounted to a survival primer on etiquette. Tracy had determined that Bob would attend many banquets governed by a complicated and symbolic protocol. Bob should not leave his chopsticks planted like fence posts in a bowl of rice because this symbolized death. He would be expected to give and receive many toasts of Chinese alcohol, and toasting adhered to its own protocol. He should hold the rim of his glass just below the glass of the toastee, as a sign of deference and respect. Every person in the room might toast him, and he had to drink with each one. New acquaintances would want to pose for photographs, possibly several, and Bob should oblige as a gesture of friendship. Finally, he had to be ready with gifts, and the gifts had to be wrapped with care (hence the commemorative wooden box that came with the bourbon).

He was supposed to serve as a consultant and tactical adviser to the team, explaining NBA strategies, diagramming offensive sets, and teaching other specialty plays and techniques. Weiss knew that a Chinese coach had overseen the team in Oregon, and he assumed the same coach would be the object of his mentoring. As a consultant, Weiss figured he could exist in a more detached realm, insulated from direct responsibility and the pressurized decisions borne by a coach, the decisions that often made coaching in the NBA so grinding. Weiss was sixty-six. A consultancy sounded fine.

Several days before leaving for Beijing, Weiss had contemplated his wardrobe. He knew the CBA was instituting a dress code for coaches, and had he been one, he would have packed his tailored suits from coaching in the NBA. But he was a consultant, and if a consultant was not expected to sit on the bench, he might not need the suits. Knowing almost nothing about his new team, his new country, or his new owner, Weiss called the person who, along with LeGarie, was most responsible for his job: Bruce O'Neil.

During the 1970s, O'Neil had coached at the University of Hawaii, his alma mater, and led the team to a winning record. But he was pushed out after three seasons when NCAA investigators discovered rules infractions. He returned to his home state of Oregon and started over, founding a production company that made instructional sports videos. A natural salesman, O'Neil traveled to Japan and discovered a big market for baseball training videos; he also sold videos to ESPN. But he missed basketball, so he sold the production company and founded the United States Basketball Academy in Oregon as a training camp for international teams. He returned to Asia to drum up business and made his first visit to China in 1995. He was exhilarated. Kids were playing all over the country. The NBA was seeping into the youth culture, and O'Neil felt like an explorer who had unwittingly stumbled upon basketball's New World.

He spoke no Chinese but visited China so frequently that he soon ingratiated himself with the Communist Party bureaucrats who ran the Chinese Basketball Association, partly by identifying the dilemma of their existence: They oversaw a socialist-era system that produced poor players and desperately needed reform, yet their jobs, status, and live-lihoods were dependent on that system. Any outsider who wanted to improve Chinese basketball, and profit from it, not only had to persuade the CBA bureaucrats to change but also reassure them that change would not render them obsolete. O'Neil took them on golf junkets to Hawaii or Las Vegas, and for several years organized tryout camps where Chinese teams could evaluate and draft Americans interested in playing in the league. In Oregon, he tailored his academy toward Chinese teams and even hired cooks from China. One of his clients was Boss Wang, who had sent over the Shanxi Brave Dragons for the summer. When Boss Wang had stormed into Oregon, looking for a former NBA coach, Bruce O'Neil was enlisted to help. He soon connected the team with Warren LeGarie, who offered up Bob Weiss for the job. Once a deal was struck, O'Neil had told Weiss to expect the unexpected in China. Now that advice was being proven wise.

"You'll need to bring the suits," O'Neil told Weiss. "You're going to be the head coach."

"I am?" Weiss stammered into the telephone. "What happened?"

Until this moment, knowing practically nothing about the Shanxi Brave Dragons had not bothered Weiss, just as the Shanxi Brave Drag-ons had not seemed bothered by knowing so little about him. Weiss had wanted a job and a chance for an interesting life experience in a foreign country. He had NBA on his chest, and that was all that mattered to Boss Wang. The Chinese coach Bob Weiss had been expecting to mentor had been fired, O'Neil now explained, so Weiss would have to run the team. The Chinese coach would remain through the transition, and the team would find a young Chinese coach who would spend the season as an assistant and be groomed for the future.

"Fine with me," Weiss said, pausing for a moment before asking the question that had not preoccupied him so much before. "What can you tell me about the owner?"

Weiss knew only the essential facts about Boss Wang. He was Chinese, very rich, had made his money in steel, and was absolutely bonkers about basketball, especially NBA basketball, which Weiss assumed counted as a point in his favor. But Weiss did not know Wang's philosophy on basketball, or whether he even had a philosophy; he knew almost nothing about Boss Wang's temperament; nor did he know how involved, or not, Boss Wang expected to be with the team. Weiss could not even pronounce his new boss's full name: Wang Xingjiang.

Weiss did know that relationships were essential in professional basketball, and, given that success hinges on personal chemistry, front office executives in the NBA usually wanted a personal relationship with the coach. When Weiss had interviewed with the Atlanta Hawks, his most important meeting came with the team president, Stan Kasten, a New Yorker with a New Yorker's distrust of anyone who appeared too unblemished.

"Bob, I've got a problem," Kasten had told Weiss. "No matter who I call, everybody tells me you are a great guy. That bothers me. I want to find one person who doesn't like you."

Weiss reached into his pocket and pulled out a pen. He scribbled a number on a piece of paper and pushed it across the table.

"What's this?" Kasten asked.

"That's my ex-wife's number. Call her."

Kasten laughed, and Weiss got the job.

Now Bruce O'Neil paused. He admired Boss Wang's toughness and his passion for basketball, but he knew his reputation for meddling and had watched him quarrel with the Chinese coach during the team's training sessions in Oregon.

"He's a very proud, passionate guy," O'Neil said. "He overreacts to certain things and oversteps certain boundaries, at least as we would see them. It's going to be a volatile situation. But you can handle it."

O'Neil then hesitated, and added, "I hope." He was laughing, sort of.

The discussion meandered to the subject of firing coaches.

"How many has he fired?" Weiss asked. He had no interest in traveling halfway around the world for the pleasure of getting canned.

The precise number escaped O'Neil but he said it didn't matter because Weiss existed in a different category. "You don't have to worry about it," he said. "You're coming from the NBA. He can't fire you.

"This is going to be your basketball adventure," O'Neil said, "and probably the biggest adventure of your life."

Outside baggage claim, hotel bellboys waved placards and looked for incoming guests as knots of illegal taxi drivers hovered nearby and eyed prospective customers among the weary travelers staggering with their luggage into the canned light of Beijing's Terminal 2. Joe, tall and lanky, a former CBA player for the elite military team, and now the Brave Dragons' interpreter, could see over the crowd as he searched for Weiss.

His English name was an anglicized version of his given Chinese name, *Jie*. He joined the team in Oregon, through a connection with Bruce O'Neil, and accepted a full-time position after Boss Wang decided to hire an American coach. Joe had accompanied the general manager, Zhang Beihai, on the expedition that led the team to Weiss. On O'Neil's advice, they traveled to the NBA Summer League in Las Vegas, an annual meat market for players, coaches, and agents. When they met LeGarie, they made clear that money did not pose an obstacle. LeGarie mentioned Weiss, and though neither Joe nor the general manager had heard of him, Weiss was NBA, and NBA was what Boss Wang wanted. Everyone agreed on a two-page contract. Weiss would earn $250,000 for eight months' work.

Now, though, Joe waited nervously. He liked smoothness in life, and he had quickly learned not to expect it with the Brave Dragons. An interpreter is supposedly nothing more than a vessel; the message is the cargo, and the interpreter neither made it, nor is responsible for its contents. But the job of basketball interpreter in China is personal in ways that sometimes pained Joe. He often had to deliver unpleasant news, and today would be no exception. Moreover, he could assume Bob Weiss understood little about the team, or about the difficulties his new job would present, so inevitably there were going to be shocks and surprises. That meant Joe would be providing services beyond mere interpretation. He would be helping Weiss survive.

The passengers from the Seattle flight trickled into the terminal. Joe had never met Weiss but recognized him from a photograph: With his bald pate and eyeglasses, Weiss might have been a visiting businessman, except that he walked like an athlete, all hips and wide shoulders; he swaggered slowly, side to side, like a retired rodeo cowboy, if one or two sizes too tall. Joe approached him, smiling and blushing, as he often did when he spoke English, as if he were embarrassed. He offered a handshake. Weiss looked relieved: He had found the only person he knew in China. He was now ready for a few days in Beijing.

"Change of plans," Joe announced.

The owner had left Beijing. The original plan of keeping the fired Chinese coach around for a few weeks to ease Weiss's transition had been discarded. Boss Wang had sent off the Chinese coach, there was no one to manage practice, and practice was in the morning. Joe had already bought tickets on that evening's flight to Taiyuan. There would be no time to attend the Olympics, nor any transition period.

Weiss sighed. He knew that he was not joining an ordinary team with an ordinary owner, so he had mentally prepared himself for the not-so-ordinary, or so he thought. But he had not counted on this. He had assumed the former coach would stick around long enough to offer a briefing on the players and the rest of the league.

"No problem," Weiss said, as he pivoted his cart and followed Joe to the check-in counter. He surrendered his luggage and stood in line to pass through security, still digesting how completely one eleven-hour flight had realigned his life. In the Seattle airport, he had kissed Tracy good-bye and hugged Stuart. After four decades as an NBA nomad, traveling through airports across the United States, he was conditioned to life on the road, to separations from friends and family. But now he was truly apart. He had known Joe for ten minutes, and was now following him around the airport like a nervous child worried about losing his father.

"Excuse me. We need to check your bag," said a security guard, speaking in broken English, pointing to the overstuffed gym bag Weiss had placed on the conveyer belt of the X-ray machine. The guard wanted to examine its contents, especially given the heightened security alert for potential Olympic terrorism. The bag was placed on a metal table, and Weiss was asked to pull open the zipper.

The gym bag represented the survivalist instincts of Tracy Weiss. She had not known what would be available in Taiyuan in the way of pharmacological products, so she had planned as if nothing would be. She had stuffed her husband's carry-on bag with aspirin, tampons for her later arrival, and a few dozen other assorted bottles and tubes. Weiss was a mule smuggling the contents of a Rite Aid.

"What's this?"

Five hundred berry-flavored chewable Tums for an upset stomach, Weiss replied.

"What's this?"

Imodium multiple symptom pills for diarrhea.

"This?"

Bug spray.

"This?"

Prescription toothpaste and dental masks, specially designed to protect teeth against pollution. Tracy was preparing for nuclear winter.

Things kept coming out of the bag: Bayer aspirin, Neosporin, moisturizer cream, Tylenol, liquid gel Advil. The guard pulled out two very large bottles filled with a thick gloppy fluid. "What's this?" he asked.

"Shampoo," answered the bald Weiss, "for washing your hair."

Another guard grabbed a smaller bottle and carried it off to a supervisor. A pink liquid was poured from the bottle and a sample of it was run through a testing machine; no one could define its content. Twenty minutes had passed. The flight to Taiyuan would be leaving soon. Finally, the bottle was handed to Weiss.

"Drink it," he was told.

Uncertain as to whether the importation of Pepto-Bismol constituted a punishable offense in China, Weiss swallowed a sip and licked his pink lips.

He and his pharmacy were checked through to Taiyuan.

As Weiss was contemplating his first practice, he knew the Brave Dragons were not as good as mediocre American players—in Oregon, they had gotten their asses kicked by semipro clubs. What he didn't know was that the Chinese players were not surprised by these ass-kickings because they had been taught to regard themselves as defective. Various explanations were given for their shortcomings: Chinese considered themselves genetically less capable of excelling at sports that require a combination of power and speed; China's period of isolation meant that Chinese players were now trying to catch up with advances in the game made in the West, especially in the United States; funding a national basketball system, one organized to encourage everyone to play, and thus broaden the talent pool, was too costly and, oddly, inconsistent with the overriding goal of the Chinese sports system, which was not to promote public participation but to win Olympic gold medals.

Humanity is such an abundant raw material in China that making use of it all is considered impractical. The Chinese sports system identifies basketball talent through a process that pairs social engineering with cost-benefit analysis. The system acts as a sieve through which almost every child in the country is poured so that a selected minority can be identified as best suited for sports. The winnowing tool is the X-ray machine. In elementary school, children undergo medical tests that include a scan of their skeletal structure, with special attention paid to their wrist bones. Doctors examine the distance between the developing bones, and that distance provides a projection for future physical growth. Kids deemed likeliest to grow the tallest are encouraged to attend government sports schools, where coaches will steer them toward certain sports, like basketball. Other kids, the ones showing narrower spaces in the bone structure of their wrists, continue attending schools focused on academics, many of which offer no team sports whatsoever.

Most of the Chinese players on the team had been caught in the sieve as teenagers. Sun Chunlei, a lumbering power forward, had been born in the port city of Yantai, in Shandong Province, across the Yellow Sea from North Korea. Shandong is traditionally an incubator of Chinese military leaders and tall basketball players, the latter sometimes described as *Shandong Da Han,* or Big Guys from Shandong. Mu Tiezhu, at almost 7'6", was a Shandong native discovered by basketball officials while working as a military border guard. Mu had never played basketball but would become a stalwart on China's national team during the 1970s and 1980s. When the Chinese team visited the United States in the late 1970s on a goodwill tour, Mu scored 11 points in an exhibition victory against the collegiate Georgetown Hoyas and later led the Chinese to a win over the NBA's Washington Bullets.

Sun Chunlei, or Big Sun, as he was called, was a large child born of large parents, and the bone tests sealed his fate. He was only nine, but the distance between his wrist bones suggested he would reach 6'6". (He actually grew to 6'8".) By the time he was eleven, he had transferred to a sports school. When a coach handed him a basketball, he did not know what to do with it. He had never played the game and had no interest in playing, and now his preadolescence was organized to prepare him to become a basketball player. The coaches woke him every morning at 5:30 for wind sprints. He was in sixth grade and he ran three miles every morning before sunrise. He hated the game chosen for him. "When I first got there," he remembered, "I couldn't take it."

Pan Jiang, the starting point guard, grew up in the industrial city of Jinzhou in Liaoning Province, in the country's northeastern rust belt, which, like Shandong, was part of China's basketball heartland. Pan loved the game, playing year-round, even when the winter temperatures fell near zero. His parents, factory workers, placed him in a sports school when he was ten. He spent nearly eight years there. The bone tests predicted he would reach 6'6", but he stopped growing at 6'2", which meant he would play point guard. The point guard is the general of the team, directing his teammates around the court, often placing their interests above his own. The position fit his temperament. He was a pleaser.

"I can get everybody involved and make some good passes," he said. "It fits my personality and my character."

More than anything, though, the job of a Chinese point guard is to please the coach. Pan had joined the Shanxi Brave Dragons six years earlier and, while trying to run the offense of whichever coach happened to be running the team, had spent most of those years as Boss Wang's whipping boy. Pan had a nice outside shot and a selfless attitude, but his chief failing was that he was not Steve Nash of the Phoenix Suns. Nash was a transcendent player who, if he was not scoring himself, intuitively distributed the ball to the right person at the right moment. Whenever Boss Wang watched a CCTV broadcast of one of Nash's games, Pan stood a good chance of later hearing exactly what Nash was and what Pan Jiang was not.

But if Steve Nash was encouraged to express himself within an offense, to experiment and dabble, Pan Jiang was required to follow orders, and strictly so. "Basically, I just did whatever they told me to do," he said. "When they told us to do a drill, we did that drill. When they told us to do something in the game, we do that. In China, we are trained to do whatever the coaches tell us."

Pan and Big Sun were the longest tenured players on the team, which meant they were the longest suffering. They had never experienced a winning season and they had watched the team collapse during the previous season, regularly losing games by 30 points or more. They had played for at least fifteen head coaches. They could not name them all. One coach had lasted only one game. Now another one was coming, though everyone knew this would be different, because the new guy was from the NBA. He was supposed to arrive for practice in the morning. The Chinese players were surly from their trip to America, but also intrigued, since no one knew quite what to expect. The NBA was evidence, offered live on television, of what they were not.

They were defective, a judgment they accepted. The question was how much they could be improved.

In the 1950s, having declared his vision of reinventing China as a Communist utopia, Mao Zedong endorsed a policy known as *ba fangwu dasao ganjing zai qing ke,* or Cleaning the House Before Inviting the Guests. He established a Foreign Nationals Management Bureau to identify and register the 175,000 foreigners living in China and then began squeezing them out through official harassment, onerous taxation policies, and political persecution. Within a few years, only a tiny number of foreigners remained. Merely speaking to a foreigner became a political act; a Chinese person conversing with a foreigner would be required to report exactly what was said.

This was cleaning the house. For a century, foreigners had humiliated China, by flooding the country with opium, demanding favorable trade policies through gunboat diplomacy, and seizing Chinese territory. Mao believed that removing foreigners from Chinese soil was the only way to scrub away the stain their presence had created. Yet even Mao realized that China needed some guests. China was a ruined, destitute nation that had missed the Industrial Revolution. Among other things, Mao needed engineers to oversee dam construction projects and military experts to modernize the Red Army. He invited the Soviet Union and other Communist nations to send advisers, and created a Foreign Experts Bureau to oversee their housing, remuneration, and political status. The Soviets were the big brother of the Communist movement and they enjoyed high status in China. They were given access to private cars and drivers, treated to annual vacations, and allowed to shop at Friendship Stores offering goods not available to ordinary Chinese. While Chinese lived in shoddy, drab apartment blocks, the Soviets lived in private apartment complexes built with Western conveniences.

But while the Foreign Experts Bureau was expected to accommodate outside advisers, it was also expected to control them. When the Sino-Soviet split in 1960 created a schism in the global Communist movement, many Soviet advisers returned to Russia, but others, sympathetic to China, remained. Deng Xiaoping, then the party's general secretary under Mao, cautioned that those who remained had to be trained in Mao Zedong Thought and instructed to focus on their work, not on Chinese politics. He called the policy *ji gan ran hong,* or Squeeze Them Dry and Paint Them Red! The terms of the relationship were clear: Foreigners were to be exploited for their expertise but not allowed to influence or interfere with Chinese affairs. When Mao died in 1976, Deng eventually emerged as his successor and began undoing the disastrous planned economy. Deng recognized that the capitalist West had raced ahead and, to catch up, he reopened China to Western expertise. His economic policies were known as *gaige kaifang*, or Reform and Opening.

Now the foreign experts arriving in China were no longer bound by shared ideology. Deng had declared that "to get rich is glorious," and China represented the greatest potential business market in the world. The Foreign Experts Bureau remained intact but could no longer manage the growing numbers of foreigners pouring into the country. Foreign investors, many from Hong Kong and Taiwan, built factories in the special economic zones Deng established in Shenzhen and other coastal cities. Multinational corporations arrived, slowly at first, but their executives were intoxicated by the same alluring potential of the huge China market that had brought European traders more than a century earlier. Yet even if China was opening itself up, the same Chinese suspicions of foreign intentions remained; foreigners still had to be controlled. During the 1980s, foreign companies entering the China market were required to form joint ventures with Chinese partners, arrangements that usually proved culturally and economically unsustainable. Foreigners relayed horror stories about Chinese partners opening secret factories to produce counterfeit versions of the same product being manufactured by the joint ventures. Chinese complained that too many foreigners were only after fast riches.

By the 1990s, China had relaxed the requirement on joint ventures, and Western business poured in, as did thousands of people who saw China as a new frontier in business, culture, and, eventually, sports. The distrust was hardly scrubbed away, but China became, again, the place where foreigners dreamed of solving the puzzle of how to succeed in the world's most populous nation, whether in business or anything else. Those who succeeded in China would be at the cutting edge of the global economy.

That, more or less, is what Warren LeGarie preached to Bob Weiss. LeGarie had spent two decades placing American players and coaches overseas, most famously George Karl, the talented NBA head coach who spent two seasons coaching Real Madrid in Spain before returning to the NBA. For years, LeGarie had steered clients away from China; he considered the league too unprofessional and too full of teams that reneged on contracts or failed to pay players. But now China had become the most coveted basketball market in the world. China meant that Bob Weiss was no longer on the NBA discard rack but standing at the front edge of the future of basketball.

The flight from Beijing to Taiyuan took less than an hour. Weiss and Joe talked about the Chinese players on the team and the upcoming season, but mostly they got acquainted. Later, when Weiss recounted the flight, what resonated most with him was how Joe had seemed to frame the season as a matter of survival, a matter of making it all the way through. Joe promised that he and the general manager were committed to Weiss, would stand by his side, as if another group of people were not.

"No matter what happens," Joe said, "we are going to help you."

Inside the airport, a young smiling man awaited. His face was so unlined and boyish that he might have been only a few years out of college. He was the general manager, Zhang Beihai, not yet thirty years old. He did not speak a word of English, but he kept smiling as he handed Weiss a large arrangement of flowers.

"Welcome to Taiyuan," he said in Chinese, and they walked outside into the hot evening air for the ride to Weiss's hotel.

They soon arrived at one of the tallest skyscrapers in downtown Taiyuan, a glass building, unremarkable except that the glass was tinted the color of a ripe banana. It was too dark and Weiss was too exhausted to notice the color but what seemed familiar was the Howard Johnson sign shining atop the building, an emblem of unpretentious Middle America gleaming in the central China night. Weiss took comfort in the sign. So much was already unfamiliar: He had moved to a city whose name he could barely pronounce to coach a team he knew nothing about, other than that it was very, very bad. He had not understood anything anyone said to him all day, except for Joe, and Joe was now leaving for the night.

Weiss rode the elevator to his room, and opened the door and walked in. The overstuffed furniture was old and stained and crowded together in the small room. He smelled the acrid odor of stale cigarettes. There was a combined bedroom and living room, and the tiny bathroom appeared to be missing essential parts. There was a small sink and toilet, but the shower nozzle poked out of a wall next to the toilet. There was no tub or shower stall; the entire bathroom was the shower stall. When Weiss flipped on the water and stepped under the nozzle, most of the water sprayed upward, where it performed a bank shot off the ceiling before splattering down onto Weiss, the toilet, the sink, and the rest of the bathroom. His shower had flooded the bathroom.

Weiss flicked on the television. He had been promised international cable service, but every channel was Chinese, except for one with news updates from Canada. He opened his Apple laptop, but the room lacked the promised Internet connection, so he collapsed on the bed, disconnected from the world he had known, and fell asleep. When he awoke in the morning and stepped outside, he learned two things: He was living in a yellow skyscraper. And the Howard Johnson was not actually a Howard Johnson. The familiar Howard Johnson sign sat atop the yellow building, but a less conspicuous English sign above the door identified the hotel as the Howell & Johnson.

Bob Weiss had spent his first night in China at a knockoff HoJo.

CHAPTER TWO

THE PURGE

Taiyuan is the boiler room of China. The furnace. Dust and soot are blown through it, whether it is billowing dust from coal mines in the surrounding mountains, or the blinking dust of the cement factories, or the dust and dirt that blow off the dry brown fields and settle over the city like a fine ash. For a time, Taiyuan ranked as the most polluted city in the world, and residents could oftentimes judge the condition of the day by the condition of their clothes. A short walk on a downtown street could stain a shirt collar. On the worst days, coal dust floated in the air like black pollen. When in 1987 provincial leaders became interested in the business of processing French fries, a local delegation traveled to Idaho and Tennessee on a fact-finding mission to study potatoes. Beyond the potatoes, two things were memorable about their trip: First, the American no-smoking rules; one man in the group would wake himself after midnight for a cigarette to compensate for lost opportunities during the day. Second, the air. It was so clean that no one had to polish his shoes during the entire ten-day trip. This was a revelation, because shoe polishing was a daily necessity back home.

On his first morning in Taiyuan, and the many mornings that followed, Bob Weiss did not immediately realize he was in an improved city. Taiyuan had surrendered its pollution title to a sister city, Linfen, a grim, industrial scar located a few hours down the highway. Taiyuan was still polluted, just less so than Linfen. In winter, when the big municipal furnaces heated the city by burning piles of coal, and the factories belched smoke into the sky, a permanent grayness still settled over Taiyuan, as if it were the city's natural state to be drained of color.

Taiyuan was the economic and political heart of Shanxi Province and once enjoyed broad political influence and social cachet in China. I once struck up a conversation with a man in the Beijing airport as we waited for a flight to Taiyuan, his home. He proudly repeated a local saying: If you want to know 1,000 years of Chinese history, go to Beijing. If you want to know 2,000 years of Chinese history, go to Xi'an. (Xi'an, currently the home of China's Terra-Cotta Warriors, was the capital of the ancient Qin Dynasty.) But if you want to know 3,000 years of Chinese history, go to Taiyuan. Shanxi Province was once a cultural and economic center that had given rise to China's banking system and its first great merchant class, men who ferried their goods to the Great Wall and dared trade with the barbarians from Mongolia.

It was also true that 3,000 years of history had wrung Shanxi dry. The country's merchants now lived on the coast, or in Beijing, and as players in the Chinese export machine they traded globally. Shanxi was landlocked and deracinated; drought had shriveled wheat fields into lunar landscapes. What money was generated in Shanxi came from digging holes into one of the richest veins of coal in the world, and as more factories and apartment towers rose along the coast, more holes were dug in Shanxi to extract the coal that fired the Chinese machine.

It was a primitive human enterprise, and it made multimillionaires out of semiliterate coal bosses. So much money had come out of the ground, and had concentrated itself so inequitably, that Shanxi distilled the country's sharpest contrasts: It was where miners earning maybe $5 a day died by the thousands inside unsafe mines, and it was where so many overnight millionaires had been created that Louis Vuitton and Cartier were anchor tenants in the newest shopping mall in downtown Taiyuan. To people elsewhere in China, Taiyuan had come to symbolize the crudest, if essential, denominator of the country's economic miracle. Chinese reporters in other cities were flabbergasted that Weiss was associated with Taiyuan, as if he were a fancy piece of new technology that had been shipped to the wrong place.

His early days were disorienting. The tumult of the city was overwhelming. Traffic was a swirling sea of cars, trucks, and people, everyone pressing forward in persistent tides, honking and lurching between lanes, bicyclists pedaling in narrow streams along both sides of the pockmarked roads. Men hauled bricks or plastic bottles or garbage on three-wheeled carts. Merely crossing the street required planning. Pedestrians would slowly push into the road, edging farther and farther outward, strangers temporarily united in a chain until they had created a human blockade that for a few moments paralyzed the crush of cars and allowed everyone to rush across. Weiss began drafting behind old women as they ventured into the fray. They seemed to have the survivor's instinct.

Slowly, he established lines of communication to his known world. He acquired Internet service and began sending his family emails and photographs of Taiyuan. His favorite was an open manhole on a busy sidewalk that had been left unmarked, day and night, for weeks. The team provided him a cell phone with limited paid minutes, and the phone chirped when time was about to elapse. "He would call and say, 'I've gotta go! I'm running out of minutes. You cannot come over here!'" Tracy recalled. Then the phone would go dead.

His contract had included a vaguely defined Personal Amenities section that provided not only for a luxury apartment but a driver on call twenty-four hours a day. In the NBA, a contract for a head coach is a meticulously lawyered document intended to protect a coach from the day he is hired to the inevitable day he is fired, and beyond. Specifics such as travel arrangements are carefully parsed, down to the levels of luxury a coach receives on road trips. Weiss had once stayed in a suite so fantastically grand that he summoned his assistant coaches so that they might chuckle over the piano, the bottles of wine, and tables of fruit and flowers. His Chinese contract left the definition of luxury to cultural interpretation.

His driver was a middle-aged man, Mr. Zhou, who collected him every morning in a dusty gray van. Mr. Zhou spoke no English, and Weiss spoke no Chinese, so they exchanged morning grunts as Mr. Zhou steered into the churn of traffic. He weaved between lanes, bleating his horn, dodging cars and people, seemingly determined to drive more recklessly than the competition. Weiss was alarmed and fascinated; either there were no rules, or the rules didn't present any meaningful deterrent. People drove as if there were no other cars on the road.

On his first morning in Taiyuan, Weiss staggered out of the van and joined the players at the team's training camp on the outskirts of the city. The practice gym was inside a converted factory on the fringe of an industrial park, not far from Taiyuan's new airport at the southernmost edge of the city. It was about ten miles from downtown; Boss Wang had chosen the location because it was cheap and away from the temptations of the city. Most taxis did not go out there, and if the Chinese players wanted to leave, they had to arrange for illegal taxis, known as black cabs, to pick them up. The Chinese players slept inside a three-story concrete dormitory painted burnt orange. Breakfast, lunch, and dinner were taken in a canteen on the first floor. The gym was an old warehouse, as high as a barn and constructed with sheet metal. Inside, two courts lay end to end with what amounted to the team weight room placed at the edge of one court: a few machines, a couple of bench presses, some dumbbells, and mats for sit-ups. Later, when foreign players arrived at the practice facility, they compared it to a prison.

Weiss's first practice was awkward. The players stared at him, slightly stunned that an NBA coach had actually materialized in Taiyuan. Weiss could not name a single player on the court, nor could he name a single team in the Chinese league outside of his. With Joe interpreting, he introduced himself, saying how genuinely excited he was to be working with the Brave Dragons, and then asked everyone to run a few drills and scrimmage. He wanted to see what he had.

The players divided into three lines at one end of the court and began running toward the other basket. The drills were universal: the weave, three-man full-court layups and two-man sets for passing and dribbling. The players ran them better than most American players; their footwork was precise and their timing was almost flawless. The problems surfaced when they faced actual defenders in a game, and their footwork and any semblance of teamwork collapsed. No one seemed to understand where to go on the floor, how to move without the ball, or how to play team defense. Everyone ran hard and played hard and had decent skills, as far as shooting and dribbling were concerned, but they played the game as if they were careening through traffic with no one else on the court.

His biggest player, Big Sun, could barely get off the ground and seemed incapable of dunking. Big Sun would anchor himself on the low post, close to the basket, and wait for an incoming pass. When the pass arrived, Big Sun would lean into the defender and pound the ball on the floor, one time, with purpose, before picking up his dribble, whereupon he was marooned. He had either to pass the ball back outside or shoot, and shooting presented a real challenge because he could barely jump. His answer was to unleash a succession of head fakes, up and down, up and down, as methodical and predictable as an oil field pump jack, until, finally, he would shoot. What happened at that point was hard to predict: Occasionally, he scored; often he missed; and sometimes the defender swatted the ball away. It would have made a fine instructional video of how a big man should not take the ball to the basket. Weiss made a mental note to find a foreign center.

Weiss clapped his hands together and called practice to a close. With two exceptions, everything he said to or heard from his players had to be filtered through Joe. There was a Taiwanese kid, Sun Huanpo—Little Sun, he was called—who spoke decent English and seemed to sop up everything Weiss said. He was the smallest player on the team and had signed a few weeks earlier to compete for the job as starting point guard. The general manager had dangled Weiss as an enticement, because the kid hoped to become a coach one day and figured that an NBA coach would teach him the higher concepts of the game. There was personal pride, too: No Taiwanese player had ever played for an NBA coach. The other player with some English was a shooting guard, Wei Mingliang, the only Chinese player who had attended college. Weiss asked for photos with the players' names. The language was so perplexing to him that attaching a name to a face demanded time and practice. It also required him to use different muscles in his mouth, so he initially depended on the language of the locker room. Sun Chunlei was already Big Sun. His other forward, Zhang Xuewen, became Kobe, for his Kobe-inspired armband. The college kid was just Wei, as in Way.

Practice presented another problem. In the NBA, training camp lasted about two weeks. Here, it was only August, three months before the first game of the season, but the team had already been practicing two or three times a day, for months. Other than a month off every season, and a short break for the Lunar New Year, the routine rarely changed. Practice never ended.

Weiss started making changes. He canceled the team's regular Sunday night meeting after concluding it was a waste of time, merely a curfew check after the players' one day off. On the court, he spent less time on rote drills, the running and layups, and more on installing an NBA-style offense and teaching team defense. The team already had a Chinese assistant coach, an older man who spoke in the gravelly voice of a lifelong smoker and sometimes wore dress shoes on the court, earning him the nickname Wingtips. But Weiss had managed to convince the general manager to hire an American assistant, Rick Turner, who had coached in an American semipro league. Turner, who oversaw conditioning, introduced a program modeled on those in the NBA in which the players ran to different stations and performed speed or strength drills at each one before moving to the next. He had tossed out the team's old regimen, which, with its heavy weightlifting exercises, seemed better suited for an American football team.

Weiss assumed he had been brought in by Boss Wang to teach the

NBA way, and that was what he was doing. He thought things were going pretty well.

Two months had passed, and Weiss had settled into Taiyuan. The October weather was quickly turning colder and the team had started tryouts for the two positions reserved for foreign players. Once the foreigners began to arrive, Weiss saw his opportunity to escape the Howell & Johnson; if the team wanted to impress and sign the best foreign players, he said, it would need to provide better accommodations. The general manager agreed and moved Weiss and the incoming foreigners to a new hotel, the Longcheng, which overlooked People's Square, the broad plaza built for mass rallies during Mao's era. Now the square was just a place for people to gather. In the early mornings Weiss could see groups of older women dancing and twirling small flags, the morning exercises common for women in cities across China. The Longcheng had a bar, a restaurant that listed steak on the menu, and rooms that provided Internet and a few television channels in English. A small sign above the bathroom sink, written in English and Chinese, presented guests with the same riddle every morning: "The Cold Water Drinkable Upon Heated. The Hot Water Non-Drinkable." The answer seemed to be bottled water.

Weiss had become a figure around Taiyuan. Local reporters had written feature stories on the city's famous new coach, and people now recognized him on the street. But more than anything, what drew Weiss into his new city was his wife. Tracy had arrived, unpacked, and announced her intention to explore. "I know the only two choices we have are to sit up in our room and wait for these next nine months to pass or jump in and assimilate ASAP," she wrote friends and family in her first email after arriving. "I am choosing to jump in and think I'll head straight for the deep end. Bob is off to practice and so I am going to try and walk and explore what is outside this building." She hit the send button and walked outside. No one spoke English and few signs were in English. She was impressed that Bob was already testing out a few Chinese phrases, though whenever a communication breakdown occurred, he simply spoke more slowly and loudly in English.

Outside the hotel, Tracy found a city in a state of upheaval, with near-epic amounts of construction and demolition under way. She felt as if she were walking through Universal Studios: the main boulevards were modern and lined with shiny new office towers but a block behind them were only poverty and dirt. Tracy was stepping through unfinished sidewalks and steering herself around work sites, when she noticed a small boy was trailing her. He was maybe eight years old and had a pack of cigarettes hidden in his sleeve. Since he wasn't in school, Tracy figured he was an orphan. Soon they were walking together. They stumbled upon a small aquarium, and she bought tickets. It was dingy inside, but there were tanks filled with fish and other creatures. They watched the seals perform and held an alligator. They joined a small crowd clapping for three young women in mermaid costumes and yellow goggles who would dive into a large fish tank, perform a couple of flips, and surface for air. The music was deafening and the audience did not stop clapping as the young women dove again and again, performing the same flips. Tracy spent an hour with the boy; she spoke to him in English, the boy smiled and answered in Chinese. When she ran out of money, their day together was over. She waved goodbye. He smiled and offered her a cigarette before disappearing back into the streets.

"I fell in love with China after that," she said later.

She wanted to see more and decided to walk to the practice facility, several miles away. Her husband had warned her about the chaos, the open manholes and the general state of vehicular anarchy. Tracy slipped into her nylon running shorts and set off anyway. Elbows chugging, legs churning, she powered past bewildered shopkeepers, gawking taxi drivers, yapping stray dogs, and giggling children. Taiyuan had seen foreigners before, but the spectacle of a 5'2" blond-haired woman motoring through the city in track gear was something altogether new.

"Guess who just walked 4 miles in her running clothes only to find out the people in this province thought I was in my underwear!?" she wrote in another email home. "I thought there was more pointing and laughing than usual but since I was tired and sweaty I just put my headphones on and my head down and tried to ignore it."

Tracy joined a local gym, hired a personal trainer. She took Bob to a party at a disco. People and animals seemed to affix themselves to her. In Seattle, the Weiss family had housed, over many years, four cats, four dogs, two birds, two goldfish, a squirrel, and five horses (stabled nearby). Tracy loved ferrets, and had owned four, including Bandit, who had required weekly acupuncture treatments for an ailing rear leg. Then there were the two rats, Cutie and Cuddles. ("They are smart, they are clean, and they are sociable," she said.) Now she found a puppy, which she couldn't resist, but nor could she keep him at the Longcheng, so she took him to the team's training compound and presented him to the two women who swept the courts. It was unclear whether they considered the puppy a welcome gift or another mouth to feed.

Tracy's Internet research had proved correct about the banquets. A week earlier, the general manager had invited them to lunch with the vice director of the provincial sports bureau, an important supporter who was eager to meet the foreign coach. When the Weisses showed up, they discovered that lunch was a wedding; actually, part of a three-day celebration of the vice director's daughter's nuptials. There were 600 guests. Bob and Tracy took seats of honor and drank wine and shots of *baijiu*, Chinese grain alcohol. Before they left, they watched two performers dressed as Mickey and Minnie Mouse walk down the aisle as part of the entertainment.

The new Chinese assistant coach arrived in the first week of October. His name was Liu Tie, and he seemed eager and gung ho. Weiss knew that part of his job was to mentor a Chinese coach for the future and he regarded Liu as his protégé and heir apparent. For his part, Liu addressed Weiss as if he were an honored teacher.

But a week after Liu's arrival, Zhang, the general manager, invited Weiss to lunch. Joe was there, because conversation would be impossible otherwise, and so was Liu. The general manager offered his usual pleasantries and then delivered his message: The owner wanted to make a change. He wanted more discipline. Weiss already knew that Boss Wang believed coaches should emphasize discipline. "I want you to rule with an iron hand," the owner had told him at their first meeting in August.

In the NBA, Weiss's reputation, of course, was as a player's coach, the opposite of a martinet, and if he hadn't changed his personality in the NBA, he wasn't going to do it in China. "Everyone has a different coaching personality," Weiss had told the owner in August. "But I'm going to get what I want out of these guys. It may not look like an iron hand, but the important thing is you get them to do what you want."

Now the general manager told Weiss that Liu Tie would run practice as well as oversee team discipline. Weiss was stunned. Liu Tie had retired as a player the season before and had never coached. Weiss was running NBA practices, teaching the players a new offense, and they were slowly getting it. Practice was paramount. Now Liu Tie was supposed to run practice?

Liu Tie interrupted the general manager. Any deference on his part had vanished; now he was giving orders. He wanted Weiss to put together a practice schedule for the next forty-five days, complete with times for drills, scrimmages, what to do and when to do it. He also had some changes of his own he wanted to introduce. "This is bullshit," Weiss answered, growing angry. He told Joe that if he didn't run practice, he couldn't prepare the team for the games. If he didn't run practice, would he really be the head coach? Joe translated the conversation. Weiss had no idea what was going on.

There had been signs. The players were surly. Here was yet another coach, even if he was from the NBA. Worse, none of them had been paid for months, something Weiss had not been told. When the players complained about the money, the general manager replied that the entire front office, including him, hadn't been paid, either. All payments to the team required Boss Wang's approval. For much of the summer, the boss had been negotiating to sell his factory, and money had been a problem. At one practice, Big Sun started skipping around the gym, yelling in broken English, "No money, no honey! No money, no honey!"

Zhang knew the money would eventually come, but what made him anxious, or what was making Boss Wang anxious, were some of the changes Weiss was making. Weiss was giving the players freedoms they never before enjoyed, eliminating some practices and meetings, like the one on Sunday night.

All of this was relevant to Zhang because his actual title was "interim general manager." If the owner had fired a line of coaches, he had fired a line of general managers, too; eight since 2002. Most of those men had come from other teams or sports organizations, recruited to bring greater professionalism or contacts or something, and they had all run into Boss Wang, often with a clash of ego. Zhang often seemed to have no ego. He almost never raised his voice or lost his temper. The boss had hired him in 1998, when he was barely out of college and was working in neighboring Henan Province as a telephone lineman, a miserable job. Boss Wang was opening a factory nearby, looking for workers who also could play ball for his factory team. Zhang Beihai, a good semipro player, landed a job.

Four years later, after Boss Wang took control of the Brave Dragons, Zhang was transferred to the front office, where he spent the next seven years working every job and bearing witness to management chaos. There was firing after firing, and the gossip mill around Chinese basketball circles reached a consensus that Boss Wang was nuts. No one ever said as much, and the boss had advocates at the league office, but the team had become a circus. Through it all, Zhang remained deeply loyal to Boss Wang. Without the owner, he would still be hanging lines on telephone poles.

"He trusted me like his family," Zhang said.

The decision to become general manager—interim general manager— had not come without reflection. He had turned it down once before, considering himself too young; even now he was not yet thirty. His wife and infant daughter still lived in Henan Province; he slept in the dorm, in a single bedroom connected to his first-floor office. When Boss Wang had declared he wanted an NBA coach, Zhang had been pleased to find Weiss. But now he was worried; players in the NBA, he believed, were more professional than Chinese players, who needed to be treated differently.

"They cannot control themselves," he later told me. "They need someone to manage them. If they are left alone, they could lose control and hurt the team."

Joe had seen the signs, too. He saw that Weiss was trying to treat the players like professionals, a radical step in China. Back in the 1980s, Joe had played for China's most famous team, the Bayi Rockets, which represented the People's Liberation Army. "Bayi was like a jail," he said. The team spent three years inside a training compound in Beijing, practicing in an unheated gym in the winter, playing games in the summer. "Even though I lived in Beijing, I couldn't go out and see my friends," Joe said. "It was a concentration camp. Every morning, we'd get up at six and run ten laps. It was so dark we couldn't see each other."

Players were treated better now, Joe thought; they lived in rooms with computers and televisions. But Chinese basketball had not really changed. A coach's paramount task was to control a team, to bend the players to his will. Under the Chinese system, everyone slept and ate together, like soldiers. This arrangement had once been common in China, when society was organized around a person's *danwei*, or work unit. People lived in dormitories attached to their state-owned factories, ate in a factory commissary, visited the factory doctor, and sent their children to the factory school. But as society loosened and government promoted real estate as an engine of the new economy (not to mention a source of seemingly unlimited official graft), city people bought apartments and cars and assumed the lives of commuting and mortgage payments that were familiar to anyone in the West. Except for professional basketball players.

"The Chinese drill to keep players doing something," Joe said.

If a coach relaxed his grip around the team, Joe thought, the reaction of the players would be immediate rebellion. They would be no different from lifers who unexpectedly find the prison gate left open.

Weiss was NBA, and the Chinese players liked him and took him seriously. One player told Weiss that he was the first coach he had ever seen smile. But Joe felt the players also sensed the grip had loosened. There were small rebellions. Weiss twice tossed Big Sun out of practice for knocking down Little Sun with cheap shots. At another practice, one of the backup point guards grabbed a brick and chased after the starting point guard. Sometimes the players loafed in drills. They were picking up the offense, but Boss Wang and Zhang worried about what was happening off the court. A Chinese head coach would live at the dorm with the players and act like a hall monitor. Weiss resided downtown. Wingtips had a room at the dorm, but the players didn't fear him.

"In China, in this league, management believes that controlling players is more important than developing their skill level," Joe said. Yet Joe was angered by how the players had reacted; their behavior had confirmed the worst assumptions of management. "They only respect you if you treat them harshly," he said, sadly. "The players do not complain. They like it."

At 6'3", lean and athletic, Liu Tie was a rarity in the Chinese Basketball Association. It had not ground him into dust. He had played for sixteen years, for a handful of teams, despite the constant practices and year-round schedule that broke so many players. Much of his prime had been spent as a shooting guard for the now defunct team sponsored by the Chinese air force, and his career had bridged a transition in which basketball was changing from a sport organized to project national glory to a sport that appealed to a new generation partly because of its subversive and individualistic edges. Liu Tie was only thirty-eight, but his values were entrenched in that earlier era. His goal for Chinese basketball was little different from the Communist Party's goal for China. He talked about helping China become a global basketball power by 2020, the same year designated by Chinese leaders for the country's arrival as a truly developed nation. Basketball had to develop along the "stronger, higher, faster principle," which "is extended across the whole nation," he would say.

As a player, Liu Tie was a prolific outside shooter and a tough defender.

Nicknamed "the Mongolian Steed," he was from the northern region of China known as Inner Mongolia, and he had the high cheekbones and wide-rounded eyes common to many ethnic Mongolians. He was born in 1971, during the Cultural Revolution, and soon after the family was sent for reeducation to a farming village in Inner Mongolia. After a few years, basketball intervened: Liu Tie's father was a good amateur player, and the county sports commission needed a coach for the county team. Dad got the job and the family was able to leave the farm for a nearby city. They moved into the team dormitory.

It was the family's *danwei*; Liu Tie grew up in the system that Boss Wang had supposedly hired Bob Weiss to change. Now Liu had moved into the Brave Dragons' dormitory. His first task would be discipline.

CHAPTER THREE

PIECES

The Tractor was sleepy. He had arrived late the previous night from Michigan, having quickly packed his bags after his agent reached an agreement for him to play with the Brave Dragons. After traveling almost twenty hours through ten time zones, Robert "Tractor" Traylor was now standing in the middle of China, his very large sock-covered feet sticking out of plastic shower shoes embossed with the logo of the Cleveland Cavaliers, one of his former teams. Rain leaked through the roof of the gym, and the Tractor was a bit bewildered as he watched the Chinese players run the court. The Tractor was listed at 6'8" but 6'6" seemed more accurate. He was a huge, burly man, yet in the NBA he had been an undersized power forward in the mold of Charles Barkley, a former first-round draft pick of the Milwaukee Bucks and college star at the University of Michigan. He had decided against practicing, as a precaution against injury, until signing his contract. He assumed that would be a formality.

It was October 22, one day before the eighteen teams in the Chinese Basketball Association had to submit their final rosters to the league office. The next day, the general manager would fly to Beijing to deliver the names, yet no one was certain which names would be on the list, or, more precisely, which foreign names would be on it, and those were the names most critical for the team's success or failure. If Mao envisioned China as a nation of classless equity, a Chinese professional basketball team is a fraternity of inequality. Foreigners so dominated past seasons that the league limited their playing time, calculating that while foreigners were needed to improve competition, they should not hoard minutes that could be dedicated to developing Chinese players. The rules operated like trade restrictions. China was willing to open its market to foreigners, but only so much, under certain conditions, and not without protecting the locals.

Yet no team could afford to have crummy foreign players. On nearly every team, the foreigners were the leading scorers and leading rebounders, irrespective of playing time. This year would be different anyway; the league office, as an experiment, was allowing foreigners to play the entire game. The old system had distorted the game and reinforced the basest stereotypes of American players as selfish. Foreigners made the most money of anyone on the court, yet their minutes were limited, meaning they felt obliged to shoot, and shoot often, to score enough points to justify their contracts and earn their next ones. Without the artificiality imposed by the time restrictions, the hope was that foreign and Chinese players might better blend together this season. The Brave Dragons had already signed their first foreigner, former Atlanta Hawk Donta Smith. Six feet seven inches tall, Smith was an excellent passer and scorer who could play every position on the court. He had spent two months practicing on weekly contracts, his mood darkening every passing week without a deal, until a few days earlier the general manager had finally offered him a contract for the season. Smith had already clashed with Liu Tie, but he signed the contract.

"My congratulations," Weiss had said to him. "Or maybe condolences."

The Tractor was a candidate for the second foreign slot, reserved for a big man, if unaware that he was merely the latest very large American who had been promised a contract to play for the Brave Dragons. Before him came players even the most obsessive fan would struggle to recognize: Tyrone Washington, Eric Turner, Sean Lampley, Norman Nolan, and Larry Turner among them. None of them held any fairy-tale notions of playing overseas to earn a shot at the NBA. The NBA had already processed them, quantified and evaluated them, and spit them out. They were castoffs, here for the same reason unemployed airline pilots from the United States had started migrating to China, India, and Southeast Asia: There were jobs there.

A wintry cold had settled over Taiyuan, and the gym was frigid. The radiators were cold to the touch. Outside, fields were starting to die, and plumes of white smoke from distant smokestacks curled in the air. On the court, a large orange bucket had been placed near the 3-point line to collect raindrops trickling through a hole in the roof. Coach Liu was on the floor with a mop as the Chinese players stepped carefully through full-court passing drills. They dodged the bucket and the mop as they ran. In less than two weeks, Coach Liu had undone two months of Weiss's work by converting his new authority over practice into authority over the team. He still presented himself as the dutiful student, the protégé, focusing intently whenever Weiss addressed the team or even taking notes when Weiss walked players through an offensive set. But he had reinstated the repetitive drills that Weiss abandoned as a waste of time, and limited Weiss to only twenty minutes each practice to install the type of NBA offense that Boss Wang admired on television. It was the same emphasis on rote repetition that shaped Chinese education, where students were graded by how closely they were able to get to a verbatim answer. Rather than worrying that the players might burn out before the season, Coach Liu had instituted a third daily practice, after dinner, for the Chinese players to shoot free throws and practice jump shots. He also ordered every Chinese player to write daily entries in a journal, subject to his review. He encouraged them to bare their souls.

"Go! Go! Go!" Coach Liu shouted as the Chinese players navigated the wet spots on the court.

I sat courtside with Donta Smith, Rick Turner, and the Tractor. Smith was nursing an injury and taking the afternoon off. Weiss walked over to ask if the Tractor was going to practice.

"Waiting on a contract," he answered. "Haven't signed it yet."

Weiss walked away, and the Tractor leaned over toward Smith.

"He didn't even know I was coming," the Tractor said. He was discovering that almost no one knew he was coming.

The Tractor's arrival was the latest unexpected moment in Bob Weiss's China adventure. He had worked through his anger over losing control of practice, if not his confusion. He thought about leaving, and had he been a younger coach, he might have. But he liked China, and Tracy was having a ball being a foreigner in a strange land. On one flight from southern China, Tracy was asked to pose for photographs as she walked down the aisle to the bathroom. She loved it. Weiss had not come to China to prove anything. He came for an adventure and he was getting one sooner than expected. He had initially been hired as a consultant, and he was now acting as one, though Liu Tie had so far demonstrated limited willingness to consult him. The strangest thing to Weiss was that he remained head coach. The new arrangement gave Liu Tie control of practice but Weiss retained control of games, or so he was promised. He would be introduced as head coach, call plays during the games, and address the media afterward. Anyone watching would assume the NBA coach was the coach.

Boss Wang had been hospitable, inviting Weiss and Tracy to dinner, but Weiss was uncertain how to read the owner. Communication was an obvious problem. One afternoon in the gym, with the owner expected to arrive later, Weiss and I were watching practice, when he asked, "How do you say W-o-n-g?" He was practicing how to say Boss Wang's name. I explained that the surname was actually Wang. Weiss opened a leather Spalding binder and wrote down the name. "Is it J-i-n-g?" he continued. "*Jiang*," I had answered, Wang Xingjiang, and Weiss had walked onto the court practicing the name of the man paying his salary.

Boss Wang was already proving to be perplexing; after the team lost an exhibition game, he spent an hour screaming and bellowing in the locker room, singling out each player, dissecting his performance and character. At other times, Boss Wang spoke to Weiss about how the Chinese league needed change and reform, how Chinese coaches wrongly shackled players as far as style of play went. Then he had brought in a Chinese coach who was quickly shackling them again.

The presence of the Tractor was a surprise because Weiss was already personally negotiating with one of his former players from the Seattle SuperSonics, a backup center named Olumide Oyedeji. He was 6'10", a Nigerian who led the Chinese league in rebounding the previous season while playing for two teams. He was an established star in China, and the Brave Dragons had offered him one of the highest salaries in the league, about $350,000 for five months' work. He had an offer for more money to play in Russia, and interest from teams in Europe, but he was willing to take less money for the stability and familiarity of playing for his old coach, Weiss. The only problem was getting him a visa to China. He lived in Orlando, Florida, but was seeking British citizenship under the sponsorship of his British wife, even though he was a citizen of Nigeria. Despite his having played a handful of seasons in the Chinese league, the Chinese government was treating Olumide like a stranger and refused to allow him to fly directly from Orlando to China. Instead, he had been directed to fly from Orlando to London to Lagos to China in order to acquire the necessary stamps, though it wasn't clear why. So when the Tractor appeared the previous night in the lobby of the Longcheng Hotel, Weiss was a little taken aback. He headed to the bar for a drink.

The Tractor now rose and walked out of the gym. He was going to meet the general manager.

It was so cold in the gym that Donta Smith was wearing a parka. On the court, point guard Pan Jiang led the players through another sprinting drill, screaming and shouting as he raced ahead of his teammates. Pan's body was so stiff that he seemed fused together, as if someone had created him by pouring cement into the mold of a basketball player.

"That boy goes hard every play, every second," Donta said, approvingly.

The Tractor pushed through the double doors of the gym and took a seat. Judging from the expression on his face, his meeting with the general manager had gone poorly. He was a very large, unsatisfied man who had traveled a long way for a contract that did not exist.

"No practice?" Donta asked.

"Ain't gonna do that shit," the Tractor answered, his voice low and bitter. "They told me the deal was done. Now they are like, 'We'd like to see you practice for two or three days.' ".

Weiss walked over for a status check with the Tractor. "They rushed me here because they said the roster had to be set by Thursday," the Tractor said. That much, at least, was true.

Forty minutes had passed, and the Chinese players were still running. The rain continued, though the orange bucket had been removed and the players were trying to step around the spot where Liu Tie had been mopping.

"If I'm out there, and I get hurt, where do I go from here?" the Tractor asked.

Liu Tie now divided the Chinese players for a scrimmage. Ever since he had arrived, he had emphasized intensity and aggression more than execution, and the scrimmage was more like a scrum. Pan played tight, hawking defense, fouling on nearly every possession. The offense was disorganized and out of control, everyone banging into everyone else like bumper cars.

"Man, pretty ugly out there without an American," Weiss said to the other Americans.

Liu Tie blew the whistle and the players grabbed water bottles. Tian, the fourth-string point guard, walked over to the row of Americans. He had arrived with two other players as part of a trade with the Guangdong team. Weiss was still trying to figure out the mechanics of the trade, since no one had left. Tian was slow, a bad shooter with poor judgment on the court. His legs were so thick and shapeless that the Americans called him

Big Calves. But he was also a prankster who walked around smirking like the kid who figured out how to cheat on the test.

"Fuck!" he shouted at Donta, pounding the ball on the floor.

"Fuck!" he shouted again, smirking and pointing at the court.

Donta laughed and slapped hands with Tian. Communication on the court was fairly basic when the Americans were blended together with the Chinese players, with everyone understanding the meaning of "shoot" or "pass" or "defense," but off the court there was very little shared vocabulary. "Fuck" seemed to transcend all cultures.

"Fuck!" Donta yelled back in what had become a team-building exercise.

The scrimmage resumed and the Americans were appalled.

"They are just running without purpose," the Tractor said. Liu Tie had told everyone to race the ball up the court on every possession without regard to pace or self-control. Neither side was bothering to run plays nor concentrating on team defense. Tian, nursing a leg injury, rejoined the Americans, smirking.

"Fuck you! Fuck you!" he shouted.

It was 5:32 in the afternoon when Liu halted the scrimmage. Through the slat of windows, the rain had stopped and the sun was dissolving behind a distant line of mountains. The gym had gotten colder.

"I feel like we are just a couple of degrees away from seeing our breath," Rick Turner said from the American row. "It'll be like one of those NFL films, and they are talking, and it is slow motion, and we come out and steam is coming off our heads."

Liu placed two orange cones on the opposite foul lines and two more on the opposite sides of midcourt, forming a diamond. The players had been running for more than two hours, but he divided them into small groups and ordered them to start running around the perimeter of the diamond. Tian was told to join in. After a lap, he began grimacing, grabbing his bad leg.

"Fuck!" he screamed. He was no longer smirking.

Donta and the Tractor watched, incredulous. An NBA team might do this kind of running during the first day or two of training camp, but the Brave Dragons had been practicing for months. Liu blew the whistle and ordered the players to run faster, and they began sprinting around the cones. Pan was sprinting and screaming, raising his eyebrows and baring his teeth, as if he were being electrocuted.

"He's going to run them again?" Donta asked. "That's too far."

The Chinese guys were gasping. Liu kept blowing his whistle, sending group after group. One of the new players from Guangdong, Ba Zhichang, known as Little Ba, started to wobble. Pan had turned pale and was coughing as Liu again sounded the whistle. Pan screamed and took off sprinting.

"Man, that is too much," the Tractor said.

Little Ba, who was 6'8", was about to faint. He was swaying so much that his legs seemed to be disintegrating beneath him, a marionette about to collapse in a heap. He was staggering around in a circle, when Liu Tie grabbed his hand and pulled him into an embrace. He grasped Little Ba around his shoulders and steered him around the court, keeping him walking, keeping him conscious, a gesture that seemed gentle and kind-hearted, until Little Ba recovered and Liu Tie ordered him to run again.

"That's a little too homoerotic for me," said Rick Turner.

"Yeah," said the Tractor.

One by one, the players kept running. Liu was timing them. When they ran fast enough, they could stop. Finally, Tian was the last player on the court. He sprinted from sideline to sideline, screaming, holding his leg. Liu Tie refused to let him stop, and when Tian staggered off between sprints, the coach grabbed his hands and pulled him back. Tian's face was red, dripping wet, and contorted in pain, almost swollen. I was certain practice must be over, that Liu Tie could not ask him to run anymore, but he did.

Liu Tie blew his whistle, and Tian ran about ten steps before he fell onto the court. Now practice was over.

The front office of the Shanxi Brave Dragons, two rooms on the ground floor of the team's orange dormitory, had the dingy impermanence of a Chinese bus station. There were four desks, a sofa and matching chair made of imitation leather, a glass coffee table caked in dust, and a dying potted tree. The tile floor was cracked and littered with cigarette butts. I settled into the chair. Liu Tie was on the sofa with a young Chinese sports agent named Garrison Guo. Garrison had arrived a few weeks earlier representing one of the Americans trying out for a job and had remained on his own tryout for a job as a second interpreter. He had helped me persuade Coach Liu to discuss his philosophy of basketball. Liu was a handsome, swaggering man, his hair shaved into a crew cut as thick and luxuriant as an animal's pelt. He smiled and checked his watch. We began.

I asked about his coaching influences, and he cited his mentor, Jiang Xingquan, known as the toughest coach in China. "First, he emphasized being strict," Liu began. "He emphasized discipline. And he emphasized the little things. And this works especially well in China. As we all know, Asian players are not as capable as players elsewhere."

I had not actually known this, or at least no one had very convincingly explained to me why it was true, but Liu Tie persisted. Asians were genetically inferior, he argued, at least as far as the physical demands of basketball, which meant that the methods of Chinese coaches were tailored to help Chinese athletes overcome their physical shortcomings.

"We have our own special ways to narrow the difference," he said. "As long as we apply these principles over a long time, we can eliminate the difference. Just like in ancient times, our ancient martial arts masters would defeat foreign boxers or martial artists from other countries."

He leaned forward on the sofa, his elbows resting on his knees, and stared at me. "Like we are doing in this gym," he continued. "We are working harder, and consistently, step by step, and little by little, we'll get better. We're consistently doing the hard work." The Americans regarded Liu as a martinet who wasted practice time on pointless junior high drills; Liu saw himself as an ironsmith pounding substandard Chinese ore into stronger, better steel.

It was not just their bodies Liu considered lacking. He believed the Chinese players had lost hope, not because they were asked to practice too hard, or because their lives were too constricted, but because past coaches had not taught them lessons a Chinese coach was expected to teach. So part of his job, as he saw it, was to restore hope. Which explained another of his habits that grated on the Americans: the long speeches at meetings or after practice. He treated team meetings as history seminars, extolling the virtues of Napoleon as a model of aggressiveness and proof that a little guy can do big things. He talked about Mao as a model of determination (as opposed to a model of destructive megolamania).

"Through my experience, through stories in my life, I can let them know what they should do when they are older, what is right and wrong, what is their place in the universe," he said, returning to China's ancient martial arts masters as a source of inspiration. "It is pretty much the same principle. We know we Chinese players are different than African American players. They are more physically gifted. We are not. But we believe that by working harder, bit by bit, it's like water dripping into a cup. Over time, you finally achieve a full cup."

Patience was paramount, he continued. A kung fu apprentice might need a decade of study before attaining true competence. Basketball might be the same.

I realized we were having a strange conversation, or at least a conversation that would run roughshod over political correctness parameters in the United States. Garrison had been helping with some interpretation, and he rolled his eyes when Liu digressed onto the kung fu warriors. Yet nothing that Liu had said was considered outside mainstream thought in China. Even as the rest of the world regarded China as a rising power, as the country most likely to dominate this century, most Chinese regarded themselves as genetically deficient, at least individually. Mobilizing the masses, not inspiring individuals, had always been the priority of Chinese leaders. The X-rays and bone tests conducted on Chinese boys like Pan Jiang and Big Sun were a systemic response rooted in assumptions of physical inferiority. No country on earth believed in Darwin more than China.

I asked about his strategy for motivating players. From observing practice, I assumed it was to run them to death. "Sometimes, I will be a teacher, a philosopher, or a strict disciplinarian," he said. "Or maybe a bad guy, like a criminal. I have plenty of roles to teach them how to grow. Maybe sometimes I will be like a brother, a true friend, or be gentle like a woman, to care for them, love them, help them grow and become more mature.

"I have one simple goal," he continued. "I have to master them, to become like me. I want them to contribute to the improvement of Chinese basketball."

Liu wanted to lift Chinese basketball in the same way China was trying to lift itself in every other endeavor. Basketball presented a greater challenge because Chinese were not naturally gifted in the sport, he said, so they must be made better through hard work and sacrifice. He told me that at night, when the Americans were at the hotel, he lectured the Chinese players on the greatness of the ancient Song and Tang dynasties, the periods often regarded as the zenith of Chinese civilization.

"This team is built on one principle," he said. "It is an army of tigers and wolves. They should fight like tigers and wolves, but they should be kind in their hearts."

Liu looked at his watch and stood up. It was time for lunch. Garrison left to make some telephone calls, and I joined Liu in the canteen where the remnants of the buffet were on the server: tofu, fish, chicken, rice. Coach Liu loaded down a metal tray and hunched over his food, shoveling rice into his mouth with his chopsticks, slurping down the juice served with the meal, his lips inches above the table. Cooking and eating are among the most languorous delights of Chinese life, but Liu believed Chinese spent too much time and energy on food. He finished in less than ten minutes. Another practice began in an hour.

When Garrison Guo first walked into the gym, I could not decide if he was posing as a sports agent or a cocaine dealer. His tinted sunglasses were propped atop a soufflé of long, wavy 1970s hair that tumbled onto the epaulets of his black jacket. His unbuttoned, wide-collared silk shirt opened to a silver chain swirling around his bare chest. He was all smiles and high fives, and every few minutes one of his two mobile phones jangled awake with Chinese pop music ring tones. At twenty-four, Garrison was fluent in English and had spent the previous season translating for the Beijing team, a job that placed him in the floating, interdependent network of foreign players and their interpreters. Being an agent had seemed like a career advancement, but he had yet to see any money out of it. Spending the season with the Brave Dragons could be appealing, he thought. He knew enough about Boss Wang to be wary but he was intrigued with Weiss. He thought Weiss represented "advanced basketball culture" and should hold seminars to lecture players and coaches on American philosophies.

"They need to connect with the thinking in the West," he had told me during one practice, as Liu Tie ordered up more sprinting drills. "The young guys are eager. They want to play like Americans."

It spoke to the fluidity of the organizational chart in the Brave Dragons' front office that Garrison, having arrived only two weeks earlier, was now acting, more or less, as the team's assistant general manager. He had not yet been offered a job, nor was he receiving anything more than an empty bed and free meals in the dorm, but he was already enmeshed in the making of the final roster.

Year in, year out, the Chinese Basketball Association standings were dominated by the same handful of teams: Bayi, the military team; Guangdong, the southern juggernaut supported by private money; Jiangsu, owned by a state steel factory in the old Nationalist capital of

Nanjing; and Liaoning. Though the power structure occasionally shifted, and unexpected teams rose momentarily in the standings—the Shanghai Sharks won the championship with Yao Ming—bad teams tended to stay bad, which made the league boring and predictable. Since the league lacked free agency, bad teams could do little to quickly improve, other than sign better foreigners or maybe an NBA coach. To inject more competition this season, the league was not only lifting the playing time restrictions on imported players but also lifting its salary cap. Now teams were spending Steinbrennerian money, in the context of China, and attracting more talented players: the Beijing Ducks were pursuing the 7'1" behemoth and former Indiana Pacer David Harrison for a once unfathomable offer of $100,000 a month. Former Houston Rockets Kirk Snyder and Michael Harris were now with teams in southern China. The Chinese basketball press was floating almost daily reports that former NBA stars, including Gary Payton, Vin Baker, and Bonzi Wells, could be headed to China, possibly even to Taiyuan.

The league also had made one more change as a direct boost to the perennial bottom-feeders: The four worst teams would be permitted to sign a third foreigner, as long as he was Asian.

Like any other Chinese entity, the Chinese Basketball Association had global aspirations, one of which was to become one of the world's leading basketball leagues. If no one yet dared dream of supplanting the NBA, CBA officials wanted to surpass the leagues in Europe and Russia and, more immediately, to become recognized as the dominant league in their own Asian neighborhood. Someone in the CBA marketing office had reasoned that recruiting players from other Asian nations would boost regional interest and help establish the CBA brand. The powerhouse teams would have rebelled if the doormats were allowed to hire a third American, European, African, or Australian; that could transform a laggard like the Brave Dragons into a championship contender. But the powerhouses could stomach the Asian policy; no one expected an Asian player to have much impact. Chinese apparently perceived, say, South Koreans to be as racially inferior as they perceived themselves to be. Asian countries, in the language of the Chinese government, were at a lower stage of basketball development.

The question was how to use this slot wisely. If Liu Tie regarded Chinese players as molten iron, whose final shape depended on heat and pounding, Weiss talked about a basketball team as a puzzle assembled by connecting pieces of different shapes and sizes. Once the pieces were fit into a whole, a team was made. This type of thinking was common in American basketball, where players are often categorized and typecast. There was the deadeye 3-point shooter, the defensive stopper, the heady point guard. The pieces became clichés. There were also pieces whose role was to counteract pieces on other teams; Shane Battier, a top defender now with the Memphis Grizzlies, made millions for doing many things, one of which was to play tough defense against Kobe Bryant, the ultimate piece, when his team played the Los Angeles Lakers. This emphasis on pieces promoted specialization and could prolong a career. Even when he could no longer score, Dikembe Mutombo, the 7'3" center from Africa, maintained his NBA career into his forties because he was a rare piece, a really big shot blocker, rebounder, and defender. Yet this specialization also created ruthless competition if you were a common piece, a 3-point shooter one shade less deadeye than a competitor, or a big man a little less adept around the basket. Every single foreigner dominating the Chinese league was a piece already discarded by the NBA.

Weiss's two months with the team had convinced him that the piece he lacked was a very good point guard, the player who brings the ball up the court, distributes it to others, and is capable of scoring. Pan played hard but struggled to effectively run and control the team. His backups had not shown enough talent to displace him. Throughout the league, even the best point guards were not capable of competing with the weakest guards in the NBA, physically or mentally. There were theories for this: Point guard is a position that requires individualism, creativity, and the ability to make decisions on the fly; Chinese players are drilled to strictly follow the instructions of the coach, and creativity can be interpreted as disobeying the coach. The Chinese sorting system also was a problem, since size was deemed the most valuable raw commodity. Yao Ming was the most extreme result of this system, regarded less as an aberration than proof of its success. The system was still looking for other 7'6" centers while effectively excluding the vast majority of kids, many of whom would eventually grow far less tall but tall enough to be point guards equal in size to most of the NBA's best.

The piece Weiss now coveted was Sam Daghlas, 6'5" and 200 pounds, the starting point guard for the national team of Jordan. Jordan, neighbor of Israel and Lebanon, beneficiary of the warm breezes of the Mediterranean, would be regarded as a distant cousin on the family tree of

Asia, at the far edge of West Asia. But in basketball, Asia was defined by Fédération Internationale de Basketball, or FIBA, the international body governing the sport, which partitioned the globe to organize regional qualifying tournaments for the world championships. Under the FIBA formula, Asia stretched from Japan to Uzbekistan to Iran before ending at Jordan. Weiss had dedicated much of his recent telephone time talking with Daghlas's agent about a deal, which now seemed set.

Except a problem had emerged. Daghlas had played college ball in the United States, and an Internet search suggested that while Daghlas did have Jordanian lineage, he might actually have come into this world in San Diego. Being Asian American or even being an Asian with an American passport would disqualify anyone from being considered an Asian in China, and the general manager was worried that the team could lose the Asian slot altogether if the league rejected Daghlas's application.

"Well, tough shit," Weiss said. "He's Jordanian."

Getting Daghlas was especially critical because of the potential alternative. Boss Wang had dispatched Joe to Kazakhstan on a talent search. Kazakhstan was indisputably within Central Asia, but it was the land of weightlifters and wrestlers, not basketball players. Yet reports had circulated back to Taiyuan, indirectly, that Joe had located a prospect, possibly another big man.

"Now we're going to start seeing Iranians and Kazakhs and who knows what else," Rick Turner complained. "So let's finish this Sam Daghlas thing."

With the general manager now en route to Beijing, Garrison was responsible for finishing the Daghlas thing. After leaving Liu Tie in the canteen, I found Garrison at one of the desks in the front office, sifting through a small stack of papers that represented the official lineage of Sam Daghlas. Garrison needed to fax Daghlas's application to the league office and was weighing the geopolitics of how best to complete the form. He pulled out a copy of a passport issued by the Hashemite Kingdom of Jordan declaring that Osama Mohammad Fathi Daghlas had been born in the capital city of Amman on September 18, 1979.

"Do you think I should use his full name?" Garrison asked. He examined the copy of the passport. The full name certainly seemed more Asian, and less American, than Sam Daghlas, as far as any Chinese basketball bureaucrat knew. Garrison deliberated. He asked my opinion and we decided, on behalf of the team, that the full name would be used. Garrison Guo, soon to become a paid employee of the team, hoped he had secured the team's missing piece.

The Chinese players wore heavy coats and shuffled slowly across the darkened courtyard toward the gym. The third practice of the day was the nighttime shooting session reserved only for them. The Americans were at the Longcheng Hotel, relaxing, and I had spent the past hour visiting with the Taiwanese player, Little Sun, who was sharing a second-floor dorm room with one of the new players acquired in the trade, a forward named Ji Le. His English name was Joy and he had already become one of the most popular players on the team. In the dorm room, Joy was wearing earphones, sitting at a small desk watching a Justin Timberlake video on an outdated desktop computer, bags of ice taped around his knees. The centerpiece of the room was a large, dusty television set, and Little Sun and Joy each slept atop large wooden crates covered with thin pallets. The toilet was a stained urinal. Little Sun cleared a space for me on his crate.

He was distressed. Liu Tie's arrival had been a pinprick that had slowly deflated him. At 5'9", Little Sun was small, if muscular, with the wisps of a faint black mustache. He spoke barely above a whisper. Before, he had been gaining confidence in scrimmages, soaking up whatever Weiss asked the players to do, eager to learn anything from a man who had touched the courts of the NBA. His teammates had taunted him initially because of his Taiwanese background. Taiwan is the island off the southeastern coast of China where the Nationalist Army fled after being defeated in 1949 by Mao's Red Army. Ever since then, Chinese leaders have shaped their military strategy and foreign policy around one day reclaiming Taiwan, even as Taiwan, now a democracy, has shown little interest in being reclaimed. Taiwanese and Chinese shared lineage and history but were divided by a bloody history. In Little Sun's first weeks of practice, Big Sun had pummeled him with cheap shots, but eventually his teammates' attitudes changed.

"The first month was very hard," he said in his simple English. "They were bitching me. They were saying, 'You guys from Taiwan are too short. You can't play in the CBA.' But I think I proved myself. I won respect."

But not from Liu Tie. Coach Liu once played for the air force team, and should China ever attack Taiwan, the initial assault would come from land-based missiles fired across the Taiwan Strait, with support from the

Chinese air force. Even if Liu Tie was not a fighter pilot, Little Sun knew his coach would consider it a patriotic duty to bomb Taiwan. Taiwanese point guards had a reputation in China for their smarts and cunning, and a few had played well in the CBA, including one who once led the league in assists. But in practice, Liu Tie mocked Little Sun for playing "Taiwan independence defense." He called him soft. The excitement Little Sun once had about playing for an NBA coach had been replaced with confusion.

"I am the first player from Taiwan to have an NBA coach teach me," he said. "I feel I have improved. That is my pleasure. But it is very strange right now. Coach Bob is just standing there."

He pulled out his journal and opened to a page where Liu Tie had scribbled criticisms in the margins. The coach had complained the players were not sharing enough about their lives, but there was only so much to share. Their lives consisted of nothing but practice. At one team meeting, Rick Turner had scribbled his own faux entry:

> Dear Diary,
>   Today I watched as we dribbled up and down the court for
> 45 minutes. This makes me feel terribly bored. So much so that if I
> have to go through another day of this, I will attempt to gouge my
> eyes out with a spoon.

Little Sun dutifully documented his thoughts about practice and never dared write about his confusion over Weiss.

"They say he is still the head coach, but he is not teaching now," Little Sun said. "I don't know why."

After I left Little Sun, I found a few players already shooting in the gym, even though the shootaround was not scheduled to start for another twenty minutes. Liu Tie's grip on the Chinese players was such that he did not even bother to attend; he knew the players would not dare defy him. Without any coaches, the mood was lighter. Soon everyone was shooting and laughing, and the sound of balls snapping through the net filled the gym. Little Ba stood behind the 3-point line nailing shot after shot, flicking his wrists perfectly. Big Calves Tian was shooting nearby, shouting out his standard "Fuck!" with every miss. We offered one another a respectful "Fuck!" as a greeting.

Joy was one of the last players to arrive, laughing and shouting out my name. He was studying English through a popular course in China called

"Crazy English," in which students are encouraged to shout as a means of overcoming any bashfulness about practicing English out loud. His mobile phone was programmed to translate English into Chinese, and he tapped his huge fingers against the screen whenever he was puzzled by a word. When I had one day asked him why he studied English—none of the other players did—he smiled. "Because I want a foreign girlfriend," he answered, laughing. But he already had a girlfriend, the most famous cheerleader in China, who cheered during the Olympics in a string bikini at the beach volleyball venue. "No, really," he had admitted, "I want to be able to talk to the American players."

In the context of Chinese basketball, Joy had moved from the Enlightenment to the Dark Ages by coming to Taiyuan. His old team was the league's defending champions, the Guangdong Southern Tigers, and attracted the best talent in China. At 6'6", he was too short and too slow to dominate inside, but he was smart and had made himself into a name player out of sheer hard work. As a child in the city of Liuzhou in Guangxi Province, he had been singled out by the sieve and steered to a top provincial sports school at age twelve. But by fifteen, his coach sent him home and told him to find another sport, since China needed athletes in more than basketball. "He said I should try water polo," Joy said. "But I think water polo is bullshit. I still thought I could be good."

He returned to a regular high school and dedicated himself to basketball. "Every morning, I woke up at 5:30. Besides school time, I practiced all the time. Then, after two years, I got a chance." His high school coach got him a tryout with the junior team of the Southern Tigers. He would steadily move up to the top team, first as a practice player, then a benchwarmer, and finally as a solid contributor for rebounds, passing, and reliable shooting. When the Southern Tigers won the previous year's championship, Joy played valuable minutes. But the team was stocked with forwards and had bigger, younger players who needed time on the court. When the general manager floated the idea of a trade, Joy had agreed. The Shanxi team was horrible, so playing time there would not be a problem. He hoped Shanxi would give him the chance to achieve his biggest goal.

"All-star, all-star," he would say, smiling.

At the foul line, Joy was making shot after shot as I stood beside him. When we first met, I had unwittingly insulted him. His home province of Guangxi is along the border with Vietnam and has a high percentage of minority groups in a country that is overwhelmingly Han Chinese.

He had the high, pronounced cheekbones common among some of the minority groups in Guangxi and had a menacing stare, when he wanted one, which was not very often. I later learned that his American teammates with the Southern Tigers had nicknamed him "Mean Mug." When I asked if he were *minzu*, or a minority, he had flinched. No, he was Han Chinese. I also asked the provenance of his English name. It was a literal translation. His parents had named their only child Ji Le, or Season of Joy.

Joy made another foul shot, and then another. He smiled, peering down at me as he said something. "Im de groof."

He made another foul shot.

"Im de groof," he repeated, grinning.

I looked at him, puzzled. He pointed to the basket and formed a circle with his thumb and forefinger. Then he stuck another finger through the whole, again and again. I wondered if dorm life was getting to him.

He kept making foul shots when I finally got it.

"In the groove," I said.

His smile was radiant. He tossed the ball off the backboard and into the basket.

"In the grove," he tried.

I corrected him. "In the groove."

Practice ended and we walked outside. It was freezing cold, and I stumbled in the dark on the short step outside the gym door. I saw the dimly lit windows of the dorm and got my bearings.

"In the groave!" Joy tried. I corrected him again.

Then he shouted it louder, Crazy English style. "In the grove! In the grove!"

Finally, shouting still louder, he hit the perfect note. "In the groove! In the groove!"

I started shouting, too, and we walked through the darkness toward the dorm. We were in the groove.

The Yingze Hotel somehow missed the rise of China. There was a strange dusty quality to the lobby, though not the usual polluting dust of Taiyuan. This was the dust of neglect, the type that accumulates in a room where time is somehow suspended, the dust you might find upon returning to your childhood home, where the same lamps remain on the same tables, the same green vase sits unmoved on the same shelf, placed between the same hardback books. Outside the Yingze Hotel, it was November 12,

2008, and China thrummed with the usual tumult and energy. Inside, it was 1955.

I had come to the Yingze to attend Media Day. The season was about to begin, and the Shanxi Brave Dragons were introducing their new coach and players. But when I stepped into the lobby I might as well have entered a museum exhibit entitled "Hotels in Early Socialist China." In that era, hotels were as rare as guests; travelers needed government permits to move between cities, which meant the only people traveling were usually Communist Party officials or the rare foreign visitor. China was a destitute and austere place, about to fall off a precipice into two decades of Maoist famine, chaos, and paranoia. The Yingze lobby was so badly lit and so determinedly undecorated that it seemed like a deliberate admonition: Do not expect any pleasure here. To one side was a dingy state-run bookstore paired with a dingier state-run travel agency. The front desk was a small counter staffed by a woman in a stern blue suit. Something seemed off. The Yingze commanded prime real estate, a short walk from People's Square, across a major boulevard from a large city park. My taxi driver told me it was the elite hotel of the local Communist Party, the hotel *owned* by the party, and if Chinese officials wanted anything out of an elite hotel, it was grandeur and pleasure, usually at a Las Vegas scale.

The desk clerk smiled and, upon my inquiring, corrected my error. I had stumbled into the original hotel, now the East Wing, but Media Day was in the newer West Wing, about 100 yards away. The Yingze turned out to be a timeline of the Communist era in Taiyuan. The original building had opened in 1955, a project overseen and designed by architects and engineers from China's Communist patron, the Soviet Union. The Yingze would quickly become Taiyuan's premier address; peasants would stand outside the gate to gawk. By the end of the 1950s, the Soviets began an expansion and poured the foundation for an octagonal west wing. But the diplomatic split between Beijing and Moscow froze the project. The Soviet advisers left with the blueprints, and Taiyuan had neither the expertise nor the money to finish the job. The foundation stood fallow for years, a cement scar in the ground, proof of what China could not yet do. Then, as the country rapidly picked up speed, Chinese architects finished the West Wing with Chinese money.

It was a cold, sunny morning, and as I approached the entrance of the West Wing, the most striking things about the exterior of the building were the large advertisements beside the entrance for Vasto, a retailer selling European-styled clothing. In one ad, a European businessman in a pin-striped Vasto suit sat atop a steed adorned in medieval mail, gripping a pool cue rather than a lance, his horse being led by a blond woman dressed in an Arthurian bikini of metal rings and steel scales. "Universal Charm," read the slogan, in English. In another ad, the same businessman wore a Vasto gold and diamond watch as two women spilled over his shoulders. No slogan was necessary. I walked inside.

The lobby was as bright and cavernous as the East Wing lobby was dark and cramped. The floor was covered in yellow marble, and a large circular chandelier radiated a soft white light. I could hear the faint chords of piano Muzak tinkling out of unseen speakers as I approached the grandly appointed front desk. Rivulets of water trickled down an ornate frieze on the wall, a few steps away from a small set of steps leading to the Yingze International Shopping Arcade, home to a Vasto store and other luxury retailers selling imported goods. The only thing missing was customers.

Every hotel had the same stores, and if the stores rarely seemed to have customers, they also never seemed to close. The salesgirls folded and refolded expensive sweaters or stared blankly from behind glass counters, preparing clothes that never seemed to sell for customers who never seemed to arrive. I assumed the stores were ornamental, intended to bestow prestige on the hotel, which probably charged a low rent, if any at all. It seemed logical that a store selling $425 knit sweaters would struggle in a nation that in 2008 had a per capita income of about $3,100. But I would later learn one explanation for the stores that made sense: The stores survived because of the economic logic of the modern Communist Party official.

If a businessman needed a permit or some other official approval, he might offer a cash bribe. But if that proved too crude, he might also present a gift of, say, a gold and diamond watch. The official would accept the gift, as well as the receipt, which meant he could keep the watch or return it for the purchase price, maybe tens of thousands of dollars, equal to a few years' salary. It was an elegant bribe. Those officials or businessmen also had to maintain wives and mistresses with gifts or with allowances to shop for gifts. Gift giving was so central to the conduct of business and official life in China that some businessmen kept wrapped gifts in the trunks of their cars, just in case. Controversies periodically surfaced over doctors who refused to treat hospital patients unless a patient's family provided a red envelope, or *hongbao*, stuffed with money. Beijing launched regular anticorruption campaigns, but the gifts kept coming.

The Yingze had evolved as China had evolved. It was still a government hotel, a setting for government business and those doing business with the government, but it had changed as business had changed.

Media Day was on the tenth floor. Four men huddled together at the front of the banquet hall beside the dais. Three of the men looked like what they were: well-fed party officials, each dressed in a suit and tie, their hair dyed black and parted. The senior man was a vice mayor of Taiyuan, while the other two were officials from the provincial sports bureau. The fourth man wore a cheap nylon jacket and could have passed for a guy loitering at a street corner labor pool. He was Boss Wang, the only person in the room worth almost $300 million. He had not bothered to comb his hair. He was so unpolished for such a public event that it seemed deliberate, as if he was offended by the softer men in suits, or at least wanted to make clear he wasn't one of them. He took a seat on the dais, and Media Day began.

The theme was quickly established: This would not be a championship season. Seated behind a long table to deliver this message were, from right to left: Zhai Jinshuai, the injured top scorer from last season; the general manager, Zhang Beihai; the owner; the three local officials; and, finally, seated at the opposite end of the table, Weiss and Joe. If the subtext of past failure hovered over the proceedings, the mood was hardly gloomy, and the reason was Bob Weiss. He was a living repository of NBA philosophies and principles somehow delivered to Shanxi Province. He looked polished in a tailored navy suit, smiling his friendly, toothy smile as Tracy sat in the back of the banquet hall with the players, snapping photographs.

Zhang began by introducing the coaching staff. He offered a mini-scoop to reporters by announcing that the team had just signed a contract to play home games at the new arena on the campus of the Shanxi University of Finance and Economics. It was the finest arena in the province, and the team would donate a percentage of the ticket proceeds to the school.

Then, reminding everyone that the Brave Dragons were inexperienced, he pleaded for patience.

"Please trust us," he said. "We're trying."

Zhai Jinshuai cleared his throat and pulled the microphone to his lips. Zhai is 6'8" and barely weighs 200 pounds. Pale and covered in acne, he looked like a Chinese Ichabod Crane, yet, when he was not injured, he was the team's most dynamic Chinese scorer. He stared down and read a prepared statement on behalf of the players. "We've hired a very high-level coach, and we're practicing very hard," Zhai said. "We will play with a spirit to never give up, never surrender. We'll give our best to take the team to a higher level.

"Remember, we're trying."

Now it was Weiss's turn to speak. If he still had not mastered the pronunciation of the owner's name, he had mastered some simple Chinese phrases. There were maybe twenty reporters from local newspapers and television stations sitting in front of the dais. A few had driven out to the training compound to interview Weiss, and he was already known around the city, but this would be his official introduction to his new fans, so as he leaned over the microphone to speak, the Chinese reporters leaned forward to listen.

"*Ni hao. Ni hao ma?*" Hello. How are you?

For the briefest moment, the banquet hall was silent. The room seemed to flinch. And then came loud, happy applause from the press. The American coach was friendly! And he spoke some Chinese! He had taken a little chance, risked a little humiliation, and the room appreciated it. He introduced Tracy, who rose to more applause in her black knit dress and string of pearls. He praised the team's management for trying to turn the team around and introduced two of the team's foreign imports. First was Donta Smith. And then, pointing to the last row, Weiss introduced the team's new center, the Nigerian rebounding machine, Olumide Oyedeji. The Tractor had left (he would eventually sign with a team in Turkey) without practicing a single minute in Taiyuan.*

Olumide Oyedeji had wasted little time in demonstrating why mercenaries are valuable in any profession. He had landed in China about a week earlier, having circumnavigated four continents, and disembarked ready to play basketball. The night he landed in Beijing, the team was in northeastern China for a preseason game. Olumide hopped a flight, reached the gym minutes before tipoff, and played all forty-eight minutes, collecting 21 points and 28 rebounds in a losing cause. Now Olumide sat quietly at the back of the room, the object of so much anticipation and calculation. If the arrival of Liu Tie had tilted the balance of power away from Bob Weiss, Olumide represented a very large counterweight. He

---

*He would remain on the international circuit until 2011, when he died unexpectedly in a hotel room from an apparent heart attack while playing in Puerto Rico.

was the league's leading rebounder, a proven star in China, and he was in Taiyuan solely because of Weiss.

"I was very touched that he would want to come here and help myself and the management turn this team around," Weiss said in introducing his new star.

"I never make predictions on how many wins, or how far we'll go," Weiss said, as the reporters hung on his words, or, more accurately, Joe's translation of those words, "but I know this team will be better than last year. We are working very hard to make this a team, to make it a group of players working together as one."

The same lines could have been delivered in Atlanta or Seattle or San Antonio. I assumed that Weiss had them hardwired somewhere deep in his subconscious after forty years of press conferences, but the room wasn't looking for originality. Weiss smiled and the Chinese journalists clapped again.

The officials came next. If it was true that the Brave Dragons had been a consistently terrible and often embarrassing team, it was also true that the team represented for Shanxi Province a rare inclusion in the fast lane along which China was so famously racing forward. China had three professional sports leagues—for soccer, volleyball, and basketball—and most of those teams were in cities along the more prosperous coast. The Brave Dragons were the only professional team in Shanxi, and their struggle for respectability reflected that of the province.

"The Brave Dragons are our pride," said the director of the provincial sports bureau. "They motivate our sports department, and they motivate our youth to play the game. And they contribute to our harmonious society." Ever since President Hu Jintao had declared that China should pursue a "harmonious society," party officials across the country had inserted the phrase into almost every speech. Basketball was no different from a new bridge or a new water treatment station in that regard.

The speeches concluded, and the floor was opened to questions. A television reporter stood and addressed Weiss: What is your biggest problem?

"Well, one of the biggest problems for me is communication," he said, through Joe. "Fortunately, I have a real good interpreter. I do not have a real good feel for the other teams in the league. Fortunately, we have Coach Liu Tie, who does know it well.

"I don't see problems," he continued. "I see challenges and difficulties, which I see as a positive. We are going to work hard to have a better team this year than we've had in the past."

Another reporter asked about Internet gossip that the team might still sign a big-name former NBA player, maybe Gary Payton. "We have not signed anyone else," Weiss replied. "This is the team I think you'll see on the floor. We have had some key injuries, some to Chinese players. Donta has been injured for the last week. It's putting us a little behind where we ought to be. But I think we very soon will come together as a team."

Then a reporter with the local *San Jin City News* took his turn. Li was pale and thin, with glasses that magnified his eyes and an uneven hairstyle that appeared to have been trimmed with lawn clippers. He had never covered basketball before, but he intuitively grasped the essential conflict of the team. "How is the blending of the American and Chinese coaching approaches working out?"

Weiss did not hesitate. "That is something we are working on very well. I think Coach and I are, you know, doing that, and I think we'll blend the two styles together."

Media Day would obviously not be a confessional. I wondered if Weiss might say something more, possibly scratch a little closer to the scab, but he didn't get a chance.

Unexpectedly, Boss Wang leaned over his microphone and blurted something out. Until now, Media Day had been an unwanted obligation for the players. They sat together in their matching yellow sweat suits and scribbled with the colored pencils on sheets of blank paper distributed to the reporters. Big Calves Tian had drawn a clown. Donta had traced a large dollar sign. They were teenagers determined not to pay attention in class.

But now the team was alert.

"This year, we can assure you we'll finish fourteenth," the Boss began. "We'll try to finish twelfth, and the best we can possibly do is tenth place."

He pushed back from the microphone. He had nothing else to say. The man who traveled to the United States to buy the league's first NBA head coach aspired for tenth place. Donta scowled after listening to Garrison's translation.

"What kind of owner is he?" Donta whispered to the back row. "He says the best we can be is tenth place?"

The Chinese players were not offended. The league had eighteen teams, and the Brave Dragons were the last-place team. Tenth place would not be easy. I later learned that Boss Wang had gathered the Chinese players together at practice and told them he would pay a salary bonus of

10 percent if the team finished fourteenth, and then another 5 percent for every slot higher.

Media Day was over. The season opener was four days off, and the road to tenth place was to begin with an away game against last year's runner-up, the Liaoning Pan Pan Dinosaurs.

The final member of the Brave Dragons was en route. Days earlier, when he had flown to Beijing to submit his roster to the league office, the general manager intended to include the name of Osama Mohammad Fathi Daghlas. But upon arrival, he panicked. He apparently could not overcome his anxiety that someone, somehow, might prove that Daghlas was less than a purebred Asian Jordanian.

Instead, the final name on the roster was Ruslan Rafaelovich Gilyazutdinov, pride of Kazakhstan. Joe had called Boss Wang with the names of two prospects, a point guard and a big man. Go with the big man, Boss Wang had ordered.

The Kazakh would arrive in China in about a week, and stories were already filtering back to Weiss and the rest of the team. One story held that Gilyazutdinov had played on the international circuit and starred for the Kazakh national team. The other story held he was a guy Joe found in a bar.

CHAPTER FOUR

BASKETBALL IS LIFE

The Liaoning Pan Pan Dinosaurs' basketball arena is shaped like a whiskey tumbler, squat with rounded glass walls, glowing on this night with intoxicating promise. For any last-place team, the first game of a new season is an absolution of past sins, a chance to begin anew, yet as the Brave Dragons trotted onto the court for warm-ups in their canary yellow track suits, it is fair to say that almost no one was giving them much of a chance to win.

The previous day the team had landed in Dalian, the biggest port in Liaoning Province, and boarded a charter bus for the two-hour trip to the Dinosaurs' hometown, the obscure industrial port of Bayuquan. The highway was a perfect black ribbon slicing through the brown deadness of early winter, the landscape already neatly folded and put away, as farmers had cleared their fields and stacked their hay into yellow mounds shaped like teepees. China's new highway system, based on the American interstate network, had grown so rapidly that, in many places, the economy hadn't caught up, the roads seemingly leading to a country yet to be built. The highway to Bayuquan was almost empty, except at the roadside, where handfuls of people huddled together, bending against the stiff Manchurian winds and clutching bags or cardboard boxes, as if standing at imaginary bus stops, waiting to be collected and delivered off the farm into that future yet to come.

They were waiting for rides to big cities like Dalian, which only accentuated the strange fact that the team was headed in the opposite direction. Dalian is one of China's showcase cities, curled around a peninsula overlooking the confluence of the Bohai and Yellow seas, decorated with manicured parks, high-rise apartment towers, and populated by more than six million people. It would be a logical hometown for Liaoning Province's only professional basketball team (as would Shenyang, the provincial capital of eight million people) if logic were dictated by the American economic rationale of professional sports, which holds that the bigger the city, the bigger the potential fan base, meaning more people to buy tickets and more people to watch local television broadcasts of games. Bayuquan was not even really a city; it was formally classified as an administrative industrial district. Bayuquan is what the future became a decade ago, when thousands of urban and industrial districts were built across China, many tossed up after central planners decided that for China to prosper, hundreds of millions of people needed to move from farms to cities. Except China didn't have enough cities to accommodate such an epochal migration, so places like Bayuquan were hurriedly paved into existence.

What Bayuquan did have, however, was the Pan Pan Security Industries Company, which manufactured metal security doors. The same urbanization policies that encouraged the hyperactive spread of high-rise apartments and office towers across China had created a thriving market for security doors; the Pan Pan Security Industries Company quickly prospered. The company's owner loved basketball, and when he got control of the provincial team, Bayuquan became the region's basketball capital. Elsewhere, the same formula often applied; in Fujian Province, the team was located in Jinjiang, rather than in the province's two biggest cities, because the Fujian team was owned by SBS, a zipper manufacturer headquartered in Jinjiang. Imagine if a multimillionaire from Chico, California (population: 88,228), bought the Los Angeles Lakers and moved them to Chico, simply because he lived there. In China, teams were located where the powerful men who controlled them wanted them to be.

The Pan Pan Dinosaurs did not seem worried about a tough game. Halfway through warm-ups, a large banner was carried onto the court to celebrate the Dinosaurs' runner-up finish the previous season. The team's young coach trotted out in a dapper gray suit to collect a trophy, as did the team's star shooting guard, a reserve on the Chinese Olympic team. The stands were packed, and if the arena was tiny, with maybe 4,000 seats, the place was vibrating. Fans didn't seem to mind the apparent lack of any heating; they were bundled in heavy coats and stomping up and down. One group of Pan Pan boosters had flown more than 600 miles from Beijing and was pounding thunder sticks so loudly that the noise echoed off the roof as the announcer introduced the home team.

On the visiting side, Bob Weiss sat at the end of the bench, silently watching, understandably a bit glum. His coveted point guard would not be joining the team and the mysterious Kazakh replacement had yet to arrive. His star Nigerian center was already feuding with management, since the first payment on Olumide's contract had not landed in his bank account and the team had not yet reimbursed his airfare for circumnavigating the globe to reach China. Weiss also had gotten clarity on the coaching situation, and the news was not in his favor. He would be introduced as head coach and would call timeouts, but Liu Tie would run the huddle during those timeouts and also handle substitutions. This did not strike team management as especially strange or insulting; it was standard practice in many Chinese government agencies that the director was a figurehead while the vice director does the work. But Weiss was annoyed.

The arrangement also created practical problems. League rules dictated that only a head coach could stand during a game. Those same rules also forbade owners from sitting on the bench and placed limits on how many people could do so. The rules were designed for a normal team, and the Brave Dragons, after a period of private deliberation, had devised a plan to ignore them. Rick Turner would be banished to the rafters to videotape the game. Boss Wang was formally designated as Team Leader, a title with uncertain responsibilities that nonetheless gave him legal standing on the bench. Now that Liu Tie was actually doing the coaching during the game, a seating chart had coalesced: Weiss, as titular head coach, took the first seat, Joe sat beside him, followed by Liu Tie, Boss Wang, then Wingtips, the second Chinese assistant coach, and, finally, the players.

What complicated the situation was the boss's mistress. Or at least I assumed, as did everyone else, that the decidedly younger woman at the side of Boss Wang was his mistress. She was in her twenties and attractive, and Boss Wang did not have a daughter, nor did the younger woman conduct herself like a daughter. Boss Wang did have a wife, a cheery woman in her sixties, so if it could not be indisputably confirmed that the younger woman was a mistress, it could be confirmed that she was The Woman Who Was Not His Wife. And regardless of title, her presence represented another potential regulations violation, depending on league policy for female companions.

The Pan Pan Dinosaurs were now on the court, awash in the banging of thunder sticks from their fans, when the announcer turned his attention to the Brave Dragons. The first player introduced was Oyedeji, number 00, and he bounded onto the court to loud applause from the Liaoning fans. He had been the equivalent of a rent-a-rebounder for the Dinosaurs the previous season, joining the team shortly before the playoffs and carrying them to the finals with his defense and unmatched work on the boards. But the Pan Pan owner had thought him too short at 6'10" to play center and had refused to sign him. Olumide hopped and grinned, and when his teammates came onto the court, he greeted each one of them with a flying chest bump. You would never have known they had met only a week or two before.

Introductions finished, the teams standing at opposite ends of the court, the loudspeakers crackled for a moment and then the tinny, recorded sound of a marching band playing the Chinese national anthem, "March of the Volunteers," spilled into the arena. The anthem was composed in 1934 and embraced by the resistance movement during the Japanese occupation of much of northeastern China, including what is now Bayuquan. Even today, nearly eighty years later, popular sentiment against Japan can be visceral in northeastern China, where families hand down stories of rapes and murders by Japanese soldiers and where Chinese schools remind students of an era when China was weak and at the mercy of its neighbors. Once, while traveling in the region with my family, we had dinner at a seafood restaurant near the Bohai Sea. It had been a typically friendly experience, with the waitresses cooing over my small children and carrying them from table to table, showing off the pretty foreigners. Later, a small girl, maybe eight years old, with pigtails, walked over to our table without a smile. She apparently had never seen foreigners before.

"Are you Japanese?" she asked.

No, we replied. We were Americans.

"Good," she said. "Because we won't let those Japanese devils win again."

When the Communists took over the country in 1949, "March of the Volunteers" was adopted as the national anthem, though its status, and its lyrics, would fluctuate with the fluctuations of Chinese politics. During the Cultural Revolution, the song's lyricist was imprisoned as a rightist and singing the anthem was forbidden. "The East Is Red" became the nation's unofficial anthem, and Mao ordered loudspeakers attached to a satellite so the song could propagandize the cosmos. "March of the Volunteers" was restored in 1978, but with edited lyrics, including a call to "raise high Chairman Mao's banner." The public didn't seem enthusiastic and the original lyrics were restored a few years later.

The sound of rising patriotic voices was now filling the arena. I was standing behind the scorer's table, on the folding bleachers reserved for reporters. There were no desks and none of the buffet-filled hospitality rooms common in NBA arenas. The Chinese reporters had placed their laptops on their knees and were connected to broadband lines running from the scorer's table so they could file live blog updates from the game. A few reporters had made the trip from Taiyuan, including Journalist Li, stalwart of the *San Jin City News*. He cleared a space for me and I listened to the singing of the anthem.

> *Arise!*
> *All who refuse to be slaves!*
> *Let our flesh and blood forge into our new Great Wall!*
> *As the Chinese people faces its greatest peril,*
> *Every person is forced to expel his very last cry.*
> *Arise!*
> *Arise!*
> *Arise!*
> *Our million hearts beating as one,*
> *Brave the enemy's fire,*
> *March on!*
> *Brave the enemy's fire,*
> *March on!*
> *March on!*
> *March on!*

It took me a moment to realize the crowd was not actually singing. Everyone was standing in stiff silence. The voices ringing in the arena were recorded. I leaned over and mentioned the lack of singing to Journalist Li.

He blushed.

"Chinese are shy," he said.

Unexpectedly, this was turning out to be a game. The Dinosaurs opened with a 4–0 lead, and the Brave Dragons seemed flatfooted and outmatched. But they soon found their equilibrium and by the end of the first quarter the score was tied. Zhai Jinshuai, his finger wrapped in a bandage, scored from the outside and Olumide dominated the boards, scoring mostly on offensive rebounds. Journalist Li spent the quarter madly typing blog updates, and when Zhai nailed a 3-pointer from the corner, Journalist Li and the other reporters from Taiyuan screamed and punched the air.

Boss Wang had started the game at the far end of the bench, sitting in a folded chair, perhaps as a concession to league policy, but as it became clear that a real contest was under way, he pushed his way beside the coaches. His companion followed, wedging herself into the bench, which triggered a chain reaction of musical chairs in which two players had to relocate to the folding chairs. By halftime, the Brave Dragons led, 40–37. The players walked slowly to the locker room and a Dinosaurs cheerleading team skipped onto the court, accompanied by the team mascot, someone dressed as a very malnourished panda.

The fans rushed toward the bathroom. I went into the lobby, where I soon began to choke. Everyone was smoking, as if the lobby were one of those small airport smoking rooms, except instead of twenty people crammed inside, there were 2,500, every person nervously inhaling cigarette after cigarette and exhaling clouds of nicotine. No country on earth has more smokers than China. When Joe had played, smoking was so heavy inside the arena in Jilin City that state television refused to broadcast games, complaining that the viewers could not see the action because of the clouds of cigarette smoke hanging over the court. New rules now banned smoking inside arenas, but lobbies were obviously exempted. Inside the bathroom, the smoke was even thicker, as men stood five deep in front of urinals, puffing away and shuffling forward, shoes sliding through the puddle of urine on the tile floor. When the smoke in the lobby became too thick, security guards opened the windows and doors, ushering in the Manchurian winds, which pushed the smoke into the arena. By the time the second half began, a front of carcinogenic clouds had settled over the court.

Donta Smith stretched the Brave Dragons' lead to 55–47 on a coast-to-coast scooping layup, one of his few bright moments. He would later limp to the bench after getting kicked in the testicles. During timeouts, Liu Tie squatted in front of the starters, barking orders in Chinese as Weiss stood at the edge of the huddle, listening to Joe's interpretation. Yet Liu wasn't doing all the coaching; I could see Boss Wang shouting in his ear, whereupon Liu would spring up and shout something onto the court. Or Boss Wang would whisper something and then Coach Liu would turn to Joe, who would turn to Weiss, who would suddenly stand and call timeout.

On the court, a pattern was emerging: Olumide was grabbing nearly every rebound and scoring easy baskets. He wasn't a natural scorer, as far as creating his own shot, but he got so many garbage baskets from rebounds that he was dominating the game. With 2:59 left in the third quarter, Olumide put back an offensive rebound for a basket, pushing the lead to 62–51 and sending an electrical current through the yelping Taiyuan press corps. By the final seconds of the quarter, the game had become a rout.

The final score was 94–74. Toward the end, popping sounds echoed off the roof, as sharp as gunshots. Dinosaur fans were streaming out of the stadium, stomping on their thunder sticks along the way. At the buzzer, the Brave Dragons rushed to center court to form a victory circle, hopping and shouting like teenagers. The bumpkins from Shanxi Province had won the team's first road victory since moving to Taiyuan. Boss Wang grinned and posed for photographs with the Chinese players. Weiss caught my eye and laughed. His expression was easy to interpret: Can you believe it?

By the time I reached the locker room, the Chinese players had left for the team's hotel. Donta and Olumide were icing their legs and stripping tape off their ankles. Olumide, who had scored 23 points and grabbed 24 rebounds, savored his revenge. "They said they could win without me!" he yelled. "The owner said they needed a taller center! It's money in my pocket, that's all I know!"

Postgame statistics usually confirm why a team won or lost, and reinforce ingrained assumptions about how teams should play the game, and how they should not. If a team is sloppy, and turns the ball over to the other team too often, it usually loses. If a team misses too many foul shots, it usually loses. By the judgment of the raw numbers on the stat sheet, the Brave Dragons should have lost, and lost badly. They had committed 28 turnovers, or about as many as a well-coached NBA team might make in three games; many times they didn't even attempt a shot before losing possession. Their foul shooting was terrible. Not a single Brave Dragon player, other than Olumide, had shown even faint interest in rebounding, and the team's best player, Donta Smith, was terrible. Yet they had won by 20 points.

Which is why Rick Turner held the stat sheet with a sense of disbelief after he had packed up his video camera and descended from the rafters. Turner had watched Coach Liu's crazy practices and crazy ideas and assumed the team would get blown out against Liaoning. He hated to admit it but he had wondered if losing might be the best thing for the team, not to mention for him. Losing might shatter whatever illusions Boss Wang had about his Chinese coach and force him to put Weiss fully back in charge. Losing might restore some semblance of order in Turner's basketball universe.

When Bob Weiss had circulated word through his network of contacts that he needed an assistant in China, he described the ideal candidate as a coach familiar with "unorthodox situations." Rick Turner's name came back. At forty-four, Turner was tall and blond, a high school point guard who had gained twenty-five pounds in the last twenty-five years, a smart and sarcastic guy who had begun in broadcasting before deciding he wanted to coach. "When you are young and naive, people tell you, 'Just do something you know and love,'" he said. "So I chose coaching."

Lacking a basketball pedigree or any connections, Turner evolved into a master of unorthodox situations. He coached a semipro team in the Seattle area, the Bellevue Blackhawks, of the American Basketball Association, to a second-place finish. The team's owner saved money by working as the public address announcer and, according to Turner, would use his microphone to mock his own players if the team was losing. During road trips, the owner gave Turner a credit card to cover the team's meals. "We had to eat every meal together because I had the credit card," Turner said. When the team traveled to Little Rock for the league finals, the manager of their hotel refused to allow them to leave because the bill had not been paid, meaning the team was held hostage in Arkansas for three days until the hometown team agreed to pick up the bill. Turner had coached other semipro teams and had adopted a philosophy he attributed to Frosty Westering, the longtime football coach at Pacific Lutheran University: Make the Big Time where you are.

"That's the philosophy I've taken, because everywhere I've been has been the little time," he said.

Turner, no longer young and naive, was broke, depending on his wife's job at Microsoft to support them and their daughter. His friends worried he was a romantic, chasing a boy's dream. He clung to a different idea: He was a good coach, and he should do something he was good at. He just needed a chance, and China had seemed to be just that. He would earn $5,000 a month, which was more than he had made during a single season in the semipro leagues, and he would have a chance to learn from Weiss. "Plus the NBA is starting to get more involved here," he said. "I thought maybe I'd be over here and make some contacts. I guess I looked at it as a proving ground."

But now he was in the rafters, doing film. The arrival of Liu Tie had undercut no one more than Turner. If Liu still deferred to Weiss, at least outside practice, he had barely acknowledged Turner and had discarded his weight program. Turner now had nothing to do during practice except rebound during shooting drills.

"I feel like my head is on the chopping block and they could send me home at any time," he told me. "I'm kind of stealing money."

Yet even before Coach Liu arrived, China was not what Turner had imagined. He knew the country would be different—the language, the food, the people. But he had assumed basketball would be roughly the same and it clearly wasn't. When Weiss had changed practice to make it less punitive, some of the players had started loafing. It was as if they wanted the hard hand Boss Wang said they required.

"These guys think that your culture matters in terms of basketball," he said. "I just think it is like sign language. It is universal. The things that work in the United States will work here, or in Argentina or Spain. I don't think Coach Weiss or I have to be Chinese to have success here. But then we talk about it and we wonder, Is that just a completely ethnocentric way of looking at it? Because if we think our way can work here, we definitely don't think their way can work in the United States.

"Maybe we're wrong."

The postgame buffet was spread across a table in the team's hotel. I found Little Sun, the Taiwanese guard, hunched over his plate, dressed in his yellow warm-ups, chewing on steamed buns. I sat down and congratulated him. He had first entered the game in the third quarter. Just before that, Liu had draped his arm over his shoulder and whispered into his ear as Little Sun stripped off his sweats, as if he were a father figure sending him into the fray with a word of kindly instruction.

Little Sun had looked pale and small on the court, yet he got a quick steal, and then a second steal from Liaoning's Olympian, scoring on an uncontested layup. But soon the bigger Liaoning guards rattled him, posting him under the basket on offense, where they had a strength and height advantage, and then forcing him into a bad turnover. He seemed uncomfortable on the court, and Liu Tie pulled him, never to return. Still, I thought he had played well enough and told him so.

Little Sun looked up from his plate. He smiled unconvincingly. The steal was lucky, he said. Coach Liu despised him. "He says, 'You don't have much time you can play because you are too short, too soft,'" Little Sun said.

Little Sun leaned across our table toward me as his eyes widened. "You know why the Chinese don't like the Taiwanese?" he asked. His dark eyelashes were long, like a doe's. He smiled. "They are envious." He mispronounced the word—in-vye-OOUS—and I gently corrected him.

"Envious," he repeated, properly. "There are a lot of businessmen in Taiwan. We are just a small island. But we have a lot of genius. I'm telling the truth." He said a close friend recently graduated from the Massachusetts Institute of Technology. "They are envious, envious," he repeated, firmly, still smiling. "We are a small island, but we can do a lot."

He told me once again how his teammates had been suspicious of him at first. "But in fact, I was not political," he said, pronouncing the word slowly. "I just want to be in China and to learn to play basketball and to learn the culture." When I had first met Little Sun in October, he had not told his parents about his problems to spare them any worries. But the pressure, or loneliness, must have been too much. "I also tell my dad and my mom," he said. "I tell them about the pol-i-tick-al problem."

Which was really a Coach Liu problem: "The first time he met me, he said, 'You guys can't have independence.' I said, 'Hey, I don't want independent. If I want independent, why am I here? I'm here to learn basketball.'" Little Sun looked at me and kept chewing on the bun. "My mom said this is good to me. After this, I will be stronger."

I told him I thought his confidence has slipped, and he agreed. "Here, sometimes, no confidence," he said of his time in China.

The dining room was now almost empty. I asked Little Sun if the players could go to bars or restaurants, if they had much free time in Taiyuan or if they must live in the dormitory throughout the year. "Of course, no free," he answered. Then he banged his fist against his chest. "Me, me," he said. "Me, I just play for eight months. Then I go back to Taiwan."

He restored himself by telling me stories of other Taiwanese guards:

a 5'9" guard who once led the CBA in assists, now coaching in Taiwan; another Taiwanese guard who played for years in China. He was part of a tradition, and even within that tradition, he was now special, the only Taiwanese taught by an NBA coach. This season was his test, and he knew it. He wanted to coach basketball. He wanted to meet the challenge of China. He smiled.

"Basketball is life," he said.

We were about to leave, when Coach Liu arrived. He filled a plate at the buffet and sat down at our table. Little Sun did not blink. Liu and I had spoken many times, but we sometimes needed someone to help interpret. I asked Little Sun to help, and he nodded. Then I began my postgame interview: What were the keys to the win?

"Today, we won because we played together," Coach Liu answered. "And everybody played good defense."

He had singled out the two areas, team unity and defense, for which he was directly responsible. I smiled and observed that it did not hurt that Olumide was unstoppable inside and that Zhai shot so well. Coach Liu did not smile. He kept eating, pushing his rice to the edge of his plate with chopsticks. "The only key points are that we played together and we played good defense," he repeated.

I had no interest in confrontation, so I praised the defense and team play. Coach Liu nodded, his face hovering a few inches above his food as he shoveled rice into his mouth. He turned to Little Sun and I could hear him say, "Ask him what he thought about Donta."

Donta had not played well. He finished with eight points and seemed frustrated. He played like someone trying to prove he was a superstar, yet the harder he tried, the worse he played. I offered Liu a sanitized version of this opinion and pointed out that Donta played very good defense.

"Six turnovers," Coach Liu replied. "He had six turnovers."

Liu finished slurping the liquid off his plate. His lips were wet and he whispered something that shook Little Sun. I asked what happened. "He told me, 'You are too soft. If you don't change your mentality, you cannot survive in the CBA,'" Little Sun said.

Liu began poring over statistics from other games on the schedule. We no longer interested him. "You can see his attitude," Little Sun said, pivoting toward me. "He cannot accept another guy's advice. He cannot accept Bob." Our conversation was making me uncomfortable. I knew Coach Liu could comprehend a tiny bit of English, having watched him clumsily try to communicate with the foreign players. I worried that Little Sun was veering toward trouble, but he kept talking.

"Everybody will say he did a good job," Little Sun said, frustrated, as the coach stayed fixated on the statistics. Little Sun's voice wavered. "But it is only the beginning, right? It is only the beginning."

Liu Tie looked up from his papers and again whispered something to Little Sun. Little Sun lowered his head and stood up. He walked over to the buffet, poured a Sprite into a paper cup, and returned to the table. He placed the cup before his coach and sat down. Liu did not acknowledge him. He sipped the Sprite and mentioned that an American player, Kirk Snyder, the former Houston Rocket, had scored 43 points that night, a huge number, for the Zhejiang Wanma Cyclones.

Little Sun turned to me. "You need to tell him that you are going to your room," he said, anguished. "I cannot go unless you go. You need to tell him."

I realized too late my complicity in Little Sun's humiliation. I stood to leave and Little Sun followed me.

CHAPTER FIVE

SHOOTING THE MESSENGERS

t was nearly 11 p.m. when I reached my room. Joe and I were roommates for the night, and I found him staring into his laptop, checking scores from around the league, his face glowing in the blue light of the screen.

"We were lucky," he said. "Liaoning is not a good team."

Joe had not been impressed. Liaoning's best players were off form, he thought, and their new Americans were not talented. One of their stars played sparingly because of a lung injury. Still, a win is a win. "It kind of looks like Liu Tie and Bob are a good combination," he said, smiling his nervous smile, sounding more hopeful than convinced.

I had spent as much time watching the action on the bench as the action on the court. Despite the regulations of the Chinese Basketball Association, every coach, assistant coach, owner, team leader, and female companion on the Brave Dragons bench had failed to remain seated. Liu Tie was up constantly, pointing at the refs, jabbering at players. Every time a player left the game, Liu greeted him on the sideline, insistently tugging at the player's hand and whispering instructions. If a player tried to pull his hand away, Liu held tighter. Boss Wang would jump up and, soon, not wanting to be left out, the second Chinese assistant, Wingtips, would jump up, too. Weiss was up and down, as befits the head coach, walking the sideline to talk to players or complain to the scorer's table, but his role was complicated. He was supposed to have authority over the games, yet the man talking in the middle of the huddle was Liu Tie.

Joe looked away from his laptop. The problem was language, he said. There was not enough time for Weiss to talk and Joe to translate. "If two guys talk, we've only got one minute, so maybe not enough time," Joe said. He returned his gaze to the laptop, tapped on his keyboard and an online version of the numbers game Sudoku appeared on the screen. Liu's practices were so difficult that the game seemed easy, Joe thought, yet the game was poorly played. Brutal practices didn't produce better basketball.

"The players have no passion," he said. "They are not playing like art. They are just attacking. Like the army."

Joe had intrigued me from the moment I met him in October. I did not share the view of Weiss, Turner, and Zhang, who questioned whether Joe was fully interpreting what they were saying, or if he was rounding it off, omitting opinions that might provoke confrontation. Without Joe, they could not communicate, yet that dependence also sowed uncertainty. During the assembly stage of the team, as different foreigners were trying out, confusion had arisen between Weiss and the general manager over which players Weiss wanted, and which ones he did not. When a few of the ones Weiss did not want unexpectedly returned for more tryouts, questions arose about Joe's interpretation. The general manager began pulling Little Sun off the court for private chats with Weiss. No one really knew what was going on. The arrival of Liu Tie had presented a different complication. Joe once worked as an assistant coach for a team where Liu Tie had been a player, making Joe his elder and making it harder for Liu to bully him. So Liu began turning to Garrison as his interpreter.

My impression of Joe was different. I found him thoughtful and reflective, familiar with the Chinese and American approaches to basketball. His English was good, though sometimes awkward, and he made the same point about Chinese basketball on the first day I met him: that it was not art. He had an idealized view of American players, of their maturity and capacity for self-discipline, and he blamed the immaturity of Chinese players for the early problems that arose for Weiss. Joe admired Weiss's coaching style, how he rarely screamed at players, and he saw the flaws of Chinese basketball as parallel to the flaws in how China developed its people. He thought the Chinese system failed to teach teamwork, that people were motivated more by self-interest and self-preservation, if out of necessity. Any sports columnist in America would say the same of American society and American sports stars, but Joe saw Americans as more likely to share and work for the common good.

"They try to hurt people here," Joe had told me early on. "Sometimes I'll try to hurt you even if it does nothing for me. At least it will eliminate you from the competition."

He had paused a moment, adding: "Maybe there are just too many people."

Joe was eighteen when he joined the Bayi team in the 1980s. The team kept him behind high walls at a time when Chinese society seemed to be finally cracking open. If there was a world beyond, he was not seeing it. He finally quit in 1986. He was struggling as a player and frustrated that the coaches could not teach him how to improve; practice was about punishment more than improvement. He decided to see what was happening outside those high walls. "I wanted to go out," he said. "I felt really hopeless and lonely. And maybe, you know, I just wanted to see the outside."

He enrolled at Renmin University, a top school in Beijing, but could not shake a desire to leave China. By the late 1980s, China appeared at a precipice, and no one could predict in which direction it might go. Communism had declined so rapidly elsewhere that China seemed to be the next place about to shrug off its authoritarian leaders. The party's reform policies had raised incomes, but also raised expectations for faster change, even as Chinese society remained seeded with the mistrust and lingering betrayals of the Mao era. "I didn't like the politics," Joe said. "People have two faces."

Japan provided his escape. Japan was a rising global economic power and introduced a special visa program to attract manual laborers, and Joe soon found himself washing dishes in Japan. He spent two unpleasant years there, but he used the time to qualify for a student visa to study English in Canada. He arrived in the summer of 1989.

"Once I got there, Tiananmen Square happened," he said, looking up from his screen.

The government crackdown against the pro-democracy Tiananmen Square demonstrations dispelled any notion that history would sweep away the Chinese Communist Party. Overnight, Chinese society froze in fear, and other countries, including Canada, responded by offering asylum to young Chinese citizens. Joe spent the next decade in Toronto and was granted a Canadian passport. Without any education, he delivered newspapers and painted houses until he developed a specialty as a guide for Chinese tourists. Toronto already had a large Chinese population and as the Tiananmen crackdown slowly receded, more Chinese visitors began to arrive.

"I've been to Niagara Falls maybe 100 times!" he said, laughing.

He had gone to Toronto with his wife. They married at age twenty-four after friends and elders had nudged them together, since both were athletes. She was a long jumper. He had never dated or remotely understood women, but he assumed that, eventually, a feeling would infuse the marriage. "I sort of thought that like the older generation, after marriage, you can get that feeling," he said. "But I never had that."

Living in Toronto meant living apart from the societal binds that kept such marriages intact in China. Joe decided they should separate. "American people, Western people, when they don't have a feeling, they agree to separate," he said. His wife thought they should have a baby and soon a daughter was born, but the condition of the marriage did not change.

He and his wife separated for two years and he considered the marriage to be finished. Then, in 1996, he met a woman visiting from the Chinese city of Zhuhai. She was a middle manager at a stock brokerage. She had no interest in traveling but won the trip through a company reward system and felt, as a manager, she had to go. Her itinerary included only the United States but the group decided to make an unplanned side trip to Toronto. At her Toronto hotel, she had noticed Joe on the elevator and when he later was one of her available choices for a guide, she grabbed him.

"I got a feeling with her," he said. "But I was still married. And she was married."

Joe turned away from where he was sitting and faced me. "Do you know the word *yuanfen*?" he asked. It roughly translates to fate or destiny. He spent three days with the woman and became convinced that their meeting was *yuanfen*. "They changed their itinerary," he said. "They flew to Canada. I don't know, but that is *yuanfen*."

Destiny would not be simple to achieve. His wife was furious, and he gave her everything, except $200. He moved back to China in 1997, with his Canadian passport. "I'm free now," he said. "If I don't like this country, I can go somewhere else. I have other options."

For a time, he did nothing. He needed to absorb his new life, absorb how startlingly China had changed. It was now a country on the move, with people suddenly untethered to their villages or families, everyone scratching to get ahead. Going outside used to mean leaving China. But now it meant going to the coast, to Guangdong Province, or going to the big cities, any big city. He had returned to a country that had woken up while he had been away. There were still too many problems, but he believed China was becoming more open and free.

"I can see the future," he said. "Before, if you made a joke about the leaders, and if somebody reported you to the policeman, they will come to your home and put you in jail. Now you can say on the street that you don't like the Communist Party or make a joke about the leaders. So much freedom."

It was past midnight, and I was exhausted. Joe was still playing Sudoku. It sounded as if he had been right about destiny. His relationship had slowly improved with his first wife; she now had a steady job in Toronto and was living with a boyfriend, a former professional hockey player. His daughter, now fourteen, had lived with grandparents in Beijing until two years ago, when she joined her mother in Toronto. In China, she had wilted under the academic pressure of school. "Homework, homework, homework: lots of stress," he said. "When she got to Canada—no homework! She feels really relieved from the pressure."

It was time to sleep, but I had some final questions. I knew that Joe and the woman on the tour had gotten married. I had met her at a dinner weeks earlier; she was tall and elegant. But what had happened to her first marriage? I asked. Joe sighed. Her divorce had not gone easily. The husband did not want a divorce but never said as much. Joe said his tactic was very Chinese: He made seemingly impossible demands in hopes that his wife would change her mind. The couple had a son, and a father in China would usually fight for custody. But he told her she had to raise the boy. She said fine.

"Then he said, 'Okay, you get no money,' " Joe continued. "She said, 'Okay, no problem.' He was really frustrated."

Finally, the divorce went through. I asked my last question: What happened to the husband? Our conversation had unfurled for more than an hour, propelled by my questions but also by Joe's desire to talk about his life, his journey, but now, as if making a blind turn, we had come to the scene of an accident. Joe paused, uncertain what to say.

"He's dead," he answered, pausing again. "Suicide."

We were silent as Joe hit the keyboard. A new Sudoku chart appeared on the screen. Then he looked down at the floor and I saw tears in his eyes. Joe could not understand why the man would take his own life. Chinese are practical. Chinese are survivors. The man had more than 2 million yuan after the divorce, a fortune in China. "He could have had a young lady, much prettier," Joe said.

I stammered out an apology. Joe smiled to reassure me and shut down his computer. No one can predict *yuanfen*.

When the team landed back in Taiyuan, the general manager and about fifty fans were waiting with flowers. Every coach and player received a bouquet, with the biggest, most elaborate arrangement presented to Weiss. The newspapers ran excited stories and fans rushed to buy tickets for the home opener on Wednesday, against the great Bayi Rockets. To anyone on the outside, the experiment seemed to be working. The new NBA coach was successfully transferring some of his high-level knowledge. But inside the team, the players understood that power was shifting to Coach Liu. Victory had exalted him. He had already introduced new rules prohibiting talking or laughing during practice. He had spent nearly an hour lecturing against complacency, invoking something from Mao about never being satisfied; again reminding the players that the Brave Dragons didn't have to be big to do big things, he veered back to Napoleon.

"He couldn't even touch the net," Weiss joked about the Frenchman.

Victory had confused the foreigners. Winning usually eliminated confusion and papered over any problems inside a team. And beating the Liaoning Pan Pan Dinosaurs had felt good. Weiss had called his ninety-year-old father, Vic, with the news. But if the fact of winning felt good, the implications of winning were disquieting. Olumide had played the entire forty-eight minutes of the game, banging around the basket, and was angry that Liu insisted he run wind sprints the day the team returned to Taiyuan.

Weiss was trying to be diplomatic. His fingerprints had not been completely erased from the win: His inbounds play had worked, and Olumide and Donta were listening to him more than Liu Tie on the sideline. But he was frustrated, and he and Rick Turner were ever more baffled by what Liu was trying to accomplish in practice once the team had returned to Taiyuan. More than half of practice was still spent on drills. Almost no time was dedicated to offense. Two players, Zhai Jinshuai and Wei Mingliang, had pulled Turner aside to ask what the hell was going on. He told them he had no idea.

Turner did not know whom to trust. He was suspicious that Joe was not interpreting everything he said, or everything that was said to him. He also thought the front office was lying to him. A few days before the team's flight to Liaoning, he had been told he could not go because his visa could not be renewed quickly enough. When he went to the visa office on his own he had gotten a renewal in a few hours. The team then bought him a ticket but chased him from the bench to shoot video from the rafters. Then he saw the owner and his companion on the bench.

Turner and I had gone to lunch after returning from Liaoning, in what might be called Taiyuan's Little America. At a downtown intersection, we deliberated among a KFC, a McDonald's, and a Pizza Hut, opting for KFC and Mexican-flavored chicken wrap sandwiches. The American fast food chains were part of a major overhaul of Taiyuan's downtown. Sidewalks were being torn up, roads were under construction, and new businesses were opening. Less than a mile away, new high-rise apartments were going up along the banks of the Fen River, which city leaders were trying to transform from a stagnant ditch into a showplace of landscaped parks. For now, it was a big construction mess, but this newer downtown, farther away from People's Square, was being fashioned as the new heart of the city. Tracy had discovered the area on one of her walks, and also discovered the World Trade Center Hotel. It was far nicer than the Longcheng, with an attached apartment tower, and she had been prodding for a move when Olumide arrived demanding the luxury four-bedroom apartment stipulated in his contract. The general manager capitulated, and the foreign contingent had moved over shortly before the season opener.

At KFC, Rick and I took a corner table overlooking the intersection. Across the street, a clothing store named Apple Man stood a few doors down from Conch Apparel, a clumsy rip-off of Coach. Rap music from America was playing in the KFC as Rick took a bite of his chicken wrap.

"It always amazes me how little difference there is between Chinese and American kids," he said. "They laugh at the same stuff. They are wired. They like girls. The same stuff pisses them off. They don't like coming out of the game any less than the American kids do."

He took another bite.

"But at the same time, we are so culturally different. It is a weird push-pull."

He was baffled that Weiss had been sidelined by the owner. "If you went through the Top 50"—the NBA had once released a list of the 50 greatest players in league history—"I bet 90 percent of these guys he has either coached, prepared for, or played with. Yet Liu Tie knows more than him? Why would you have a guy like him and then not use him?"

Turner was offended by Liu Tie's arrogance, and didn't think he knew much about coaching, as far as diagramming plays or organizing practices went. But he did not dismiss him. He could see that the Chinese players responded differently to him than to Weiss. "They weren't afraid of Bob," he said. "They fear Liu. Personally, I don't think that is good. To rule by fear is not really ruling. You don't have the will of the people. I'm not trying to get political about it.

"And then again, coaching is not really a democracy."

We finished and started walking back to the World Trade. We turned down a side street, away from Little America, and passed a block of six-story walk-up apartments. It was a sunny day, and we came to the gate of an elementary school. Throngs of kids in matching yellow caps were cramming back through the gate after going home for lunch. We walked through them, giants wading through the Lilliputians, and they peered up, blushing and smiling their glorious smiles at the unexpected sight of two foreigners, everyone shouting happily at us in their primary school English.

"Hello! Hello! Hello!"

"Hello!" we shouted back.

Winning had been rare enough for the Brave Dragons that paying bonuses was an unusual event. But now a victory had been achieved, and bonuses were due. Liu Tie had taken control of bonus money, too. For foreign players and coaches, bonuses were specified in their contracts, with different amounts for home and road wins; Olumide now got $1,200, the biggest bonus on the team.

The Chinese players existed under a more arbitrary system. Their bonuses were smaller and calculated at the discretion of the coach. Liu reserved the biggest bonus for himself and Zhai Jinshuai, who had 22 points as the team's high scorer after Olumide. The bonuses got progressively smaller as Liu doled out different amounts to different players, depending on playing time and his assessment of their performance. He placed Little Sun near the bottom. The trainer was given the next to lowest bonus. Beneath him came the translators. Joe and Garrison were told to split the same amount given to the trainer.

Joe accepted it. Garrison was furious. He had signed a contract before the Liaoning game and was working twelve hours a day as an intermediary between the foreign players and the team. Joe advised him not to complain. Liu was young and insecure, Joe argued; this was how he exercised power. But Garrison was young, too. He approached the coach about a bigger bonus. He thought he had earned one.

The bonus stayed the same.

"All you are doing is talking," Coach Liu told him.

Garrison Guo estimated it took him about a week to learn what he calls the fundamentals of English. He was entering middle school in Zhengzhou, the capital of Henan Province, one of China's biggest and most backward provinces. His teacher announced that any student who tested well on an entrance exam could qualify for one of the city's top schools. Garrison's parents were workers with only a basic education. His mother was an administrator at a shopping mall; his father had kicked around different jobs before landing one as a manager at a gas station. They wanted better for their son. It was the middle of the 1990s, and China was taking off. The depression that had settled like a cloud over the country after the Tiananmen massacre began to lift and China began to develop faster.

Sons and daughters of farmers would be the mules of Deng's vision, pouring off the fields to work as laborers in the new generation of factories opening along the coast. The ancient yoke to the land was irrevocably broken; the countryside was dying and millions of peasants saw the factory as a first, grueling step toward a toehold in the city and, from there, a chance to scratch out a better life. China's race to the city, still gathering speed, would become the greatest migration in history, with hundreds of millions of people on the go. But families already in the cities aspired to more than factory jobs for their children; they had already made it off the farm, and moving up in the city required skills and education. Garrison's father wanted his son to get into the better school, but the entrance exam posed a problem. English was a required subject, and Garrison had never paid attention to English.

"I didn't even know A, B, C, D," Garrison recalled.

His father hired a tutor and Garrison turned out to be a natural, scoring 27.5 out of 30 on the entrance exam and earning a placement in the Foreign Language School of Zhengzhou.

Timing can be ruthless in China. Had Garrison Guo shown an aptitude for English two decades earlier, his family might have been persecuted in the final, angry eruptions of the Cultural Revolution. Had he come of age a decade earlier, when China was just opening its door, he might have met the same confused uncertainty that pushed Joe to go outside. But when as a teenage boy he arrived for his first day at the Foreign Language School of Zhengzhou, his timing was absolutely sublime.

When I first met Garrison, he was still working as an agent; we shared a taxi back to practice one afternoon. As the dented red cab rattled through Taiyuan traffic, dust and noise seeping through the cracked window, I

Bob Weiss and Brave Dragons owner Boss Wang had never spoken or met when Weiss arrived in Taiyuan to coach the local team. First impressions mattered, and both men came prepared with gifts. Boss Wang presented a box of tea. Weiss offered bourbon.

Taiyuan is the capital of Shanxi Province, which is the coal heartland of China. Coal has brought riches to some people in Taiyuan, but it has also draped the city in a gray curtain of pollution.

Boss Wang did not want the Brave Dragons players exposed to any of the temptations of Taiyuan, so he converted an old factory outside the city into a dormitory and training gym. The Chinese players lived eleven months of the year in the concrete dormitory, living two to a room. The gym was a huge warehouse in the rear of the compound. In winter, it was so cold that players needed to wear coats when they were not practicing.

A Taiyuan street scene

Forever caught in the middle between two cultures, the team's interpreters—Joe and Garrison Guo—were the bridge that bound together the foreigners with the Chinese. Here, Bob Weiss and Joe field questions during Media Day at the Yingze Hotel in Taiyuan, a few days before the season-opening game.

Little Sun, left, the Taiwanese point guard of the Brave Dragons, spoke English and sometimes helped out, as here when Zhang Beihai, the general manager, talked with Weiss.

Garrison Guo, a fluent English speaker, became the team's second interpreter to help with the growing number of foreigners.

Olumide Oyedeji, the team's star center (from Nigeria via the NBA and a host of other international teams), became one of the team's most beloved players for the way he embraced Chinese fans. During a promotional event held at a local elementary school, Olumide showed that he was still a kid.

Zhang Beihai, the general manager, spent the season putting out the fires set by Boss Wang.

Joy, or Ji Le, was the team's most indispensable Chinese player, and had hoped that playing for the Brave Dragons would help him become an all-star.

The Brave Dragons cheerleaders

The team mascot

The Brave Dragons bow to the crowd.

When Boss Wang decided the team needed some tough Chinese discipline, the coaching clipboard was handed—temporarily—to Liu Tie, left, here with Garrison Guo and Weiss during a game.

Whoever was called coach at any given moment, the foreign players kept listening to Weiss. Here, Donta Smith (second from the left), Olumide (next to Weiss), and Weiss joke during the final minutes of a victory. To the right of Weiss are Big Sun, power forward, and Zhai Jinshuai, wing player.

Liu Tie ordered the players, as part of their conditioning, to carry one another up a winding staircase that led up a mountain to an ancient temple.

David Stern, commissioner of the NBA, shakes hands with Jin Zhiguo, the chairman of Tsingtao, after the two men signed a corporate branding partnership in 2008.

Ruslan Rafaelovich Gilyazutdinov, "Big Rus," the Kazakh center, who first signed with the Brave Dragons when he was working in a bar, did not live up to expectations. Here he sits with Rick Turner (right), Weiss's American assistant.

Located on a busy downtown Taiyuan sidewalk, Bob Weiss's favorite manhole, which remained uncovered for weeks

Bob Weiss's wife, Tracy, had spent most of her life nurturing a menagerie of animals in the United States, whether dogs, cats, ferrets, or rats. In China, she helped two players secretly adopt puppies. They named them Prince and Princess.

asked Garrison what he thought of the experiment the team was under-
taking by hiring an NBA coach. I had spent only a week with the team
and was still trying to make sense of what I was seeing. Garrison had an
outsider's perspective, I figured, and was familiar with the culture of the
Chinese game.

He had nodded out the window, toward the rising dust.

"An American coach is like a seed of a very good American plant, an
American species," he said. "But if he wants it to grow a flower in the soil
of China, it is very tough. Other seeds from other countries have a hard
time growing here." It was an unexpectedly poetic response.

The taxi kept pushing along, detouring past construction sites or
veering onto and off of dirt roads, and the noise was loud enough that
we were shouting as much as talking. Garrison was curious about me.
Why had I come to such a crappy place to follow such a crappy team?
I explained that I was interested in the interaction between Americans
and Chinese, playing a game both countries loved. I wanted to see the
cultures entangled.

I had thought it a benign answer. Garrison responded by bringing up
the Opium War. Every Chinese child is taught that China's defeat by
Britain in the First Opium War of 1839–42 marked the beginning of a
"century of humiliation" that would render China too impotent to resist
trade demands and military aggression by European powers and Japan.
Decade after decade, the Western powers and Japan came to plant flags
on Chinese soil, claiming concession districts in port cities like Shanghai,
Tianjin, and Canton (later Guangzhou), as China lay prone and exposed,
unable to resist. This legacy of foreign exploitation and Chinese weakness
would shape the coming century in China, propelling the rise of the Communists and Mao. Today, many younger patriotic Chinese invoke this history as proof of Western hypocrisy and are eager for a powerful, globally
respected China, if partly out of a desire for some historical score settling.

As the taxi puttered forward, I braced for a lecture on American arrogance. But Garrison had taken different lessons from the Opium War. He
thought it had demonstrated Chinese arrogance and exposed the unwill-
ingness of the imperial rulers to adapt to the modern world. Because the
Qing rulers had assumed Chinese superiority in all endeavors, they were
blind to the modernization under way in the West, including in developing weapons of modern warfare.

"That's why we had lost to the foreigners 100 years ago," he said. "The

Chinese people didn't believe that other nations were better. We still believed that we were the best."

The Opium War confronted China with the undeniable fact that global power, and global supremacy, were shifting rapidly to the West. How to respond was the question. Violent resistance to Western influence would periodically boil over in movements such as the Boxer Rebellion, but the broader response would be an attempt to strengthen the country, to catch up, by appropriating Western expertise. Yet learning foreign technical knowledge required learning foreign languages, especially English, which was becoming the global language of science. Introducing English meant introducing Western culture itself, Western beliefs, religions, and, eventually, entertainment. No wonder that English would often be regarded as a threat to traditional Chinese culture.

Long before the founding of the People's Republic in 1949, the Chinese aristocrats of the late Qing era showed only faint interest in foreign languages, as a means to facilitate trade. When the Qing established the first foreign concession district in Canton in the early 1800s, the foreigners were barred from studying Chinese with Chinese teachers. By mid-century, having suffered defeat in the Opium War, the Qing opened language schools in Beijing and Shanghai that ascribed to the maxim of zhong xue wei ti, xi xue wei yong, or Study China for Essence, Study the West for Utility. The initial students were louts and sharpies looking for a piece of the trading business but English steadily attained greater cachet, especially toward the end of the century, with growing numbers of Christian missionaries. The very first missionary, the Scotsman Robert Morrison, had lived in Canton at the opening of the nineteenth century and dedicated himself to translating the Bible into Chinese and producing the first Chinese-English dictionary.

Foreign concession districts soon spread to other ports, often as a result of treaties pressed on the weakened Qing, and English spread with them beyond Canton to Amoy (now Xiamen), Shanghai, Shanhaiguan, Tianjin, and Qingdao. In some cases, Chinese elites whose fortunes were dependent on trade bankrolled missionary schools to teach English to their children. Shanghai would become the sinful embodiment of the conjoining of East and West.

After Mao took power in 1949, Russian became the dominant foreign language, given China's political alignment with the Communist big brothers of the Soviet Union. In the 1950s, the country's few English linguists were dedicated to translating scientific and technological manuals;

by one official estimate, China had only 450 secondary school English teachers in 1957. When Mao broke from the Soviet alliance in 1960, language teachers were retrained to teach English rather than Russian, but the revival was short-lived. Amid the chaos and destruction unleashed in 1966 by the Cultural Revolution, English was stained as a bourgeois tool of capitalism. Schools were shuttered across the country and all teachers became targets of the Red Guards, the groups of marauding students mobilized by Mao to carry out his ideological terror campaigns. Teaching English was regarded as an especially grave offense.

"I am Chinese," read one banner from that era. "Why do I need foreign languages?" Another declared: "Don't learn ABC. Make revolution!"

Schools reopened in 1968, and Mao signaled a new acceptance for English by expressing his regret that he had not studied foreign languages as a youth, commenting, "It is good to know English." Even then, English curricula were infused with propaganda and politics, as students memorized stilted phrases glorifying Mao and the superiority of class struggle. It would take the end of the Cultural Revolution, and the death of Mao, to liberate English from the confines of propagandizing. Under Deng, English became a tool for doing business—and for getting rich.

Like so many Chinese coming of age in the late 1990s and early 2000s, Garrison Guo was interested in getting rich.

When Garrison enrolled at the Foreign Language School of Zhengzhou, his textbooks contained the usual stilted English passages to memorize and recite. But Garrison's education in English would be primarily shaped outside his textbooks. The school had foreign teachers who listened to foreign music, and Garrison began to hang out with them. He studied the lyrics to "Everybody" by the Backstreet Boys and started singing karaoke with friends.

"I felt very cool," he said. "If a student could sing in English, he would be very popular."

In high school, at age sixteen, Garrison had befriended two foreign exchange students who taught English, one from the United States and the other from Poland. They dedicated themselves to providing him with a broad-based immersion course in global youth culture. The Polish boy offered him marijuana. (Garrison says he refused.) The American taught him CPR. Both of them taught him to speak with the same kind of English that many Americans use.

"They taught me all the dirty words like bitch, eat it, nuts, slut, prostitution, hooker, whore, son of a bitch, and asshole," he said. "That's when I started talking slang. I would say, 'What's up, man?' I was a very typical teenager. You wanted to be cool, fashionable, and modern. You wanted to do things so that people will like you."

He enrolled in a local university in Zhengzhou, the first person in his family to attend college, and English quickly thrust him into the spotlight. He competed in English-speaking competitions and became a songwriter and rapper. When he entered a national rap contest, he wrote his own music, created his own elaborate outfit, and won his regional competition. He went to the finals in Beijing prepared to perform a number that somehow combined a saxophone, a basketball, and nunchakus. The producers told him not to bother. They said the only thing that mattered was how he looked. It seemed plausible; most of the performers in the regional competition had been male models. But when he showed up for the Beijing competition, everyone had a gimmick. He bombed.

"I saw all kinds of things," he said. "People were dancing with snakes. Even a soldier was marching in front of the judges."

He kept bouncing from thing to thing. He tried to study overseas in Sweden but his financial aid package fell through. He was probably too restless for the classroom, anyway, too eager to get out into the world. He had worked as a summer counselor at his university's basketball camp, which had led him to a job offer as an interpreter in the CBA.

Basketball had found him even before he had found English. At age eleven, he would play by himself at night on a court near his house. "There was nobody there," he said. "No lights. I worked on my hook shot and my dribbling, over and over. I was never tired. Later, when I was depressed, as I quarreled with my family, basketball was with me. Every time I was sad, I would take my basketball to the court."

His mother fell sick when he was a child. Arthritis left her unable to continue working, bedridden and angry. He rebelled, often fighting or arguing with his parents, and would flee to the basketball court, even when it rained. But basketball would also push him to English.

"I watched the NBA for the first time," he recalled. "I saw Michael Jordan and Charles Barkley. I thought, Whoa, how amazing are they? I want to be like them. I want to play basketball. I was so small and skinny. But I tried harder than anyone else. The ball was so heavy. That's why I learned the hook shot."

The bonus infuriated him enough to spark a small rebellion in Garrison. The evening before the home opener against Bayi, he spent the night in an empty bedroom in Olumide's apartment, a jailbreak from the dorm. We sat at the kitchen table, eating bananas as Olumide was taking his morning nap in his bedroom. I mentioned that I was soon having lunch with Boss Wang and asked Garrison if there was a question he wanted me to ask.

"Ask him if he would like his daughter to marry Garrison," he said, joking. Boss Wang didn't have a daughter. It was a little example of why Westerners sometimes think Chinese have a tin ear for humor. Garrison was trying, with humor, to say that he wanted Boss Wang's money. But then he corrected himself. He didn't want the owner's money. He said he wanted to earn his own.

When he studied English, he was expected to memorize famous aphorisms. Now he cited Charles Chaplin, as he called him.

"People have to believe in themselves. That is the secret to success."

He moved to Lincoln. "Towering genius disdains a beaten path. They seek regions hitherto unexplored."

He paused, frowning. "Hi-ther-to? Is that word right?"

He began again. "What I believe in is there is greatness asleep in every man. When that greatness awakens, miracles happen."

He pointed to his chest. "It's true everyone in the world is unique. They just don't realize it. When they realize it, they can do great things."

I had lost track of the authors of his epiphanies. I asked him who deserved credit for the last one.

"That is Garrison Guo," he said, grinning a wide grin.

Olumide Oyedeji spoke English with a British accent. The issue of his accent arose a day or so after I moved in. Olumide's wife and infant daughter were arriving in a few weeks, and in the interim Olumide was letting me live in one of the empty bedrooms. Olumide would say something to me in his deep and mellifluous voice only to quickly detect, perhaps from my frozen, uncertain reaction, that I hadn't understood him, or that I was pretending I had as a way of being polite, which he considered merely frustrating. "Do you understand?" he would ask me, his eyes widening, his chin tucking back into his neck. He loved to talk, and the thought that I might not precisely understand him was frustrating because it impeded conversation. He concluded the issue was his accent, his *Breee-tish* accent.

I had never encountered a British accent quite like it. China conditioned a foreigner to different permutations of English, the same way Chinese were conditioned to the hackneyed Mandarin spoken by most foreigners. But Olumide's words seemed subject to an unpredictable chemical reaction upon contact with oxygen. It was as if they arrived a long moment after they left his mouth, as if the sound were lingering in the air, vibrating, deliberating whether it would coalesce itself into something recognizable or collapse into something melodically incomprehensible. He said *PREEE-zun* for prison, when he explained that one of his rivals in the Chinese league had spent some time in *preezun*. He said *ohpe* instead of hope, as when he warned that Coach Liu must be careful not to grind the Chinese players into sand or they might lose *ohpe*.

He learned his English growing up in Nigeria, in Ibadan, where he was born on May 11, 1981, as the only son in a family with five daughters. He told me that he was descended from African royalty, and if I never proved or disproved this, he did have a distinctly regal bearing. When he joined the SuperSonics as a second-round draft pick, everyone called him "O" or "Double O," mostly, he would say, because they were too lazy to figure out how to pronounce his name (oh-LOOM-i-day). This was a shame, because his name is imbued with heroic meaning in his native Yoruba language; Olumide translates as "My warrior has arrived." A slightly different translation would be "My savior has arrived," which was probably how his mother saw it.

His mother was a devout adherent of the Christ Apostolic Church, which, like English, had come to Nigeria on the same tide of British colonialism that found its way to China in the nineteenth century. She prayed four or five times a day and ran a strict household. As a boy, Olumide was given a choice: If he chose to attend church, he would be fed. If he chose not to attend church, he would have to find his own food. He went to church. In his apartment in Taiyuan, he kept a Bible in his bedroom and, on the coffee table, another Bible, which offered a passage for every day of the year. One evening after we discussed Liu Tie, chewing over what Olumide considered the coach's innumerable and obvious failings ("He doesn't understand basketball!"), the big man shuffled back to his bedroom when I heard him exclaim, apparently still stewing and commingling his religious background with his distinctive interpretation of English, "Jesus! G-E-S-U-S. Jesus!"

In the geopolitics of the team, Olumide was counted as an American. When Weiss discussed the team with the Chinese press, he often commented about "the two Americans." Olumide did own a home in Orlando, though he rarely saw it, and he had spent four seasons with the Sonics and the Orlando Magic. His Americanness was more a statement of his place in the basketball world, a verification of his status as a bond with a higher rating. In truth, he had turned pro at sixteen and played in Russia, Germany, South Korea, Slovenia, Kuwait, Spain, Puerto Rico, Nigeria, Saudi Arabia, Bahrain, Israel, and elsewhere. His four years in the NBA were the highlight, even if he spent most of his time on the bench. He was a piece that didn't quite fit; he was a "small" 6'10", and if his rebounding was ferocious, his offensive skills were raw. He had not moped when the NBA dumped him. It clarified things. Basketball was a business, which made him a basketball businessman.

He was "looking for money and trying to explore different ideas and different mentalities," he told me.

He was also looking for a washing machine. The game against Bayi was hours away and his Brave Dragons jersey had bled in the wash.

When word came that the general manager wanted to see him, Rick Turner understood it was not good news. "I knew either I was going home or it would be the junior team," Turner said. It was the junior team, the kids on the other court. Turner would take over as head coach. It didn't make sense to have so many coaches for the main team.

The general manager seemed embarrassed as Joe translated his words for Turner. But the decision had come from Boss Wang. And the job had certain restrictions created by Liu Tie: The junior team practiced twice every day but they never played games. They had no season. Turner's entire job would be to run drills.

Joe did not bother to mention that he had been demoted, too. He was now Turner's assistant coach.

CHAPTER SIX

FIGHT

A gain and again, Michael Jordan scored. It seemed like a miracle, a man so sick, yet so relentless, ruthless even, so determined to prevail, to win a basketball game. He took the ball behind the 3-point line, squaring his shoulders, feinting one time, two times, before rising for the shot. Good. He slashed into the lane, propelling himself upward through a crowd of Utah Jazz players, only to float for an extra instant and toss up a shot. Good. Again and again: good, good, good. Only during timeouts would Jordan weaken, covering his head with a towel, once too tired to lift a cup of water. Or toward the end, as he walked off the court, draping his arm around his teammate Scottie Pippen, a man clinging to a raft. To watch Michael Jordan in Game 5 of the 1997 NBA Finals was to wonder if he might simply collapse. His flu was so bad it was stunning he played. Yet to watch him was also to wonder if he was incapable of collapse, if anything existed, on a basketball court, greater than his will.

Boss Wang watched the game on a small television in China. He was not yet so unfathomably rich, and a deal would disintegrate because he skipped a meeting to watch the game. But he would not forget what he saw, and more than a decade later he would still grow excited at the memory, his enthusiasm less about Jordan's talents, his unmatched skills, than about the sheer brutish force of his will.

"Jordan was very famous," he recalled. "He made a lot of money. He had his own jet. He didn't have to play the game for money. He just wanted to fight. He fought for something other than money. There was something in his heart. He wanted to show how tough he was, how special he was."

What made that game resonate so much for Boss Wang was that he saw something in Jordan, a feral spirit, maybe even a greatness, which he believed existed in himself.

It was, admittedly, an opinion not universally shared.

The waitress brought our tea. We sat at a corner table in the coffee shop of Boss Wang's hotel, on the opposite side of the Fen River, not far from the new provincial museum, a massive structure built with coal money and filled with relics of the ancient Shanxi civilizations. Joe had arranged the meeting and we waited near the front desk, both of us nervous and pacing, until Boss Wang came out of the elevator in expensive blue jeans and a gray coat, his shoes clacking against the marble floors, breaking the silence of the lobby. He took my hand.

"We are friends," he said. I considered it as much a warning as a greeting.

I had asked for the meeting to discuss basketball and his life. The home opener against Bayi would start in less than twelve hours.

I had assumed I would be meeting with a madman. What I got was someone harder to define.

"I grew up in the countryside," he began. "It was before Reform and Opening. In the 1960s, the countryside was very poor. It was hard to fill up your stomach. So to keep from thinking about my stomach, I played basketball. The hardest period in China was 1960. I was twelve. I had started primary school when I was eight. I ate anything. I peeled the bark off the trees. I took seeds out of the ground. There were no vegetables in the soil. A lot of people died."

What Mao had called the Great Leap Forward, his misguided collectivist campaign to transform Chinese industry and agriculture, would kill more than 30 million people. Teachers canceled physical education because most students were too weak from hunger. People ate worms and rats. People ate people. People were falling down dead as party propagandists cheered the success of the nation's productive forces. By the time the famines ended and the hunger finally eased in 1962, Wang Xingjiang was sixteen. He had survived. It was time to go out.

"I started my independent life," he said. "I left my family. I shaped my own character from then on. I started to rely on myself."

His father was a farmer in Hebei, a province stretching northward from the dusty plains above the Yellow River to the mountains around the national capital of Beijing. Boss Wang wanted nothing to do with farming. After leaving home he enrolled at a four-year technical school in the provincial capital of Shijiazhuang to train as an accountant. He assumed he would be assigned a government office job in China's planned economy, a notable feat for a farmer's son, but his graduation in 1966 came only weeks before Mao unleashed the Cultural Revolution. Wang was swept away in the national hysteria. He was sent to a small factory in a rural county, Wuji, on the outskirts of Shijiazhuang, where his accounting background was rendered useless. Mao wanted to reorganize society around the idea of perpetual revolution, to reeducate the urban elites by sending them to learn the simple, essential skills of the countryside. Wang became a mechanic and a fitter, repairing heavy machinery.

"Whatever Mao said, we followed," he recalled. "He controlled everyone's minds. So when Mao said educated people should be reeducated on factories and farms, we thought at the time that it must be the right thing.

"I spent eight years at the factory. It hardened my mind and made me tough. I learned how to run a factory. And I kept my connection with basketball."

His interest in the game had taken hold during his time at the technical school. There, he organized a tournament, but he did not play. When the games began, he sat on the sideline, watching, until a player confronted him. "You just watch us," the player said. "You are tall. Why don't you play? You are wasting your talent." The words stung. He would hardly be considered tall today—he was perhaps 5'9"—but in that era, when weaker teenagers had fallen dead, the suggestion that he was wasting his potential was more than an insult. It was a political rebuke. He began practicing with a fury, and even with little formal coaching he became captain of the school team. When Wang first was sent to the factory, basketball was suspended across China, as the Cultural Revolution meant the closing of schools and a prohibition on activities regarded as bourgeois. It would take Mao's overture to America in 1971 to resurrect the game. When Mao invited the United States table tennis team to China for an exhibition, a gesture that opened the door for Nixon to visit the following year, it was the strongest signal inside China that people would not be punished for picking up balls and playing sports.

The Cultural Revolution had upended the country's human geography. Cities were drained of much of their human capital, as professors and accountants were plowing fields or working on assembly lines in the provinces. Basketball was no different; basketball had always been a city game, and a sport of the military, but the Cultural Revolution dispersed the country's best players and many landed in Hebei Province, including in the counties around Shijiazhuang. Factories had already quietly begun to field teams, and factory bosses snapped up the top players as employees.

Wang was a starting player for his factory's team, earning 20 yuan a month, less than $5. In that era, it was a decent wage but not enough to feed himself and send something back to his parents on the farm. Although people were no longer starving, hunger remained a dull pang. Food was still defined by scarcity, vegetables were rare, and people in the north survived winter by eating *baicai*, or Chinese cabbage, known in Beijing as *ai guo cai*, or Love Your Country Vegetable. While he was playing for his factory, Wang learned that officials were forming an elite county team and that every player would be rewarded with six months of free food. Making the team also meant players could stop working in factories for at least three months every year in order to practice. Wang befriended the army recruiter who also ran the county sports program and got a tryout. He made the team.

"Basketball gave me the chance to leave the factory and eat for free," he said. "Basketball changed my life."

His marriage would, too. In 1972, he married the daughter of a Communist Party official in the city of Xingtai, a steel center in Hebei with several large state-owned factories and a competitive basketball league. The couple initially lived apart, a fairly typical arrangement, since they were assigned to positions in different counties, but Wang's father-in-law slowly exerted his political influence to unite them in Xingtai. It was a small but telling example of the special privileges available to Communist Party members, and Wang had married into the club. After his transfer to Xingtai, Wang was assigned to a division of the city's construction bureau that built buses. He also joined the construction bureau team to compete against some of China's best players. Bosses in Xingtai would hire top players with no-show jobs and good salaries; Wang remembered that one coal mine hired four former players from China's national team. There were no gymnasiums but factories draped lights over outdoor courts and sold tickets for games.

"There were no movies, no television, nothing to do," Wang recalled. "A basketball game would attract a lot of people."

It was 1976. Wang Xingjiang was a new father of a son, Songyan. He had no reason to imagine everything was about to change again.

Mao envisioned steel as a symbol of China's socialist might. Industry was the muscle of Western capitalism, and Mao wanted to prove Communism was stronger. He ordered the construction of large steel mills and other heavy industries, hewing to a Stalinist development model, and then introduced his own industrial campaign in 1958 as part of the Great Leap Forward. He declared that China would double steel output in a single year, surpassing Great Britain as a producer. Across the country, peasants and factory workers frantically built small mills, sometimes backyard blast furnaces, and melted down pots, scrap metal, spoons, and anything they could find. It became a disaster that crippled Chinese industry.

But if Mao's methods would be discredited, his vision of China as an industrial power, an unmatched producer of steel, would be realized five decades later. By 2008, China was by far the world's top producer and consumer of steel, with a capacity to produce more than 700 million metric tons annually. China's economy had become insatiable, and anyone in the business of feeding it could get very rich. From Deng's symbolic embrace of market reforms, China had evolved into a messy hybrid, a blend of private and state-owned enterprises, with tight regulation in some sectors as well as vast, vaguely defined gray areas of opportunity for an entrepreneur.

Wang Xingjiang did not immediately jump into steel. First he had to jump into the sea. The expression, *xia hai*, originated from ancient poems about sailors who had risked their lives by going out to sea. But by the 1980s, the phrase signified the cadres, the so-called Red Hat Capitalists, who left their government jobs and jumped into private business for a chance to get rich in Deng's new and churning ocean. Wang had been transferred to the city materials bureau, a job that carried him around the country to purchase buses or heavy machinery for the Xingtai government. He had become a *ganbu*, a party cadre, and his young son attended the elite elementary school reserved for the children of government officials. By the early 1980s, he had decided to jump.

"I saw the chance," he said. "I could make some money." At that point, he had none.

When Deng lifted the boulder off Chinese society, the immediate reaction was to look upward, everyone squinting at the sun, frozen, waiting to see if the boulder would come crashing back down. But as change started to arrive, people began to move, to scramble toward the factories that were rising along the coast, or to do a little business. Almost no one had any money to speak of, and getting money took *guanxi*, or connections. Plenty of peasants would get rich by dint of hard work and business acumen. But those with the early advantage were the officials who would benefit from their government ties after jumping into private business. Wang was one of them. If people were starting to move in China, Wang wanted to give them a ride. His break came when a friend at a government credit union loaned him enough money to buy a used bus. He established routes through the industrial corridors of Hebei Province.

"We started with one bus, then two, then three," he said. "Then I had more than twenty."

He expanded into trucking. Hebei was the steel center of China, and he began delivering rebar from factories in Xingtai to other cities in Hebei and neighboring provinces. He was now *Wang Laoban,* or Boss Wang, and by the early 1990s he thought he was a rich man. He took a trip to Europe and wandered into a jewelry shop. There, as he would later tell the story, he saw a large, beautiful pearl. It captivated him, but when he asked the price, he could not afford it. He realized he was not such a rich man after all.

He returned to China and went into steel. Steel, like coal, would become an engine of the Chinese economy. Economic planners in Beijing categorized steel as a nationally strategic industry that should be dominated by the state. But the state-owned mills were enduring a painful restructuring and would be slow to respond to a market about to change radically. In the mid-1990s, China's prime minister, Zhu Rongji, ordered the bloated state sector to begin shedding workers and other obligations. Tens of millions of workers were laid off, particularly in the northeastern Rust Belt, and enterprises began dismantling the "iron rice bowl" benefits of schools, health care, and housing, the security net of the *danwei* system. As part of this, enterprises transferred the titles of tens of millions of apartments to residents, usually at below market prices. Whether by design or dumb luck, this transfer of property marked the birth of a private real estate market in China and would underpin the biggest economic expansion in the history of the world.

With new equity in their old apartments, urban residents began buying new, better housing. Developers built apartments in every city in China. Demand surged for concrete, cement, and steel, but the state-owned sector could not respond fast enough. China had to import steel to meet demand. Private operators saw an opening. Even before the real estate boom, Wang had discovered there was more money to be made in making rebar than in moving it. When he had returned from Europe, he got another friendly loan and began importing steel billet from Ukraine, becoming a middleman who supplied the raw materials that Chinese factories processed into steel wire. By 1995, he had saved enough to buy his own steel factory in Henan Province.

Steel placed Boss Wang in the messy, chaotic center of the rise of China, a place of incredible opportunity and moral ambiguity, filled with dreamers and schemers. Owning a steel factory in 1995 was akin to being a modern-day warlord. A private mill owner had to be able to cut deals with local officials, guarantee his own supply of raw materials, and secure credit; had to be comfortable in the gray zones of an authoritarian state; had to be tenacious, hardworking, a tough son of a bitch. In 2006, investigators arrested Boss Wang, his brother, and managers at a factory he had opened in Shanxi. The factory had been using fake receipts to avoid taxes on purchases of raw materials, a violation that was shouldered by the brother, who went to jail. Boss Wang was released.

Steel would make him very rich, and owning a factory offered another fringe benefit. He was one of the earliest of a small group of modern-day Chinese who could pursue a wild fantasy of self-expression and get away with it. One Chinese millionaire, for example, built a replica of the U.S. Capitol as his home. Boss Wang simply organized his own basketball team.

He had first discovered a wider world, as far as basketball went, when he joined the county team in the early 1970s. The coaching improved, and he learned specific drills to hone certain skills. He also got access to the team's small black-and-white television and began watching occasional games from other countries. He had not realized he was playing a global game.

"We did not know about the NBA," he said. "But people told me that American basketball was the best."

When NBA basketball did start appearing on Chinese television, Boss Wang was transfixed and became determined to implement the lessons he was learning. In 2002, he had bought a new CBA team and merged it with players from his factory in Henan. He left Henan after officials in Shanxi Province offered him land and tax incentives to open a new factory in Linfen, the industrial city south of Taiyuan. Bringing the team was part of the deal. Shanxi was dripping with coal money, and provincial leaders wanted a pro basketball team to boost the province's image.

When he bought the team, Boss Wang inherited some talent, but those players had signed contracts that were now expiring. Most of them left. At the same time, the Bayi team finagled the rights to his best player; when Boss Wang filed a lawsuit, Bayi beat him in court. He felt screwed. He arrived in Taiyuan in 2006 with Big Sun, Pan, Kobe, and a few others. As a steel boss, Boss Wang had been an outsider, compared to the big state mills, but he considered the steel industry a good model for the basketball league. Private entrepreneurs had proved that they could compete against the state monopolies that controlled the steel industry; in basketball, he would have to make the same breakthrough, even though he felt constrained by the system. He couldn't obtain new players because the Chinese league had no free agency. He felt the league needed to be more like the NBA, more commercial, if it wanted to improve.

He hired coaches and then exploded when they failed to make changes that seemed plainly obvious to him. He meddled in practice, berated his players for making mistakes, and ran the team the way he ran his steel mills—as a fiefdom defined by hard work and ruthlessness. It did not take long for him to earn a terrible reputation among Chinese coaches—having fired so many of them—which matched his opinion of most of them. He thought they were too insular, too willing to soak him for money, and too resistant to learning from the NBA, which finally led him to America and to Bob Weiss. Yet he had sidelined Weiss after only two months and replaced him with an inexperienced Chinese coach intensely resistant to learning from the NBA.

We had been talking for more than three hours. We had moved to the hotel restaurant and eaten lunch. Boss Wang leaned across the table, closer to me, when I asked about his experiment with Weiss. "Bob brought a lot of modern principles and ideas from the NBA," Boss Wang said. "He is accustomed to dealing with lots of high-level principles. Our players are very young, very raw. They couldn't understand what Bob wanted them to do. They couldn't follow Bob's ideas on the court."

Coach Liu did understand, he continued. He knew how to implement the NBA principles through drilling, and Liu Tie was helping the players execute Weiss's ideas. He thought the partnership was working, and the players were more confident.

"Maybe they feel they have an NBA coach standing behind them and a young Chinese coach," he says. "Maybe they feel like there are a lot of people trying to support them. I felt they were lonely before and felt abandoned on the court. Now they have support."

He sounded almost grandfatherly. Or delusional.

I asked about the Bayi game, and he smiled. Bayi's players took note of Shanxi's opening win and had spoken about the team with respect. "A lot of people are saying Shanxi's team is like a nail in the wood," he told me, grinning. "It is not easy to pull out."

He asked my opinion about an idea he had been pondering. What did I think about benching the foreigners in the first quarter against Bayi?

Playing Bayi always demanded a gimmick. Bayi had no foreigners, since hiring imports would be akin to the People's Liberation Army depending on foreign mercenaries to fight battles. That meant that any team playing Bayi had to play under the old rules, in which foreign players were limited to six combined quarters. Boss Wang's idea was to play Chinese against Chinese for the first quarter. He said the Chinese players could keep the game fairly close for a quarter, then the advantage would swing to Shanxi for the rest of the game. Bayi would be tired, while the foreigners would be rested and eligible to play the rest of the game.

"The coaches do not like this," he said, "but it is my idea."

I asked if the team would employ his strategy. He pulled back from the table, smiling.

"Oh, the coaches will make the decision, not me," he said.

We walked to the cashier. The game was starting in a few hours, and Boss Wang was leaving for the team meeting. I had barely noticed the strange decor of the restaurant. Pieces of fake seaweed were hanging from the ceiling, which was plastered with beige-colored stucco intended to resemble sand. Shells were placed in the stucco. The floor of the ocean was staring down at us. We were upside down in the churning sea.

The foreigners had a new van, more of a minibus, to accommodate their growing number. Ruslan Rafaelovich Gilyazutdinov, the Kazakh, was sleeping on the back row, a Russian pulp novel rising and falling on his chest. He had arrived in Taiyuan a few days earlier and immediately reported to the practice gym for a late night workout ordered by Liu Tie. The coaches wanted to see what their Asian could do. The answer was not much. He was in terrible shape, a large, lumbering cinder block of Central Asia who nearly vomited after a half hour of Liu's running drills.

His value to the team remained an open question. He wasn't dressing for the Bayi game.

The minibus was moving along a newly improved road. The incessant tumult of construction in Taiyuan had produced a divided six-lane thoroughfare, Binhe East Road, stripping along the eastern edge of the Fen River, running south to north as a connector between the new airport and the new downtown, slicing beside the new high-rise apartments in the process. Driver Zhou must have felt bored; the road was devoid of bicyclists or mules or rickshaws or old women stumbling into traffic. He glided past one of the riverside parks where workers were building a replica of a large pagoda.

Weiss sat near the front, staring at a printout of a long email that arrived that morning from his financial advisor. The news from America was grim. The collapse of the subprime mortgage industry was still rippling through the American economy, wreaking havoc on real estate prices. Foreclosures were shooting up. The new president-elect, Barack Obama, faced a banking crisis before taking office. In Seattle, Weiss's home was on the market but no one was even taking a look.

"The key thing he said," Weiss said of the email, "was to keep your revenue stream alive."

For a moment, everyone was silent.

The night before, the defending league champions, Guangdong, had destroyed the team from Yunnan Province by 40 points. The Chinese press was already holding up Guangdong and Bayi as defenders of the national honor by not depending on foreign talent. Guangdong had two foreigners, but the team was built around Chinese stars, including four members of China's Olympic team. The opening weekend of games had seemed a little like the Opium War. "Foreign Players Go Crazy!" screamed the banner headline in *Titan Sports,* the country's leading sports publication. The former Houston Rockets Michael Harris and Kirk Snyder had become overnight superstars. Snyder, playing in coastal Zhejiang Province, had become such an instant celebrity that the general manager of his team was trying to block press interviews because "if there are too many articles, it will have an influence on our domestic players." *Titan Sports* responded to the interview ban by following Snyder to a restaurant in Shanghai and running a full-page story on his thoughts about seafood prices.

Harris was playing for the Dongguan New Century Leopards, a team expected to contend for the championship. The Leopards had a mix of top Chinese players and had also signed an American center, Jamal Sampson, to pair with Harris. The Chinese press was hyping the Leopards' upcoming game with powerhouse Guangdong as a battle between East and West.

"They are powerful," snapped Du Feng, the star forward for Guangdong, when asked about the new foreign stars on the Dongguan team. "But don't you think we are powerful? We're not like other teams who rely on foreign players. The key for us is preparing well."

The one team getting almost no attention in the national basketball press was the Shanxi Brave Dragons.

Driver Zhou turned the minibus into the campus of Shanxi University of Finance and Economics and stopped at a service entrance behind the arena. The Brave Dragons marketing department had already been at work. Team posters were hanging outside the service entrance. One had Big Sun driving to the basket, another Pan Jiang dribbling on the wing. Donta Smith pointed to a life-size poster near the door.

"Look!" he shouted. "*Ba-bu Wee-Suh!*"

It was a photograph of Weiss, with a ball embossed with the CBA logo cupped in his arm. He was wearing a blue New York City firefighter's sweatshirt and staring ahead with a determined look, captain of the ship.

He grabbed his clipboard and walked into the gym.

"It's hell being an idol," he said.

The crowd stirred when the two teams walked onto the court for the opening tip. There were the great Bayi Rockets, led by the league's greatest domestic player, Wang Zhizhi, a 7'1" center with a lethal outside shot, the first Chinese to play in the NBA. Next came Li Nan, veteran of four Olympic teams, the leading scorer in league history. During introductions, the Taiyuan fans had cheered politely for Bayi, so powerful was the Bayi brand, so intertwined was the team with China itself.

Basketball had been the sport of the Chinese military since before 1949, when the Red Army general He Long organized competitions among different army brigades. Bayi became the army's elite team; the name *ba yi* translates as 8/1, or August 1, the founding date of the People's Liberation Army. For decades, Bayi skimmed off the best players in the country, many of them from poor families, by offering lifelong employment, bonuses like fur coats or even a Mercedes. Players received high military ranks without the obligation of military service. Following the formation, in 1995, of the Chinese Basketball Association, Bayi won seven of the first eight league championships, the only defeat coming in 2002 to Yao Ming and the Shanghai Sharks. Beating Bayi meant you had beaten the People's Liberation Army.

Yet if the Taiyuan crowd stirred at the sight of Bayi, they were also reacting to the all-Chinese starting five for the home team. A murmur swept through the seats as the fans craned down at the Shanxi bench. Olumide Oyedeji was still in his yellow sweats. Donta Smith sat beside him, elbows on knees. Up on press row, the Taiyuan reporters assumed they were witnessing the unorthodox strategy of the new foreign coach. I could see Boss Wang on the bench, still in his expensive jeans and gray coat, pinched between Liu Tie and Wingtips.

The arena seated about 4,000 people, with the different seating sections divided into red, yellow, or blue. It could pass for an arena at a small college in the United States, except that gyms in the United States usually turn on the heat in late November. During the pregame, the Brave Dragons cheerleaders—known in Mandarin as the La La Duis—danced in halter tops and spandex pants, then pranced quickly off the court to slip on their matching blue parkas. Fans had poured into the arena, most of them men, nearly all of them wearing the same brown or black jackets that pass for wintertime male couture in coal country. Almost no one took off their jackets, given the frigid temperature, and the fashion effect was the same as a winter dust storm. The arena turned as brown as the fields outside.

The referee tossed up the ball to start the game, and the crowd howled. Bayi controlled the tip, and Pan Jiang attacked on defense like a feral dog. At the morning practice, Coach Liu had pulled Pan aside. Pan was already Boss Wang's whipping boy, and Liu was not happy with his defensive intensity, his will to fight. Liu Tie had crouched into a stance and slammed his hips against Pan, slapping at his arm, to show him what he wanted. Now Pan was pressing against the Bayi point guard, banging against his hips, raking at the ball. Whistle. Foul. A minute later, Pan hacked again. Whistle. Foul. A backup replaced him. The backup hit a Bayi guard so hard that the guard was rolling beneath the basket. A pattern had been established: Nearly every possession, Shanxi was attacking on defense, pushing, crashing around the court.

Offense was another matter. The Taiyuan fans, rather than witnessing the unveiling of a high-level NBA offense, were watching complete disorganization. Everyone stood in place, uncertain where to go, what to do.

Liu Tie had effectively deconstructed Weiss's offense. The problem was that he had not constructed anything in its place. The frontcourt players were frozen under the basket. The guards were throwing up wild shots. Kobe threw an errant pass into the stands and the fans started laughing. Luckily, Joy was in the groove. He made a 12-footer. He hit a 3. He was as disciplined as his teammates were out of control. He made a steal on defense. He scored 12 points and the Brave Dragons led halfway through the quarter. Bayi was rattled and called timeout. Boss Wang sat silently on the bench, legs crossed, as the players celebrated around him. His gamble appeared to be paying off.

Then came the Wave. The music came out of the sound system like the scream of a jet engine, a screeching techno version of what once was Beethoven's Fifth. At the corner of the court, a paunchy man in a blue sweatshirt, Ren Hongbing, the Brave Dragons' deejay, was pounding on a soundboard, shaking his head to the beat of the music and shouting for everyone to get up. They did. As if an electrical current were crackling through their pants, the spectators in section after section, brown and black jackets flying upward, arms flailing, a roiling sea of giddy potbellied coal bosses and everyone else, smiled and laughed and reached for the roof. In America, the Wave had devolved into a canned act, no longer novel enough for anyone to risk spilling a beer, but it was a sensation in Taiyuan. The Shanxi University of Finance and Economics was trembling.

It took a moment for everyone to realize the game had resumed, and not in Shanxi's favor. Bayi was pressing full court, unnerving the Brave Dragons' guards, who started turning the ball over. Wang Zhizhi was hitting everything, almost nonchalantly, and would finish the quarter with 15 points. Bayi also was returning the favor on defense: A Brave Dragons guard was knocked to the floor by a vicious foul in front of the Bayi bench. The Bayi coach was a dashing figure, arms crossed in a tailored suit, his nose tilting slightly upward, his head covered by a dark blue beret. He glared down at the player on the ground, disgusted, as if he had been served cold coffee at a Paris bistro.

Bayi kept coming, scoring on baskets by Wang Zhizhi or going to the foul line. Shanxi was struggling to get off a shot. Weiss slumped on the bench, staring at the floor. Liu Tie rubbed his hands over his head in frustration. Bayi led 39–29 at the end of the quarter. Defensive intensity had not translated into good defense. The Brave Dragons had 16 fouls, a ridiculously high number.

Donta Smith and Olumide Oyedeji stood up and and stripped off their yellow sweat suits.

We were standing in pee. At halftime, I followed the Taiyuan press corps into a small lobby reserved for police, soldiers, journalists, and the stadium crew. Everyone was smoking. The People's Liberation Army soldiers were smoking. The cops were smoking. The photographers were smoking. The Communist Party hacks were smoking. I found it difficult to breathe. When our small journalistic party attempted to enter the bathroom, we could not breach the door. Cops and soldiers were peeing and smoking simultaneously, so we waited beside the lavatories in a small adjacent room. Our shoes stuck to the floor. No one seemed to notice. We discussed the game.

Bayi led 65–53. Olumide and Donta started sluggishly. The Brave Dragons were piling up fouls. We shook our heads at what had been a monumentally sloppy half.

On the court, the Brave Dragons cheerleaders, having shed their parkas, were finishing a number, grinding their hips and shaking their shoulders as the deejay played "Don't Push Me" by Sweetbox.

> *Don't cage me in,*
> *Don't tie me down.*

Clouds of nicotine moved out of the lobbies and settled over the court. The game clock showed the second half starting in less than a minute. The Bayi Rockets were getting loose, shooting layups and jump shots. The Brave Dragons were still in the locker room, talking, or being talked to. One of the scorekeepers sent someone to get the team. With only seconds until the buzzer, the familiar yellow jerseys appeared. One of the first players onto the court was Donta Smith. He was squinting. He waved his hand in front of his eyes to clear the smoke.

With 8:39 remaining in the third quarter, Bayi led 72–53 and the cheerleaders were shivering in their parkas. Then the foreigners took over the game. Olumide began vacuuming up every rebound, waving his arms to draw the fans out of their seats, tumbling to the floor or crashing into the courtside photographer, always grimacing in pain, seemingly in need of medical evacuation, only to rise up each time and trot down the court. When two Bayi players offered to help him up, Olumide slapped their hands away. The Shanxi crowd roared.

Then Donta Smith scored on a jumper, followed by a 3-pointer. He slammed down a dunk, pounding his fist against his chest, shouting at the roof. From press row Journalist Li turned to me and mouthed a single word: *Qiaodan.* Jordan. Donta moved to point guard and kept scoring. He and Weiss had huddled on the sideline and crafted an impromptu offense, placing shooters like Joy on the wings to create space for Donta to drive and score, or dish outside for open shots. When Donta finished the third quarter with a driving baseline dunk, Bayi's lead was halved, 94–85.

Shanxi was still reckless on defense, but now the character of the fouls seemed to change. There was a very questionable whistle against Joy. A teammate drew a whistle after barely touching a Bayi player.

"Hei Shao! Hei Shao! Hei Shao!" Black Whistle! Black Whistle! Black Whistle! The fans were shouting at the referees, screaming the Chinese expression for corrupt officiating.

It was 100–98, Bayi leading. Six minutes and 45 seconds remained. The crowd was bellowing. The Taiyuan press corps was in a state of frenzy, not from the approaching deadline nor from typing blog entries but from screaming, pounding their fists against the table and raising their arms in triumph after a Brave Dragon sank a 3-pointer to take the lead, 101–100.

One minute and 27 seconds remained, and Bayi had again pushed ahead, 110–108. Beating Bayi for the Brave Dragons would mean felling Goliath. A Bayi player kicked the ball, an infraction, but the referees ignored it. The fans shrieked. Seconds remained. Shanxi had a chance to tie or pull ahead. Donta received the ball in the post area, close to the basket. He spun, shrugged off a foul, and took a tough shot. The ball rose toward the basket but clanged off the rim. A Bayi player grabbed the rebound and was fouled. He made both shots. Shanxi rushed down the court and missed a foolish 3-pointer. The Brave Dragons fouled again.

Final score: Bayi 116, Shanxi 110. Wang Zhizhi led all scorers with 33 points, while Donta scored 24 in only three quarters. The crowd filed outside as the deejay mourned the loss with the theme from *Star Wars.*

Bayi shot 65 free throws, Shanxi only 21. At the postgame news conference, a reporter noted that Shanxi seemed to commit a lot of unnecessary hand fouls. Was this the NBA method, playing this type of defense? Weiss was asked.

Weiss absorbed the question. His assistant, Liu Tie, oversaw the team's defense, he replied. He praised the team's tenacity, their will to fight. "But they have to learn the difference between aggressive and overaggressive," he said. "They've got to know when to pull back. We can't have other teams shooting this many foul shots against us."

Another reporter reminded Weiss that Shanxi had been one of the league's worst teams. Did the players really believe they could win games against teams like Bayi?

"They should believe it now," he said. "We can win against anybody."

The news conference ended, and Weiss walked down the corridor to the locker room. The door was closed but a voice could be heard inside. Someone was shrieking. Weiss opened the door and stepped inside. I stole a quick glimpse. The players, sweating and exhausted, were sitting in chairs, backs against the wall of the room. Boss Wang was moving from player to player, dissecting their performances, lecturing them one by one. The door closed, but the voice still rang through the hallway. He would talk for another hour.

At the edge of the court, the ushers were standing in a line as a supervisor conducted a postgame review. On the court, the cheerleaders had changed into street clothes and were standing in formation. The lights were off, the music was off, but they began to move in unison on the darkened court, practicing, hips grinding and shoulders shaking in the silence.

CHAPTER SEVEN

SELLING AIR

Not long after Bob Weiss landed in Taiyuan, David Stern, the commissioner of the NBA, walked into a Beijing conference hall to conduct the business of basketball in China. It was August 23, the day before the gold medal game between the United States and Spain, what for Stern should have been a moment of triumph. He had spent twenty years cultivating China, and the NBA was now one of the most popular and recognizable foreign brands in the country. The American team of NBA stars was about to win the gold medal in a thrilling final, yet even the Spanish team bespoke the NBA's global domination. The Spanish roster included Pau Gasol, the starting center for the Lakers; his brother, Marc Gasol, soon to be the starting center for the Memphis Grizzlies; and two players about to be selected in the NBA draft, Ricky Rubio and Rudy Fernandez. No matter which team Chinese fans rooted for, they were rooting for the NBA.

Stern did not seem triumphant, however. He had a global vision for the NBA, one that extended beyond North America into Europe, where he had long wanted to place teams, and especially into China, where 300 million people supposedly were playing basketball, a number roughly equal to the entire population of the United States. For the past year, the NBA had made its biggest and riskiest global bet in China, forming a Chinese subsidiary and pursuing its own Chinese league, and the Olympics were tantamount to a product launch. A day earlier, Stern met with officials from the Chinese Basketball Association to discuss a partnership on a possible league. The Chinese media had been buzzing about a possible announcement, but nothing had happened. Instead, as he took his seat of honor inside the conference hall, David Stern was about to sell some beer.

The event was the union of the NBA and Tsingtao, one of China's leading beer brands, and the wedding party sat on opposite sides of a stage as a local television personality presided. The room was already saturated with virtual booziness, as if the wedding reception had already taken place. Stern had been running late, so the waiting Chinese journalists were entertained with a Tsingtao infomercial showing tipsy foreign tourists clanging tankards, everyone stupendously jolly during Tsingtao's annual Oktoberfest celebration along the Chinese coast. Next came images of a single, shimmering Tsingtao, quivering with tension until the cap finally exploded off the wet green bottle. Music blared off the ceiling and the images of inebriated foreigners and ejaculatory beer bottles were repeated again and again, spliced with game footage from the NBA, until Stern finally arrived. A group of Chinese drummers pounded out a welcome, banging away as performers beneath a paper lion burst through a rear door and twisted toward the podium. "The lion dancing will bring good luck to the cooperation between you two," the mistress of ceremonies shouted as the paper lion settled at the foot of the podium. Stern gazed down, puzzled then bemused, before smiling and rising to speak.

"This is an alliance between the best of sports and lifestyle," he pronounced. His new partner, Tsingtao's chairman, Jin Zhiguo, beamed and declared that the NBA was an ideal mate for brand positioning, brand attractiveness, and brand association. "It's really hard to imagine that life as we know it today would be as wonderful without the NBA or Tsingtao beer," he concluded. Then the drummers resumed their banging as the paper lion clambered to life for the ceremonial exchange of gifts. The Tsingtao delegation presented the NBA side with a statue of a horse pulling a Tsingtao beer wagon, while the NBA's deputy commissioner, Adam Silver, reciprocated with an NBA ball signed by the American team. Stern and Jin stepped off the stage to dot the eyes of the paper lion with a calligraphy brush while a troupe of Chinese streetballers in NBA jerseys performed some dribbling and passing tricks. Finally, mercifully, it was over.

"Beer represents fun," the mistress of ceremonies declared in her deliberate English. "Basketball is, of course, fun. We'll have double fun after your cooperation."

It was a goofy, schlocky event that also happened to represent how the NBA makes money in China. The NBA and Tsingtao were signing a branding partnership, the corporate version of a high school romance in which the cheerleader gets to wear her boyfriend's letter jacket. Tsingtao was agreeing to stamp each of its millions of beer bottles with the familiar logo of the NBA. Ordinarily, this might be considered advertising, which would mean that the NBA would pay for the privilege, since millions of beer bottles represent lots of advertising, but a branding partnership is different, happily so for the NBA. NBA basketball is so popular in China that Tsingtao was paying an unnamed sum for the privilege of using the NBA brand. By the time of the Olympics, branding partnerships represented the largest share of the $75 million in annual revenues earned by the NBA in China. When corporations like Tsingtao partnered with the league, the NBA granted them a package of marketing products: advertising time during broadcasts of NBA games in China, the chance to participate in NBA promotional events around the country, and the right to adorn their products with the trademarked image of the NBA logo. In China, the NBA logo was considered synonymous with America itself; one survey by a consulting firm rated the NBA as one of the ten brands Chinese consumers most identified with the United States. The league's popularity had turned logic upside down. The NBA wasn't selling a tangible product, such as a Nike shoe or a Spalding basketball. The NBA was selling air, and doing so at a nice return.

Now it wanted to create more air. Any multinational corporation with the kind of name recognition and success enjoyed by the NBA would have tried to create more products to sell in the Chinese market, which helps explain why the NBA decided it wanted a Chinese league. Economically, a league would create new revenue streams from tickets and concessions, yet, most of all, a league would create new content, new air, which could be packaged and sold in China. The potential existed for a whole new tier of branding partnerships for a China league, new trademarked merchandise that could be sold to Chinese fans, as well as new television contracts. NBA executives also reasoned that an NBA league would bring a more exciting style of play to Chinese fans and improve Chinese basketball by exposing Chinese players to better coaching and training methods. It seemed like a just reward; the NBA was the reason basketball was so popular in China.

But a league is very different from air. China already had one, under management of the Chinese government. A partnership certainly made sense, if judged by the cold logic of mutual need. The Chinese league needed help making money and improving the quality of play; the NBA had the world's greatest players and moneymaking was encoded in its corporate DNA. The NBA needed help getting government approval for a league; the Chinese league was the government. Yet this logic went only so far. The real issue was control. The Chinese league saw the NBA as both a model and a threat. In Taiyuan, Bob Weiss was running into the hard, invisible wall of Chinese culture. His expertise was to be exploited but also contained. Now David Stern was hitting a wall, too. When he left the Tsingtao event and walked toward the elevator, Stern was followed by a small cluster of reporters, including me. We wanted to know about his meeting with the CBA. "We had a very good meeting with the CBA yesterday," he said, a bit testily. "Generally we are discussing having a potential league. But there is no timetable." The situation, he said cryptically, was "very complex."

Born in New York, raised in the New Jersey suburbs, David Stern earned a law degree at Columbia and joined the NBA as outside counsel in 1966. He became commissioner in 1984. His legal background dovetailed with the different challenges facing the league. He negotiated a drug testing policy with the players union and hammered out a revenue-sharing agreement between players and owners that created a team salary cap. When the owners locked out the players during a labor dispute in 1998, Stern grew a beard as a symbol of his discontent. More than his peers who ran professional baseball and football, Stern was widely recognized in the United States and beyond, partly because of his long tenure and partly because of the stagecraft created for the annual NBA draft, carried on live television and followed intently on the Internet. Stern greeted each first-round draft pick for a posed handshake: the short, grinning Jewish commissioner shaking hands with a procession of enormous players, most of them black, nearly all of them gigged up in outlandishly tailored suits.

The draft was evidence of how Stern's NBA had become a marketing machine with global ambitions. If the promoters of baseball and football often debated which one was America's favorite sport, or which was the most truly American sport, Stern spoke of basketball as a global game with the NBA perched at the top of a global order. Now kids playing basketball around the world dreamed of their handshake with David Stern, and when some of those kids began showing up on draft day, befuddling American announcers with their strange-sounding names, gigged up in their own ridiculous outfits, the breadth of the NBA dream machine became clear. The NBA *was* America itself, or what America claimed to be: the place where anyone from anywhere could compete against the best in the world and get rich doing it. The draft became a tool to tether different countries to the league; any player imported into the NBA from a foreign country also exported the NBA back to his country, which is why the 2002 draft was so important. When David Stern shook hands with Yao Ming, the first pick in the draft, the NBA believed it had pushed open the door to the greatest basketball market in the world.

Stern had first knocked on that door in 1987, when he arrived at the headquarters of China Central Television in Beijing with a videotape of highlights from the NBA All-Star Game. Stern couldn't yet visualize what China would become—who could?—but he had already started exploring the international market, including the then Soviet Union, where he was negotiating with sports officials over the star Lithuanian center Arvydas Sabonis (who would later play for the Portland Trail Blazers). In the United States, basketball was the country's third most popular professional sport, but as American sports slowly started trying to attract a global audience, Stern had an advantage. Basketball was played almost everywhere and had been an Olympic sport for decades; China had sent a basketball team to the Games in 1936. And as the politics of the Cold War melted, the economics of globalization were starting to become clear. If the NBA didn't try to capture the global basketball market, another league would.

"We were participating in a sport that had already had a global presence," Stern said. "And, of course, it became apparent as globalization occurred that there were economic opportunities that could be accessible to products that cross borders easily."

At CCTV, Stern had an appointment with Li Zhuang, the man overseeing foreign programming in culture, entertainment, and sports. Two years earlier, Stern had met a delegation of Chinese basketball officials visiting the Basketball Hall of Fame in Springfield, Massachusetts, but his expectations were low for any immediate returns from his visit to CCTV. China's reform period was just starting and the country did not yet have anything close to a market economy or a middle class. The CCTV building was a bland white tower on the west side of Beijing, in the bureaucratic heart of the city. Stern and a staffer arrived at the gate and offered their names to the guard. The guard made a telephone call while Stern waited. And waited. "Mr. Li said he had no record of a meeting with us," Stern recalled later. "We sat in the lobby for two hours."

Ultimately, Stern got his meeting, and eventually his deal, even if it didn't seem like much of one. He was pitching a demo tape of an NBA highlight show. The league would provide one tape every week for free. The NBA would get half of any ad revenues attached to the show, but Stern expected little if any money to materialize. He would later say that giving away the show was partly a goodwill gesture. But he also wanted exposure and CCTV could deliver an audience unlike any other.

Television first appeared in China in 1958. In the United States, television was emerging as the nation's most powerful cultural force during the 1950s as audiences watched *Gunsmoke,* Jack Benny, and Lucille Ball. In China, the country's lone network, Peking Television, operated on a closed circuit and broadcast political updates and ideological directives to a select group of high officials. Party leaders soon recognized the propaganda value of the new medium and steadily expanded Peking Television's coverage area while provincial governments also started new stations. For all programming, the government instructed the stations to promote the political agenda of the leadership. And when Deng Xiaoping announced his reforms in 1978, the only hint of coming change in television was cosmetic; the name of Peking Television was changed to China Central Television, or CCTV.

Then something entirely new happened in 1979 in Shanghai. For the first time, an advertisement was broadcast on Chinese television. The ad was hawking a local brand of rice liquor and represented a clumsy introduction to the entirely new concept in China that television could be a tool of commercialism. By the time David Stern arrived nearly a decade later, commercials had become common, though the political agenda of the network remained the same. No department was more heavily censored, or more politically sensitive, than news, as a young employee named Ma Guoli had discovered. Ma had graduated from Beijing Broadcasting Institute in 1982 and was ordered to report to a teaching position on the east side of the city. But Ma lived on the west side and bicycling to his new job took three hours every day. "The government was required to give you a job, but the job didn't depend on your interests," he said. "I asked them to reconsider my situation." They reassigned him to CCTV. After a few years in the news department, Ma engineered a transfer to the tiny sports division, a stepchild within the larger operation, a less politically complicated assignment that Ma thought might provide better job security.

By the late 1980s, CCTV still had only a single channel, CCTV1, which carried only sixty-five minutes of taped sports programming a week, much of it an amalgam of carefully edited international highlights of bullfighting, horse racing, and race car driving that was broadcast on Tuesday nights. One problem was a lack of content. China had no domestic professional sports leagues, which meant CCTV had little to work with, other than qualifying tournaments for the Olympics or the World Cup. When China hosted the World Cup Table Tennis championship in 1987, CCTV provided extensive coverage. Newspapers were starting to carry accounts of foreign leagues but CCTV had neither the budget nor the sophistication to purchase broadcast rights. Reforms in the 1980s had allowed CCTV to import certain programs from countries including the United States and Japan, among them *The Man from Atlantis* and *Animal World*. But sports had only its limited programming.

The highlight show from the NBA was a start. Every week, someone in the NBA's New York office placed a tape inside an envelope and mailed it to Beijing. There, editors at CCTV extracted about fifteen minutes of highlights and dubbed Chinese commentary. Chinese fans already knew about Larry Bird and Magic Johnson from newspapers, but CCTV could show them the most exciting moments of their games. The problem was getting the tape. Shipping took two weeks. Editing took two more. Highlights were aired in China a month after the games had been played.

"There was no UPS," Ma recalled. "We just had normal mail."

When David Stern returned from China, he had to figure out how much this new market was worth. The NBA had no idea how to price advertising. In 1990, CCTV's total advertising revenue amounted to less than $1 million. Advertising was in such an infantile stage of development that NBA executives found themselves asking advertisers for advice on pricing in China. "We would go to the Coca-Cola guy and say, 'We'd like to sell this to you. Can you tell us how much it is worth?' " Stern recalled. "We didn't know how to value a thirty-second spot."

What did become obvious was the popularity of the NBA. Those highlights packaged in New York included footage of Michael Jordan during his championship era with the Bulls. Before Yao Ming, Jordan was the first star to captivate Chinese fans and his arrival on Chinese television was perfectly timed. By 1992, an aging Deng Xiaoping was worried his economic reforms were stalling. Deng had unmatched influence, if no official government title, and he embarked on what became known as his Southern Tour. At stops at special economic zones along the southern coast, Deng called for deeper economic reforms and exhorted the nation to develop faster. Soon, new policies fueled a nationwide construction spree, especially along the coast where foreign investment soared, as almost every multinational in the world opened factories to benefit from cheap labor, good infrastructure, and friendly policies. Within a decade, China emerged as the workplace of the world.

Deng's tour shook television, too. New stations had proliferated across China and were supposed to be producing their own programming. But the programs were bland and amateurish, and many stations continued to subsist largely on government subsidies. After Deng's tour, stations were ordered to improve the quality of their programs, expand their use of advertising, and reduce their dependence on the government dole. This meant that stations needed to contemplate what their viewers might actually want to see. They also needed credibility with advertisers and found it in the form of foreign brands. Nike was now outsourcing some of its shoe manufacturing to the new factories on the Chinese coast—and drawing criticism for the labor conditions of Chinese workers—but it had started cultivating China as a market, too.

Terry Rhoads, then a young Nike employee, traveled the country and watched kids in polyester pants playing basketball on dirt courts. No one had any skills, but everyone loved to play. "I remember at Nike we felt, Wow, we have so much work to do," Rhoads recalled. "We were fortunate that the NBA was giving away its programming. Jordan was like osmosis. He was seeping into the consciousness of Chinese youth, this godlike man who could fly."

Nike had already made Michael Jordan the centerpiece of the company's advertising strategy, and the spots for Air Jordan shoes had changed sports marketing and helped transform Jordan into a global figure. In 1994, few Chinese consumers could afford the Air Jordan shoes, but Chinese television stations wanted the ads anyway. "Those Jordan ads were so popular that TV stations were contacting us and asking if they could run them for free," Rhoads recalled. "The stations wanted to demonstrate to other advertisers that they were top-shelf." Soon, so many Air Jordan ads were running on stations across China that Rhoads got a call from Nike's regional headquarters. The bosses were pleased that the company was getting so much exposure in the new China market but also concerned about the cost. How was Rhoads paying for all these ads? He happily told them he wasn't.

Television was turning sports into a cultural force in China, and an economic opportunity. ESPN and Star Sports were moving into Asia with new channels that carried such an endless lineup of soccer that Thailand soon became home to some of the world's most fanatical fans of the English Premier League. This same public enthusiasm for sports was building in China when Ma Guoli became head of sports programming at CCTV. Soon the network expanded coverage of the Olympics and began airing taped soccer matches from the Italian league. The Chinese sports fan was essentially up for grabs. The NBA was now mailing tapes with more highlights and longer segments from games, even as the same delays persisted. "Michael Jordan was the emperor of the NBA, and we didn't feel good if newspapers could tell the story of the final before us," Ma said. "We could only show the tape one month later. It was embarrassing." At one point, Ma arranged for China's leading state-owned airline, Air China, to deliver tapes of the NBA Finals, reducing the lag time to a week after editing. Finally, CCTV carried the 1994 NBA Finals between Houston and New York, the first live coverage of a championship series.

Ma knew the moment was right to create an all-sports channel and even blurted out the idea on a live program to the annoyance of CCTV's president. When Ma made a formal proposal for a channel, CCTV's oversight committee turned him down, saying the idea was premature. But a few months later a new frequency became available for a handful of channels. Ma's proposal was still lying around the offices at CCTV, and his bosses quickly ordered him to resubmit it. Soon China's answer to ESPN would be born. Known as CCTV5, the channel debuted on October 1, 1994, the forty-fifth anniversary of the founding of the People's Republic of China.

Now that Ma Guoli had a channel, his problem was finding enough sports to put on it. He didn't have the budget to compete with ESPN or other channels to buy broadcast rights to major international competitions or leagues. The NBA had whetted an appetite in China but Ma couldn't afford to buy full rights to the NBA. His one advantage was Chinese sports. He had a monopoly on broadcasting any sport in China. And China was about to create its own commercial sports league.

David Stern had recognized that sports could be packaged, delivered across borders, and sold like any other product. Television made this possible, and television's biggest sporting stage was the Olympics. When the decision was made to allow professionals to play at the 1992 Olympics in Barcelona, the NBA had its chance to wow the world. The "Dream Team" led by Magic Johnson, Michael Jordan, and Larry Bird was the greatest assemblage of basketball talent in history and eviscerated the Olympic field to win the gold medal in what became a marketing coup for the NBA. NBA stars were now global celebrities. The NBA was indisputably the greatest and most glamorous basketball league in the world.

For China, Barcelona was a disaster. The Chinese men's team finished last, losing each of its five games by lopsided margins, a dismal performance that should not have been surprising, given that funding had been slashed for domestic basketball after the 1988 Games in Seoul. Chinese sports officials, focused solely on winning more total medals, had decided that the chances of medaling in basketball were low and redirected money into sports such as diving, target shooting, and women's weightlifting. It was a strange time to decide that basketball represented a bad investment. Sports were becoming a global industry and American sports leagues were becoming cash machines with revenue streams from television rights, merchandising, ticket sales, concessions, and corporate sponsorships. But the careers of China's sports bureaucrats rose or fell solely on whether the Chinese team won Olympic medals, not on profits. When they began redirecting money to smaller sports, many basketball officials asked in vain to introduce commercialism as a means of replacing the lost money.

"We said, Okay, you take care of little brother and little sisters," one of them recalled. "We said they should let big brother earn his own food. But they wouldn't let basketball go to the market."

The humiliation at Barcelona changed that. In 1992, two ranking Chinese sports officials, Wang Junsheng and Xu Feng, joined with a Brit named Richard Avery of the sports agency IMG to introduce a commercial soccer league in 1994, followed the next year by a new commercial basketball league, the CBA. Midwifing the CBA into existence required a typically Chinese coupling of experimentation and resistance to experimentation. The national sports ministry controlled the league and government basketball officials retained authority over games, schedules, and the rules. This was the resistance. But the league's budget came through a contract with its commercial partner, IMG. This was the experiment. IMG paid the league an annual fee for marketing rights. In turn, IMG generated revenue from television rights and corporate sponsorships, and among the potential corporate sponsors, none were more interested than cigarette companies. No country on earth manufactured or consumed more cigarettes than China, and foreign tobacco companies jumped at the chance to identify themselves with the new leagues. Philip Morris financed the soccer league as a promotion for Marlboro, while British American Tobacco, or BAT, sponsored the basketball league to advertise its Hilton brand. No one seemed to mind or notice the linkages between tobacco and lung cancer; it was already common for Chinese coaches and players to smoke a cigarette or two at halftime.

Nothing like this had ever been tried in China. Under Mao, sports were intended to promote physical strength and instill revolutionary fervor. The idea that a sporting event should be organized to attract fans and generate revenue was a dramatic conceptual departure. None of the infrastructure for a commercial league existed. No one knew how to produce a game for television. No one knew how to sell a game as if it were a tangible product, say a quart of milk. "No one knew what advertising boards were or what press conferences were," recalled Kenneth Lim, who worked for IMG. "No one knew anything about marketing."

For IMG, even the most threadbare marketing concepts seemed fresh and exciting in China. When attendance began to dwindle at soccer matches, IMG introduced the giveaway. The first 10,000 fans buying tickets for a soccer match were rewarded with a free red Marlboro cap. Owning a Marlboro cap meant owning something foreign, which meant something of value and social cachet. "We would draw a stampede of 45,000 people," Lim said. "They wanted the hats. And it got them excited about the games. Even today, you can still see people wearing those hats around China."

The balance of power was starting to shift: Fans were customers, and customers now mattered. Commercializing sports meant empowering fans, since the money they paid for a ticket entitled them to be entertained. The games needed to be entertaining because there was now competition for the public's attention and money. Movies, television, restaurants, and other diversions were becoming common in even the smallest Chinese cities. Public gatherings in China had traditionally been organized to bear witness to the power of the state. The crowd was supposed to be obedient and provide affirmation for whatever the Communist Party wanted affirmed. Now fans were pushing and shoving for hats and other freebies at games organized around the idea that sports should be fun. Police saw the freebies as a security risk and insisted on veto power, out of fear that angry fans would throw things on the court or even riot. Hilton once tried to give out oversized foam Number 1 hands stamped with the Hilton logo; the cops said no way.

"We would make sure the sponsors had something acceptable," said Bill Moriarty, who worked for IMG on the basketball league. "The rule was, if they can throw it, don't let it in."

For anyone accustomed to the old model, the CBA felt like a radical departure, yet it was not radical enough. Initially, IMG found enough sponsors to pay the CBA fee and make a modest profit every year. But finding new streams of money was especially difficult in China. National television rights went to CCTV5 and, initially, the league had to pay the network, rather than vice versa, to broadcast games. Since no other national television network existed—nor was allowed to exist—the CBA could not seek other bidders. Provincial governments or other state entities continued to control most teams, and none of the teams, whether private or state-owned, were allowed to market independently in their home cities. Moreover, sports bureaucrats still cared more about preparing the national team for the Olympics than the smooth operation of the CBA. Officials might unexpectedly cancel or postpone part of a CBA season to allow the national team more time to practice. In a putatively commercial league, the needs of the state still prevailed.

The crisis came around 2001. Big Tobacco was under siege in the United States for illegally marketing to teenagers and lying about the health hazards posed by nicotine. Tobacco companies, banned from sports marketing in the United States, also withdrew from the Chinese leagues, and IMG departed after a contract dispute with Chinese officials. The CBA was rudderless and short of cash, and the national team had not made much progress since Barcelona (the Chinese would lose to South Korea in the 2002 Asian Games, an unthinkable humiliation). Meanwhile, the popularity of NBA basketball was only growing in China, especially after Yao Ming joined the Houston Rockets. CCTV5 soon began carrying live regular season games, drawing audiences that dwarfed the number of people watching the CBA.

Chinese basketball was in a crisis at precisely the wrong time. In September 2001, Beijing won its bid to host the 2008 Olympics and the Chinese government declared the staging of the Games to be a paramount political priority. Beijing would spend $43 billion on new roads, subway lines, bridges, parks, and sports stadiums. Ancient *hutong* neighborhoods would be razed and replaced with forests of sleek glass skyscrapers as Chinese leaders were determined to show the world a new, modern, and rising nation. A similar urgency swept through the sports bureaucracy; if winning medals had always been a political priority, the pressure to win was now far greater, including in basketball.

By 2002, the NBA smelled momentous opportunity. From the outset, when David Stern cut his deal with CCTV, television had allowed the NBA to dominate the basketball market in China. For a new generation of brand-conscious Chinese teenagers, the NBA was as much a lifestyle brand as a sport, representing a hip, urban attitude. Allen Iverson, the rebellious, tattooed scoring guard for the Philadelphia 76ers, became one of the most popular NBA players in China; Chinese kids bought copies of his jersey or his brand of shoe. The NBA logo, an afterthought in the United States, became an imprimatur of cool in China. "You could just tell," recalled Mark Fischer, the managing director of NBA China from 2004 to 2008. "The more we put into China, the more we would get out. You could just feel that this place was ready for a brand like the NBA."

The key was placing a Chinese player. Having a successful Chinese player in the league was essential if the NBA wanted to cement its relationship with Chinese fans. It was one thing to root for foreigners on television; it was something else to root for one of your own, competing for national pride on the international stage. The first Chinese player had been Wang Zhizhi, who was unexpectedly drafted in 1999 in the second round by the Dallas Mavericks. Two years of negotiations ensued between the Mavericks, the NBA, and the Chinese military before Wang joined the Mavericks at the end of the 2001 season. In his first game, Wang collected a pass at the top of the key and swished a 3-point shot. But injuries and a lack of speed made him a marginal NBA player. His lack of success, coupled with his quiet, aloof temperament, also presented problems for the league's marketing machinery.

"Chinese love winners," Fischer said. "They love guys recognized as stars. But Wang Zhizhi was quiet. We had a hard time marketing around him. Yao Ming was another story. He had a kind of charisma, and when he became the first pick in the 2002 draft, and especially when he became an All-Star his first season, that's when we had something to rally around."

The NBA had first noticed Yao at the 2000 Sydney Olympics when he was a teenage center for the Chinese team who rejected a shot by the American forward, Vince Carter. Once Yao was drafted into the league, China became first priority in Stern's global plans. In 2004, the NBA inaugurated the China Games, a pair of preseason matchups in Shanghai and Beijing between Yao's Rockets and the Sacramento Kings. Chinese newspapers expanded their coverage of the NBA and sent reporters to the United States to follow Yao. New basketball magazines appeared to meet the growing public appetite for the game, while Internet fan clubs sprouted for players like Kobe Bryant. Other NBA stars began touring China on behalf of shoe companies or simply to promote themselves in the China market. When the retired Michael Jordan came to China, the crowds were so huge that police in Beijing canceled an event at a popular outdoor court near the Forbidden City.

The NBA also seemed to have found an ally in the bespectacled former college professor now running the Chinese league, Li Yuanwei. Li's arrival in 2003 was regarded as a victory for reform; he replaced Xin Lancheng, a classic Communist Party bureaucrat who distrusted foreigners and favored continued government control of the league. Li and Xin had been rivals inside the league office before Xin had gotten the top position. While Xin ran the league, Li spent three years in bureaucratic purgatory at a teaching position at Beijing Sports University, where he specialized in "basketball management," studying how leagues in Europe and South America were making profits and producing internationally competitive teams, even as China seemed stuck.

"We were losing money and morale was low," Li later told me. "Everybody was frustrated. We had almost no idea what was going on outside China."

Having now replaced Xin, Li began to look outward. He hired a former NBA coach, Del Harris, to lead the Chinese men's team in the 2004 Athens Olympics, and flew to America to visit David Stern and study the NBA. He deeply admired the NBA business model but chafed at what he considered the arrogance and sometimes condescending tone of Stern and many NBA executives. He was annoyed that the NBA announced its China Games without consulting him. When he attended the 2004 NBA All-Star Game, Stern asked Li to appear with him at a press conference announcing the China Games. Li refused, since doing so would be tantamount to CBA approval; he wanted to signal that the Chinese league must be respected. Stern was irritated but later made amends before the preseason game in Beijing, pledging to cooperate closely with the CBA, Li recalled. The relationship seemed in good standing.

Li had already decided the CBA needed major structural change. He commissioned a firm in Shanghai, Zou Marketing, to examine successful basketball leagues and draft a plan to improve the Chinese league. Zou was a small outfit run by three men, Frank Sha, Tor Peterson, and Terry Rhoads, the former Nike employee. Their proposal, completed in 2004, was called the North Star Plan. By Chinese standards, it called for a revolution. "The big issue in our minds," recalled Peterson, "was that government interests and private interests were colliding in the league."

The North Star Plan examined the full breadth of Chinese basketball, from how players were developed to the ownership structure of teams to the conflicts sowing dysfunction in the league, none more disruptive than the political mission of the league to produce a national team that would bring glory to China. League officials were expected to act as government bureaucrats and businessmen, an inevitable conflict. Officials make policy. Businessmen try to make money. The North Star Plan eliminated the conflict by creating an independent, commercial league in which the Chinese Basketball Association would oversee the league from a distance, with a status akin to a board of directors. The league would be incorporated as a holding company, with every team required to meet certain standards. Teams would buy shares in the league and revenues would be equally distributed. Teams would also submit to audits from the league office, while the league office would be independently audited, too.

The idea was to create checks and balances of the kind that didn't yet exist in the relationship between the Chinese government and the Chinese people. Official corruption was endemic in China, a trend magnified in sports, especially soccer. Match fixing was such a stain on soccer that Chinese fans became disgusted and lost faith in the league. Without transparency, Zou argued, basketball could be ruined, too. "One reason for these rules is showing the fans that this is serious," Peterson said. "You are saying, 'We take this very seriously and we will not allow coaches and players to disrespect the game.'"

In drafting the plan, Peterson and Sha met regularly with a special CBA panel to review the proposed business model or discuss suggestions for how the league could better develop talent. Again and again, Peterson was confronted by cultural assumptions about the physical inferiority of Chinese athletes. "We just told them that there actually is no physical barrier to creating a top basketball team with Asian blood," he said. "There was no reason that a group of Chinese players could not beat the United States national team one day. The Spanish beat them. Argentina's national team beat them." China simply had to find a style of basketball of its own. It needed its own basketball identity. It also needed to find a better way to develop talent. By using medical tests to identify teen-agers mostly likely to grow tall, the system shuttled prospects like Pan Jiang and Big Sun into sports schools. From there, the best players were recruited for the junior teams of the professional clubs, which produced the raw material supplying the national team. This meant the talent pool was actually tiny. Maybe thirty professional teams across the country kept junior teams. If each team kept thirty players, then fewer than 1,000 play-ers were being trained.

"That's just not a lot in a country of 1.3 billion people," Peterson said. "We tried to create a plan to solve player development issues and systemic issues."

Li Yuanwei was impressed. But when the sports bureaucracy consid-ered the plan, the answer was no. Zou Marketing was told that China wasn't ready. No one mentioned that the North Star Plan would have pushed many basketball bureaucrats out of power. "You can't understand something if your job depends on you not understanding it," Peterson said. "At the end of the day, I think they had a really difficult time. Lots of things would have been restructured and privatized."

Publicly, Li Yuanwei praised the North Star Plan as a blueprint for the future, without discussing the radical parts of the blueprint that would be ignored. Privately, Li was deeply disappointed. When I met him at a Beijing hotel in 2009, he continued to hope the league would someday reflect the North Star blueprint. "That's our final goal," Li said. "Other-wise, we face a deadlock. But in reality, the current system doesn't allow us to do that. Nor does it encourage us to." He added, "We are in a special transitional time. If we are determined to have a market-oriented league, we've got to solve this gradually."

By 2006, Li Yuanwei was doing the easy pieces of the North Star Plan, such as adding cheerleaders and dividing the league into northern and southern divisions, but little more. Li knew the system needed change, yet he also knew trying to force change was a pointless exercise. He concen-trated on shoring up the league's finances and signing a marketing agree-ment with a Swiss conglomerate, Infront, which was expected to attract new sponsors for the league.

The NBA now had an office in Beijing, and was expanding rapidly, signing new television contracts with stations across the country, pur-suing branding partnerships and selling NBA merchandise. In the late summer of 2006, Stern visited Guangzhou to watch the American team play exhibition games as part of a warm-up for the World Championships. Meeting with reporters, Stern boasted that NBA revenues in China were growing by 30 percent and described China as "our most important and largest market outside the United States." Business was so good that NBA executives in New York had been quietly discussing the possibility of a China league. It made perfect sense, yet no one had dared say it out loud.

Among the many talents attributed to Stern by his admirers is the star player's gift for making the right decision at the right time. Mark Fischer regarded Stern as a visionary strategist and masterful negotiator. "He can negotiate and present with anybody," Fischer said. "He could sell ice to Eskimos. He's amazing at saying the exact right thing for every situation, for every audience. In many ways, David Stern is the smartest person I've ever known."

Yet at the Reuters Media Summit in November 2006, Stern unwittingly said the wrong thing at the wrong time. In two interviews, as Stern discussed his desire for a bigger NBA footprint in China, he floated the possibility, almost as an aside, of a league. "The model that we're working on now is the placement of all our assets in China in an enterprise with all NBA rights," he said. Reuters quoted Stern as saying this new Chinese entity would oversee the NBA's business in China and have the ability to operate a league "such as NBA of China."

In another situation, another country, Stern's comment might have been received as inconsequential, or even as a tactical mistake by tipping his hand, yet in China the consequences were immediate. *China Daily*, the country's official English-language newspaper, quickly reprinted one of the Reuters articles. Stern's staff at the NBA office in Beijing was startled. Chinese basketball officials were blindsided and alarmed. Several Chinese team owners held an emergency strategy session and wondered if Stern knew something they did not. Had he somehow gone around the CBA and gotten permission for a league? No one knew. Only as days and weeks passed would it become clear that the NBA didn't have permission at all.

Li Yuanwei was furious. In China, personal relationships mattered deeply in business, and while he admired Stern's league, Li had remained wary of Stern and distrustful of his promises of cooperation. During Stern's visit to Guangzhou, Li later recalled that Stern had needled him about the Chinese team's performance during a recent trip to Europe. The Chinese had played poorly and lost to Spain by 47 points. A year earlier, the CBA had signed the marketing contract with Infront, even though the NBA had also bid for the contract. "You see," Stern said, as Li later recalled the meeting in his memoir, "you work with the Swiss, and you lost by 47 points. That's just very shocking!" When the translator relayed Stern's joke, Li said, he had almost stormed out of the meeting.

As he digested Stern's unexpected comments about a league, Li realized the NBA commissioner had miscalculated. "I was astonished," Li told me. "He had never said this before to us. If he had said he wanted to cooperate with the CBA, then that would have been understandable. But he didn't say a word, which meant he knew nothing about China."

Several months later, in early 2007, David Stern and Li Yuanwei appeared together at a news conference in Shanghai. It was tempting to think of them as a couple that had averted a bad breakup though, publicly, there had never been a spat. Yet a new tone was obvious. No longer did Stern speak of the NBA's desire for its own China league. Now the theme was partnership and cooperation and how both leagues could benefit from collaboration. Maybe they could share a league. Li Yuanwei seemed pleased. He later joked to me that Stern was "now my best friend."

With reason. The NBA's ambitions in China had grown. By early 2007, NBA lawyers were conferring with Goldman Sachs over a proposal to form a subsidiary, NBA China. No longer would the NBA be an outsider, a foreign multinational; if it created a Chinese subsidiary, the NBA would be proving its commitment to China, and also creating the business infrastructure that could lead to potentially far greater riches. The Olympics were less than two years away and a giddy optimism had infected the sports marketing world. The commercial potential of Chinese sports was now nakedly obvious, and expectations were rising that finally China was going to open the door to real commercialization. No one expected major changes so close to the Olympics; the optimism was about what might happen *after* the Games. Many people thought the Olympics could have a catalyzing impact on reform and that the government would finally begin decoupling sports from politics.

The NBA certainly did. Months earlier, an opportunity had unexpectedly landed in the NBA's lap. Across Beijing, stadiums were rising through clouds of construction dust as a new Olympic Green was being carved out of the northern tier of the city. Beijing's Olympic organizers were not simply building stadiums. They wanted to make statements.

Rising side by side, the National Stadium, known as the Bird's Nest, and the National Aquatics Center, known as the Water Cube, were so daring and original that visiting architecture critics breathlessly described them as portents of a new Chinese age. No one offered such praise for the basketball arena. Located on the west side of the city, the original design envisioned a building masquerading as a television set; the exterior facade would be covered with digital screens televising round-the-clock game coverage and commercials during the Games. Inside would be a six-story mall with shopping, restaurants, and nightclubs. The International Olympic Committee was alarmed enough that the project kept getting scaled back. But the more important problem involved the builder, a Beijing firm, Cencons, which had suffered losses in another venture. Faced with a cash flow shortage, Cencons sold the property to a Chinese land development company, later named Air China Real Estate, or ACRE. The company owned an adjacent property and saw the potential to build a shopping mall on the extra land around the arena. The only problem was that ACRE knew nothing about basketball.

But the NBA did. One September morning in 2006, a former Boston bakery chain owner named Matthew Carberry left his suburban home in Beijing for nine holes of golf. Carberry had arrived in China three years earlier and reinvented himself. He had followed his wife after IBM relocated her to Beijing and had quickly built a network of friends and contacts around the city. He was a natural entrepreneur and salesman who tried different things before he landed in real estate as a foreign face inside ACRE. Carberry's morning golf partner was Mark Fischer, who was now living in Beijing and overseeing the NBA's operations in China. Fischer and Carberry had never met, though they lived in the same housing compound and their children attended the same international school. Carberry arrived with a pitcher of homemade fruit shakes and a proposal: The NBA should partner with ACRE on the Olympic arena.

From that morning round of golf would begin five months of discussions and meetings that culminated in a deal in February 2007. Joined by Carberry, Cai Tong, head of ACRE, flew to New York and signed an agreement with David Stern that granted management rights over the Olympic arena to the NBA. The old designs were jettisoned. Architects hired by the NBA would redesign the arena to meet the league's specifications. The Beijing Olympic Committee would still manage the arena during the fortnight of the Games, but the NBA offered consulting advice on in-game entertainment and helped import cheerleaders, music soundtracks, and tumbling teams for the halftime show. For the NBA, the deal seemed like a marketing coup; the Olympics had always been considered the best stage to showcase the league to Chinese fans, and now the NBA would control the stage for years to come. The arena, known as Wukesong, would eventually be called "the Home of the NBA in China."

. In the NBA, arenas were not merely basketball courts; they were carefully designed cash machines, especially the newest ones, like the Staples Center in Los Angeles. Wukesong offered the NBA a chance to transplant its economic formula onto Chinese soil. The game was the spectacle, the draw to lure patrons (and to be converted into content for television). Once spectators entered the arena, they entered a piece of real estate painstakingly designed to separate them from their money. To do this, arenas were subjected to an encyclopedic list of specifications dictated by a doorstop-thick NBA manual. The manual was the NBA's guardian of quality, protecting what league officials called "the integrity of the game," but it was also a blueprint for profit.

Nothing demonstrated this more than concessions. The failure of many CBA arenas to sell concessions would have been unthinkable in the NBA. Concessions were profit centers granted inalienable rights in the NBA manual. There must be at least one "point of sale," or cash register, for every 150 patrons, and each point of sale must be granted at least four linear feet of counter space. To supply concessions, an arena also must reserve space for kitchens, beer storage, and refrigeration. An NBA franchise in the United States might earn one third of its revenues from tickets and concessions. Most CBA teams charged less than a dollar for a ticket and sold nothing.

But what also excited the NBA about the Olympic arena was the potential for naming rights once the Olympics were over and, presumably, a NBA China league was up and running. Naming rights were the richer cousins of the marketing partnerships signed by the NBA and corporations such as Tsingtao. Except the transaction was reversed; if a marketing partnership meant Tsingtao paid to place the NBA logo on Tsingtao beer cans, naming rights meant a corporation would pay to place its logo on an NBA arena. When stadiums began selling naming rights in America, the backlash was predictable and futile. Purists were horrified at the crassness. Commercialism seemed to have run amok. Football teams were playing in stadiums named after potato chips and oil-change chains. But naming rights, if anything, were the brutally logical extension of what sports stadiums had become: boxes designed to advertise and sell products. They were television sets where people actually entered the box. In China, the NBA viewed the Olympic arena the same way a butcher viewed a cow, as something to be maximized and carved into different cuts, so that each slice could be assigned a different value. If naming rights to the whole arena could be auctioned, other parts of the building could be auctioned, too. Maybe a Tsingtao Lower Concourse could be created, which would have concession stands selling cups of Tsingtao beer over four linear feet of counter space.

The Wukesong arena was bricks-and-mortar proof that the NBA had something besides air to sell in China. By October 2007, a small group of NBA executives and investment bankers from Goldman Sachs had toured Hong Kong and mainland China. They called it the Road Show. In New York, Goldman bankers and NBA executives had decided to structure the Chinese subsidiary as a private offering in which selected corporate investors would receive preferred equity, a guaranteed return, dividends, and an out clause. ESPN invested from New York, but otherwise the NBA wanted Chinese partners as "strategic investors" whose advice and connections would be as valuable as their money. At the same time, a subsidiary represented a potential payout for NBA executives. In the United States, the league was privately held, and although executives were well compensated, their income was limited to salaries and bonuses. NBA employees would be granted shares of the new Chinese subsidiary, and if the subsidiary went public one day, those shares could reap millions of dollars.

"This was an opportunity, potentially, to reward some people," said someone close to the process.

Yet a problem had to be addressed: How much was a Chinese subsidiary worth? More than anything, the NBA existed as a brand in China. It sold content (games) to television stations, operated an NBA.com website, sold jerseys and other merchandise, and pursued corporate marketing partnerships. In the United States, the NBA was a sports league *and* a marketing business. In China, marketing was almost the entire operation—and certainly a profitable one. In an investment overview provided by Goldman to one prospective Road Show investor, a graphic showed that NBA revenues in China had shot upward from $9.5 million in 2004 to $53.2 million in 2007, with projections for $78.3 million in 2008 and $149.3 million by 2010.

But the ability to project perpetually bigger revenues depended on determining how the basketball business would grow in China. Partly that value came from gazing into the future and seeing the same demographic trends that made everything seem valuable in China; the annual economic growth of at least 8 percent, a steadily enlarging middle class, the expansion of Internet and television media, and, most of all, the birth of a consumer society assumed to have tastes similar to those of consumers in the United States. The problem wasn't any lack of appetite for NBA basketball; it was overcoming the systemic obstacles to satiating that hunger. Basketball games might seem to be apolitical, innocuous events, but they contained worrisome ingredients to a Communist Party that placed tight restrictions on freedom of assembly. Yet it seemed safe to assume that change was happening every day in China, and investing in basketball was betting that China inevitably was being reshaped by the wider world.

Goldman informed potential investors that the NBA wanted to raise $230 million in equity, which would constitute 11 percent of the new NBA China, leaving the remaining 89 percent with the NBA. This meant that Goldman had valued the unborn NBA China Inc.—a basketball company without a basketball league—at more than $2 billion. Completely out of the air.

No one seemed to doubt it was worth it. The Chinese system was failing miserably at producing good basketball and failing even worse at making the game profitable. The NBA brand was so popular that the league envisioned fitness and entertainment centers in China called NBA Cities, as well as chains of stores, lounges, and restaurants. "The pitch was: This can be huge," said one person familiar with the presentations. "The NBA is a brand. They are selling a brand. It is almost like selling Louis Vuitton bags."

By the end of the Road Show, the NBA had raised $253 million, surpassing its goal, and landed the elite of China's private and state-owned business establishment as partners: Hong Kong's richest and most politically savvy businessman, Li Ka-shing; the Bank of China; China Merchants Bank; and Legend Holdings, the parent company of Lenovo computers. While everyone was excited to be allied with the NBA, the subject of the Chinese league never went away. The Goldman overview mentioned the league under the banner of "The NBA's Presence in China." It read: "Potential to establish an NBA-affiliated professional basketball league in China following the 2008 Olympics." That was it.

"It was sort of the elephant in the room during these meetings," one participant recalled. "The NBA always positioned a role or stake in the

China league as a potential upside, although never as a promise. But everyone asked about it, the subject always came up."

In May 2008, inside the Grand Hyatt, the sleek and airy hotel on the Avenue of Eternal Peace in the heart of Beijing, Tim Chen presented the NBA's proposal for a China league. Born in Taiwan, Chen had been recruited from Microsoft to become chief executive of NBA China, partly because of his reputation for finessing the Chinese bureaucracy into granting whatever approval or clearance his company needed.

Inside a conference room, Chen and other NBA officials sat across from Li Yuanwei of the CBA. Chen explained that the NBA wanted to create a new Chinese league with eight teams. Teams already competing in the CBA would be given the priority to join but would be required to pay a $50 million fee. Ownership of the new league would be equally divided between the NBA and CBA, with the NBA receiving an operations fee and the CBA receiving a management fee. Importantly, Chen said, the new league would carry the NBA brand.

Li Yuanwei listened with two other CBA officials. He knew the global consulting firm McKinsey had advised the NBA on the proposal—reportedly for a $1 million fee—and was not surprised. "Within minutes, I realized this plan was totally a product of the American mind-set and self-involvement," he later wrote in his memoir. Chen argued that David Stern had made a big compromise by not insisting on a controlling share of the league. But Li thought the plan demonstrated again how the NBA did not regard his league as a true partner. To Li, the concept was unrealistic and not feasible: What would happen to the existing CBA? What about the CBA's current teams and sponsors? As for the $50 million fee, none of the CBA teams could afford it.

"If we want a new league, the CBA is fully capable of going forward alone, so why do we need to cooperate with the NBA?" Li asked, mockingly. Li knew very well that the Chinese league needed a great deal of help and had long considered the NBA as the best model. As far back as 2003, Li had even floated the idea of some sort of partnership. But now he was irritated and asked Chen whether the NBA had contemplated the impact of the proposal on the Chinese league. He later recalled that Chen seemed embarrassed by the question.

There was nothing further to discuss. Three months remained before the Beijing Olympics, and Li was absorbed with preparations. He had no time to concentrate on a new league and thought the plan needed a major overhaul. For now, the issue would be pushed aside. Before he left, Li couldn't resist making his own joke at the NBA's expense.

"How about you guys give the CBA only $500,000," Li teasingly told Chen, "and we'll definitely come up with a much better plan that could even become a reality."

David Stern was hardly giving up. Two months after the Olympics, Stern stopped in London to announce a new partnership with AEG, the global sports and entertainment conglomerate, to operate twelve new arenas in China. Then he flew to Guangzhou for the latest staging of the China Games—a preseason game between the Golden State Warriors and the Milwaukee Bucks—where he announced that the NBA would design and manage a new state-of-the-art arena in Guangzhou, as well as another arena in Shanghai. Counting Wukesong in Beijing, the NBA would now control stadiums in China's three premier cities.

In Beijing, where the Bucks and Warriors played a second game, Stern announced a new deal to stream more NBA games over the Internet and then took questions from Chinese reporters. Everyone wanted to know about a possible league. Stern said he was in discussions with Infront, the Swiss marketing firm, as well as the CBA, about "mutual cooperation." Without offering any specifics, Stern predicted that "there will be announcements in the next several months" and described the stadiums as pieces of a grander plan. "If we do get to the point where we have that cooperative league, we'll have the buildings already," he said. Yet over the next several months, there would be no major announcements.

Stern wasn't the only person who was stymied. Ma Guoli, the father of CCTV5, was now regarded as the godfather of Chinese sports. He left the sports channel in 2005 to manage the television production of the Beijing Olympics and then was hired to run the China office of Infront, the Swiss firm handling the marketing for the CBA. Ma's professional life had come full circle. CCTV5 and the CBA had been born together and their relationship had once seemed mutually beneficial. CCTV5 needed content; the CBA needed exposure. Just as the CBA was trying to make itself relevant by copying the NBA, CCTV5 had emulated global sports networks like ESPN or Star Sports. It copied the same garish stage sets, offered the same highlight shows, and sold advertising for the same products—cars, razors, tires, and basketball shoes.

Yet Ma understood the critical difference between CCTV5 and its Western role models. CCTV5 was a division of the Chinese government, a megaphone for the Communist Party's propaganda machine. China had scores of provincial or city television stations, but CCTV was the only national network permitted by the government, an arrangement partly designed to protect the Communist Party's grip on information. Yet this lack of competition was a critical problem for a commercial basketball league. The economic formula created by the NBA—one the CBA hoped to replicate—depended on television contracts for huge amounts of revenue. Teams got richer and players got richer when the league's television contracts got richer from bidding contests among competing networks. But in China, where CCTV was the only national network, there were no bidding contests. Ma Guoli had built CCTV5 into a television power; now, without any leverage, Ma had to persuade his old channel to give more money in television rights for the CBA.

"I joke with our people that for TV rights maybe I can ask CCTV to pay 10 percent more than before because of my relationship," Ma told me. "But no more. I know the situation. This situation—I don't know when it can be changed."

Finally, the Olympics also coincided with the end of Li Yuanwei's five-year term presiding over the CBA. Like others, Li had expected the Olympics to usher in major reforms in Chinese sports and introduce more commercialization. But unexpectedly, the opposite happened. China's top sports officials, having seen Chinese athletes win a record fifty-one gold medals, concluded that the system did not need to be changed at all. They underscored this point through their selection of Li's successor—Xin Lancheng, the man Li had replaced in 2003. Li could rightly claim to have overseen a small revival of the CBA; the finances were now secure and television ratings were rising. But Xin's return was a triumph of the old system over the new. Reform was pushed aside; talk of an NBA league was tabled.

"I never imagined this would happen," Li wrote in his memoir. "Five years of exploration seem to be wasted. If I knew this, I would not have taken the job in 2003."

Yet one small experiment was still under way in Taiyuan. Like David Stern, Bob Weiss had the NBA brand on his chest and he was already inside the Chinese league, witnessing for himself the difficult process of blending together two very different strains of basketball.

CHAPTER EIGHT

RUMORS

The rumors surfaced on the Internet, a smattering of unsubstantiated reports on a handful of Chinese basketball blogs speculating on a tidbit of gossip that seemed to defy logic. Boss Wang was preparing to sign a former NBA star. Similar gossip had floated about during the preseason, but now the rumors carried an unusual specificity. The new player would arrive in about a week, on December 12. His salary was reportedly $80,000 a month, among the highest in the league. And his name was Bonzi Wells, the former playoff hero for the Sacramento Kings, the former Houston Rockets teammate of Yao Ming, and one of the signature bad boys of the NBA. If he was now past his prime, Wells was a name player, a genuine though exasperating talent, who would rank as the biggest star to ever play in China, assuming he actually was coming to China. The whole idea seemed nutty. Why make a change now? The Brave Dragons were *winning*.

Quite unexpectedly, the team was the surprise of the CBA. Eleven games into a 50-game season, the Brave Dragons had won seven, lost four and were an early contender for a playoff spot. True, the coaching arrangement was still a mess, and Boss Wang was meddling more and more. But Olumide was leading the league in rebounding at 19 per game, and Donta Smith was arguably the league's most versatile player, scoring, rebounding, and dishing out assists to his Chinese teammates, who were finishing the job. In Taiyuan, success had startled the fan base. The local press was portraying Weiss as a Western guru (Liu Tie was also credited), while Olumide had easily become the team's most popular player. A knot of fans in Brave Dragons jerseys waved photos of the big Nigerian during home games and serenaded him with cheers. When Olumide dove for a loose ball or fell hard to the court—and falling theatrically to the floor was apparently stipulated in his contract, given how often it happened—Taiyuan gasped. Then, as Olumide slowly rose, grimacing or shaking out a potentially injured limb, the cheers filled the stadium. Olumide would smile and trot down the court, waving his arms at the crowd, and even sometimes shouting out in Yoruba. Of course, no one had a clue what he was saying.

The strangest thing about the Bonzi Wells rumor was how neatly it demarcated the divisions within the team. The Chinese players knew all about it. They started reading snippets of gossip a few days before on the Internet. The foreigners, who could not read, write, or speak Chinese, had absolutely no idea. I had first heard about it from Joe a few days earlier. Practice was canceled that morning and Rick Turner and I were puttering toward the practice gym in the minibus, following the frozen Fen River beneath a morning sky so clotted that the faint outline of the sun was barely visible, a milky white pearl trapped behind the gray haze. Turner was starting his second week coaching the junior team, a thankless job. Leading a team that never scrimmaged and never played games was the coaching equivalent of being the rat in the wheel.

Joe was already on the court when we arrived and the junior team players were doing layups. Christmas was less than three weeks away, and Rick wanted to make a short visit home. His daughter was sending emails saying all she wanted for Christmas was Daddy. Rick needed a few days off and assumed his absence would not matter since the junior team only practiced, but he could not get a meeting with Zhang Beihai. The general manager kept avoiding him and the uncertainty left Rick stewing, as did Joe's advice.

"As long as you stay here, nothing is going to happen," Joe advised him. "If you leave, I don't know what is going to happen."

As Joe saw it, Rick would already be gone if not for the intricate and unspoken social codes that governed Chinese life, codes Chinese intuitively know how to navigate. The owner had no more use for Rick and had left his fate with Zhang Beihai. Usually, this would mean a succinct firing, except firing Rick would be embarrassing, given that Rick, a foreigner, was Weiss's chosen assistant. Firing Rick would represent a loss of face for Weiss, which, in turn, would mean a loss of face for Zhang. By keeping him, even in a do-nothing job, Zhang was saving face for everyone. He was doing Rick a favor, even if Rick felt wronged and slighted. Joe had accepted his own demotion as something beyond his control. *Mei*

Banfa—there is nothing I can do. Confrontation was pointless. Survival is what mattered, staying employed and making it through the season.

"In the Chinese way, sometimes they don't want to talk directly," Joe said as we stood together, watching the junior kids lope up and down the floor, as clumsy as foals. They practiced fifty weeks a year, sometimes seven days a week, repeating the same dribbling or running drills, again and again, as if they were factory workers asked to master every job on an assembly line. I wondered how long it took these kids to begin to hate basketball. Probably longer than it took to hate working in a factory.

"I always tell the players that everything doesn't happen like you wish," Joe said. "So just enjoy the best parts."

Midway through the practice, the team accountant arrived in search of Rick. His visa needed to be renewed and he needed to go to the visa office before it closed. Rick seemed startled, if pleasantly so, as he trotted off the court, smiling with relief in my direction: *Maybe they aren't trying to can me.* The players started running another drill, and Joe leaned over to me.

"I hear we may be getting Bonzi Wells," he said.

I was incredulous and said so to Joe. Joe believed it would happen. I left the practice gym certain the rumor was a hoax and returned to the World Trade.

From down the hall floated a staccato of sharp popping sounds. Rat-tat-tat-tat-tat. Rat-tat-tat-tat-tat. I followed the noise, which sounded like a machine gun.

"Fuck!"

Donta Smith was at the end of his bed with the curtains drawn, sitting shirtless in the dark, shaking a joystick and glaring at his television. He was slaughtering virtual Nazis in a video game, "World at War," but was pinned down inside a farmhouse in what appeared to be virtual Poland. He had just gotten blown away. If the rumors were correct, and if Bonzi Wells really was coming to Taiyuan, the league quota on foreign players meant that either Olumide or Donta would be going. Given that Olumide accounted for most of the team's inside scoring and rebounding, Donta would be the odd man out.

When he was with the Atlanta Hawks, Smith had a short taste of what he now called "the Life." He roamed the nightclubs in Buckhead or downtown Atlanta under the social directions of the more veteran players. He was a country boy from Kentucky, and in Atlanta his eyes were opened. "It was *crazeeeee*," Donta recalled, smiling. Now "the Life" meant nights at the World Trade. He ate in the hotel, or at McDonald's, and watched movies, played video games, or talked to friends through instant messages or Skype.

He really didn't seem to mind. He had learned to adapt growing up in the town of La Grange, about twenty miles outside Louisville. By age seven, he was stuffing his house key and a few dollar bills into his sneakers for emergencies. His mother sometimes disappeared for work, which in her case was selling drugs in Louisville, and on those nights she didn't come home Donta would shuffle down the street and stay with a friend. He knocked and the family let him in.

"When I was with her, everything was crazy," he said of his mother.

She was a dealer, not a user, and if only from the perspective of a child, she met her basic obligations. She fed and housed him. He remembered visiting neighborhoods in Louisville where his mother sold drugs. People knew him because they knew her. They were her customers, and when the kid came around, they were almost protective. It was a chaotic, confusing life for a little boy and by the time Donta reached elementary school, his mother was in the penitentiary.

"I don't remember seeing her a lot," he said. "I would go and talk to her through a glass. I didn't like being behind the glass. When I saw her, I would cry, and then she would cry." When she was transferred to a lower security prison, mother and son were able to meet in the same room. "I could touch her," he said. "I never cried when she was in that one."

When he first joined the Brave Dragons, Donta came off as another American scorer slumming for a paycheck in China. He could be moody and petulant, and he seemed to prefer to keep his distance. Only gradually did he begin to smile, and it took Tracy Weiss to realize those dark moods weren't who he really was. She decided he was guarded, even sweet, and a long way from Kentucky.

"He's only twenty-five," she said, "and he's in China."

At Oldham County High School, Donta had played football and basketball. He had moved in with his father, a devoutly religious man who did not tolerate any foolishness. As a senior, Donta was already 6'5" and played wide receiver well enough to whet the interest of some major football schools. Basketball, though, was the game he loved. He dumped football after his basketball team lost a tough game against the school's archrival, Shelby County. He was distraught. "The emotion I felt that day—I knew I was a basketball player," he said. He signed with Southeast Illinois Junior College, averaging 26 points a game, and was ready to transfer to play for Rick Pitino at the University of Louisville when his name started popping up on mock NBA draft boards.

Donta was a versatile swingman who could play guard or forward, which made him a piece with value in the NBA. Prodded by friends and his own curiosity, Donta declared for the draft and the Hawks took him in the second round. He signed a two-year contract, with a team option for a third year, bought a house, and waited for his chance. His first NBA basket came on an alley oop dunk against the Milwaukee Bucks. "The Bucks called a timeout, so I got to cherish the moment a little bit," he said. His best game came against the Lakers. "I had 11 against the Lakers, and we beat them."

The Hawks situation seemed perfect. They had drafted four new players as a foundation for the future: Josh Childress, Josh Smith, Donta, and Royal Ivey. They became friends, and the veteran point guard Kenny Anderson began calling them "the Toys 'R' Us Clan," except they never got a chance to grow up together. The Hawks traded for five veterans, and Donta spent two years on the bench. "I played my role. I came in and practiced hard. It was good for me, because I got to watch the guys. But I at least thought I deserved a shot."

What he got was Bulgaria. He played five months in the Euroleague after the Hawks declined to pick up the option for the third year of his contract, returned to the United States for a failed tryout with the Sacramento Kings, and then circled back to Bulgaria in December. He was shooting a layup, when he felt a pop in his knee. In Atlanta, a surgeon discovered the same type of microfracture that had ended, or altered, the careers of other players.

"When I woke up and he told me, I could have cried," Donta said. "I felt like my soul left me."

His mother had been living in Atlanta, in his house, when Donta was in Bulgaria, and now she cared for him as he rehabilitated his knee. They had reunited during his senior year in high school, after she was released on probation. He had respected and admired his father but had ached for his mother.

The knee healed more quickly than expected. By spring 2008, Donta was cleared to play. "I went straight to the gym," he said. "I felt like I was a kid all over again." By summer, he needed a job. His Bulgarian team still owed him money, so his agent got him a tryout with the best team in China, the Guangdong Southern Tigers. He was signed, but almost immediately traded to Shanxi.

It took Boss Wang a while to decide to keep him. The Boss ordered an MRI of Donta's knee at a local hospital. Word began to circulate that the knee was unstable. Zhang Beihai prodded Weiss about other NBA players, including, at one point, Bonzi Wells. But once the season started, the thought of dumping Donta seemed ridiculous. He was why the team was winning. He made everyone better. He figured out what his teammates could do, and put them in a position to do it. Nearly every 3-pointer that left the hands of Wei Mingliang, the shooting guard, started as a pass from Donta. Whenever Olumide found himself open inside for a dunk, he usually had gotten a nifty pass from Donta. When the team needed a steadier hand at point guard, Donta filled in. When they needed scoring on the wing, he moved to the wing.

Zhang Beihai became a believer. After one win, Weiss gave the general manager a chest bump in the locker room. "Hey, Bonzi called," Weiss said, jokingly. "What do you want to tell him?"

Dripping with sweat, Zhang beamed. "*Smiss* stays," he answered.

Even Boss Wang seemed to come around. In late November, the team traveled to the eastern port city of Qingdao for a Friday night game. Thanksgiving fell the day before the game and the foreigners gathered at a Crowne Plaza to celebrate with an actual turkey dinner. They were also celebrating Donta's birthday. Boss Wang arrived and paid for everything. He put his arm around Donta, posed for a picture, and declared him part of the family.

Ruslan Rafaelovich Gilyazutdinov was not certain what he was a part of. It was all very strange, or, as Big Rus liked to say in his heavily accented English, It was *booooooolsheeet*.

Yet unlike the other foreigners, Big Rus was actually less appalled with the circus of the Brave Dragons. He had seen worse. He had played in Iran. He had played for a coach in Kazakhstan who was a former soldier. "It was terrible," he said. "He didn't know anything, but he thinks he knew everything. Big bullshit. We had lots of meetings. Same shit. Before the game, after the game."

His father had been a volleyball player, a member of the Soviet team before the breakup of the Soviet Union, who had then played abroad in Cyprus. There, he took young Ruslan to see a game in the Greek professional basketball league where one of the foreign imports was the former Atlanta Hawk Dominique Wilkins, once famous for his windmill dunks. Ruslan had been playing volleyball for six years, but he dropped the sport immediately after watching Wilkins. "When I saw what he does, I want to play basketball."

The problem was that Kazakhstan was not a basketball country. It won Olympic medals in wrestling and judo, so the government put money into those sports. Basketball players were lucky to make $2,500 a month for a six-month season. When Joe offered $5,000 a month and bonuses, Big Rus saw a chance, even if he was in terrible shape because he had not played in almost a year and wasn't doing any running because of the Kazakh winter.

Taiyuan struck him as modern and cosmopolitan. He had once played in China in a youth tournament and remembered it as a terrible place. "It was like . . ." he continued, fumbling over the English phrase, "Age Stone. Age Stone? Stone Age. But now it is so much more cultural. Now it is so clean I like it better than Iran."

In the Iranian league, he had played near the Caspian Sea in the Gorgan region. "Terrible city," he says. "Not city. It looks like big village. In Iran, there is nothing to do. I go to practice. After practice, I go to shop and to buy some food. After that, I go to game. That's it."

He promised that he would be in top shape in two more weeks. Then he would show everyone what he could do.

Tracy was worried about all of the Chinese players. To her they were boys tossed into basketball prison, and she wanted to save them the same way she wanted to save the stray dogs and cats on the streets of Taiyuan. She sometimes carried hot dogs in her pockets to feed the mangy strays she came across on her daily walks, but there was little she could do for the players. When the country celebrated National Day in October with a week off, the Brave Dragons practiced every day, twice a day. "I wish our NBA players could spend just 1 week here to gain a little better appreciation for what they have," Tracy wrote in an email home. "Bob's concern that I will want to leave here with an adopted baby is somewhat warranted," she wrote in another. "However, it is more likely that I will bring home a young twenty-year-old to room with Stuart [her son]. I grow more fond of these young men every day and it is difficult to watch what they go through, and they never question it."

Of all the players, Little Sun, the Taiwanese point guard, spent the most time with the foreigners, because of his grasp of English and because he, too, felt foreign. After Coach Liu's arrival, Tracy had watched Little Sun endure the pressure and she had sent emails trying to encourage him. "I don't have confidence because coach Liu always say: you are to small, and also too soft on the defence," Little Sun wrote back. "He will not let me play more time on the court he said , he always talk about poliics of tawain independent to me ,that's booshit! Whatever just focus on the positive, its easy to say but difficulty to do."

She told him to just keep trying.

By late afternoon on Friday, December 12, the two photographs were spreading across the Internet. The first was inconclusive. It showed Bonzi Wells dressed in a wool hat and blue jacket, staring directly at the camera with an expression registering somewhere between stunned and angry. He looked like a man who had awoken from a bad dream to discover his wallet had been stolen while he was sleeping. It was a tight shot, showing no one else but Wells. He appeared to be inside an airport, but it could have been any airport in any city.

It was the second photograph that clinched it. Now Wells was outside. The sky had a familiar leaden color. Wells seemed startled and was running away from a handful of people chasing him with tape recorders. They were Chinese journalists, and there, practically tugging at his sleeve, trying to push himself in front of the American star, was one especially persistent reporter: Journalist Li.

Bonzi Wells was in Taiyuan. He was the new American ambassador of basketball.

CHAPTER NINE

THE AMBASSADOR

onzi Wells had been in China for barely four days, and Mark Zhang was his assigned body man. Unfortunately, Zhang had lost him. Zhang called Bonzi's mobile phone and knocked at Bonzi's seventh-floor apartment at the World Trade. Nothing. That Bonzi Wells could be erratic or moody was no surprise but already he had confounded his new Chinese employer. He had refused to play. The Brave Dragons had lost three straight games and the new savior had yet to slip on a uniform.

Mark Zhang, chubby and earnest, his hair shaved into a buzz cut, very much wanted the whole Wells thing to go smoothly. Zhang worked for the Starz Sports agency and had already worked with NBA stars. Starz Sports had been founded by two intimates of Yao Ming and often partnered with one of Yao's agents in America, Bill Duffy. Nearly every name player in the NBA seemed interested in getting something going in China—an endorsement deal, a clinic, or appearance opportunities. When Duffy or another agent sent someone over, Zhang was often on the receiving end. He had escorted the guard Baron Davis (who would sign a shoe deal with the Chinese sportswear company Li Ning), as well as the NBA's top point guard, Steve Nash. He had taken Nash to Beijing's most famous streetball court, where Nash had disguised himself in a knit cap and played some pickup. Zhang had chaperoned Shaquille O'Neal, Shane Battier, and Luis Scola, too.

Now Duffy had sent over Bonzi, but this would be a different exercise. It was one thing for an American star to pass through China on a prospecting tour; Wells was coming to play. In the broader context of Chinese sports, Zhang thought this was a good thing. China's sports market had lagged behind other sectors of society, as far as opening up to the market was concerned, and reform was critical if Chinese basketball was going to catch up. Reform meant more commercialism and exposing Chinese players to better competition. Bonzi Wells represented the best competition ever to play in the CBA.

But Wells also had a reputation, and Zhang had worried that a player with Wells's temperament might not slide so seamlessly into the Chinese league. Normally Zhang would cold-call teams and manufacture a bidding war to drive up the price for a player of Wells's caliber. But now he worried his agency's reputation might suffer if something went wrong; he didn't want a general manager complaining about being misled if Wells lost it in China. Zhang wanted the team that signed Wells to do so of its own free will. So he planted a story in *Titan Sports* floating the fact that Wells was interested in playing in China. Then he waited for his telephone to ring.

It rang, several times. He responded to each query with the same answer: Yes, Wells is a major talent, but be certain you want him. Check him out. He is an American player who might require special arrangements. Do an Internet search. Then decide. "He's definitely a good player," Zhang would tell each caller. "But whether he fits your team—that's your job and your coach's job, not my job."

Some teams checked the Internet and did not call back. A few others kept nibbling. The one team that never hesitated, that kept calling, eagerly, was the Shanxi Brave Dragons.

"The owner was a big fan of Bonzi," Zhang would later recall. "He kept calling us and promising everything. And he put it all in the contract."

A media onslaught ensued, at least by the media standards of Taiyuan. Reporters from national newspapers and leading websites were now arriving to bear witness to Bonzi. Where once Taiyuan existed outside the basketball consciousness of China, it was suddenly the place to be. The hype only grew after Yao Ming himself blessed the Bonzi experiment. In the Rockets' locker room, Yao told a herd of Chinese reporters that Wells was a big talent and still had a big game. He expected him to put on quite a show in China.

The clip was aired across China: the great Yao, iconic figure of the global game, the breakthrough Chinese star whose talent and dignity had won over fans in America, giving props to the man being crowned as the greatest American to ever play in the Chinese league, assuming he would play.

Now if only Mark Zhang could find him.

Bonzi Wells would not have been America's first choice as ambassador-at-large for America's game. Gawen DeAngelo Wells, born in 1976 in Muncie, Indiana, had cursed coaches, cursed fans, cursed referees, brawled with fellow players (spitting on one), and had once been named by *GQ* magazine as one of the country's "Top Ten Most Hated Athletes." Any Chinese general manager combing the Internet would have found a damning rap sheet, a complicated blend of defiance and contrition, and at least one humanizing anecdote: He got his nickname from his mother because of her love of chocolate bonbons.

He had come into the NBA out of Ball State University. Twice in college, he was named conference player of the year, even as he was ejected from games for arguing with referees. After a loss against Central Michigan, he slapped an opposing player who had tried to shake his hand. He was so combustible that his coach sent him to a psychologist to work on his temper. But at 6'5", 210 pounds, Wells also had a unique skill set; at either shooting guard or small forward, he was a tough rebounder and defender, and an explosive scorer who could post up smaller guards near the basket. The Detroit Pistons made him the eleventh player selected in the 1998 NBA draft. On the day of the draft, he arrived in the Green Room, the holding pen for likely top picks, with his family and friends donning matching fedoras. The sports columnist Bill Simmons would later describe his entourage as "all looking like extras in a Notorious B.I.G. video."

Wells was traded before his rookie season to the Portland Trail Blazers, a proud franchise that soon veered so badly out of control that the team became known as the "Jail Blazers." Criminal charges and controversies quickly piled up: marijuana arrests for Rasheed Wallace, Damon Stoudamire, and Qyntel Woods, who also pleaded guilty to animal abuse charges after staging dog fights in his home. Wallace was suspended for threatening a referee. At one practice, Zach Randolph and Ruben Patterson got into a fight (the club having signed Patterson despite his no contest plea to an earlier felony sexual assault charge). Popular players like Steve Smith, Jermaine O'Neal, and Arvydas Sabonis either left or were traded. Portland, epicenter of earnest Pacific Northwest crunchiness, had supported the Blazers for years; now fans started to recoil at the team's aura of thuggishness.

In such a poisonous atmosphere, Wells earned a media reputation as a "bad chemistry guy." A Blazers beat writer described him as a fake and a con man. In his first two seasons, he was fined or suspended at least five times, once for giving the finger to a fan and again for cursing the coach Maurice Cheeks after Cheeks removed him from a game, establishing a pattern of clashing with coaches, especially those with reputations as disciplinarians. He was suspended for spitting in the face of Danny Ferry (and for calling him a "honky") and also suspended for being involved in a fight with an opposing player, Chris Mills, at the end of a game. When he was later traded to the Memphis Grizzlies, Coach Mike Fratello suspended him during the 2005 playoffs.

What sustained Bonzi was the cold calculus of the NBA—he could play, and most teams will overlook most anything for someone who can play. Moreover, a few voices out there argued that if Wells was complicated and often unable to control his emotions, he wasn't really a terrible guy. A Chinese general manager would have found a smattering of stories describing how a "misunderstood" Wells was trying to turn things around, to get his act together. He had been thrown unprepared into the NBA glitter, this argument went, and had acted out. He would occasionally say as much himself. Now he was trying to mature. He still lived in Muncie and had donated money to keep the local community center from closing down. He cried when the court was named after him. He was still basically a small-town guy.

His greatest moment as a player precipitated his greatest humiliation. By 2006, he was with the Sacramento Kings, thriving under the more relaxed coaching style of Rick Adelman, when the eighth-seeded Kings met the defending champion San Antonio Spurs in the first round of the playoffs. Expected to lose badly, the Kings pushed the Spurs to a deciding seventh game largely because of Wells, who averaged 23 points and 12 rebounds a game. Spurs coach Gregg Popovich called him "a one-man wrecking crew." The Kings lost the deciding game, but Wells was redeemed, and at a felicitous moment. He was a free agent, and the Kings offered him a five-year deal for roughly $38 million, a major payday.

He didn't accept it. His new agent, William Phillips, pushed for $50 million and told the Kings that Wells had other suitors. Apparently, he didn't, or at least not at that price. The Kings signed a cheaper player, and Wells fired Phillips. He signed with the Rockets for two years for a total of $4.5 million and was mocked for his arrogance and stupidity (though he was hardly poor, having earned about $35 million in eight seasons). It was a hard thing to shake. He arrived in Houston overweight and had problems with Jeff Van Gundy, a coach with a reputation as a hard-ass. When Adelman arrived as coach the following season, Wells was jubilant, arriving in great shape and seemingly poised for a great season. But he suffered injuries and never found the right niche with the Rockets before being traded midseason to the New Orleans Hornets. When his contract expired, Wells had no other offers.

Duffy first tried to place him in Spain, but after negotiations broke down he turned to China. When Wells played in Houston, he had signed a shoe deal with Anta, a Chinese brand that was a sponsor of the Chinese Basketball Association. He was benefiting from the Yao effect: Almost any player on the Rockets was attractive to Chinese shoe companies, given the obsessive coverage of the team on Chinese television. But his trade to the Hornets complicated the deal; Anta had wanted him because he was a Rocket. Coming to China and playing in the Chinese league might help resurrect things with Anta. It could also give Wells a chance to prove himself worthy of a second chance in the NBA, assuming he played well and could keep his head.

Bonzi would admit to knowing almost nothing about China. He had initially thought his new team was in *Taiwan,* not Taiyuan, and his companion, Daphne, was excited to learn that Taiwan was an island with great weather. Wells had seen a video clip of the team and was impressed with Donta Smith. He looked forward to playing with him. He knew Weiss was the head coach. This was important, since an NBA coach would understand how to use him, and Weiss had a reputation as being a good guy, a player's coach.

Bonzi had no idea he would be greeted in China as such a giant star. He knew nothing about the team's Chinese assistant coach, and little about the owner, except that he was someone who was really rich and loved the NBA.

He would later tell me he had figured he could do anything for a few months.

Hours before Bonzi was to arrive in Taiyuan, Rick Turner was completing another morning in purgatory. The Brave Dragons were in the far western region of Xinjiang preparing to play the league's second-place team, and Turner had spent the morning chaperoning the junior team with Joe. Practice finished, Turner headed toward the minibus, when Joe mentioned, offhandedly, that Bonzi Wells would be arriving later in the afternoon to join the team on a guaranteed contract. Turner had heard all sorts of rumors, for months, so many rumors that he was inured to them. But now something was really happening. He was floored.

"That kind of sucks for Donta, doesn't it?" he asked and climbed into the minibus.

The losing streak would gather momentum that night in Urumqi. It was a close game but Xinjiang was too strong. At tipoff, Donta still knew nothing about Wells, or that Wells was already at the World Trade in Taiyuan, though he had noticed his Chinese teammates buzzing about something. Even Liu Tie seemed strangely distracted and had pulled Donta aside before the game.

"I hope you get 50 points tonight," Liu Tie told him.

"I knew something was going on," Donta would later say.

By the time the team arrived in Xi'an for the next game, Donta knew. The general manager then called a meeting to inform the team of what everyone already knew. Garrison cried as he did the interpretation. Donta did not. He said what you are taught to say in the NBA: that basketball is a business, and that this was a business decision, no hard feelings. His agent was already in contact with a top team in the Australian league. Under normal circumstances Donta would have turned in his uniform; but Bonzi was not ready to play. Donta also was still under contract. In Xi'an, Donta played and scored more than 30 points in another Brave Dragons loss.

The losing streak came during a tough stretch against top teams, and even without the Bonzi distraction, winning would have been difficult. But the team's flaws, its lack of preparation, were also being exposed. Coach Liu did not know what to do. The endless drills and full-court running could be explained as the hammer he was using to pound out steel. Or they could be described as time fillers from a coach who had never coached before and had no experience diagramming an offense.

When the team was winning, Weiss had managed to install a simple high-low set in which Olumide flashed out to set a pick for Donta, who either drove for a basket or dished out to the wings for Wei Mingliang or Zhai Jinshuai. It was crude, but it worked. Zhai and Wei had prospered. But whenever one of them got on a hot streak, Coach Liu would inexplicably bench him. It was hard to know if he did not know what he was doing or if he knew exactly what he was doing and didn't want any of his

Chinese players to break out as a star for fear they would outshine him. Several players suspected the latter.

The loss in Xi'an lowered the Brave Dragons' record to 7-6, with a home game three days off against Shandong. Practice was scheduled for the following morning. Everyone was going to meet their new teammate.

Bonzi Wells had never been missing at all. He had just gotten tired of Mark Zhang after spending his first two days in Taiyuan sharing a two-bedroom apartment with him. Bonzi stopped answering Zhang's calls and locked the door to the apartment. Bonzi slipped on his earphones, turned on his music, and ignored the buzzing of his iPhone until the team returned from Xi'an and Bob Weiss knocked on his door.

Weiss seemed as bewildered and astonished as the rest of the Chinese basketball world that Bonzi was now parked inside the World Trade. Before the season opener, when Boss Wang was still nervous about Donta's knee, Weiss had emailed Bonzi and later called him at the general manager's request. But neither Weiss nor Wells seemed to take the conversation very seriously, and since then Donta had become arguably the league's best player. After the loss in Xi'an, reporters had peppered Weiss with questions: Did he know? When did he know? Like everyone else, he had had no idea.

Bonzi told Weiss he liked what he had seen of Donta on tape. "We can't lose that guy," he said. Weiss smiled and explained that teams could have only two Americans, meaning that Wells would be replacing Donta on the roster. "He didn't know he was knocking someone out of a job by coming here," Weiss said later. He also didn't know that Weiss was head coach in name only. He discovered that the next day.

It was Monday, December 15, leaving two days of practice and a game day shootaround for Wells to get acquainted with his new teammates before the game on Wednesday night. Wells expected to run through the offense and scrimmage so that he could familiarize himself with the other players. Instead, Coach Liu ordered running drills and spent half an hour practicing the pick-and-roll, the type of drill that Wells did in junior high in Muncie.

"Bonzi ran about three of them and said, 'Will you tell him that this is a complete waste of time?' " Weiss recalled.

Liu Tie explained that he wanted to check whether the ten-year NBA veteran grasped the fundamentals of the game. Wells did all the running drills, and when the team practiced Tuesday, the drilling continued. Then it was Wednesday, game day, and the great Bonzi Wells had still not scrimmaged a single play with his team.

He announced he could not play. Weiss didn't disagree.

Donta Smith, still under contract, had unexpectedly become best friends with the man replacing him. They stretched together, ate dinner together, and joked together on the court. Against the Shandong Lions Bonzi sat courtside, and Donta dominated yet again. He scored 41 points, passed out assists, grabbed rebounds, and played like a man about to be freed from prison.

But a pall had settled over the rest of the team. Shanxi lost another close game. The Brave Dragons were 7-7. The Qingdao Double Star were coming to Taiyuan for a Friday night game. Finally, the greatest American ever to set foot in the Chinese league would play. Maybe.

It was Friday morning. The Brave Dragons were stretching on the court before the shootaround. Bonzi Wells was wearing a red Anta hoodie and a black wool cap, stretching beside Donta. The day after the Shandong loss, Coach Liu had organized a short, half-court scrimmage, but Bonzi had now been in China for a week and had not played a game of full-court basketball. Thursday night, he announced he was still not ready to play. "I cannot play until I practice with my team," he told Weiss. "I've got to get a run with my team."

Bonzi's not playing presented a problem for Zhang Beihai. The general manager was standing beneath the bleachers, talking on his mobile phone, not far from my seat on one of the courtside pink sofas. The league office in Beijing had called yesterday. A top official was coming from Beijing, someone big, someone who wanted to see Wells's debut. Now Zhang was huddled with the coaches and Garrison, strategizing. Weiss broke from the huddle and walked over to Bonzi, who had taken a seat on a pink sofa near me.

"You know one thing that hits me?" Weiss began. "We're gonna be traveling tomorrow. You're not going to get to practice before the next game. You could start tonight and then we could take you out after five minutes."

Wells listened and said something I could not hear before Weiss walked over to talk to Donta. They talked for a minute and started laughing. Donta had already signed a new contract in the Australian league with a team in Melbourne. His agent had told him not to play that night, no matter what Bonzi did. He could get injured. Weiss walked off the court to rejoin Zhang and Garrison.

"Uh, no," Weiss answered. "Bonzi says no."

When Bonzi first arrived, Boss Wang and the general manager had convened a meeting with the coaches. By then, even as Weiss remained frustrated with the coaching arrangement, a sense of cooperation had developed. And on the issue of Bonzi, the coaches were unified: They wanted to keep Donta.

"You pay me a generous salary, and I feel obligated to give you my opinion," Weiss had told Boss Wang during the meeting. "When we leave this room, we're united as one. But I wanted to tell you this is a dangerous moment. This may not take us up. It may take us down."

After listening to his coaches, Boss Wang had not budged. "We're keeping Bonzi," he had replied. Yet now eight days had passed and even Boss Wang was wavering. He was frustrated that Wells wouldn't play. He couldn't be certain he still *could* play.

Power was already subtly shifting within the team. There were small signs that Boss Wang was cooling on his Chinese coach, and growing wary of his ambitions. Weeks earlier, Liu Tie had hired a friend to coach the players too young for the junior team, the handful of fourteen-year-olds and fifteen-year-olds who spent afternoons practicing their dribbling. Within the team, this hire was interpreted as Liu's first tiny move toward empire building, toward developing a support base. Boss Wang had noticed. He fired that coach.

The frictions between Liu Tie and the players, especially Olumide, also had worsened. After a loss, a frustrated Olumide had thrown a water bottle, accidentally breaking a mirror in the locker room. Liu began shouting at him and told him to shut up. "Don't you tell me to shut up," Olumide had screamed back. "I'm a father. I'm a *man*. You can't tell me to shut up."

Bonzi left the pink couch and joined his teammates on the floor. Standing a few steps from me, Weiss told Garrison to relay a message to Wingtips. "Ask him what he thought of Bonzi yesterday," Weiss said and kept talking. "He's strictly an eighteen-foot iso guy," the terminology for a player who is good one-on-one but not a team player.

Garrison began his interpretation. I wondered how he was going to translate "iso guy."

"This is very dangerous," Wingtips agreed. "Very dangerous."

"He hasn't even run up and down the floor," Weiss said. "We haven't seen him. And Smith's agent is telling him not to play."

The players were now loosening up. Bonzi fired a 3-point shot that clanged off the rim. Wingtips turned away, disgusted.

Liu Tie divided the team, putting Bonzi, Donta, Olumide, Big Rus, Big Sun, and Joy at one end to shoot foul shots. The rest of the Chinese players ran a drill where each man popped out to receive a pass and shot a quick jumper. They were almost robotic in their precision, making shot after shot.

Mark Zhang had been observing practice, too, keeping more of a distance from Bonzi, yet still keeping watch. He sat down beside me on the pink sofa, all smiles and enthusiasm, and handed me a business card. I asked if Bonzi would play that night.

"Working on it," he said, smiling again.

Mark had decided to shrug off Bonzi's initial standoffishness. He understood that an athlete like Wells needed his space and had moved out of the apartment. He told me that Wells would fit in soon.

"I think the problem is a lack of communication between the team, the coaches, and the player," he said. "Everybody needs to communicate better."

He smiled at the thought.

After the shootaround, Weiss and I went to a café named, in English, the Decently Stylish. The Decently Stylish was a short walk from the World Trade and had become our hangout. The manager delivered us to our usual table, and Weiss began venting.

"What a fucking clusterfuck," he said. "What needs to be done is the owner needs to come and watch Bonzi scrimmage because once they let Donta go, a week later they are going to come to me and say, Okay, who can you bring in for us?"

For weeks, Weiss had maintained his equanimity. He usually laughed off Liu Tie's practice regimen, figuring the situation was beyond his control, and he had found ways to have an impact with the players. He had worked with the young guard Duan Jiangpeng on moving without the ball on offense and also discovered a flaw in Duan's foul shooting. Duan was looking at the floor for an instant before he shot. Weiss got him staring only at the basket and his foul shooting improved overnight.

But Weiss was not laughing now. "We're just so ill prepared," he said. "They think they are being prepared. They aren't doing anything."

Before Turner got sidelined, Weiss had pushed to make him a real video coach, breaking down every game so that the team could properly examine and correct mistakes. But that idea was rejected. Lunch arrived, but Weiss was growing more agitated.

"I mean, we didn't do a thing today," he said. "We did layups."

We left the Decently Stylish and crossed the street to return to the hotel. Weiss now had a regular Chinese table tennis partner and, through Tracy, had started to make friends with people at her health club. He liked Taiyuan. If once he was timid wading into traffic, now he barely looked up, jaywalking through the oncoming cars, charging ahead with the rest of the mob.

"The country is great," he said as we wove through traffic. "I love the people. But it is so frustrating to have a Top Four team and watch it be destroyed."

We took a second-floor shortcut through the World Trade, a route that reached the apartment tower in the rear by passing through an indoor lobby called the Shanxi Mobile Information Plaza. The plaza was a mobile phone showroom, bigger than a football field, and the blue neon lighting lent a weird noir quality to the space. There were very few customers. Women dressed like flight attendants sat behind a row of desks selling service agreements.

Weiss and I slipped into a narrow hallway leading to the apartment tower. The walls had blue and white signage with slogans in Chinese and English, inspirational messages for employees.

"Communicate a Boundless World and Construct an Information Society," read one in English.

"Striving to Become Creator of Superior," stated the second.

"Responsibility Makes Perfection," declared the third.

Hours before the game, Bonzi Wells received a call. His presence was requested at the practice facility. Boss Wang wanted to see him. More than that, Boss Wang wanted to play with him.

It was a private game with few spectators, and later, after word leaked out, the elemental question that would never quite be answered was: Why had the owner wanted a game? Did he want to test whether Bonzi was in shape? Or did he simply want to be able to say he had played with the great Bonzi Wells?

Mark Zhang later recalled an unusual eagerness in the owner. He smiled when Bonzi arrived and introduced himself as a "super-fan." He had already been playing half-court pickup with a handful of kids on the junior team. He told Bonzi to jump in.

Wells did. But he made it clear this would be a straight game. He wouldn't back down just because the owner was on the court. Wing-tips refereed, and the game began. It lasted only about fifteen minutes, enough time for the sixty-one-year-old Chinese steel boss to bang against the pride of Muncie. Both seemed satisfied.

Later, Wells said the owner was too old and too short to guard a former star in the NBA. His game was nothing special. But Wells gave him credit for his will. The old man played like a bull.

"He was *strong*," Wells said.

Li Yuanwei, commissioner of the league, arrived about fifteen minutes before tipoff and took a seat in the coal millionaire section. Bespectacled and professorial, Li was the mystery guest, a visitation akin to David Stern showing up at the last minute for a Minnesota Timberwolves game. Li visited a different game every week and had put Taiyuan on his schedule for the debut of the great *Bangqi Weiersi*, as the sporting press had dubbed Bonzi Wells. That Wells was not debuting was a bit of an inconvenience.

Wells was already seated in what had become his customary place, one of the chairs at the end of the scorer's table, near the Brave Dragons bench. This section had gradually mutated into a penalty box for the banished: Rick Turner had a regular seat, along with Big Calves Tian, who no longer dressed for games, and, on this night, Big Sun. He had been demoted for the game after Boss Wang screamed at him for being too soft.

Donta had trotted onto the court, looking a little dazed, and melded into the layup line. Up on press row, every seat was taken. Television crews had set up a row of camera tripods and the number of newspaper writers had doubled, everyone anticipating that Wells would finally play. The *San Jin City News* had placed that day's edition over every seat on press row to highlight an article by Journalist Li comparing Donta and Bonzi.

"Wells or Smith?" Journalist Li wrote. "That is the question." He concluded that keeping Smith would be the safe, practical choice. Going with Wells would be daring, romantic but risky. He fretted that the season hung in the balance.

Wells was bent over in his seat, bobbing to the beat of his iPhone. The deejay, Ren Hongbing, blasted music and the Brave Dragons cheerleaders ran onto the court in camouflage army pants and sequined halter tops. When the team was announced, the crowd signaled its choice, or at least its respect, by giving Donta the biggest ovation. He was now the hometown boy. The Chinese national anthem was played. No one sang. Bonzi bobbed to his headset. Coach Liu had a final word with the starters and then Donta walked over for a solidarity shake and shoulder bash with Bonzi.

Then the game began. As in Peking Opera, the symbolism and gestures told the story. The first quarter opened with the quandary of the protagonist. Donta started sluggishly, distracted and not yet immersed in the game, perhaps weighing summer in Australia versus winter in Taiyuan. The crowd madly cheered everything he did, having assumed that this was his final game, even as public fascination deepened about his brooding replacement sitting offstage. At one point, a television crew walked onto the court and pushed a camera toward Bonzi's face for a close-up. He glared and waved them away.

The second quarter introduced the drama's supporting players. Olumide missed a foul shot and fell back gasping, shaking, and hopping in what could be called his frustration dance. The crowd cheered. Zhai Jinshuai, the demoted scorer, came into the game shooting. Then an unexpected figure arrived in the penalty box: Joe. He had not attended a game since his demotion but now he took a seat, a moth to the flame. Then another unexpected move: the Kazakh was sent into the game to replace Olumide. Enough time had now passed that everyone, with the possible exception of Big Rus himself, realized that he was not going to be the Asian secret weapon. Instead, he had become the team's cult hero. Fans loved him the same way fans in the NBA love it when the last guy on the bench gets in the game. The *San Jin City News* ran a picture of his newly shaved head beneath a one-word English headline: "Cool."

He blocked a shot. He made two foul shots.

Ren Hongbing could not contain himself. "Rus!!!" the deejay yelled, waving to the crowd. "Do you think his haircut is coooolll!?"

"Yes!" the crowd bellowed.

The third quarter introduced the unexpected plot twist. Donta was on the bench with an ice pack on his knee. The crowd murmured. Big Rus had entered a trance. He grabbed a rebound and scored. He took a pass from Olumide and flushed a dunk. He launched a long 3-pointer and it crashed against the backboard. Trance broken. Except the ball landed in the hands of a teammate for an easy basket. Assist, Big Rus. Boss Wang laughed and gave Rus a high five when he returned to the bench, winded but triumphant.

The fourth quarter brought the return of the hero. Donta was back in the game, limping. Qingdao led 80–76, but Donta drove for a dunk. He threw down another dunk. He passed to Joy for a basket. Not to be outdone as far as injury theatrics, Olumide made a foul shot and limped down the court. He dove for a loose ball and then hobbled down the floor as if stricken by gout. Donta made an incredible spinning move, scored, and got fouled. The Brave Dragons led 96–91, with fifty seconds left. Timeout, Qingdao.

Ren Hongbing seized his moment and pushed a button on his soundboard: Beethoven's Fifth. The Wave. Bedlam. Coal country ecstasy. A roiling water bed of brown jackets.

Donta made two foul shots and a dunk at the buzzer. The Brave Dragons won 106–95 and improved their record to eight wins and seven losses. Fans ran onto the court and engulfed Donta. Ren Hongbing rushed to his side with a gift, a jade bracelet; Ren had bought it himself. Fans began to hug Donta, to touch him. A few people were crying. Donta was touched, if bewildered, since he could not understand a word anyone was saying.

After midnight, my phone rang. It was Weiss. He was looking for Donta and Bonzi. He wanted to make certain they were both on the early morning bus for the trip to Tianjin.

I asked if there was clarity yet on who was staying with the team and who was going.

"Not yet," he said.

Boss Wang had decided before the game to keep Donta. Liu Tie had even formally welcomed him back to the team. But now the owner was wavering again.

"He's also made another decision," Weiss said. "We've got a new head coach."

I was stunned. Who? I asked.

"Me."

We hung up. Later that night, Boss Wang chose Bonzi. Weiss was irritated, if not surprised, and took the elevator down to Donta's apartment to deliver the news. He was going to Australia after all.

No one could quite pin down why the owner made the decision he did. One explanation was that the commissioner, Li Yuanwei, had personally recommended taking Wells, reasoning that such a big star would bring good publicity for the league. The team had played better than expected and perhaps the boss thought Wells might push them into the Top Four.

But I was inclined to believe a different explanation. I later had a long lunch with the owner's son, Songyan, who reminded me that when Wells played for the Trail Blazers, one of his teammates was Scottie Pippen, the longtime Chicago Bulls sidekick of Michael Jordan. Boss Wang figured that Wells had absorbed from Pippen some of the lessons of Jordan. By keeping Bonzi Wells, Boss Wang was only three degrees of separation removed from the great Jordan.

Bonzi and his new teammates were going to Tianjin in the morning. Quite unintentionally, the debut of the greatest American to play in the Chinese league would have a historical symmetry. More than a century earlier, American missionaries with the YMCA had arrived in Tianjin preaching that strong bodies could make a strong nation. To prove their point, they had brought a newfangled game called basketball.

CHAPTER TEN

BIRTHPLACE OF THE GAME

The trains come and go from Beijing South Railway Station, but the size of the crowds never seems to change. It was Sunday afternoon, December 21, and sleek white bullet trains were departing for Tianjin, three or four leaving every hour, with another three or four arriving to complete the circuit. The station was lagniappe from the Beijing Olympics, built for fans traveling to see matches at the Olympic soccer venue in Tianjin, about ninety miles away. Many of the Olympic stadiums in Beijing would become white elephants, empty and evanescent, but Beijing South, the city's fourth railway station, was another piece of hardware for China's race into the future, another reminder of how differently scale was defined here.

The concourse was a cavernous rectangular plaza the length of several football fields beneath a curved steel roof with a translucent plastic hole in the center. A milky light filtered through the hole onto a grove of artificial palm trees where passengers in heavy coats sipped tea in overstuffed chairs. Winter air rushed through the sliding glass doorways leading down to the tracks. Up on the big digital boards, the train schedule turned over every few minutes, more trains coming, more going, a metronome of relentlessness, a turnstile of humanity. Ticket sellers told me every seat to Tianjin was sold out for the next several hours, despite every hour having so many trains. Sunday night was especially crowded because weekenders were returning to Tianjin. People kept pouring into the concourse. People replenished people.

I took a seat to wait for my train. Humanity is commonly considered an excess natural resource in China. There are too many Chinese, the Chinese often say. A Beijing taxi driver muddling through midday traffic will inevitably complain about the volume of people in China, shaking his head at the inconvenience. Deng's recipe for progress encouraged this calculation; he recognized that even rapid economic progress could not sustain so many people. Progress would require more growth and fewer people, which led the Communist Party to introduce the one-child population policies that seemed so inhumane to outsiders, so unthinkable. Chinese leaders in response said they were doing the world a favor. Preventing the births of 300 million people meant 300 million fewer mouths to feed, 300 million fewer claimants for jobs, land, and water. It was ruthless practicality in a country where people are measured in bulk.

A door slid open and people pushed toward an escalator leading down to the tracks. A young couple embraced. He was wearing designer eyeglasses and an expensive suede coat. She was petite in a wool coat. They were yuppies, the one-child generation born from Deng's calculation, the economic beneficiaries, the generation said to be more individualistic, more selfish and demanding. This new generation of urban Chinese say they want only a single child; having more was too expensive, too inconvenient. Then the couple was gone and replaced by more people pressing toward the escalator, moving anxiously to their precious seats as others remained in the concourse, glancing at the big digital boards, waiting.

A rail clerk approached a woman sitting beside me.

"Are you going to Tianjin?" the clerk asked. "Do you want to get on the 5?"

"Yes," she said, hopping up, "but I have a ticket on the 6."

No matter, the clerk said. The woman grabbed her bag and walked toward the gate as I followed uninvited. The ticket taker tried to shoo us away but we pointed toward the clerk, who was trolling the packed concourse, tapping other startled people on their shoulders. Another ticket taker waved us through, and we rushed past, down the escalator, into the cold of the tracks, and found . . . no one. The landing was empty. The white bullet train was purring. I stepped in and found . . . no one. A minute later, other people arrived, everyone a little giddy, having slipped behind the wizard's curtain. We left the station with the car little more than half full.

In precisely thirty minutes we arrived in Tianjin. The bullet train had streaked through the winter darkness at speeds reaching 322 kilometers an hour (just over 200 miles an hour). The train suddenly shivered with a startling whooooosssshh!! as we ripped past another bullet train racing toward Beijing on a track only a few feet away. It was a thrilling ride.

These high-speed train networks were being constructed across the country, a steroidal central nervous system connecting steroidal cities designed to mobilize a populace encouraged to regard itself as a surplus commodity.

When we pulled into the station, Tianjin was prostrate beneath a foot of snow. I walked out of the station in search of a taxi, a thin crust of ice cracking in places under my feet, and a small red cab finally collected me for the ride to the basketball arena. The debut of Bonzi Wells was taking place in about two hours. Snow was still coming down as we puttered through the city's old colonial concession districts, preserved today as a tourist attraction, streets lined by stolid gray-brick apartments left by the British or columned, baroque houses once erected by the Italians and the French. The Americans left a much smaller physical mark, a three-story brick building erected almost a century ago by the Young Men's Christian Association.

The Tianjin YMCA was a modest building but the Y's ambitions in China were determinedly immodest. The Americans did not come for Chinese trade; they came for Chinese souls.

In 1895, David Willard Lyon, twenty-five and newly married, arrived by ship in the city of Shanghai. He was an anomaly not merely as an American in China but as an American born in China. His parents were Presbyterian missionaries who lived in the city of Hangzhou until Lyon was ten, when the family returned to the United States. Like his parents, Lyon would dedicate himself to spreading the Gospel, attending McCormick Theological Seminary in Chicago, where, among other things, he became president of the student branch of the Young Men's Christian Association. The YMCA then sent him back to China.

Lyon was part of a global evangelical outreach by the YMCA, which was promoting a muscular brand of Christianity rooted in ideas of service and the belief that citizens of a nation must be physically strong for a nation to be strong. He was trained in Springfield, Massachusetts, at what is now known as Springfield College. In China, any type of American missionary faced a difficult task. Preaching blind faith for an unseen God whose son died and returned as a redeemer was a decidedly foreign concept for a peasantry taught to worship their ancestors and revere the emperor as a deity. Many Chinese wanted more than abstractions. One Christian missionary in Yantai brought back apple seeds from the American West. Yantai had always produced a small apple, and when the missionary planted the new seeds, he promised local peasants that God would help grow a bigger one. Even today, the big, juicy Yantai apple is famous in China.

Lyon's seed was the idea of self-empowerment through physical strength. His timing was perfect. China's military humiliations and the steady encroachment of foreign powers onto Chinese soil had sparked intense intellectual ferment and introspection. Where once Chinese intellectuals had taken as self-evident the superiority of Chinese civilization, now social reformers began to question traditional Chinese beliefs. Even as resentment festered over the presence of foreigners, many Chinese intellectuals looked to the West for methods that could be used to modernize and strengthen China. Few comparisons were more grating than the most basic: Chinese were physically weak compared to Westerners.

Qing rulers spurned physical exercise. Refinement was prized, and even the symbol of the Qing—the long ponytail, or queue, worn by men—would for many Chinese reformers come to symbolize the decadent rot of the imperial era. In one famous story, a Chinese athlete competing in a high jump competition kept clearing the bar only to see it knocked over again and again by his queue. Enraged spectators yelled, "Cut off your queue!" The next day, the athlete returned, having sliced off the queue, and won the competition. The Qing's rejection of physical exercise seemed further proof that the imperial order was oblivious to modern thinking. Social Darwinists were starting to apply the concepts of natural selection and evolution to nation-states; as with biology, politics and diplomacy were disciplines where only the strongest would survive, a potent argument for increasingly nationalistic Chinese intellectuals humiliated by the "Sick Man of East Asia" insult.

"The people of our nation are weary and spiritless, our bodies emaciated by disease," wrote one reformer, Xu Yibing. "Alas! These deficient, weak, exhausted bodies—what in the world would happen if they were pushed into the unforgiving competition of men in this evolutionary world of strong countries and strong physiques."

Lyon chose Tianjin for his new YMCA after deciding that the national capital, Peking, was too rooted in traditional thinking. Tianjin had a large foreign presence and several universities from which Lyon hoped to attract young Chinese to his new endeavor. It was also where the Qing government was introducing "modern" educational principles that would attract students from around China. "Working among these students means influencing the coming great men of 'new China'—men who will be scattered all over the Empire in their various posts of influence," Lyon later wrote a friend. His thinking was plain: If the Y could indoctrinate the country's new elite, the elite, in turn, would spread the principles of the Y throughout China.

In December 1895, Lyon founded the Tianjin YMCA at a ceremony attended by about 100 students from local universities. To commemorate the day, Lyon introduced a game created four years earlier by James Naismith in Springfield. Naismith had been asked to invent an indoor game as a diversion for young men during the cold New England winter, something wholesome and vigorous that would keep them out of trouble in the growing cities of America. It took some time but soon he nailed a peach basket against a wall, divided up a group of young men into two teams, and handed them a ball. Basketball was born. As the Y began introducing the new game in America, men like David Willard Lyon began to carry it around the world.

Lyon left Tianjin in 1898 but other Americans arrived to continue his work. At its pinnacle, the Y had branches in at least thirty Chinese cities, including Beijing and Shanghai, as well as 170 student associations with a combined membership approaching 50,000. Before the Y, modern sports had barely existed in China. Foreign merchants or diplomats had brought tennis and cricket to the treaty ports controlled by foreign powers, but they played only for amusement and among themselves. Now the Y introduced basketball and another new game, volleyball, and translated the rule books into Chinese so the games could be easily taught at every branch.

In Tianjin, the Y also pursued Lyon's goal of influencing a new generation of Chinese leaders. One of the most influential would be Zhang Boling, a former sailor in the Chinese navy who had resigned in embarrassment after the disastrous loss in the Sino-Japanese War. Having witnessed the incompetence and impotence of the Chinese navy, Zhang wanted to end Chinese backwardness through modern education. A passionate Chinese nationalist, Zhang joined the Tianjin Y, converted to Christianity, and founded two schools dedicated to strengthening China by learning from the West, Nankai Middle School and Nankai University. One of the students studying on a scholarship was a slender young man named Zhou Enlai, who would later join the country's underground Communist movement and ultimately become prime minister under Mao.

Merely introducing sports was one thing. Making sports a tool of national empowerment and spreading the influence of the Y was another, and for that the Chinese YMCA found a powerful rationale in the Olympic movement emerging from Europe. Drawing inspiration from ancient Greece, the French aristocrat Pierre de Coubertin was resurrecting the Olympic Games as an international competition organized in the name of friendship and goodwill. By 1896, the first "modern" Olympics were held in Athens. For the Chinese Y, the Olympics were based on modern ideas about competition, national strength, and chivalrous behavior, yet ones that derived moral authority from ancient virtues. Here was a stage for the leading nations of the new century to compare and compete. C. H. Robertson, an American who had arrived by 1908 to run the Tianjin Y, saw the Olympics as a marker for gauging China's progress. Hoping to catalyze China's athletic movement, Robertson began a campaign focused on three questions:

When will China be able to send a winning athlete to the
    Olympics?
When will China be able to send a winning team to the
    Olympics?
When will China be able to invite the world to come to Peking
    for an international Olympic competition?

The three questions resonated in Chinese sports through the coming century. Zhang Boling became one of China's most ardent Olympic enthusiasts. Different YMCAs began holding the country's first sporting tournaments as Y leaders organized elite teams to represent the country. A team of basketball players from Nankai University, known as the Nankai Five, became famous for defeating a team of American soldiers. In 1910, the Y organized the First National Athletic Games in Nanjing, a tournament that would ultimately become the equivalent of a national championship to select teams for the Olympics. The First National Athletic Games attracted 150 athletes and more than 10,000 spectators.

Though the vast majority of Chinese knew nothing about the Olympics, and continued to know nothing for decades to come, Robertson's challenge had sparked a sports movement that gestated among a small but influential group of Chinese nationalists. Some ultimately embraced the Olympics as a way of joining the world. Others saw the Games as a way to beat the world. But all regarded the Olympics as an arena in which to restore China's national dignity.

To truly spread its movement, and the word of God, the YMCA

needed to become a Chinese organization. This was central to the YMCA vision, and the localization process was under way in 1914 when the Tianjin Y opened a new three-story brick headquarters with the country's first indoor basketball court. Three years earlier, Zhang Boling had been elected chairman of the YMCA board, while Chinese physical education directors were being trained in athletics, anatomy, physiology, hygiene, and Bible study.

Inevitably, given its ambitions, the Y became entangled in the politics of the era. When the Qing Dynasty collapsed in 1911, ushering in the tumultuous republican era, China began making halting steps toward a more democratic political system. Lecturers at the Tianjin Y advocated progressive campaigns promoting public education or warning against smoking opium. When the American educator John Dewey toured China, lecturing on democracy and education, he also spoke there. For a moment, the Y even had the support of Sun Yat-sen, the revolutionary who became the first president of republican China. He was a Christian who spoke at the Shanghai Y in 1915 and later encouraged the Chinese YMCA to emulate Joshua and lead the Chinese people to Canaan. Sun promoted his Christian faith as essential, rather than antithetical, to his revolutionary beliefs.

"The revolution is just like fire and the religion is oil," he once said. "People just had noticed my revolution, but ignored my belief. If there is no oil, there will be no fire."

Having sought to woo the new Chinese elite, the YMCA now had the opening it had so carefully cultivated, except it closed very quickly. Sun struggled in vain to unify the country until his death in 1925. The underground Chinese Communist Party had grown into an insurgency against the ruling Nationalists, who were proving no better than the Qing at fending off foreign encroachment. Japan had created a puppet regime in Manchuria and was claiming more Chinese territory, including, eventually, Tianjin. When full-scale war broke out with Japan in 1937, the Tianjin Y was impressed as a Japanese military headquarters. Other Y buildings in other cities were seized and American secretaries were forced to flee. More than a decade of war, deprivation, and upheaval would end with Mao founding the People's Republic in 1949.

The Y was a rare exception to Mao's campaign to expunge foreign influence from China, partly because of its success in becoming a Chinese organization. Zhang Boling became a leading figure in China's new sports bureaucracy. But although it survived, the Y was effectively gutted, severed from the YMCA in the United States, as Mao ultimately placed religion under state control. What did remain, if now no longer intertwined with Christianity, was the concept of sports as a tool of nation building. And basketball.

Luo Shilong had heavy-lidded eyes and the faintly stained teeth of a dedicated smoker. When he shambled through the door, I was struck by his size. He was tall and thick; he'd once played in Tianjin's local basketball league. He also was an atheist, which spoke to how much the Tianjin YMCA had changed since the days of David Willard Lyon. Luo now ran the Y.

The Y was in the suburban district of Wanglanzhuang, inside a faded pink villa in a housing compound of other pink villas, across the street from a depot for city buses, and distinguished only by a sign reading "Tianjin Young Men's Christian Association." Downstairs, in what should have been a living room, there were a few scattered pieces of furniture and a Ping-Pong table covered in bound stacks of paperback books. In an upstairs bedroom, a middle-aged woman was doing paperwork and answering the phone. In a city of 11 million people, the Tianjin Y now had five employees and about 300 members. The pink villa was empty and silent, without any sports facilities and without a basketball court.

"We have a very limited budget," Luo said, smiling. "If you want to donate some money, I'd love to have it!" Luo's connections got him the Y job about a decade ago. He had worked as a vice party secretary in the Association of Chinese Youth, a government umbrella organization representing state-recognized service groups, including the YMCA. I suspected the job was a sinecure because there didn't seem to be much work to be done. The group owned another villa where old people gathered for poetry readings, singing, and knitting classes. His staff also coordinated a network of volunteers who visited the sick and elderly. "We want them to feel that someone still cares for them," he said.

He had invited me into a second-floor bedroom converted into a room for receiving guests. The woman answering the telephone arrived with cups of tea as I asked Luo about Christianity. Tianjin has about 100,000 Christians, he said, citing official numbers, and the Y now had twenty Christians who were allowed to meet for Bible study, if not for worship. For that, they must attend a state-sanctioned church. "We're not a church," he said. "We're only a club."

Splintering the Chinese Y from Christianity was a precondition of its survival. When Mao took over, the Y was placed under the sphere of the party's youth organization, the Communist Youth League, whose followers studied the writings of Mao as a secular religion. "All of the young people at that time were members," Luo said. "You were considered bad if you were not accepted by the Youth League." I mentioned to Luo that a Y diluted of Christianity didn't seem like a real Y. He disagreed. He said the Y's purpose was never strictly as a proselytizing organization in China but that "the Christian ideology, the Christian spirit, the spirit of God" were part of why the Y still existed. "No matter what the initial agenda that pushed the YMCA to China, they brought good things: modern civilization, modern education, and modern sports," he said. "Maybe from a religious perspective, God is happy."

Luo sipped his tea.

In 2005, Luo organized a celebration of the 110th anniversary of the Tianjin Y. Now fifty-two, Luo had grown up in Tianjin; as a boy, he was taught nothing about the city's colonialist legacy or about the Y. When Luo and others began pulling together materials for a commemorative book, they were startled by what they discovered. The Tianjin Y had helped shape modern China. "In the past 100 years, China had such a chaotic history," he said. "It is rare that you can find anything that has existed continuously during that history. The YMCA has existed during the whole period, or at least the Tianjin Y has. There has to be a reason. We want to figure out why."

Materials had been sent over from the YMCA archives in Minnesota, including letters from Americans who established the Y and other documents. Graduate students in Tianjin were translating the documents into Chinese, and Luo had organized annual seminars on different themes: the Y and Modern Education in China; the Y and Modern Civilization; the Y and the Creation of Modern Sports in China. The stacks of paperbacks downstairs were the written records of these seminars. I complimented the scholarship but suggested that the YMCA's ambitions were never fulfilled in China, as history and Mao got in the way. Luo again disagreed. He believed the Y helped deliver modernity to China.

"We call it the Western wind blowing East," he said. "All the Christian groups brought their beliefs here. But China has its own civilization. If you want things to take root, the organization has to be localized."

Luo's other project for the Y was more ambitious. He wanted to reclaim the original three-story building, home to China's first indoor basketball court. It had been under lease to a government preschool since 1958, on less than advantageous terms, despite the building's prime location in the Nankai district, one of the city's most desired addresses. Luo thought he could make a killing by renting the building to a bank. Or, possibly, he could renovate it for use as a real YMCA. I asked if we could visit the building. Luo agreed, after we stopped for lunch.

Lunch was in the Heping District, once the city's colonial quarter, a quaint collection of colonial era buildings, a time capsule and historical dollhouse preserved inside Tianjin. Our restaurant was inside a nineteenth-century building now called the Garden Hotel, and the old wooden staircase creaked under our feet as we walked past period photographs of the old British opera house, the trolley route, and other colonial landmarks. The owner was a friend of Luo's who was trying to evoke Victorian England to attract tourists. We sat on dining chairs with needlepoint seat cushions as the waitresses brought us a steaming pot of tomato soup. A Nationalist agent once lived in the building, Luo mentioned, smiling, a spy against the Communists.

We sipped our soup. Luo was a student of history and had earned a master's degree in Ming and Qing history at Nankai University. In his job with the Association of Chinese Youth, he traveled widely, visiting thirty countries and studying service organizations to learn what could and could not be applied to China. He had a good impression of Americans as well intentioned and charitable, though he learned not to discount the cultural differences, even the small ones. On his first visit to the United States, he attended a dinner in San Diego. The guests had finished eating when the hostess circled the table, asking if anyone wanted second helpings. Luo smiled and declined. In China, a hostess would have understood that Luo was merely following custom, demonstrating humility and deference, and the hostess would have kept insisting that he eat until he relented, each person fulfilling social expectations. But the American hostess took him at his word, assuming he meant what he said. He never got a second helping during the entire trip.

"The first time I went to the United States," he said, laughing, "I was always hungry."

He visited the United States five more times and visited the Metropolitan Museum of Art in New York during an exhibition of photographs of Shanghai taken during the 1920s. The Shanghai photographs were part of a larger exhibit on different world cultures, and it worried him that they were the ones selected to represent China. "I realized why Americans don't understand China at all," he thought at the time. He began to draw his own conclusions about the differences between China and the West.

"Western people talk about love in a Western sense," Luo said, putting down his spoon. "You give your heart to somebody. You use love to get close to someone. Chinese talk about love, too. But we also talk about respect. We use love and respect together. But in a sense, respect means: I'll keep a certain distance from you."

Waitresses arrived with vegetables and a meat dish. "Western people talk about tolerance," Luo continued. "If you make a mistake, and you realize it, you are forgiven. It is a gesture of generosity, evidence that the person doing the forgiving has an open heart. Well, Chinese people talk about being restrained. They say, Yes, you are making a mistake, and you are hurting me. But I won't get mad at you."

The difference made me wonder if the West can possibly change China, as so many Westerners have tried to do, as the Tianjin Y once tried to do. "We have changed, and we are learning from Western culture all the time," Luo said. "A lot of Western values are already adopted by China. But the influence is always mutual. It's like you open a door between two rooms. Air will naturally flow between them."

Luo's mobile phone suddenly awakened with a musical ringtone. It took me a moment but then I placed it: the Village People singing "YMCA." On one of his American trips, Luo visited Los Angeles and bought Lakers souvenirs for his daughter. She was a teacher at Peking University in Beijing, the nation's most prestigious school, and a member of a Chinese fan club for Kobe Bryant. Like his daughter, Luo preferred the NBA to the Chinese league. When I mentioned that the NBA wanted a league in China, but was having problems, he smiled faintly. During the anniversary of the Tianjin YMCA, Luo asked his Y counterparts in America to make an overture to the NBA about participating. He thought Tianjin would be perfect for an NBA-affiliated camp for talented Chinese high school players; the Tianjin YMCA could easily have gotten the necessary licenses, given his government contacts. But he never heard back from the NBA.

"The most important strategy in China is to cultivate your own community," he said. "You've got to have your own people first, especially in China. The NBA should learn from the YMCA during the past 100 years.

You seep through the grassroots level. The YMCA was pretty smart about that. They were pretty practical."

He neglected to mention a relevant fact: The international YMCA no longer ran the YMCA in China.

The Y building was in the Nankai District, which had a few scattered period buildings but was now another construction zone of the New China. Tianjin was booming, with an economy that grew last year at 18 percent. A half dozen skeletal yellow construction cranes clustered over the downtown. A new residential compound called the Courtyard Above Tianjin was rising near the frozen Hai River, a forest of half-built high-rise towers. Nearby, workers were finishing a shopping mall that covered a city block on East Street. The Y was a tidy brick structure with a white marble entrance and windows with flower boxes, not far from a Carrefour hypermarket. Luo parked in a small lot and we entered through the basement. I heard children.

"The building was designed by the YMCA in the United States," Luo said as a line of preschoolers straggled into the basement hallway behind a teacher, everyone giggling at the unexpected sight of a foreigner. "You can see similar buildings all over the world. Japan's is very similar."

I followed Luo upstairs and noticed the hardwood flooring. Wood was a scarce enough resource in China that nearly everything built in the last half century was made of brick, concrete, and steel. In Beijing, an earthquake zone, houses were built with concrete roofs. But this flooring was made of the thin hardwood strips of a basketball court. At the second-floor landing, Luo pushed open a door to a large room that was now a cafeteria. Preschoolers were sitting on tiny plastic stools, sipping juice and having an afternoon snack. They looked up, adorable, another Chinese generation.

When the Y was built, it was the tallest building in Tianjin and a social center for wealthy Chinese and expatriates. The cafeteria was once a social hall. The first movie shown in Tianjin was screened here.

"This was the best nightclub in Tianjin a hundred years ago," Luo joked.

One of the administrators of the school, Yang Yuqiang, led us into another room, which seemed strangely familiar. The ceiling had been lowered and a small stage had been erected at the far end, with large posters from the last performance: the October 1 celebration of the sixtieth anniversary of the People's Republic of China. The preschoolers had staged a patriotic show for their parents.

"Little Flower, One by One, Our Hearts Point Toward the Motherland," the posters read.

The room was narrow, a rectangle less than half the size of an NBA court, and then I realized why it was familiar: the running track. Anyone who has belonged to one of the older YMCAs in America knows the elevated, cantilevered running track built above the basketball courts. I once belonged to a Y in Alabama with the same kind of track. This was where YMCA secretaries once taught Chinese boys to toss a ball into a basket, where basketball in China was born.

"We call it the multifunction room," said Yang Yuqiang. "The ceiling used to be taller than this."

Yang walked onto the floor and motioned toward the opposite ends of the running track. Baskets were once bolted on each end. We stood silently for a minute and a custodian arrived with a plaque, written in Chinese. Yang said it would soon be affixed to the wall as part of a dedication ceremony. It read:

> Basketball was created in the United States in 1891. Four years
> later in 1895, YMCA missionaries introduced basketball in
> Tianjin. Here the first Chinese indoor basketball court
> was built in 1914.

We admired the plaque and took another moment in the room. I wondered what those YMCA missionaries would have thought of what they achieved, and what they did not, having come here preaching that strength of body equaled strength of nation, that a nation knocked to its knees by modernity could stand itself back up. They aspired to build red-brick YMCA buildings across China and bring the Chinese people closer to God. They traveled to a country that defied their understanding, propelled by their faith and their belief in the power of that faith.

Yet it was the practicality embedded into their vision of faith that appealed to many Chinese, a path to rebuilding a country as much as saving souls. The Communist Party appropriated their ideas, and China did stand itself up again, if not in the name of God. Like the NBA a century later, the Y had come to China selling something intangible, and if the Y had no interest in money or profit, it did want to change China, to make it more like us. It had built its own network of basketball courts across the country—a precursor to the NBA's plans for new arenas around China—and had hoped those YMCA centers would radiate as beacons of Christianity and tools of a Chinese rebirth. In the end, that would be too much to ask for; I wondered if the NBA was also asking for too much.

It was time to go, and I followed Luo onto East Street. He was still fascinated by the NBA.

"I suggest to the NBA that they should learn from their ancestors, the YMCA secretaries," he said. "You can't focus too much on making money. That is too nearsighted. You should have a long-term plan. Then, one day, you'll see the flowers bear fruit."

Bob Weiss was standing on the sideline, near the scorer's table, a good fifteen feet from the bench. He was coaching now. The distance was a statement of independence. No more whispers to stand up and call a timeout. No rubbernecking when someone else made a substitution.

Outside, snow was still coming down, which had deflated the national debut of Bonzi Wells. The expected sellout had been reduced to a few hundred diehards, including about fifty men who were beating thunder sticks for Bonzi. The arena was large, frigid, and mostly empty, with an oval concrete floor, an awkward configuration for the rectangular court. It was like watching a basketball game inside a very large indoor rodeo, minus the fans and cows.

The Brave Dragons were introduced. Olumide hopped off the bench and loped onto the floor, greeting every teammate who followed with his customary chest bump. Like the rest of the team, Olumide was uncertain what to make of the new imported star. The team was wearing their red road uniforms, and Wells wore Number 42. When he was introduced by his Chinese name, he trotted out for his chest bump with the Big O.

Bangqi Weiersi!

The Tianjin crowd exploded. No one appeared to be rooting for the home team. Wells stripped off his warm-ups and walked out to midcourt. The men with the thunder sticks were screaming. A few fans were wearing Rockets jerseys. Bonzi was thick in the chest and shoulders, overweight by NBA standards, but more heavily muscled than anyone on the court. He outweighed the Chinese player guarding him by maybe thirty pounds. When he played in the NBA, Wells's role was clearly defined: to provide a burst of offense, often off the bench, as well as rebounding and some tough defense. In Taiyuan, he had asked Weiss about his role for the Brave Dragons.

"They expect the Americans to play forty-eight minutes and get 30 points," Weiss had said.

"I play about thirty minutes and get about 15," Bonzi had replied.

Now the ball was tipped and the game was under way. The Brave Dragons came down the court. The starting five were Pan, Joy, Kobe, Olumide, and Bonzi. They had barely played together. Pan pushed the ball across midcourt and passed to Wells. Everyone reflexively stopped moving and bore witness to the great star. He squared, launched his first shot in China, and missed badly.

Gradually, he found his game. He made a steal for a breakaway dunk. He slammed down a dunk and made a 3-pointer. Olumide drew two defenders and whipped a pass outside to Bonzi for another 3. He had scored 10 points in ten minutes.

Weiss was a different man. He stood the entire first quarter, barking at Pan or calling Bonzi over, intently focused on the game. Liu Tie did not leave the bench. He wore a parka to stay warm. Boss Wang sat beside him, jawing in his ear as Liu nodded silently. At one point, Boss Wang patted him on the knee.

Bonzi was now shooting on almost every possession. Pan dribbled up the court, standing at the top of the key, waiting, until Bonzi came over and collected the ball. Everyone was frozen, intimidated, except Olumide, who was visibly frustrated as Tianjin crept back into the game, trailing 26–25. Timeout. Bonzi walked very slowly back to the huddle where the players were circled around Weiss. He was yelling at them with Garrison trying to keep pace before the team returned for the last seconds of the first quarter. Weiss had called a clear-out for Bonzi to operate on his own and try to beat his defender for the last shot, but Bonzi fell down and the quarter ended with the Brave Dragons leading 29–27. Bonzi claimed he was fouled and argued with a ref. Bonzi shouted in English. The ref shouted back in Chinese.

A pattern took shape: The Greatest American Ever to Play in the Chinese league was scoring but laboring, too. He did not have a natural shooting stroke; he had a hitch in his motion, and at one point tossed up three bricks in a row from behind the 3-point line. He was shooting too quickly because he was exhausted and did not want to waste energy by driving to the basket.

Still, as the game had progressed, he had put the Brave Dragons up

64–55 with a nice spin move. He hit a 3-pointer, missed one, and then hit one at the buzzer before the end of the third quarter. He had 30 points and the Brave Dragons led 82–67. His fans were beating their thunder sticks as the two teams walked out for the final quarter. Victory seemed secure.

"Warning! Warning! Number 42."

The game commissioner pointed at Bonzi Wells. The commissioner had risen from his chair and stepped onto the scorer's table. He represented the voice of authority. During a timeout, the referees had trotted over for a quick evaluation. If coaches wanted to argue a point, they walked down the sideline to plead their case with the game commissioner. Every game had a different commissioner, and tonight's commissioner could have been a Vegas lounge singer: He was holding a microphone and wore a white dinner jacket, his hair swept over his forehead as he tried to restore order. Throughout the game, Wells had barked at the referees, complaining about foul calls until the commissioner had intervened.

"Next time we'll give you a technical foul," the commissioner warned.

Wells was dripping in sweat, furious. A player for the Tianjin team made two foul shots. As the Shanxi lead had evaporated in the fourth quarter, Bonzi grew increasingly agitated at the refs. He was getting no respect and no calls.

"Always follow the rules," the game commissioner intoned, stepping off the table.

The Brave Dragons' lead had shrunk to two points. There were twenty-five seconds left in the game.

Bonzi brought the ball upcourt and was immediately fouled. He walked slowly to the foul line as his cheering section slammed together their thunder sticks. He had shot so many times that his arms must have felt limp.

The referee handed him the ball. Journalist Li was typing blog updates as Bonzi bent his knees and flicked his first foul shot toward the goal. Good. The thunder sticks crashed together. Weiss watched from the sideline as Wells pounded the ball against the floor and stared at the basket. His wrist snapped. Good. Four-point lead.

Now the Tianjin guards raced up the court, seconds ticking down, and one of them pulled up and fired a 3-pointer. Good. One-point game. But the clock expired. Shanxi won, 107–106. Bonzi Wells was 1-0 in China. On the bench, Boss Wang was grinning.

The postgame news conference was conducted in a small room in the basement of the arena. Elated, Weiss offered some valedictory comments and praised Bonzi for playing almost the entire game, despite not having played competitively for so many months. Then Wells took the microphone and the Chinese reporters edged forward. He had scored 48 points in his Chinese debut, though he took 46 shots to do it. It was not always pretty.

"It's a whole new culture," he said. "I'm just learning, but I'm going to get better every day. I really appreciate my fans. I've been here for about two weeks, and it just feels great. I haven't felt this much love in a long time."

He thanked Weiss and thanked his new teammates. Then he pointed upward and thanked God.

CHAPTER ELEVEN

MERRY CHRISTMAS

The knock on Rick Turner's bedroom door came about 1 a.m. He was watching the end of a movie and barely awake. It must be Donta, Turner thought. Donta had spent the evening packing for his morning flight to Beijing and on to Melbourne, home of his new Australian team.

"Uhh, Rick? Could you come out here?"

It was Joe. He was in the living room with the assistant general manager, the team accountant, and a bleary-eyed Donta. The team had not known Donta was actually leaving. His agent had arranged the flight, and Donta figured the agent could handle any other unfinished details, so he had planned to get up in the morning, get to the airport, and get out of China. But now the team had sent an official delegation to persuade him otherwise: They wanted him to stay in Taiyuan as an inactive player, a safeguard in case the Bonzi experiment blew up. He could practice and still draw his salary if he would just stick around. Donta had thanked everyone, but his answer was no, an unequivocal, emphatic no, which is why Joe knocked on Rick Turner's door. He needed a lawyer.

Turner stumbled out in a T-shirt and camouflage boxer shorts. He was being asked to draft an agreement dissolving Donta's contract. He had never studied law, but he could write in English, which was enough. He tore a piece of paper out of a notebook and began writing out the final terms, including a last payout for Donta. The accountant copied the agreement in Chinese and handed Donta a fat stack of 250 $100 bills. It was more than Turner had made in his entire coaching career.

"I'd be lying if I said my mouth didn't water," Turner would later admit.

Everyone shook hands, and as the Chinese delegation moved to leave, the assistant general manager turned for a final question. Could Turner move out? The apartment was too big and the team would rent him a one-bedroom down the hall. Sure, Turner agreed, though it presented a problem. He was leaving, too, in less than five hours. He was going home for Christmas. He had finally gotten his meeting with Zhang Beihai, after sending a long email explaining why he needed to return, how his daughter's birthday was on December 28, even as he emphasized that he would stay if leaving meant losing his job. Joe had repeated his warning. Leave and they will not let you come back, he said. Stay and they will not dare fire you. It was the Chinese way.

When he got his meeting, Turner made his case. "I'd like to come back," he said, "but I was told you don't want me to come back." No, no, not the case, the general manager had promised. He understood why Christmas was important, and the junior team's schedule would not be interrupted by his absence. Another coach, Coach Zhao, had been working with the youngest kids, but he could help Joe with the junior team until Turner returned. All the general manager asked was that Turner make it back by January 5. Turner promised to return much sooner.

The strange thing was that Turner really did want to come back. True, part of the allure was that he did not have a job in America. And, true, leading a team of Chinese teenagers who are not allowed to play games represented an especially devious form of coaching torture. But being here was a great adventure, a taste of another culture, a daily soap opera. It was misery, but it was fun, too. He thought he was getting through to some of the players, making progress, and it was still *his* team. His confidence remained intact. He believed he was a good coach. He had a track record to prove it. He just needed a chance. So far, coaching a bunch of teenagers inside a converted warehouse in the middle of China was the best chance he had gotten.

He got his stuff together so the team could move him into the new apartment and soon afterward went to the airport with Donta. They shared a flight to Beijing and then parted. Tracy was also going to Seattle for Christmas and they planned to meet for a drink.

In Seattle, Turner's family gathered for the annual Christmas party. His daughter had a daddy on her birthday. Turner raced around town, trying to catch up with everyone he had missed during the previous five months and was having drinks in a bar with a friend the night before his return flight to China, when Bob Weiss's number appeared on his cell phone.

He was excited to answer it. Maybe Weiss had convinced the owner to let him return to the senior team. Or maybe Weiss was just passing along the latest nuttiness. The maybe he hadn't expected was that Weiss was not bearing good news. Joe had just called him to say Turner would not be allowed to return. The team would put Turner's belongings in a box and ship them back. Weiss apologized. He had not seen it coming, either.

"I was supposed to be on a plane in less than twelve hours and the plug had been pulled," Turner wrote later. He wondered if Zhang Beihai had lied all along, or if he had just changed his mind. He left the bar and returned home to find an email from Joe:

> Rick
>
> I just got a call from Mr zhang he wants me to tell you that the second team and the teenage team will merge to one team and coach Zhao and me will coach this team so they don't need no more help. I hate be picked to tell you this i am sorry.
>
> joe

Turner had wanted to take the Trans-Siberian Railroad from Beijing to Moscow once the season ended, and then jump on Eurail to London before flying back to Seattle. But now he was in Seattle and it seemed as if the last six months had never happened.

The box of his belongings sat for weeks in the front office, untouched and pushed to the side, as if it contained hazardous materials. Rick was initially patient when his things failed to arrive in Seattle, writing polite emails. He was told the shipment was going out soon. It didn't.

Turner had left mostly clothes and a few personal things. He had finally gotten his Anta swag, the shoes, sweats and other freebies coaches live on. He wanted them. Finally, after another week of nothing in the mail, Turner wrote a furious email, angry and hurt, demanding his stuff.

No one in the front office wanted to touch it because no one knew if the team would actually pay for the shipment. Finally, Joe took the box to the post office and paid the freight himself. The box arrived a few weeks later.

CHAPTER TWELVE

BODIES

Men touch each other in China. The habit usually catches foreigners unaware. You might occasionally see two young men walking down a sidewalk, holding hands. Or maybe they are draped over one another, an arm hooked over a shoulder, laughing or whispering, sharing a small intimacy. Young women are the same, walking arm-in-arm or holding hands, sharing an umbrella, giggling in a protective cocoon of sisterhood. Usually, the men are from the countryside, where this kind of physical contact is common and without any sexual connotation. The anthropologist Susan Brownell, who ran track at Peking University during the 1980s, recalled communal showers where one female teammate pressed herself against a wall in the frisking position as another woman softly scrubbed her back. When Brownell attended student dances, men usually danced with men and women with women. This changed during the next two decades, as a nightclub in Beijing became little different from a nightclub in New York, yet even in 2008, the sight of men strolling down a city street holding hands was not that uncommon.

Bonzi Wells had noticed. His teammates sometimes touched each other. Nothing remotely sexual, but still: touching. They gave each other neck rubs. They were always hanging on each other at practice, which made Wells uncomfortable. Then he walked outside onto the streets of Taiyuan and saw the occasional twosome touching each other, fingers loosely intertwined. It just seemed strange. He mentioned it to Weiss, to the other foreigners on the team, to me. He asked: Are all these guys gay?

Bonzi was entering his fourth week in China and he had not yet assimilated himself into his new team or his new country. Two nights before,

Bonzi played what Weiss described as one of the worst quarters of basketball he had ever witnessed. The Brave Dragons were on the road in Xi'an, and Wells was awful, especially in the first quarter. He had five points and five turnovers. The gym had been cold, and Wells had not bothered to warm up. He played with such a groggy lack of interest that Weiss benched him for part of the game. The Brave Dragons lost, and Boss Wang ranted for an hour in the locker room. He screamed and hollered and berated every Chinese player, as usual, but this time he screamed at the foreigners, too. When Olumide rose to confront him, the owner shouted for him to shut up.

It ended there, but Boss Wang finished his screed with an ultimatum: Beat the Beijing Ducks in the next game or all the foreigners would be sent home.

The team returned to Taiyuan the following day and Zhang Beihai and Weiss huddled in the lounge of the World Trade. Weiss fortified himself with two Manhattans. A kinship had developed between the two men. They were lashed to the same mast on the same battered ship, trying to ride out the same storm. Now the Bonzi experiment was turning into what the coaches had most feared. Boss Wang had believed Bonzi would elevate the team into the league's elite, but the team had gotten worse: three wins and four losses since Bonzi arrived, with the Brave Dragons fighting for the final playoff spot.

Bonzi had altered the chemistry of the team in a way that defied easy solutions. The team was worse with him but helpless without him. He was the only scoring option. Hardly anyone did anything on offense except watch Bonzi and wait for him to shoot. The Chinese players sometimes seemed terrified on the court. The two Chinese players most likely to score, Wei Mingliang and Zhai Jinshuai, both wing players, were now on the court less often because they didn't blend smoothly with Bonzi. Donta Smith could move to point guard, creating minutes, and shots, for Wei, but Bonzi was a pure scorer.

And he was scoring. That was what made it even more confounding: Bonzi was doing exactly what everyone had said he was supposed to do. If you discounted the ugly game in Xi'an, Bonzi was the league's most unstoppable force. He had single-handedly beaten Fujian with 52 points, including 13 in overtime. He could be breathtaking to watch, and China was watching. CCTV was now televising almost every Brave Dragons game. Crowds loved him. Ren Hongbing had confected a special medley for Bonzi by blending Peking Opera, American hip-hop, and Chinese pop.

The chorus, roughly translated, was this:

> *Bonzi, Bonzi, Bonzi!*
> *Kill, Power, Bonzi!*

"This may be the first time in the CBA that something like this was specially made for a player," Ren proudly told the Chinese press.

Weiss was frustrated but sympathetic to Bonzi. "It's not his fault, game-wise," Weiss said. "He is what he is—a scorer. Donta made all the other Chinese players better. He made Olumide better. He gave Olumide four or five dunks a game."

Olumide's scoring and his touches on offense were down, as was his cheery demeanor. Before, he had been one of the biggest stars in the league, and the marquee player for the Brave Dragons, but now the attention, and the offense, had shifted to Bonzi. Bonzi had demanded, and gotten, first-class seats on airplanes. Bonzi had demanded, and gotten, a suite for road games. "Being the bad boy pays off," Olumide had grumbled on one flight after Bonzi sat in first class. Eventually, wisely, Olumide used the situation to demand similar perks and got bumped into first class, too. But his falling numbers were another matter. Numbers represent food for a basketball mercenary.

He was now joined in Taiyuan by a full complement of Nigerians. His wife, Miriam, and their infant daughter, Ana, arrived with his best friend, Ogoh, and Ogoh's pregnant wife, Joy. Everyone lived inside Olumide's apartment, which became the Little Nigeria of Taiyuan. Additional Nigerians would materialize, a favorite aunt or someone from the Nigerian embassy in Beijing, and the kitchen was stocked with bags of rice, different cooking powders, and boxes of frozen meats for preparing what Olumide called "hard-core" Nigerian food. Given that much of Nigeria is a tropical savanna with average wintertime temperatures of about 80 degrees, Olumide kept the apartment heated high enough that my glasses sometimes fogged over as I walked through the door.

Ogoh was a short, muscular man, soft-spoken with an appealing serenity who once played guard for the Nigerian national team. Like me, Ogoh was affixed to the Brave Dragons despite having no obvious or practical use. Technically, his role was Olumide's personal trainer, as stipulated in a clause in Olumide's contract requiring the club to cover certain expenses for said trainer. Yet I had spent months with the team and never actually witnessed Ogoh "train" Olumide. When I had once gently asked about the "training" regimen (which Olumide had described to me as very cutting-edge), Ogoh answered that most of the work was done during the "off-season." This deepened the mystery since Olumide played basketball ten or eleven months every year on multiple continents, essentially eliminating the "off-season." Whatever, I had concluded Ogoh's role was that of friend and one-man posse. Wherever Olumide went, Ogoh went with him.

The morning before the Beijing game, the team gathered for practice. I went on the chance that Boss Wang might show up and fire everyone. The team had lost a heartbreaker in Beijing two days after Bonzi's debut in the blizzard in Tianjin. He had almost pulled out a miracle victory with a steal and the go-ahead foul shots in the final seconds—only to watch Beijing score the winning basket at the buzzer. This would be a home game, which would help, but Weiss was edgy at practice; he thought a mass firing was distinctly possible. I took a seat beside Ogoh and waited for Boss Wang the way you wait for an approaching hurricane, uncertain of the extent of the coming damage. But practice began without any sight of him.

Weiss was working on transition offense, rotating the first and second teams. Bonzi's leg was bothering him and he hobbled through the drills. Like Weiss, Ogoh did not blame Bonzi, solely, for the team's problems. "A lot of the players are not getting as involved as they should be," he said. "The only one putting in some effort is him." He pointed at the skinny young guard Duan Jiangpeng. "The others are just content to watch. The others think: Hey, he is the great Bonzi. He should do all the scoring."

Weiss stopped the drill to chew out Big Sun for making a lazy pass. On the opposite sideline, Liu Tie was alone, pacing, head down, hands in pockets. He was quiet now, almost ashen, since his demotion. I knew he was proud and did not raise the subject but I heard from others that he was devastated. He thought he had earned the owner's trust but had concluded instead that no one could earn his trust. Overnight, his relationship changed with the players. Now he was one of the guys. He played cards with Wei and Big Sun in the airport waiting room. Or he invited players out for dinner and told them not to worry about the curfew, just to relax.

Now the first team was back on the court. Bonzi had lost ten pounds and looked thinner. He hated Chinese food in America and liked it even less in China; he vomited after one meal. His diet consisted of one Western-facsimile meal a day supplemented by Red Bull energy drinks. Between sets, he walked over and sat down beside me.

I asked what he thought of his Chinese teammates.

"He's good," he said, pointing at Duan Jiangpeng. At twenty, Duan was playing his first season in the CBA after being promoted from the junior team. He was 6'4", maybe 175 pounds, and had emerged as the team's best second option as a scorer. At the beginning of the season, Weiss and Turner thought he was too cowed to contribute much, but Duan had gotten better every week and was faster and better on defense than Wei and Zhai.

"What about Zhai?" I asked.

Zhai was running with the second stringers. He scored 22 points in Bonzi's first game in Tianjin and I thought maybe he had regained his strut, except he had since done little as his confidence and minutes had dwindled away.

"Who is that?"

"The guy in the blue hoodie."

"He's scared. They're all scared."

Weiss called for the first string, and Bonzi walked slowly back onto the court. He had tweaked a knee, and after running a few offensive sets he took a seat under the basket to watch his teammates. Kobe took a pass and swooped in for an easy layup—which he missed.

Bonzi glared at him. Kobe had become Bonzi's pet project. Easily the most athletic Chinese player on the team, Kobe was the team's defensive stopper who guarded the top foreigner in every game. When the team played Xinjiang, one of the league's strongest teams, Bonzi thought his Chinese teammates were intimidated by the foreign players as well as Xinjiang's massive Chinese center, Mengke Bateer. His message to Kobe had been simple: Don't be scared. He tried to build him up, telling him that he might be talented enough for the NBA. He wanted him to be aggressive on offense and defense the following night against Beijing, when he would be matched up with Dontae Jones, one of the league's leading scorers. Jones didn't play defense and Bonzi thought Kobe could score against him.

Kobe rebounded his missed layup, then put it in, and looked over at Bonzi for approval. Bonzi nodded and walked back over to join me on the sideline.

"Half these guys don't know how to play basic basketball," he said, con-

The brain trust. Left to right on the bench: Bob Weiss, Garrison Guo, in and out coach Liu Tie, Boss Wang, and Wingtips, a Chinese assistant.

Bob Weiss with his driver and the foreigners' van

Taiyuan on a rare clear day

Forward Big Sun in the team's weight room. It consisted of a few bench presses and barbells on the sideline of one of the practice courts.

onzi Wells's midseason arrival with the Brave
Dragons became the sensation of the Chinese
Basketball Association. Once ignored, the
Brave Dragons became the focus of a media
frenzy, as Chinese reporters descended on
Taiyuan to chronicle the successes and travails
of the onetime NBA star.

an Jiang, the Brave Dragons point guard

Ren Hongbing, or Red Soldier, the team's
deejay

Zhang Xuewen, or Kobe, was the athletic power forward who became the subject of a battle of wills between Boss Wang and Bonzi. To his right is Duan Jiangpeng, the guard who by season's end was considered one of the best young prospects in the league.

Bob Weiss literally warming up in the Hawaii Room, the only heated room in the team's arena

The Taiyuan crazies. Few teams, if any, had such a rowdy fan base.

The three-story YMCA building in Tianjin is the birthplace of basketball in China. Built nearly a century ago, the building is now a preschool.

This room was once the first indoor court in China. Note the elevated running track built into every YMCA.

Hoppy, the Don King of Chinese squirrels, who was saved from the cook pot by Tracy Weiss

Part field general, part Vegas lounge singer, a game commissioner (in the white suit) is the arbiter of games in the Chinese league.

American import Tim Pickett on the floor after getting injured in the critical game against Shandong.

When Brave Dragons fans started pelting the floor with lighters and other debris—wondering if the critical game against the Liaoning Pan Pan Dinosaurs was on the up-and-up—ball boys and ball girls tried to clean up the debris, even as the refs wanted to get the game over with.

The Brave Dragons rejoice in the dying seconds of the season finale. Tenth place never felt so good.

Bob Weiss, heading home to Seattle after the season

Bode the dog, formerly of China, currently residing in Seattle, Washington

tinuing where we left off. He had been impressed with several Chinese players on other teams, but he considered his teammates too young and too green.

He was still startled that he was even here. "I didn't know anything," he told me. "They asked me in November. I said, 'No, I don't want to go to China.' But they got me by saying I could get some of the Anta money back. And maybe some other deals. I said yes on Monday. I was on a plane on Wednesday."

He was stunned by how the Chinese players lived. "The life they live is so different," he said. "The shit they have to do. There is a twenty-six-year-old Chinese guy who is thinking about retiring. They have to live here fifty weeks a year and practice with the same guys. That's like prison.

"I guess if they came to our place, they would find things that are different in our culture."

He watched the Chinese players as they ran up and down the floor, banging into each other. "If we had a good point guard, my life would be easier," he said. "I've got to be the point guard. I've got to facilitate everybody. I've always just been a scorer. But that shit will wear me out, having to score 50 every night."

He said he wanted to build a rapport with his teammates but that it wasn't easy. Language was the biggest problem, but he was also still incredulous about the touching. "I tell them, 'You guys are crazy. You aren't ever supposed to touch another man.' It's okay to give a five or a smack on the butt after a good play."

It was at this moment that Bonzi called for the team's trainer, Yuan Zaibin, to massage his ailing leg. Barely 5'7", with bottle-thick glasses, Yuan lived in the dormitory in a small bedroom attached to what constituted the medical wing: a single room with a massage table and some outdated machines used to apply sonic waves to an injury. He recently rented a small apartment near the facility for his wife and infant child. Yuan was one of the most popular people in the organization, forever upbeat, if not entirely trusted by the foreigners as a medical practitioner. When Weiss first arrived, a player left practice with an unknown ailment. Weiss approached Yuan for an explanation. The answer he got, which may or may not have been lost in translation, was "His ass is blue." Weiss never did figure out the problem.

But the suspicions about Yuan were really suspicions about the wholly different way Chinese coaches and players approached conditioning and caring for their bodies. In his early days running the team, Liu Tie had taken the team on a two-hour drive into the mountains west of the city, where the players unloaded at the bottom of a steep incline of stone steps leading to an ancient temple. Then Liu separated the players into two-somes and ordered one player to piggyback the other up and down the steps, running. To the foreigners, this was stupidity, an invitation for injury. To the Chinese, it was just another day at practice. Before every game, on several teams, you would commonly see the Chinese players in a circle for their stretching routine, while the foreigners did their own warm-up drills. Sometimes a foreign player would shoot from inside the stretching circle of his teammates. It was as if they were different pieces of machinery.

Bonzi had been checking his emails on his iPhone as we spoke and then put it in his lap, when Trainer Yuan arrived, smiling, and began rub-bing Bonzi's leg. He rubbed around the injured knee and then moved up toward his thigh and groin, rubbing, rubbing, his fingers kneading the muscles, when Bonzi suddenly jerked back and shoved him, cursing. It happened so fast that I was startled. So was Trainer Yuan, who assumed that Bonzi was joking the way Chinese players do. He playfully shoved Bonzi back. Now Bonzi was irate and shoved him even harder, and only then did I realize what had happened. The iPhone was on Bonzi's lap, and Yuan had reached to move it. Bonzi thought Yuan was trying to grab his penis. I now tried to intervene—this was just a misunderstanding!—but Yuan's face was starting to cloud as he pushed Bonzi back again, still play-fully, but confused.

"Get away from me, motherfucker!" Bonzi shouted and shoved Yuan to the floor. "Don't touch me!"

The gym went silent. Liu Tie and a few players were standing under the basket, gaping. The trainer was now furious. He jumped up, red-faced, shoulders pitched back, fuming, staring in fury at a man who outweighed him by 100 pounds.

"Get away from me!" Bonzi yelled again. Yuan walked down the side-line and took a seat. He was enraged and glared silently at Bonzi.

Bonzi leaned forward and glared back at Yuan.

"What are you mad about?" Bonzi shouted. "Bring me some fucking ice! Ice!"

Yuan rose from his seat and opened a cooler. He scooped out a small bag of ice and slowly walked toward Bonzi. Bonzi was the star player.

Trainer Yuan was not. He bent down, placed the ice on Bonzi's knee and wrapped it with tape.

The gym was silent except for the sound of tape being ripped off the roll.

When practice ended, Bonzi walked outside to the bus. "Coach," he told Weiss, trying to make light of what happened, "I need to fill out a police report. I got fondled."

Soon enough, the story spread. Everything else about Bonzi had.

He had no idea, of course. Any foreigner in China exists somewhere within a sliding scale of unknowingness. That many Chinese regard their culture as impenetrable from the outside is what makes China so seductive to some outsiders, those for whom China becomes the ultimate puzzle to be solved. For others unknowingness is almost self-defense, a coping mechanism. Then there are the innocents, tossed into the sea, ignorant of the language, unaware of what is happening around them, grateful that McDonald's and KFC have made it over. Bonzi fell into this category.

He knew he was a big story in China. He just did not know what those stories were saying. Almost none of the foreigners did. The Chinese government censored the Internet on any subject judged politically destabilizing by the Communist Party, but otherwise the Internet was a megaphone, a pulsating hive of chat rooms and discussion boards and news reports that constituted the central nervous system of the country. When Wells had first arrived in Taiyuan, a *Titan Sports* reporter had followed him and Zhang Beihai to the supermarket. It was as much an ethnological exercise as a journalistic one: When another shopper accidentally bumped a cart into the American star, *Titan* reported that "Bonzi did not get angry but made a gesture to let the person go through."

"I heard he had a bad temper," the general manager told the paper. "I did not expect he would be such a gentleman."

The character study continued at lunch at a nearby KFC, where more unexpected evidence surfaced of his good nature: He had placed the trash from his meal on his tray and personally delivered it to the garbage.

"He's really not bad!" Zhang Beihai had exclaimed.

The narrative had already been written before Bonzi arrived: Here was the Ugly American come to China, a man of prodigious physical talents, if also a prodigious temperament. Here was the American Id. He would be watched on the court, and studied off it.

When Yao Ming first arrived in the NBA, the scrutiny was far greater.

Yao was the top pick in the NBA draft, and scores of Chinese reporters had followed him to America, trailing him everywhere along with
an American press that observed him with a skeptical fascination. Not
one reporter had followed Bonzi to China, nor was any national prestige
attached to how he performed, as had been the case with Yao. For those
few American basketball blogs paying attention, Bonzi was just another
past-his-prime star now looking for a paycheck overseas.

But like Yao, Bonzi would be judged in his adopted country as an
ambassador of sorts. Yao knew this, of course. The NBA was invested in
his success and had helped prepare him. Even so, he faced stereotypes. He
was the Great Wall of China, more robot than man, a freak produced on
the assembly line of the Communist sports machine. What transformed
his image was not just his eventual success on the court but the way he
demonstrated his individuality. He was funny. He was not a robot. He
was proof that Chinese were individuals.

What awaited Bonzi was a Chinese press already conditioned to American players who typified the American stereotype of selfish and spoiled.
Bonzi's arrival was exciting because he conferred status on the Chinese
league, confirming its rising global standing, which meant Bonzi would
be examined as a cultural ambassador, too. This was an unspoken part of
the basketball experiment in China: Could Chinese and foreigners play
together?

When Wells first postponed his debut, reports surfaced that "many
people" considered him as *shuadapai*, or, roughly speaking, acting like a
huge diva. His second postponement "only deepened the suspicion that
he was just *shuadapai*," *Titan* concluded.

The big Web portals now posted reporters to cover the games or even
attend practices. Autographs became fodder for blog updates: first, the
exclusive that Bonzi didn't seem interested in signing them, and later,
once he had signed a few, the follow-up revelation that he just wrote a
lazy B followed by a squiggly line rather than a neat rendering of his
name. ("I've always signed like that," Bonzi protested later.) Then there
was his relationship with the sporting press. Mutual loathing might accurately describe his relationship with many basketball writers in the United
States. Now the Chinese press was eager for an interview, an exclusive,
anything, but Bonzi was only talking during his postgame remarks. He
even turned down CCTV. Whether he knew anything about CCTV, or
understood the ramifications of turning it down, is unlikely. But that, too,
became a story: Bonzi Turns Down CCTV.

His inaccessibility transformed Wells into a test of Chinese journalistic manhood. Two weeks earlier, at the morning practice before the last-second loss to Beijing, a huddle of Chinese reporters had stared at Bonzi from the edge of the court. It was as if they were passing a bottle, gathering their courage. Bonzi was leaning against the scorer's table, headphones on, when one of the reporters approached me. Did I think Bonzi would talk to him? Probably not, I answered. He stared at Bonzi and took a breath. He was a young guy. "If I do not try, I cannot respect myself as a journalist," he said, and walked toward the scorer's table. At almost precisely the instant the reporter reached the outer edge of Bonzi's personal space, some sort of journalist radar must have pinged inside Bonzi's head. He pushed off the scorer's table, never looking up or indicating any awareness of someone approaching, and joined his teammates at midcourt. The young reporter returned to the huddle with his self-respect, if not an interview.

Inevitably, Bonzi's presence inflamed the sporadic media sniping about foreign domination on the court. "Foreign Players: The CBA's Ball Hogs," crowed *Oriental Sports Daily*, which catalogued Bonzi's "cold war" with the media, his snubbing of CCTV, and his estranged relationship with his teammates. "Are the CBA's Foreign Players Devils or Angels?" asked *Guangzhou Daily*, concluding that foreigners, with a few exceptions, could be royal pains in the neck whose ball hogging retarded the development of young Chinese stars.

Bonzi's media blackout had effectively reproduced the same alternating story lines in the Chinese press that shaped his public image in the United States. There were stories saying he was a jerk. There were stories saying he was misunderstood. A few of his teammates tried to defend him. "The Internet says he is one of the NBA's Top Ten most notorious personalities, ranking at number seven," Joy told one paper, trying to be supportive. "It says he acts like a big celebrity. But that's not the case. He's actually quite a good guy."

Most of his other Chinese teammates were privately less charitable. They thought Bonzi was weird. They still couldn't understand why he locked himself in his room.

Nearly all the Chinese players had computers in their rooms that tethered them to the Internet, which, in turn, tethered them to the youth of China. There were more than 400 million Internet users in China, and when Joy was a reserve on the Guangdong team, he became one of the several CBA players to write a blog on the league's website. He discussed everything from movies to diarrhea to night school classes to the Sichuan earthquake. His latest entry was about the Fujian game and how it would ruin his season. His headline was: "Crap—I Got Injured."

He had accidentally stepped on the foot of Fujian's point guard and badly dislocated his ankle, damaging the ligaments. He had never been seriously injured, but now he was out indefinitely and would fly to Hong Kong for medical treatment. So much attention was focused on Bonzi, and his impact on the team, that few people considered the impact of Joy's absence. He rebounded, passed, never made dumb mistakes, and hit open shots. He was what coaches call a "glue guy," meaning he kept the team together. Now he was gone.

"This is the worst nightmare," he wrote. "Perhaps God had seen me playing so hard and wanted me to take a good rest."

The timing was terrible. Joy was playing well. In Guangdong, as a bench player, his confidence had suffered. At one point, the father of one of the team's stars pulled Joy aside at practice to encourage him to be brave on the court.

"You should be confident at all times," the father had said. "Otherwise, you'll never get better."

On his blog, Joy began writing about his self-doubt. He was curious and honest and almost goofily thoughtful. He wrote one post about the benefits of thinking like a dog. "We know that when a dog is chasing a Frisbee, he has only one thought in mind. Success. He wouldn't think about his past failures. He wouldn't lose sleep for a night or worry whether he would catch the Frisbee the next day. A man would be concerned about what other people would think about him if he failed to catch the Frisbee. He would also ponder who would be disappointed if he didn't catch it."

He concluded: "Sometimes people should be willing to think as a dog. Have you ever seen a dog dismal or upset that he didn't catch a Frisbee? Have you ever seen a dog give up because he had already tried once? I suggest, that as a dog does, when you are the victor, at least pat yourself on the head, or roar under the moonlight, as a reward to yourself, even if your achievement is tiny."

Soon the Web was writing back. "On our team, I must learn my position and what character I possess," Joy wrote. "I can't compete on offense with players from the national team and foreign players. Some bloggers said I should be more decisive and braver. Good suggestion.

"Thanks for all the advice."

His breakthrough moment came the previous season when the Guangdong coach unexpectedly put him in the starting lineup of a game. At the end of the game, he scored eight points as the other team kept fouling him, assuming he would buckle under the pressure. But as Joy kept making foul shots, the home crowd began chanting "MVP! MVP!" He raised his fist in the air in triumph.

The trade to Shanxi had initially stunned Joy. But then he thought that maybe this was his chance. "If your hard work could help the Shanxi team play better, wouldn't that be an amazing experience? Wouldn't that make you feel fulfilled and valuable?" he wrote.

But now his foot was in a cast. He would not return for several weeks. And by then so much would have changed.

Joy was not the team's only invalid. A few hours after morning practice, I joined a medical expedition to the Shanxi Medical University Secondary Hospital. Big Rus hurt his ankle a week earlier and had yet to see a doctor. Trainer Yuan had assumed it was a sprain, and that the swelling would subside, except it had not subsided. His ankle remained as large and discolored as an eggplant.

The trainer led our delegation. He seemed to have shrugged off the morning episode with Bonzi as we took the van to the hospital. Garrison had come along for interpretation. He was dressed in his latest fashion statement: a fur-lined sweater, a Chinese incarnation of a coonskin cap, and large aviator sunglasses. He had just reunited with his girlfriend, Amy, and was practicing saying "I love you" in Russian.

The injury to Ruslan Rafaelovich Gilyazutdinov did not constitute a death blow to the team. He was still out of shape, and other than those few good moments in Donta's last game, he had not done much. Despite being almost six feet ten inches, he could barely jump, making about half his dunk attempts during layup drills, which admittedly put him in the upper echelon for the team. Rick Turner had amused himself by keeping stats of dunking percentages during warm-ups; before one early game, discounting Olumide and Donta, the team had missed nine of thirteen dunk attempts. Uncontested.

What I had come to appreciate about Big Rus was that, despite an abundance of empirical evidence proving otherwise, he remained convinced that he was an elite international player. He was never intimidated on the court and never hesitated to take the ball to the basket. If he was confronted with his limitations—say his inability to score in a game or his inability to stop his man from scoring—Big Rus usually identified the flaw not in himself but with factors beyond his control—the team, the coaches, maybe even the owner. He seemed stunned that they could not see in him what he saw, which was major league talent.

"This is *booooollsheeeeet*," he would say, smirking.

The emergency room was a dimly lit corridor overcrowded with people. We were taken into a small room with three black pallets. On one, a woman was sound asleep as her husband checked messages on his telephone. Another belonged to a bedraggled, delirious man circled by family members. Big Rus heaved himself onto the third. A doctor ordered an X-ray and sent us down the hall to the radiology department. We passed an old, hunched woman in a wheelchair who had been abandoned in the hallway; patients were diverting around her as if she were a stone in a moving stream. One man in a surgical mask was lugging a folding chair for waiting in lines.

Big Rus was disgusted. Of all the foreigners, he was the most impressed with Taiyuan, but the hospital appalled him. Dirt and grime were smeared on the lime green walls. An old man shuffled by with a gash on his cheek that was dripping with pus.

"Dat guy *smehls*!" Big Rus complained, scrunching his nose.

What he actually smelled was the bathroom. He had taken a seat near the bathroom door. A toilet had flooded and urine had pooled on the floor. The other toilets were caked in grit and feces, and the odor was spreading through the corridor. Then a steel door slid open, and Big Rus was saved by radiology. He stepped inside and placed his huge purple foot on the X-ray table. The X-ray showed no broken bones.

We followed Trainer Yuan out of the emergency room to a rear courtyard and walked to another wing of the hospital. Patients were coming and going, and cars pushed through a narrow parking lot. I suddenly realized that we had lost Big Rus. He had stopped to hold the door for a man who was piggybacking his sickened wife back onto the streets. Big Rus dodged an oncoming black Passat, and we managed to reach the other wing. When the elevator arrived, people poured out. I counted fourteen. The elevator was beeping. We tried to push in but the beeping continued, so Yuan and I took the stairs. It was five floors up, and at the landing beneath the fifth floor, Yuan paused to catch his breath.

"China's medical system for ordinary people," he said, breathing hard, his thought incomplete.

"*Bu tai hao,*" I offered, finishing for him. Not too good. He agreed.

On the fifth floor, Yuan searched for a doctor, while Garrison, Big Rus, and I loitered in the waiting area. The wall was covered with a large propaganda display about hospital services. One photograph showed earnest, white-frocked technicians staring at computer screens as a patient was being placed inside an MRI machine. The patient was a stone-faced, angry man with a strangely swollen neck.

"Rus, look," Garrison said, pointing at the man. "Coach Liu."

Yuan returned and took Big Rus to see the doctor. I had not spoken to Liu Tie in a while, and I asked Garrison how he was doing. He said Liu was now just trying to preserve his job. His demotion taught him that he had much to learn about dealing with an owner, though this particular job was difficult no matter who held it.

"It's like a pair of shoes made of iron," Garrison said. "It is going to be hard, no matter who tries to fit into them."

Yuan and Big Rus returned, clutching the X-rays, and we waited for the elevator. It arrived and ejected another swarm of people. We joined the swarm getting on. The bell sounded. Garrison motioned for four people to follow him off the elevator into the hallway. I assumed he was going to take the stairs. But no; he lined up his four followers beside the elevator door.

"Now, walk back on, very slowly," he said.

They were silent as they tried to slide weightlessly back aboard. The elevator was not fooled. The bell rang.

Yuan and I took the stairs.

The doctor had delivered bad news. Big Rus was out for three weeks.

"*Booooools*heeeet!" Big Rus declared as we were leaving the hospital. "One week and half. I'm going to call my father. He'll know what to do."

When she had gone home for Christmas, Tracy had been surprised by how *strange* the normalcy of Seattle had felt. Where was the chaos? Where was the crazy energy? Where were all the people? She found herself missing Taiyuan, and missing the players. She was already emailing regularly with the handful who could write in English and to her they often seemed like typical adolescent boys. When she caught them eyeing a flight attendant in a tight skirt on a flight back to Taiyuan, she started laughing and they started blushing. While she was in Seattle, point guard Jin Jiming wrote confiding that he and another player had smuggled two puppies into the dorm and had named them Prince and Princess. Jin Jiming's career with the Brave Dragons was basically over; he had been demoted to the junior team, though at age twenty he was too old to play for them. He was trying to get traded to another team and, as yet, Boss Wang had not released him. He had natural talent as a player but also a hot temper—he had been the one who chased another player with a brick a few months earlier—and the Chinese coaches had given up on him. Off the court, though, Jin Jiming was mild and achingly polite, and Tracy adored him.

"I'm so glad you were back," he wrote Tracy after she returned from Christmas. "We are in the gym Everyday. Prince and Princess just had bee vaccinated, so they could not have a bath. They don't smell good, and a little dirty. If you don't mind that, I will take you to play with them. They are dying to see you. And we really appreciate to take photo with you. See you this afternoon." So that afternoon, Tracy slipped into the dorm and played with Prince and Princess.

The Nigerians were having dinner at Mao's House, which qualified as Taiyuan chic. It was across the street from the World Trade, a two-story restaurant with a giant bust of the Chairman in the first-floor lobby. The walls were exposed brick, and the main dining area had an understated elegance unusual for Taiyuan. It did not, however, have heat, so the manager had placed outdoor kerosene heating towers throughout the room. I had been invited as a friend and interpreter. We took a table and asked the waiter to roll a tower near Ana's stroller.

Olumide oversaw the ordering, which involved about twenty minutes of negotiations in Yoruba, English, and Chinese before food began to arrive. Soon afterward, a man in a red sweater appeared with a small box. He was middle-aged, with strings of hair pulled across his head, and he could not stop smiling. He was a fan. The box was Chinese rice liquor, or *baijiu*, and he wanted to share a toast with Olumide. He asked me to deliver a message: The success of the team was wonderful for Taiyuan. Taiyuan had too much pollution, and too many coal bosses, but the team was something that had lifted the city. He wanted to say thank you, and he wanted Olumide to know that he loved the way he played, the way he hustled and dove on the floor.

As I repeated the message in English, a broad smile spread across Olumide's face. He rose from his chair and took the man's hand, and I snapped a photo of them. But the matter of the toast remained. *Baijiu* is alcoholic battery acid; Olumide rarely drinks. I improvised and explained that Coach Weiss forbade players from drinking the night before a game. Much was at stake against Beijing tomorrow, I said gravely, and Olumide needed to be sharp. The man nodded and left the box behind.

More food arrived, and so did the fan, again. Now he wanted Olumide to meet his friends. We walked down a narrow hallway where the restaurant had rooms for private parties. The fan opened a door and Olumide ducked inside. At the sight of the Nigerian rebounding machine, everyone jumped from their chairs, men and women, an otherwise perfectly sane group of family and friends now giddy.

"Drink! Drink!"

"We must toast!"

I offered up the no-drinking policy and Olumide posed for more pictures, wrapping his big arms around husbands and wives, his incandescent smile warming the unheated room. A few men toasted him just the same, slugging down shots of *baijiu* in his honor, and we left the room to a small round of applause as good wishes for the following night, when the Nigerian pride of Taiyuan would take on the Beijing Ducks.

No one would be getting fired this night. Kobe was playing his best basketball. Before the game, Bonzi had lectured him at midcourt, and Kobe came out attacking, driving past Dontae Jones for easy scores. Bonzi was also a different player; he was passing, distributing the ball, even as he kept scoring with ease.

I sat beside Journalist Li. He was curious if I thought the team was better with Bonzi or Donta. I made the point that Bonzi was an incredible scorer but that Donta was a better team player. He agreed but then started typing on his laptop. He tapped me on the shoulder and pointed to a message in broken English on the screen: Engage Wells, Shanxi team maybe regret sometimes. Not engage Wells, Shanxi team maybe regret all life.

The first quarter ended with the Brave Dragons leading the Beijing

Ducks, 32–19. Beijing then made a run, but Bonzi found a teammate for a 3-pointer. It was going beautifully, until Bonzi grimaced and fell to the floor, clutching his ribs. Trainer Yuan hustled onto the court and helped Bonzi hobble off the court. He sprawled himself on the floor in front of the bench, literally at the feet of Boss Wang, who did not look down as Yuan massaged Bonzi's ribs. At halftime, the Brave Dragons led 46–39.

When the teams returned for the second half, Bonzi was healed. He scored on drives, buried midrange jumpers, and hit his 3s. With 2:32 remaining in the game, the Brave Dragons led 94–79, and the voice of Ren Hongbing echoed through the arena.

"Chi fan le ma?" the deejay asked the crowd. Have you eaten?

No!

"Nimen yao chi shenme?" he continued. What do you want to eat?

And the crowd yelled as one, *"Beijing Kao Ya!"*

Beijing Duck!

The final score was 98–83. At the postgame news conference, the room was filled with reporters, even a foreigner from Agence France-Presse who was writing a piece that would be distributed around the world. He asked Bonzi about his rib injury.

"I've been playing the game long enough to understand injuries are just part of the game, and you just play through them," he said. "I've got to be smart and understand my body."

He said he was also getting a better understanding of China.

"I've been here about a month, so I'm getting accustomed to it," he said. "It was a big culture shock at first, but I'm starting to understand my surroundings. Since I've been here, it's been all business. I haven't had any fun yet."

He smiled.

"I'm looking forward to some fun."

Fun was on the way. The Brave Dragons won their next game against Tianjin and improved to 13 wins against 11 losses. Bonzi also seemed to be making a small effort at a charm offensive. Weiss had prodded him to work on fan interaction. At practice, a father and son had approached him for a photograph and autograph. There was a moment of uncertainty as Bonzi looked at the father. Then he smiled and posed for the photograph. No autograph, though. Miracles don't happen overnight.

He also had granted his first interview for a cover story in the Chinese edition of *Sports Illustrated*. The magazine dispatched a young reporter who could speak English, a woman whose English name was Coco. Photographers arrived at the practice facility and blocked off half of the junior team court. A large gray backdrop was erected at the foul line, so that Bonzi could pose in different positions—holding a ball, standing on an unseen ladder so that he could imitate a dunk, extending his arm in a defensive pose. Coco spent forty-five minutes talking with him beside the court. Her article would lean toward the misunderstood genre.

The junior team was sitting on the sideline watching the photo shoot. But Coach Zhao was still running the fifteen-year-olds through some dribbling drills on the other half of the court. Each boy was dribbling two balls, between his legs, from the end line to the photo canvas, then back. The photographer had climbed onto a ladder to shoot downward as Bonzi posed in front of the gray canvas, but just then the canvas rippled and the shot was ruined. One of the fifteen-year-olds had fumbled the dribbling drill and the ball had crashed into the canvas.

CHAPTER THIRTEEN

YAO'S HOUSE

How America is organized economically follows a logic many Americans regard as universal. Power, wealth, and expertise aggregate in cities, which produce money and innovation from the efficiencies of having so many people concentrated in one place. Usually, the bigger the city, the more power it has, whether politically, economically, or culturally. When professional basketball began taking root in the 1950s, there were teams in cities like Fort Wayne, Indiana, and Syracuse, New York. But over time these teams moved to Detroit and Philadelphia and, eventually, every professional sports league basically reflected the economic hierarchy of the country. Like any other entertainment business, professional sports chased customers, whether as ticket buyers or television viewers, and the most customers were in cities with the most people. There were exceptions to the rule, and the hierarchy of cities was hardly static, given the periodic shifts in the economic landscape, but this was how the sports market worked.

No city in China was bigger than Shanghai, with its roughly 22 million people. When the Brave Dragons arrived in the middle of January for a game with the Shanghai Sharks, our airport bus glided along an elevated highway as if we were arriving at the mezzanine level of the city of the future. Apartment towers rose in every direction. For miles we drove toward the old city, passing thousands of buildings, until we were above the low, pitched roofs of the old colonial enclaves, the concession districts once carved out along the Huangpu River by the French, British, and other foreign powers. Rising from the other side of the river stood modern China's revenge: the jagged, futuristic skyline of the Pudong district, with the cantilevered Jin Mao Tower at eighty-eight stories and the shimmering blue sheath of the Shanghai World Financial Center at 101. Pudong had been a swamp when Deng Xiaoping visited during the 1980s and demanded that Shanghai develop faster. It had.

Bonzi Wells sat in the back row of the bus, staring silently out the window.

"You aren't in Taiyuan anymore, Bonzi," Weiss said, admiringly.

We were the hicks coming to the big city. We had coal dust on our shoes. Except logic was strangely reversed: We were the team with the big payroll. We had signed the expensive foreign players. We had the fat-cat boss with the fat-cat wallet. Strangely, Shanghai was one of the most cash-poor teams in the league. It could afford only one foreigner and had gotten him at a discount. The Sharks had the league's worst record and were mostly ignored by the Chinese press, other than an ugly postgame brawl earlier in the season in which the Sharks' captain, an Olympian named Liu Wei, led his teammates to attack Gabe Muoneke, the foreign star of the league's other doormat, the Yunnan Bulls. Suspended for 10 games and fined 50,000 yuan (about $7,700), Liu was not especially repentant, citing a Chinese aphorism to suggest that the league had taken action only because of his fame and because Muoneke was a foreigner.

"A big tree catches the wind," he said.

What made the pathetic state of the Sharks especially bewildering was that Shanghai was the greatest city in China, a financial powerhouse, sophisticated and cosmopolitan, dripping with disposable income. Kids played basketball across the city. The NBA was enormously popular, and Nike and Adidas regarded Shanghai as a marketing laboratory and as probably the greatest basketball market in Asia. Nike plastered billboards of Kobe Bryant outside the Grand Gateway Mall in the city's Xi Jia Hui district and along the swank shopping street of Huaihai Road. Adidas was running a campaign with Dwight Howard. Yet the Shanghai Sharks struggled to attract 1,000 fans for home games. There was even talk that the Sharks might simply cease to exist.

It didn't make sense, because Shanghai was Yao Ming's hometown, home to millions of basketball fans, and the Sharks were his former team. How could they be so bad on the court and so impoverished off it? The answer was that the people who ran the team couldn't care less about whether they won games or attracted fans. The people who ran the team were the city leaders of the Communist Party, who also ran Shanghai.

"This is where Yao Ming lived."

Yu Xiaomiao stood in Room 302 of a pink concrete dormitory of the Shanghai Sports Institute, one of the city's eight government athletic training centers. Around the corner from a decaying textile mill, the Sports Institute was in the city's Xuhui district, far from the moneyed glamour of Pudong and the French concession. Xuhui could have been any Chinese city, a knot of drab streets lined with yellowed concrete apartment blocks, a sameness born of the necessity of warehousing people, which was how most people lived in Shanghai, wedged into small spaces.

Yao's room was small, maybe fifteen feet by ten feet, and empty except for two metal desks and two chairs. The Sharks still lived in the dorm, along with other athletes using the training center, but Yao's room had been converted into a front office. It was an innocuous, charmless room that still evoked a wistful nostalgia from Yu Xiaomiao.

"Now that Yao Ming is gone," Yu said, "no one comes. It's because of our record." He paused, smiling in advance as he made a gentle joke. "Now we feel lonely."

Yu was in his sixties, with salt-and-pepper hair, dressed in khakis and a knit sweater, the preppy Westernized appearance favored by some Shanghainese. His father had managed the city's sports programs under the Nationalists, including the basketball gym on Tibet Road built decades ago by the YMCA. When the Communists took over in 1949, Yu's father kept the same job, under different bosses, and Yu became one of the city's top basketball players until he was sent to the countryside during the Cultural Revolution for reeducation with the peasants. When he returned, Yu taught physical education at a local university and became an official in the city's sports bureaucracy. He joined the Sharks in 1996 and served as "team leader" during Yao's era.

His nostalgia for Yao was hardly surprising. Before Yao, the Sharks were mediocre; with him, they became a league powerhouse. Twice, Yao led the Sharks to the finals against Bayi, losing each time, before finally beating them for the championship in 2002. Until then, Bayi had won every title since the founding of the league, and China's former president, Jiang Zemin, once the party secretary of Shanghai, had described Bayi as the flag of the People's Liberation Army.

"How could you pull down the flag?" Yu said, repeating the question that hung over the league in that era.

It took Yao Ming.

When he left for the Houston Rockets, the Sharks sank back into mediocrity, and then worse. Yao still visited his old dorm, his old team, whenever he returned to Shanghai. For his marriage, Yao invited his old teammates and coaches to a reception at one of the gilded banquet halls of the Portman Ritz-Carlton hotel. But without Yao on the court, the Sharks had little except his close friend, Liu Wei, the point guard. At one point, the league almost relegated the Sharks to a B-level league as penalty for poor performance. By this season, the Sharks were widely regarded as a joke.

"Yao Ming was like a very large piece of jade," Yu said. "We were selfish. We didn't want him to go. And his teammates wanted him to stay so we could win more championships. But all the officials wanted him to go abroad because it was an honor to Shanghai to send out this basketball talent. So now we are last."

We walked out of Yao's room and Yu locked the door. The hallway was narrow and dimly lit, and it was easy to imagine Yao Ming hunched over, trying not to bang his head against the low ceiling. The Sharks players lived on this floor, one below the coaches, sharing rooms, meals, and a curfew. In the most vibrant city in China, with a nightlife that pulsed early into the morning, the Sharks lived under guard, an existence little different from that of the Brave Dragons, except that temptation was closer.

"Their lives are boring," Yu said as we walked out of the dorm. "This is the early stage of China's basketball reforms. So we don't want to let them completely free yet. They would go to bars, to Internet cafés and would be drunk."

Professional basketball had come to Shanghai not because of the impulses of the marketplace, or to please the city's legions of basketball fans, or because companies like Nike considered the city a big pot of gold, but because the Communist Party bureaucrats who ran the city did not want to lose face. When the Chinese Basketball Association was created in 1995, Shanghai was not included, an omission noticed by a high-ranking city party chief named Gong Xueping. Shanghai would be embarrassed if it was not part of such a high-profile initiative, and Shanghai's party bureaucrats would be especially embarrassed. Even in those days, in the mid-1990s, when Shanghai was a symbol of a changing China, the impulse that mattered in the birth of the Shanghai Sharks was the incentive structure of Communist Party officialdom.

Like someone rummaging through the garage for spare parts, Gong set about conjuring a team from available government resources. First, he needed players, so he visited the city's sports bureau. Shanghai had the equivalent of a provincial team that competed in government tournaments, and Gong gave the sports bureau an ownership share in the Sharks in exchange for players, as well as room, board, and practice facilities. But the sports bureau team was not very good, so a handful of players were also recruited from a defunct army team in Nanjing and, for a foreign flourish, an Eastern European forward was lured out of the Russian league.

Next, the team needed publicity. Gong had headed the city's branch of the State Administration of Radio, Film, and Television, a job that gave him regulatory power, and influence, over the city's state-controlled media. He contacted Oriental Television, which would later become the government-owned Shanghai Media Group, or SMG, the second most powerful channel in China, after CCTV. Prodded by one of the city's most powerful officials, SMG also agreed to take a stake in the team and to televise games. Finally Gong cajoled the city's airport authority into taking the smallest stake, 10 percent, in exchange for providing free airfare to away games.

Gong had performed a bureaucratic miracle. He had massaged and manipulated a Communist Party bureaucracy with little interest in basketball into sponsoring a professional team organized around the pretense of operating like a commercial enterprise. The Shanghai Sharks made their debut in the second season of the CBA.

The Sharks seemingly had everything necessary to become one of the league's top teams in a city known for entrepreneurship and savvy management. Instead, the team was a disaster. Gong had not created a basketball team but had engineered a bureaucratic Frankenstein's monster.

The man placed in charge of the team as general manager was Gong's former classmate, an ex-television cameraman named Li Yaomin. Li had no experience in sports management but he did have the spirit of a promoter. In the early days, when the team struggled to attract fans, Li once drove out to People's Square and offered to take people by bus to the game. He had the team install tollbooths outside the arena where fans could toss in coins for a ticket. He was a natural showman, but despite his instructions to run the team as if it were a private enterprise, he soon discovered that the Sharks actually operated as a neglected appendage of the government.

Or, more precisely, it was an appendage of three government agencies enlisted more out of bureaucratic obligation than any desire to create a real commercially oriented sports team. When other teams began hiring foreign players at higher salaries, Li wanted to go after top talent. But he had to ask permission from both the sports bureau and the television station, neither of which had the interest, or understanding, to improve the team. When one of his top Chinese players became unhappy with his salary, Li wanted to give him a raise. Instead, he was traded. When Li tried to sell advertising to local companies, he was thwarted by the CBA's monopoly over marketing contracts.

The Sharks became an inadequately marketed team with mediocre talent trying to lure fans in a city with little patience for mediocrity. Basketball was popular in Shanghai but bad basketball was not. SMG began to show the games at irregular hours, Li said. At one point, Li said he sold only twelve tickets for a game, with only seven of those people showing up. "Actually, about 100 people were at the game but only those seven paid," he recalled. "We had given a free tour to some PLA soldiers to get more people for the game."

The hope was Yao Ming. When Yao was born in 1980, he weighed eleven pounds, twice the size of the average Chinese newborn, and the news was quickly relayed to sports administrators. His parents were former players from Shanghai's men's and women's teams who had been nudged toward marriage by coaches. The couple named their newborn boy Ming, which means bright, but one former Shanghai coach had thought the more appropriate name should have been Yao Panpan, or Long Awaited Yao. "We had been looking forward to the arrival of Yao Ming for three generations," one retired coach said.

Yet though Yao became the sports bureau's most precious asset, the family suffered for several years. Like so many people of her generation, Yao's mother, Fang Fengdi, had been one of the legion of Red Guards who heeded Mao's call for revolution by berating teachers, intellectuals, and some party officials. In Shanghai, Fang had led a public denunciation of a party official, Zhu Yong, who spent five years in a reeducation camp, enduring considerable hardship. After Mao's death, and the end of the Cultural Revolution, Zhu was politically "rehabilitated" and became a sports administrator, a position that enabled him to inflict a measure of revenge on Yao's mother. She had once been captain of China's national team, which normally would have assured her a good job in the sports system, but Zhu assigned her a menial position. The family barely subsisted, making it difficult to feed such a large boy.

The tension between Yao's family and the sports system never quite eased, but by age thirteen Yao joined the sports bureau's junior team. He was 6'5", awkward and painfully thin. He had disliked basketball until his mother took him to see the Harlem Globetrotters. It was the first time he had seen people having fun on the court. Yao's interest in the game grew as he grew. By seventeen, he was over seven feet tall and joined the Sharks.

"Yao Ming was a once-in-a-century talent," Yu Xiaomiao recalled. "The government officials paid lots of attention to him."

Yao became part of what was marketed as the Great Wall of China: Wang Zhizhi, the star of Bayi, at 7'1"; Mengke Bateer, then playing for the Beijing Ducks, at 7'1"; and Yao, the youngest and greenest at 7'5". Crowds started coming to Sharks games just to see the team's giant young center. By his third season, Yao led the Sharks to the finals against Bayi and established a personal rivalry with Wang Zhizhi. Ratings rose on television, and party bosses at SMG and the sports bureau were suddenly willing to invest more in the team. Players saw their salaries jump sharply; in Yao's final season, when the Sharks won 20 consecutive games, Li said players earned bonuses for every victory of about 3,500 yuan, or almost $500. Add it up and the bonuses totaled more than the salaries for most Chinese players.

By the beginning of the 2001 season, Yao appeared to be headed to the NBA. Wang Zhizhi had already signed with the Dallas Mavericks and Mengke Bateer would spend half a season with the Denver Nuggets. But Yao was considered the most valuable prize. By spring of 2001, after leading the Sharks to a second consecutive trip to the finals, Yao and his family wanted to apply for the NBA draft. But at a news conference in May, Li Yaomin announced that the Shanghai Sports Commission was not ready to let Yao leave. The team's director gave several reasons for the decision, including one that might have seemed minor to anyone unfamiliar with the Chinese system: Yao's obligation to represent Shanghai in an upcoming domestic tournament, the Ninth Chinese National Games.

"We all know that this year is the year of the Ninth National Games," the director said, "and Yao Ming was nurtured by Shanghai single-handedly, so of course Shanghai hopes that Yao Ming can contribute."

The Chinese National Games mattered to Chinese sports bureaucrats because their careers depended on them. For participants, the National Games were equivalent to national championships, but for sports bureaucrats, winning medals brought prestige, bigger budgets, more resources, and promotions. Whichever provincial sports bureau won the most medals was essentially doing its patriotic duty, which created a very different incentive structure for popular sports like basketball: the Shanghai Sports Commission wasn't especially motivated by ticket sales or marketing or creating an exciting environment for Sharks fans. Medals were the motivation.

It also meant the Chinese Basketball Association existed at the bidding of the National Games. Many CBA teams were still controlled by provincial sports bureaus, so the teams, minus their two foreign players, represented their provinces in the National Games. Even most private teams had an arrangement; the Guangdong Southern Tigers, for example, had a contract to represent Guangdong Province in the National Games. To accommodate the tournament, the CBA revised or abbreviated its schedule so that provincial teams could train. There was no question what mattered more.

For officials in Shanghai, losing Yao before the Ninth National Games in November would have meant losing any chance for a medal. He played the entire tournament, leading the Sharks to the finals against Bayi, which represented the army. Playing Bayi meant another confrontation with Wang Zhizhi, who was ordered to skip the NBA training camp of the Dallas Mavericks to play in the tournament. In the deciding game, Yao dominated but Bayi won by a single point. Shanghai's sports bureau got a silver medal.

Five months later, Yao led the Sharks to their CBA championship victory against Bayi, and team officials unexpectedly announced that he would be eligible for the NBA draft in June. Li Yaomin made all sorts of demands, angering the NBA and Yao's family, but Yao would make it out. Shanghai basked in the honor of his selection, as did the Sharks, but the team was already an orphan in the bureaucracy. "The government did not care about the team anymore," Li said. "We were in a weaker position with the government. If we wanted something, they said no. And the television station only gave us a fixed budget every year."

At the training center where the Sharks lived, the team's status sank immediately as money and resources were shifted to Ping-Pong and the volleyball teams, considered better medal contenders. Yet if sports officials were not willing to invest in the team, they were not willing to sell it, either. When Yao had played, the Sharks had had private suitors, some of whose interest was mostly in attaining the rights to the star center, yet even after Yao left, the Sharks were considered a very desirable property. The private owner of the Fujian team had expressed interest, as had foreigners, but the bureaucracy seemed paralyzed by the prospect of selling something considered a state asset: Who would represent the province in the National Games? What would happen to the jobs of the sports officials who ran the team? How much should they sell it for?

The Sharks instead went searching for money and found it in the pockets of one of China's richest men, Zhou Furen. A basketball nut worth more than $2 billion, Zhou had built a steel and fertilizer conglomerate in Liaoning Province and wanted to buy the team outright. Short of that, he agreed to sponsor the Sharks for 15 million yuan a year, or about $2.2 million. The deal gave him marketing rights but no ownership stake, an arrangement that eventually frustrated him. Zhou was among China's growing class of entrepreneurs—he was an acquaintance of Boss Wang's—and he bristled at the resistance put forward by Shanghai's sports bureau. He wanted to fire a coach, but the sports bureau refused. He had ideas about developing players, but the sports bureau would not listen. He was paying for a team that he could not control and could not market.

"The development of the CBA is similar to the development of the economy here," Zhou told me. "We need a better system. Now we have a market-oriented economy, which means we need to have a commercial league."

By the time the Brave Dragons arrived for the game in Shanghai, Zhou had decided to quietly abandon his sponsorship at the end of the season. On the afternoon I visited Shanghai's training center, Yu Xiaomiao knew the team would soon face a crisis. He thought Chinese basketball needed to truly embrace the market and that the NBA's popularity made it inevitable that the Americans would play a bigger role. The CBA had to be severed from the National Games, so that the league could truly become commercial. He saw the Sharks at the precipice of extinction, which he considered a potentially good thing.

"I am optimistic," he told me as we walked through a training center that embodied the old system. "I believe there will be a turning point and the team will enter the market. In China, there is a popular phrase: Put someone in a dark alley and then you can learn to survive. So either we die or survive."

One lesson of Shanghai was simple. If you lose the country's greatest player, your team is going to get worse. Another was that China's old basketball system was failing, even as it remained too entrenched to be discarded. But Shanghai also was a reminder of the perils of assuming that what is logical in one country is also logical in another. In Shanghai, the greatest commercial basketball market in Asia, the only fans who mattered were the bureaucrats of the Communist Party.

The Sharks played in a small gym at the edge of the French concession. It had fewer than 4,000 seats, and maybe half were sold for the game against the Brave Dragons. By comparison, the stadium in Taiyuan seemed like Madison Square Garden. I sat in the mezzanine with my friend David; we had been deputized as team videographers because Weiss couldn't find anyone else. A few fans dressed in Sharks jerseys waved banners from the seats above the baskets as the Shanghai cheerleaders danced to music from the hit American movie *High School Musical*. David was a former basketball player who still followed the game and had lived in Shanghai for more than three years, yet the thought of attending a Sharks game had never occurred to him. This was his first CBA game.

The ref tossed up the opening tip and any drama soon disappeared. The Brave Dragons led 31–19 at the end of the first quarter. David was appalled at what he was seeing. "They are really not very good, are they?" he asked me. I put my finger to my lips. We were taping the action and the audio was on; it was probably best for team morale to keep the commentary to a minimum.

Many of the fans were cheering for the great Bonzi Wells. "Bonzi— Yao Miss You" read one placard in English. Other fans wore Rockets jerseys and started chanting "Bonzi Go Home! Bonzi Go Home!" By the fourth quarter, the fans chanted "All-Star, All-Star!" Bonzi was playing his most controlled game and finished with a modest 22 points and a load of rebounds and assists. The final score was 105–92.

The highlight of the game was the postgame press conference. Television crews crowded into the basement of the stadium, eager for footage of Bonzi. But when Weiss arrived, he brought Wei Mingliang, who had finished with 16 points. The Chinese reporters immediately complained, but Weiss explained that Bonzi was getting "treatment" from the team trainer.

The most telling comment came when a Sharks team official introduced Weiss to the reporters and praised the Brave Dragons. "Thanks to the Shanxi team for importing a very famous player," the official said. "It helped us sell tickets."

CHAPTER FOURTEEN

CORNER POCKETS

On the court, the home team was enduring an old-fashioned whipping so convincing and absolute that not even the Wave could resuscitate the Taiyuan fans. The game had been advertised as a marquee matchup, if also a morality play: Bonzi Wells and the Brave Dragons versus Michael Harris and the Dongguan New Century Leopards, a contest between the two former Houston Rockets now laying waste to the Chinese league, between the Good American (Harris) and the Bad (Wells). Good won easily. The final score was 127–112. Harris finished with 43 points and scored so effortlessly that at times he was laughing on the court.

All the buoyancy after the easy win against the Shanghai Sharks was now punctured. Only a week had passed but the season was collapsing, the elements of the Bonzi experiment now proving unstable. Losing badly to Dongguan followed achingly close losses against two league power-houses, Jiangsu and Guangdong, and meant the Brave Dragons now had 14 wins and 14 losses. Losing three straight games against three of the league's best teams was not altogether unexpected, but Bonzi's arrival had altered expectations, none more than those of Boss Wang, even if the same problems of chemistry and blending the players together had not been solved.

What made the situation more excruciating was that sometimes Bonzi *could* almost beat teams by himself. He dominated the Jiangsu Dragons, which had one of the league's best point guards and best foreign players. Had the refs called an obvious foul in the final seconds when Bonzi was hacked while driving for the winning basket, the Brave Dragons might have won. Against Guangdong, Bonzi scored 17 points in the first quarter and kept the Brave Dragons ahead until the final minutes, when, exhausted, he began turning the ball over and his shots stopped falling. His body literally ran out of fuel; his entire intake of food and drink on game day had been one can of Red Bull.

"One-man basketball defeated by team basketball," triumphantly declared Xinhua, the government's official news agency, after Guangdong's win.

The loss to Dongguan could not be so easily rationalized. Michael Harris was not particularly well known in the United States. He had played at Rice University, a school known for academics more than sports, and in the pros had played only briefly with the Rockets. Yet he was a talented, disciplined player, never forcing his shots and blending nicely with his Chinese teammates, among them one of the country's most promising young point guards and a 7'1" forward, Zhang Kai. Bonzi played like a man who hadn't eaten in two weeks. Harris played like Michael Jordan. Which might help explain, at least indirectly, the punch.

It came during the second quarter, with the Leopards leading by 11 points. From press row, I only saw the burst of commotion that came an instant after the punch. Players on the Brave Dragons bench seemed stunned. From a distance, it appeared that Weiss had placed himself in front of Boss Wang, who was stomping his foot and barking at the team, his head shaking like a yapping dog. Fans behind the bench had jumped up, shouting and pointing at him.

Boss Wang had hit a player, Kobe.

That Zhang Xuewen was the most *American* Chinese player on the team went beyond his nickname. He played the way Americans played, or at least he could move the way Americans moved. Kobe was almost the only Chinese player to dunk in a game. At times, he was the only Chinese player to consistently dunk during *warm-ups*. Against Beijing, he had made a reverse dunk so breathtaking that even he seemed stunned. It wasn't simply that he had made it, but that he had even *attempted* it, that the machismo that boiled inside the best dunkers, the best players, also boiled inside him. He still played as if his mind could not keep pace with his body, yet what separated him from most of his Chinese teammates were the flashes of potential, which is what made him a rare point of agreement between Bonzi and Boss Wang. They both saw something in him.

Where they differed was how to get at it. The punch was part of Boss

Wang's method. It was an act of discipline, like paddling a disobedient child. Never mind that it happened during a nationally televised game in what is supposed to be a professional basketball league. Kobe had grown up in Taiyuan, the son of a volleyball player, and his interest in basketball blossomed when as a ninth grader his team won a championship. What he remembered from that championship was one play, his dunk in the finals, and that dunk changed the way he regarded the game and himself. When the Brave Dragons recruited Kobe, his father wanted him to stay in school and go to college, but Kobe was more interested in basketball than studying and joined the junior team. He was sixteen, and virtually a ward of Boss Wang.

Now he was twenty-two and having his breakout season. He started most games and played without fear on defense. It was offense that presented the challenge, where he sometimes seemed to play out of control, hurtling toward the basket like some misfired missile. Weiss would stare dumbfounded. Yet this was what Boss Wang wanted. If Weiss was no longer a figurehead coach, neither had he managed to completely curb the owner. Boss Wang remained on the bench, occasionally making substitutions. At the practice facility, Boss Wang met privately with the Chinese players to lecture them on how he wanted them to play, or what he had seen on television. "He changes his mind all the time," said one player. "He watches the NBA in the morning and he changes his mind in the afternoon. We learn from the Lakers one day and San Antonio the next."

He wanted Kobe to attack the basket: attack, attack, attack. He chided players for cowardice, for being intimidated by Bonzi, especially the guards, who seemed too afraid to take charge of the team. For a while, Boss Wang ordered the point guards to prevent Bonzi from bringing the ball up the court since doing so wasn't his job. In one game, an obedient backup point guard literally tried to wrestle the ball from Bonzi, who angrily swatted him away, bewildered again by the strange way the Chinese played basketball.

Against Dongguan, Kobe slashed to the basket whenever he had a chance to score until his defender finally eased off and conceded the 3-point shot. When Kobe got the ball, suddenly finding himself wide open, he took the shot. He missed. What happened next I only reconstructed later, after talking to players and coaches. Boss Wang called a timeout, or he ordered Weiss to call one. As the players walked off the court toward the bench, Boss Wang confronted Kobe, screaming and swinging at him.

"What are you doing? What the fuck are you doing?" the owner shouted. "I told you not to shoot the three."

At which point something unexpected happened: Kobe shouted back, "I only shot one."

There were actually two punches, possibly a third, landing squarely on Kobe's back and shoulder. Weiss quickly intervened, sliding between owner and player, and Kobe seemed at the edge of tears, if more from shame than pain.

At halftime, Boss Wang barked at Kobe in the locker room. "If you don't want to listen to me, go home," he shouted. "Everybody can go home."

By now even the foreigners understood that listening to Boss Wang rant was an occupational hazard of playing for the Brave Dragons. The Chinese players accepted it and even were willing to argue that the lectures were meant to be constructive. "We understand that he has good intentions and he does it out of love for us," one player told me. "But it's still like your mother nagging you every day." The foreigners felt doubly penalized; they listened to him screech in Chinese, not understanding a word, and then listened to Garrison's edited interpretation. Donta Smith had tried to let the words bounce off him. Weiss stared at the clock. But Bonzi was not willing to play along. At postgame meetings, he wore his headphones and bobbed to music as the boss screamed. During one half-time meeting, Bonzi stormed into the locker room and shouted at Garrison to relay a message to Boss Wang: "Tell that motherfucker he's got to get his ass in the stands."

Garrison hesitated and slowly began translating. Boss Wang listened, nodded, and the team returned to the court. Afterward, Weiss asked Garrison about his translations. "I told him that Bonzi thought we needed to play better defense," Garrison said.

Now, though, Bonzi stood up and confronted the owner in front of the team. "You cannot do that shit in the game," he said. "All the fans saw you hit Kobe."

"I paid you to come here," Boss Wang answered, "and I wanted you to help us to win games. But you are not the boss. I am. I pay for everything."

This time Garrison said nothing. Bonzi stomped out of the locker room.

The Chinese players watched in amazement. Most of them hated Bonzi, even as his talent awed them. He demeaned them by how little he respected them on the court. Playing with him did not make them better; it made them realize how powerless they were. Yet they also saw that Bonzi, unlike anyone else, was not afraid of the owner. If anything, it was the other way around.

Halftime ended and as the players returned to the court, Boss Wang and Bonzi approached one another in the hallway, angrily, and Bonzi hurled a half-filled bottle of water toward the owner. The bottle landed harmlessly, but the Chinese players watched in astonished silence.

"The owner was afraid of Bonzi," Little Sun told me later in his simple English. "Everybody think: Who dared to fight with the owner? Who dared to throw a bottle at the owner? Only Bonzi. Bonzi, he is a *man*."

Usually, when the general manager, Zhang Beihai, came to the World Trade after a loss, his job was to soothe the foreign egos rankled by another outburst by Boss Wang. But sometimes he came to deliver a message, and the morning after the punch he was carrying a message for Weiss. First, he opened with praise. Weiss had done a fine job. Could he return next year? Could he work with the Chinese players if they toured America this summer?

Weiss thanked the general manager and said the summer sounded like a good idea.

"But let's wait and see on next year," Weiss said.

In a few hours the team was departing for the airport, so now Zhang Beihai got to his real business. Bonzi throwing the plastic bottle was a physical challenge and, as the owner saw it, a physical attack. More than that, it was mutiny. The owner's authority had been challenged in front of the other players, and now Boss Wang worried that discipline would unravel. The general manager now agreed that bringing in Bonzi had been a mistake, yet losing him would cripple the team. The team was returning to Liaoning Province to play the Pan Pan Dinosaurs and then the league would take a ten-day break to celebrate the Lunar New Year, China's most important national holiday. Typically, this was when struggling teams cut highly paid foreigners or when foreign players, frustrated with China, went home to visit family and never came back. Bonzi had already bought his ticket to Muncie.

Was there anyone else Weiss could bring over, another faded NBA star, in case Bonzi did not return, or if the team decided it did not want him back—Gary Payton, Steve Francis, Dikembe Mutombo? Weiss respected Zhang Beihai, but this was like humoring a child who thought that simply by asking, a former NBA All-Star would show up in Taiyuan for the holidays.

"It would be more of the same," Weiss answered.

The general manager returned to the question of discipline. The owner thought the players needed a firmer hand and he wanted Liu Tie to resume coaching in practice and during the games.

Weiss had been rehired and fired during the same cup of coffee.

"Well, you'll lose both of them," Weiss answered. "Olumide and Bonzi. I'll do what you want. But I'm telling you what I think."

The day before, Olumide had threatened to boycott the game against Dongguan. He was frustrated by the owner's postgame shouting and by the way his role had diminished since Bonzi had arrived, and the front office had responded by dispatching Garrison to Little Nigeria as an envoy. The big man listened as Garrison pleaded. He relayed sympathetic Internet chatter from fans who thought Olumide should get the ball more. He talked about how Olumide could get endorsement deals if he stuck around. He even brought an offer from the general manager: the team would fly the entire Nigerian delegation to the resort city of Sanya on the Chinese island of Hainan for Lunar New Year. Olumide was unimpressed until Garrison finally stood up from the brown sofa to leave.

"You believe in God," he had declared. "Ask him."

The thought of God Almighty interjecting Himself into the player personnel decisions of the Brave Dragons seemed to please Olumide. Garrison was an atheist, but he picked up the Bible on the coffee table and started looking for a passage he had once read, something about faith and love, and Olumide disappeared into a rear bedroom. He returned with another Bible in one hand and tiny Ana in another.

"First Corinthians," he answered, finding the passage. "First. 13.13. 'And now these three things remain: faith, hope [pronounced *ohpe*] and love. But the greatest is love.'"

He then handed the Bible to Garrison.

"Okay, so what about the tickets?" Garrison asked.

God had given Garrison his opening. If Olumide agreed, Garrison would also go to Sanya, along with his new girlfriend.

"To Sanya?" he asked, pleading.

For a moment, tiny daughter in hand, the Warrior was silent. And then slowly a big, regal smile filled his face.

"Tell them that it must be a seven-star resort, on the beach," he said.

"Seven-star?" Garrison asked. "Are there seven-star hotels?"

"And tell them I want a flying boat," Olumide added without explanation, as if one were possible.

Weiss's coffee with Zhang Beihai had ended amicably. Weiss defended his tenure, arguing that the team had done well, considering Joy's injury, the transition to Bonzi, and the toughness of the schedule. But he actually felt some relief. He genuinely liked Zhang Beihai and offered what he called a piece of "personal advice": If another opportunity arose in Chinese basketball, Zhang Beihai might be well served to take it. The general manager laughed.

"This is my chance," he answered, "and I know that chance brings obligations."

Later, when the team gathered at the airport, Weiss approached Liu Tie and presented the Chinese coach with the black marker he used for diagramming plays. He started laughing, and Liu Tie laughed, too, and rolled his eyes.

At the hotel in Bayuquan, Weiss broke the news to Bonzi and Olumide. Bonzi did not deliberate for long. He had dislocated his pinky against Dongguan. Suddenly, the pinky was bothering him.

"Tell them I can't play," he said. "I need two weeks to recover."

Weiss relayed the news and then went to sleep in the team hotel. The next morning Wingtips told him that the team had reconsidered. This was a bad time for a change, right before such an important game.

"Bad news," Weiss told me when I arrived a few hours before the game. "I'm back in."

The Pan Pan Dinosaurs and the Brave Dragons had developed something close to mutual hatred. The season opener had been a stunning upset. The Dinosaurs regarded themselves as an elite team and had never imagined losing to a team like Taiyuan, much less losing by more than 20 points. When the Dinosaurs came to Taiyuan for a rematch, the Brave Dragons had won again, and one of the Dinosaurs' star guards, Yang Ming, had been carried off the court on a stretcher. Now the two teams were battling for a playoff spot.

I returned to the same bleachers reserved for the press during the season opener. Now every spot was taken by a reporter, and nearly every reporter was a young, pretty girl, fresh out of college, working for a different website eager for updates on Bonzi. I squeezed myself into a spot beside a young, cheery woman who worked for a local newspaper. She introduced herself by her English name, Pooh. I noticed the screen saver on her laptop was a large photograph of Winnie the Pooh.

Nearly all the female reporters knew Garrison, or wanted to know him, because he was considered the best path to Bonzi. Garrison had been complaining to Zhang Beihai that it made no sense for him to live with the Chinese players since his job was to translate for the foreigners. He was spending hours every day driving back and forth. Zhang Beihai had ignored him until Bonzi began complaining that without an on-site interpreter, he was a hostage in his apartment. The general manager had then relented and ordered Garrison to find a room somewhere downtown for $25 a month. No apartment or room was even remotely possible at that rate, so Bonzi agreed to let Garrison live in the spare bedroom of his apartment, under certain rules: No guests. Knock before entering.

Garrison had celebrated by starting a blog, www.wohebangqiweiersi .com, which translated as www.MeandBonzi.com. He did not mention the blog to Bonzi or to the team's management, but he had used his first entry a few days earlier to position himself as the best source of inside Bonzi news: "Garrison 'charges' into Wells' camp," read the headline.

Starting today I want to record stories about Bonzi in China, stories about him and me, and the many interesting things that happened on the team. That's the way I am. Salute to Chairman Mao, to pragmatism and realism!!

I am going to move into Bonzi Wells' camp. Many stories are still waiting for me to dig them up, who knows, you are never gonna know . . .

Bonzi opened the game with an airball. The Liaoning crowd hooted but Bonzi soon took control, hitting a 3, making a steal for a dunk, and scoring 16 points in the opening quarter. But Yang Ming was having his revenge from the stretcher game and scored easily against the Brave Dragons' guards. With every shot, Pooh jumped off her seat to cheer.

"*Jia you! Jia you!*" she shouted, the Chinese cheer that translates literally as "Add oil! Add oil!" but that effectively means, "Go team!"

The first half ended with the Brave Dragons leading 48–46. Kobe, who had started the game, had regressed; at one point he dribbled down the court for an apparent layup, only to reverse and dribble back out to the wing, where he made a crosscourt pass that landed in the seats. Weiss removed him a few minutes later, and Boss Wang pulled him down for a few words on the bench before letting him go. There were no punches.

The second half started with more baskets by Yang Ming. Pooh clapped and screamed beside me. Then it happened: Kobe took the ball on the wing, slashed to the basket, and rose, twisting through the air for a reverse dunk over two defenders. It was stunning. Entire games pass without a Chinese player dunking, and Kobe had performed an NBA-quality jam in traffic. He seemed stunned and then exhilarated, pulling out his jersey in pride as he trotted down the court. The Shanxi bench had erupted, and Boss Wang punched the air. Bonzi stood on the court and conferred his ultimate gesture of respect: a look of surprise and genuine admiration.

Pooh, on the other hand, was not happy.

She was even more disappointed when the game ended, the Brave Dragons on top, 86–83. Boss Wang was beaming. Bonzi triumphantly tossed his headband into the crowd. The next day, the Chinese players would get their first break from basketball in eleven months. They would have four days off.

Weiss and I walked to a local pool hall to celebrate. It was a dingy shop at the end of a row of dingy shops near the arena, and the owner sent out a runner to buy us beer. Garrison arrived with Bonzi and the two foreign players for the Dinosaurs, and soon a tournament was under way. The stakes were one pink Mao 100-yuan note per game. Each bill was stamped with the face of Mao.

Pool is played most everywhere in China, usually outdoors. Tables are placed on sidewalks or in alleyways. It is not uncommon to see scores of tables outside beneath a makeshift tent or awning to protect against the midday sun. Like basketball, the rules are the same as in the United States, and so is the size of the table, but the differences lie in the subtleties.

Weiss had already spent a few hours deciphering the table. He discovered the pool hall earlier in the day, during a walk around Bayuquan, and had played with some of the locals. No one could communicate, other than to point, but Weiss was tickled, playing pool in a shithole town in eastern China. His frustration with the dysfunction of the team was matched by how much he enjoyed China. In Taiyuan, he had a regular Ping-Pong circle, including a local television reporter, a young woman barely five feet tall, one of the best players he had ever faced. He loved it.

Bonzi, on the other hand, had not yet played on a Chinese table. He drew me as an opponent. He began by running in several balls on short, direct shots. He hit them hard, crashing into the back of the pocket, and then taunted me with some trash talk. But then he began to falter. The balls bobbled off the sides of the pockets. He kept missing shots, and I slowly caught up. "That would go in in America," he said after another shot tickled out of a pocket. He began to complain. The sticks were too short, too light. The tables weren't right. The sides of the corner pockets were curved.

I sank the eight ball to win the game and placed Bonzi's pink money in my pocket.

He increased the stakes to 200 yuan. I agreed and broke. He kept trying to hit the ball hard, growing more frustrated, and he kept missing. I won easily, and he crumpled up two 100-yuan notes and tossed them into my hand.

Last game. Finally, Bonzi adjusted. He slowed down. He hit balls softly. He worked the corner pockets carefully, compensating for the curve. He was still talking trash. No force on the planet seemed capable of changing that. But now he was playing a different game. He won, and I returned his 200 yuan.

In China, even if the table seems the same, you've got to learn to adjust.

The Brave Dragons were as happy as I'd ever seen them. The team was 15 and 14, in a four-way tie for seventh place, and the bus was ripping down the highway toward the Dalian airport and four days of freedom. The landscape was still brown and lifeless, still months from springtime, and a dusting of snow swirled over the rooftop as we roared south. Two players were arranging tickets on their cell phones. Another sat toward the back, dead asleep, mouth agape. Up front, Weiss sat near Liu Tie and Wingtips. Last night, after the win, Wingtips had called Weiss and Garrison over to his table during the postgame meal.

"Your burden will continue," he had said in his graveled voice, smiling.

We drove into Dalian, where the driver made a detour. The guard Duan Jiangpeng was hopping a train home. A few websites had begun listing Duan's name as one of the young Chinese players who might one day be capable of playing in the NBA. It was the sort of speculation that periodically arose when a young player began showing promise, and Duan had improved more than anyone else on the team. The driver punched a button and the teenage star stepped onto the street with his duffel bag, searching for a taxi in the light snow to carry him to the train station.

Together almost fifty weeks of the year, the rest of the team dispersed at the Dalian airport before Boss Wang could change his mind. Wingtips was flying to Shanghai. Big Sun was going to Shandong Province. Yu, Kobe, and Big Calves Tian were headed to Beijing before returning to Taiyuan. Wei was taking a train from Beijing to join his parents in Baoding. Everyone was going home to see family. Across China, one billion people were on the move: tens of millions of migrant workers who left the countryside for work in factories; tens of millions who left their families for work on construction sites; young girls, still teenagers, who left home to wait tables in restaurants or, failing to find anything better, took work in beauty salons that were actually brothels. Lunar New Year was when an ancient nation reverted to its original shape. Everyone went home.

I flew to Beijing with the foreigners. In the Beijing airport, Weiss caught a flight back to Taiyuan. He and Tracy were joining the Nigerians for the beach trip to Sanya. Finally, there was Bonzi. At the luggage carousel in Beijing, he assumed his usual position, sitting alone, staring into his iPhone. Garrison went to collect Bonzi's baggage but would not be escorting him any farther; he needed to catch a flight to Taiyuan and then pack for Sanya. So I assumed the role of Bonzi's body man. We were talking at the luggage carousel, waiting for Garrison to return with the luggage, when a chubby man in a suit and tie approached us. He wore the red sash of an airport employee. He stood about two feet from Bonzi, staring and smiling—no, beaming.

"*Bangqi Weiersi*," he said.

I nodded. Yes, it was the great Bonzi Wells.

Bonzi was annoyed, if trying not to be. The man kept grinning and staring. I mentioned to Bonzi that personal space was defined differently in China. He seemed to have realized that and the chubby man finally walked away. "When I first got here, I had no idea what was going on," he said. "People were crowding me and grabbing at me and pushing." He motioned with his forearm. "So I was pushing back."

A minute later, the chubby airline employee returned. He informed me that he spoke English. Then we spoke in Chinese. He pointed his mobile phone at Bonzi from a distance of about four feet and began snapping photos, one after another.

"Doesn't he know that is rude?" Bonzi asked, increasingly annoyed.

I mentioned in Chinese to our friend that in the United States it was considered impolite to stand directly in front of someone snapping scores of photographs without his or her permission. He nodded and kept snapping. I pointed to his sash and asked what service he provided for the airport. "Luggage collection," he said. "Luggage collection."

We escaped by pushing Bonzi's luggage cart outside the security perimeter. My job as body man was to escort Bonzi to the international concourse, Terminal 3. We searched for a shuttle to take us there, but an agent from Starz Sports was unexpectedly waiting for Bonzi, a man who introduced himself in English as Michael. He was joined by Coco, the *Sports Illustrated* reporter who had profiled Bonzi. Bonzi was startled that they were here, and I imagined a vast unseen machine of sports agentry trying to anticipate the needs of a volcanic basketball star.

On the shuttle, Bonzi and I took seats on the back row. Coco had brought some posters of *Sports Illustrated*, which was hitting the stands later that week. Bonzi was the cover boy, and Coco made a point of saying she had personally arranged to make the posters and bring them to Bonzi as a gift before he returned to Muncie. Bonzi didn't grasp what she said, and Coco seemed hurt, so I translated from English to English and he got the message: She had done him a favor. Bonzi smiled and sprinkled Coco with some charm as the shuttle rumbled toward Terminal 3.

Terminal 3 was a showpiece built for the Olympics, the largest, most architecturally stunning airport terminal in the world. Now it was mostly empty. Bonzi was flying to Chicago, and we approached the United counter, where the most famous basketball player in China presented his passport. United had no ticket under his name. The Brave Dragons front office was supposed to make the arrangement, but the clerk said no ticket was registered under the name Wells. To his credit, Bonzi was calm. But his support team—us—swung into action. I called Garrison and told him that we needed to contact the team accountant, but Garrison was stepping onto his flight and could not make the call. That is when Michael of Starz Sports silently took over. If Mark Zhang was friendly and talkative, Michael was a silent hit man. He had already gotten the team on the phone and was haggling with the counter clerk. Bonzi liked him.

As we waited, Bonzi sat on the luggage scales. He hadn't yet seen Coco's article, but she offered her thesis: He was misunderstood, and his angry expressions and animated gestures toward officials and coaches were just his emotions boiling over. Coco interpreted these outbursts as a cultural difference; Americans were more direct, while Chinese were less confrontational and more acculturated to smile and never be so direct. Yet then her English brought a bluntness she probably did not intend.

"Everyone says you are a monster," she said. "But I do not think so."

"Monster," said Bonzi. He repeated it softly, shaking his head.

The moment dissolved. Bonzi's ticket was still unaccounted for. He said he would have to buy his own ticket and that now he was not coming back to China. He was joking. "There's my story," Coco said, smiling. "Bonzi Wells says he is not coming back." Then I wondered if hers was merely a courtesy call to deliver the posters. Why are you taking such a large bag? Coco asked Bonzi. She was suspicious. Bonzi said he left three more back in Taiyuan. He had brought a lot of suits and ties because he usually dressed up in the NBA but now he realized that players wore nothing but sweats in China. So he was taking things back.

Finally, Michael cleared the ticket. The team had misspelled Bonzi's last name using "i" instead of "l." Bonzi Weiis. My job was done. Bonzi gave me a shoulder bump. He said he would see me when he got back. This time he would be bringing a camera because he wanted to get pictures of all the crazy shit he'd been seeing in China.

The great Bonzi Wells walked toward security, having checked his very large bag. Coco left with Michael, and I walked out of Terminal 3. I also had plans for Lunar New Year. I was spending it in Taiyuan with Ren Hongbing, the team deejay, and his family. I wondered if we'd be celebrating with the Wave.

CHAPTER FIFTEEN

RED SOLDIER

This must have been what war sounded like. Taiyuan was vibrating. It did not seem unreasonable to wonder if each of the city's three million residents had been issued a drum and ordered to stand outside and beat it. What had actually happened was that many of those people were lighting firecrackers or bottle rockets or cherry bombs or whatever else. Dull booms punctuated the steady percussion of the fireworks. Then, an instant after each boom, a splash of color crackled in the sky. Sidewalk vendors stood hidden behind gaudy towers of boxed fireworks. Grown men were lighting roll after roll of firecrackers, never mind that the launch sites were downtown streets, or that they were grown men. The acrid smell of gunpowder hung over the city. A giddy anarchy had taken hold. The Year of the Rat was ending. The Year of the Ox was soon to begin.

This was my sixth year in China. I'd lived here long enough to know there was only so much I would ever know. Most foreigners who chose to live in China succumbed to an obsession about the place. China appealed to the maven, the polymath, the autodidact because of how insistently it withheld itself, charging outsiders a price of admission for every step deeper inside, forcing them to prove their worthiness through mastery of successively more complicated levels of language, custom, and culture. Mastery was so hard earned that those who managed to bore deeper inside the hard stone of the culture often became gatekeepers, too. Any dinner party of seasoned expatriates in Beijing was sprinkled with little demonstrations of expertise, of Chinese phrases carefully dropped into conversation, of knowing discussions of this political figure or that, of chuckling recitations of this adventure or that one in distant places whose names elicited knowing nods. China hands cannot resist keeping score. But the obsession was genuine because answering one question inevitably led to another and another, which inevitably boiled down to the most essential ones: How were we similar? How were we not?

I'd always wondered about the moments in Chinese life where Chinese take joy in *being Chinese*. Society was bound by love of family and food, but China was consumed by a churning relentlessness, a pressure cooker wrought by the national mandate of restoring Chinese greatness. Ask an Indian intellectual in New Delhi why the capital's libraries are mediocre or their infrastructure was poorly built and he might shrug and say, "We Indians are not especially good at that." The Chinese, or at least their leaders, could not accept such a lack of ambition or national will; for China to reclaim its place in the world, China must be great at every endeavor. Yet the price was that daily life was a grinding stone. Everyone worked hard, often separated from family, as rebuilding and rebranding Chinese greatness was a round-the-clock enterprise. Drive past a construction site at 3 a.m. Men were working. Drive past a textile factory at 4 a.m. Women were working. Work, work, work, work. When was the payoff?

I came to believe Chinese New Year was the best representation of that single moment when people could exhale, the purest representation of the Chinese soul. Migrant workers put down their hammers or walked away from their sewing machines and went back to the countryside, like some of the Brave Dragons players. Gifts were bought. Houses were cleaned to sweep away bad luck. Firecrackers were lit as symbolic reminders of the mythical beast called Nian, who centuries ago had feasted on livestock and crops until farmers realized he was frightened by the color red and the cracking noise of fireworks. Those running the race to the future paused to remember the past. I once spent the eve of Chinese New Year at a farmhouse in a mountain village a few hours outside Beijing. My family rented rooms from a local farmer as a getaway from the city. It was not a typical second-home arrangement; we paid $40 a month for four unheated rooms lacking a bathroom. My landlord grew corn and held a second job as a carpenter making coffins. When you shook his hand, you noticed he was missing parts of a few fingers. On the big night, he and I drank many celebratory shots of *baijiu*, so many that I was happily asleep when my wife, Theo, began shaking me at midnight. Get up! You are missing it! she said. I staggered out to see our tiny village in rare ecstasy.

Fireworks exploded out of the drab dirt courtyards of every farmhouse. Snowflakes of color burst over the silent mountains, and I could hear laughing and shouting echoing through our narrow valley. This was happening in every village in China. This was the moment.

To reach Taiyuan, I had left Beijing in the morning and also left behind the notion of municipal restraint. Beijing was hardly a pyrotechnical slouch, but it did restrict where and when people could buy and blast their arsenals as an ancient city's precaution against fire. Taiyuan was an ancient city with no such policy. From my room on the twenty-eighth floor of the World Trade, I watched men bend over and touch the sidewalk, fiddling with matches before quickly stepping back and craning upward as another bottle rocket shot off the ground, spiraling, spiraling, spiraling up to a wobbly summit where it exploded in a puff of smoke. Puffs of smoke floated in every direction. Because all the factories and mines were closed for the holiday, the air was unusually clear of pollution, revealing the skyline of a city curled inside a ring of mountains: the yellow glass tower of the Howell & Johnson rising a few blocks from People's Square; the jagged steel tips of the new downtown skyscrapers; the high-rise apartments peering over the park of stunted, brown trees along the frozen Fen River; and the grids of old, flat-roofed socialist-era apartment buildings, square and depressing, conveying the institutional gloom of a prison.

Ren Hongbing collected me at 10:30 p.m. Midnight marked the New Year, the moment when the full arsenal was unleashed, and we would celebrate with his extended family. He was tickled that I was joining them as an honored foreign guest on this most auspicious evening. He greeted me as *Yangge*, or Older Brother Yang, the honorific bestowed on me by the Chinese players. We squeezed into his small car and moved through the city until we arrived at a housing block of government apartments. Every apartment had a small balcony, from which people were lighting long strands of firecrackers that crackled like machine guns: Pow! Pow! Pow! Pow! Pow! Pow! In the narrow dirt alleys between the apartment buildings, fathers were firing Roman candles as children bent so close to the flame that their faces glowed in the yellow light. I could feel a light sprinkle of ash falling from the sky.

Ren Hongbing was laughing as we ducked into a dingy stairwell and climbed up to his family's apartment.

We had first met before the season. I had seen him in the front office and had assumed he was one of Zhang Beihai's minions. These were the handful of guys who unlocked the gym, renewed visas, ordered food, dealt with sponsors, booked travel, and managed the books. When Boss Wang was around, they organized his pickup games, playing if needed, and generally cowered in his presence. Individually, they had different jobs, but collectively they served, along with the general manager, as an institutional buffer between Boss Wang and everybody else. Inevitably, this meant they had to clean up his messes. When paychecks were late, as was more common than not, the accountant bore the complaints and threats and whining of the players. The money is coming, the accountant would promise, never mentioning that he hadn't been paid, either. There was an assistant general manager who carried around a lot of keys and sometimes drove the van for the foreigners. There was a media man, the two farm women who swept the floors and cleaned the toilets, and the old man with the angry scowl who locked and unlocked the front gate and apparently represented security.

So when the season began, I was surprised to see Ren Hongbing behind his soundboard at the corner of the court. I was flabbergasted after first experiencing his show. It was consciousness-altering. Typically, the role of music during a basketball game was similar to the role of music during a movie, which was to manipulate the emotions of the audience at critical moments. In movies, music conditioned and prepared the audience for whatever plot twist was coming. Certain types of music signaled danger. Others signaled romance or sadness. Another was designed to quicken the pulse—the cavalry is coming! The same principle applied to a basketball game. A game deejay used one type of music to excite the fans when the home team was rallying and another type to reawaken the fans if the team was struggling. The deejay might use one noise for a 3-point basket and another for a dunk. Doing all this required coordination between what the audience was seeing and what it was hearing. It hinged on conditioning, so that the audience equated certain musical cues with certain emotions, the way Pavlov's dogs were conditioned to equate the sound of bells with dinner.

I was not conditioned for Ren Hongbing, at least not at first. I felt dizzy as I tried to connect what I was seeing on the court with what I was hearing as he twisted knobs on his soundboard. My emotions felt more pummeled than manipulated. In theory, the music or musical prompts should play a supporting role to the game itself, yet the music never seemed to stop, regardless of what was happening on the court. Ren Hongbing had a completely different catalogue of musical cues and a completely different sense of timing. The music was so loud that I found it hard to hear Journalist Li beside me on press row. Worse, I couldn't tell how the music was supposed to make me feel at a particular moment of the game. It seemed, initially, without any logic or shape. There was some screeching Peking Opera, some saccharine Chinese pop ballads, some techno stuff from Europe, and some hip-hop from America. And, of course, the Wave. It was all a raucous, incoherent mess, or so I thought.

Once I had visited other arenas, where the deejays usually played only the music approved by the league, I slowly realized that Ren Hongbing was thinking quite a lot about what he was doing. He was experimenting, trying to find out how musically to best blend something Chinese with something Western. His experiments could be excruciating at times or, as I would come to appreciate, they could be small moments of genius. He could even be considered an artist.

As a teenager, he had been rebellious and his parents pushed him into the People's Liberation Army to drum some discipline into him. When he was discharged after two years, he went on a walkabout, drifting around the country, without a job or money or prospects—yet, unbeknownst to him, with the benefit of very good timing. It was 1992 and China was about to take off. His wanderings carried him to Guangzhou, the city of hustlers and fast fortunes on the Pearl River, where social attitudes were far less constrained than in Taiyuan. One night, he went to a disco. He would later say his life was forever changed.

As a boy, Ren loved singing and playing the guitar, but music was hardly a career. His parents were factory workers, and China was still untethering itself from the old, planned economy in which the state assigned jobs. Doing something solely because it made you happy and fulfilled, especially if it was unconventional, was a fairly daring concept. At the disco, Ren was transfixed by a Dutch deejay named Johnny who stood behind a board of switches and blended together music of different styles and nationalities, creating something original, if not wholly unfamiliar. Ren was transfixed. He approached Johnny at the end of the show but they could not communicate; Johnny did not speak Chinese. The following night he returned with an interpreter and a proposition: He wanted Johnny to be his teacher. Could he apprentice under him?

Johnny took measure of this strange man whom he could not understand and without hesitation said no.

"I didn't know this kind of thing could be a career," Ren would recall. "When he said no, I went to his apartment every day for a month to ask him to be my teacher. He was moved by my passion. We became teacher and student."

Johnny eventually took in his new student, too. Ren was homeless and practically penniless, except for money sent by his parents. Johnny played gigs until early in the morning and arrived back at the apartment to find Ren awake, having bought Johnny hot food. They would eat and experiment on the soundboard until dawn.

"He would sleep all day," Ren said. "I would practice during the daytime on his soundboard without turning on the sound because I didn't want to wake him. If I made mistakes, I would go to the club and listen to my teacher and then return to the apartment to practice."

He first learned how to mix two songs together. When his dexterity improved and his imagination expanded, he began mixing five different tracks and his apprenticeship ended. He played at popular discos in Beijing, Shanghai, Guangzhou, and Hohhot and earned a following in the underground culture of Chinese pop music. When he made it to the final round in a national deejay competition, Johnny offered to take him to Europe and expose him to other musical influences. Ren said no.

"I felt some regret, because in China I couldn't learn the newest techniques and the equipment wasn't the best," he said. "But I didn't want to leave my home, my country."

He was born in Taiyuan, toward the end of the Cultural Revolution. During the Maoist era, parents often named their offspring after whatever patriotic campaign was under way. In the 1950s, during the country's first five-year economic plan, many babies were named Jiangu, or Build the Country. During the Korean War, babies were named Yuanchao, translated as Aid Korea. But the Cultural Revolution left perhaps the biggest mark. I befriended a farmer from central China who during the Cultural Revolution had renamed himself as Zhandou, or Struggle. In Beijing, I occasionally rode with cabbies named Wen Ge, short for Cultural Revolution. Ren's parents had also chosen appropriately revolutionary names. Their firstborn, and only daughter, was Hongying, or Red Heroine. Next came Hongyu, or Red Fighter, followed by Hongwei, or Red Guardian. Last came Ren Hongbing, or Red Soldier. These names would later seem like strange historical artifacts, and it said something about the pace of change in China that a baby named Red Soldier grew up to be a man who made a career by mixing tracks of Sweetbox with tracks of Taiwanese pop.

Ren's chosen occupation perplexed his parents. They had financed his apprenticeship, but traveling the country to mix records together at discos didn't seem like stable or even normal work. "They thought it was strange," he admitted.

His break came when the Brave Dragons moved to Taiyuan in 2006 and approached him to be the game deejay. He almost turned down the job, fearing he knew too little about basketball, but he auditioned during a game and proved so popular that he was hired. He loved the atmosphere, and the excitement, but the job was initially less creative than he had hoped. The CBA restricted what a deejay could say and also provided teams with digitized cheers that closely emulated those in the NBA. Deejays could play an English track of "Deeefennse! Deeefense!" when the visiting team had the ball. Every team also had the same halftime ritual in which two fans competed in a shooting contest. Many of the cheerleaders danced to the same songs, no matter their team. It was Big Brother saying: We need to be hip; here is the approved guidebook on how to get there.

Ren was too restless for that. Early in the season, he invited a famous deejay from Taiwan who spent three days in Taiyuan and cajoled Ren to put his creative juices to work, to let loose.

"He told me that I could have my own free style of play," he said. "He told me to put my personality into playing the music. But he didn't tell me how. What you hear is all me."

Profanity was forbidden, and he couldn't cross any political lines, but he decided to use the game as his canvas. He already had a style but he was searching for a new language. He wanted to blend the mix of the team into his mix of music. He asked every player his favorite music, movie, or video game, especially things from their childhoods. Kobe remembered a favorite childhood video game with a catchy techno track. Ren found it. Olumide loved to dance and liked Russian disco from his teenage career in Siberia. Ren found Russian disco. He played part of the Hallelujah Chorus of Handel's *Messiah* whenever Bonzi made a 3-pointer.

He knew everything would fall apart if the audience felt excluded, if the language of his cues was too disconnected and unfamiliar, so he sprinkled snippets of culturally iconic Chinese music throughout every game. When an opposing team called a timeout, he played a famous song—synonymous with a dullard—from the movie *Da Hua Xi You,* a Hong Kong parody of the Chinese classic *Journey to the West.* He dabbled so often that he occasionally got lost in his own musicultural mélange.

Against the powerhouse Guangdong team, he played a track from *Huang Fei Hong,* a popular movie, before realizing that the movie was in Cantonese, the native language of the Guangdong team. He had committed musical treason.

"No one complained," he said, "but it was a mistake."

He became a little bit famous in Taiyuan. Professionals and friends praised him and said nice things to his parents. They started coming to games and seeing how much fun everyone was having and how the crazy noise their son was making was integral to the fun. Soon Red Fighter and Red Guardian became regulars, and Red Heroine came, too. Their baby brother, Red Fighter, was the musical madman of Taiyuan.

"We are the only team now to have individuality in our music," he would tell me, "to have our own musical style."

Red Guardian was in the kitchen, wearing an apron and pinching dumplings. New Year's custom in northern China called for serving dumplings after midnight, and Red Guardian and his wife were pressing the dough into little crescent moons. He was short and muscular, like a wrestler, and he grinned and welcomed me to the apartment. I was feeling a tinge guilty for invading the family during the Chinese equivalent of Christmas and Thanksgiving blended together, but I could see I was regarded as one of the unexpected, if pleasing, novelties of what Ren's career had provided the family: a foreign guest on New Year's Eve.

The apartment was small but pleasant, and other than Red Heroine, who was spending the evening with her husband's family, everyone was there. Ren steered me to the sofa, in front of the television, where a seat of honor had been prepared beside his other brother, Red Fighter. Then he started pushing food on me. There were nuts, hard candies, sesame seeds, and slices of dried beef on the glass coffee table.

"Eat! Eat!" Ren demanded.

I ate. Red Fighter pointed to the plate of food and grinned. I ate some more. The terms of engagement for the evening were established.

Ren's pregnant wife brought me a glass of soda. At twenty-five, she was almost a decade younger than her husband and usually helped him during games. They met on the Internet, as part of an online video gaming group that matched experts with novices as a mentoring exercise. She was a dancer in Henan Province and a video game novice. He was an expert and they spent two years communicating through instant messaging, never meeting or seeing a photograph of one another. When she messaged to say she was going to travel around the country, he invited her to stop in Taiyuan. They were married soon afterward.

I nibbled on a slice of dried beef and hunkered down beside Red Fighter and Ren's father to watch the CCTV New Year's Gala. The closest experience in the United States was watching the Detroit Lions on Thanksgiving Day and, like the Lions, the Gala had its share of critics. It was a variety show of singing, dancing, skits, and stand-up comedy that managed to be the most complained about television program in China even as it was arguably the most watched television show in the world, with an audience of anywhere from 400 million to one billion. The carping, which usually boiled out of Internet chat rooms, generally focused on the show's determined lack of creativity and daring. Ultimately, the show was accountable to government censors, and the Communist Party understood enough about propaganda to use a captive audience of hundreds of millions of people to its benefit. Last year, the Gala featured a long panoramic shot of the unsmiling nine members of the Politburo Standing Committee as well as a gentle reminder of the unfinished business of reuniting Taiwan with the motherland.

Certainly no one in the studio audience dared express anything but happiness with the show. In 2007, with midnight drawing near, the hosts completely bungled and mistimed their lines, interrupting one another and growing visibly annoyed. At least the audience was on cue; everyone burst into applause. Yet, like the Detroit Lions on Thanksgiving, the show was an indelible part of Chinese New Year. Minutes before midnight, Ren's parents were laughing at all the jokes, as the rest of us hurried down the stairwell with fireworks.

Outside, it was Pearl Harbor. People were lighting strings of firecrackers that dangled out the windows of their apartments, snakes that crackled and hissed. People squeezed into the narrow alleyway, blasting bottle rockets or Roman candles. I could hear every sound: the booming thuds, the insistent whistles of the bottle rockets, and the rattle of the firecrackers. The noise was so deafening that I covered my ears as gunpowder and burned paper rained down on top of us. I checked my watch. It was midnight.

"This," Ren shouted into my ear with glee, "is Chinese New Year!"

It was astonishing. Ren bent over beside a parked car and lighted a string of firecrackers. The thought occurred to me that this was not the safest thing to do, but the thought passed. I had never heard or seen anything like this. Beijing was for pikers. Colors flashed overhead, and the dull windows of the apartments shimmered in the reflected splashes of yellow or green or blue light. The whole city seemed to be shaking in joyous celebration.

We returned to the apartment as the shelling continued, and I took my seat. Now it was time for dumplings. My own bowl of dipping sauce was on the table, and Red Guardian placed a huge plate of dumplings in front of me. Then another plate, a molehill of dumplings. None of the ten other people who crowded into the apartment was eating yet. That was my job. Everyone smiled and nudged me as still more food arrived on the table: nuts, dried raisins, candied kiwis, cookies, blackened sunflower seeds, chopped shoots of garlic, and more sliced beef. Ren nudged me toward the slices of beef. His father had cured it. Red Fighter pushed a dumpling at me. I dipped it in my sauce bowl with my chopsticks and swallowed it whole. I ate another, and another, and another.

Eating is an essence of being Chinese. By eating I was praising my hosts. By insisting that I eat, my hosts were extending their hospitality and their friendship. In a country where at least 30 million people died of famine, food was more than mere sustenance. When you arrived at the home of a Chinese villager, the greeting was usually, *"Chi le ma?"* Have you eaten? Food was an obsession, an offering, a demonstration of renewal, an emblem of wealth. I kept eating dumplings, and the family joined me. Red Fighter slurped down dumplings. Red Guardian appeared from the kitchen with another plate. Ren was pleased.

I was distracted enough by the food that I didn't immediately detect the smoke. It took me a few minutes before I noticed a faint smell. I assumed it was from outside. The fireworks. But the smell grew stronger and clouds of smoke started filtering into the apartment. I noticed Red Guardian and Red Fighter huddled together in the hallway. I mentioned the smoke to Ren.

"No, no, no problem," he said, pushing more dumplings at me. "It is nothing."

I kept eating. Red Guardian and Red Fighter had disappeared from the hallway. I noticed a flash of light in the window and could see flames reflecting in the window of the apartment directly across the alley. I walked to our window, looked down and discovered that our building was on fire, very much on fire. A shed connected to a ground floor apart-

ment was fully ablaze, and the blaze had moved out of the shed into our
building. Now the smoke in Ren's apartment was denser and his father
started to cough.

"I think we have a problem," I told Ren.

Red Fighter and Red Guardian were in the bathroom filling plastic
laundry tubs with water. One after the other, the brothers filled a tub
and then rushed down the stairwell. Ren was anxious but determined to
fulfill his role as gracious host. He picked up a plate of dumplings and my
bowl of sauce and led me out of the smoky living room into his bedroom.
It was the room farthest from the window and the incoming smoke, and
we stepped inside. A life-size wedding photo of Hongbing and his wife
was taped above their bed. Hongbing placed the dumplings and sauce on
the windowsill and invited me to sit on his bed.

"Eat!" he said. "This is not a problem. I'll go take a look."

He closed the door. I found myself wishing that Ren's parents had also
given birth to Red Firefighter. I ate a few dumplings and contemplated
my predicament. I was Ren's guest, and I did not want to embarrass him
or for him to lose face. I also did not want to die on the third floor of
a burning building. I ate a dumpling and walked into the smoke-filled
hallway. Ren was in the kitchen pouring water into a pot. He saw me and
tried to shoo me back into his bedroom.

"Enjoy yourself!" he said.

I thanked him but suggested that maybe I should pitch in. He was
not convinced. Then I tried another tack. I suggested that as a writer, a
journalist, I should witness the fire. Doing so was my professional responsibility. He relented, and we hustled down the steps. Families were still
lighting firecrackers in front of the building as we raced around the corner to the rear of the building and the scene of the blaze. Ren tossed his
bucket into the flames and I noticed a shower of water from above: Red
Fighter and Red Guardian were now dumping their buckets out the window. A window frame on the first floor was melting from the heat.

A police officer arrived, his face lit in the reflection of the flames. I
asked if he was busy tonight. He laughed. More neighbors had now
arrived with more water and the blaze seemed to be subsiding. Finally, a
dozen firefighters arrived from an opposite alley. In the smoke and darkness, they looked like aliens, with the white lights atop their helmets bobbing like fireflies. Their truck was too big to navigate the alley so they
were unfurling a very long hose from the truck. It took about ten minutes.
Red Fighter and Red Guardian were dumping more buckets out of the

window when the firefighters finally turned on their hose. They missed and sprayed us instead.

A few minutes later, the fire was doused. Ren smiled, took me by the elbow, and led me back upstairs. The apartment was still filled with smoke, and Ren's father was holding one of the water buckets and watching the final credits on the Gala. He said it was a great show.

"Sit down!" Ren said to me, and I obeyed. "You haven't eaten any dumplings yet!"

Less than two weeks later, another fire occurred, during the Lantern Festival, which marked the end of every Lunar New Year holiday. This one was in Beijing, as fireworks torched and gutted the not-yet-completed Mandarin Oriental Hotel. The fire attracted international attention because the hotel was part of the complex built around the new, futuristic headquarters of CCTV. Among superstitious Chinese, the blaze was not considered a good omen.

CHAPTER SIXTEEN

LOL

Bonzi did not come back. Maybe Coco was right about his big bag. Maybe our airport chest bump meant farewell. Maybe Bonzi Wells touched back down in the United States of America, settled into his Midwestern cocoon of Muncie, and said to himself, as he might phrase it: *There is no motherfucking way I'm going back to that crazy country to play for that crazy team owned by that crazy motherfucker.* It seemed plausible. And, really, who could blame him? He was mismatched with the team he was supposed to elevate into a champion, hated the food, misunderstood the culture, and had neither the interest nor the temperament for the role of basketball ambassador. He was the anti-ambassador, more likely to start a war than prevent one. He had come to China to show he could still play, make a few bucks, and maybe salvage a shoe deal. He had gone two out of three. The shoe deal apparently went nowhere.

Yet Bonzi's departure meant a very public experiment had ended, badly, which meant someone had to be blamed. The obvious parties blamed each other. Bonzi claimed he had intended to come back but the team had been unreasonable. He was supposed to be in uniform for the Sunday night game after the New Year's break, but then different issues arose, including a medical appointment in Indiana for his injured finger, a salary spat, and a snowstorm. It was hard to know what to make of these excuses but it was clear Bonzi wanted a few more days in Muncie and a few less in Taiyuan.

Boss Wang did not want to be jilted. He doubted that Bonzi ever intended to return and wasn't certain he wanted him to return. Still, he instructed Zhang Beihai to bring him back. Garrison played intermediary, calling the United States in search of Bonzi, who almost never picked up and seemed to have deliberately disappeared. When Garrison reached Bonzi's agent, the message was relayed of Bonzi's need for a few more days, which only made Boss Wang more suspicious and paranoid, which explained his secret contingency plan.

The secret contingency plan was named Tim Pickett. A muscular shooting guard who starred at Florida State University, Pickett was waiting in the gym when the rest of the team returned to prepare for Sunday's game. It quickly became clear that this stranger with a nice outside shot represented the Bonzi Wells insurance policy. If Bonzi failed to return, as the front office suspected would happen, Pickett was the new starting shooting guard for the Brave Dragons. If Bonzi did return, Pickett would have the benefit of a few days in Taiyuan. At one point, Pickett was told to go back to America and flew to Beijing. He was waiting in the Beijing airport for his delayed flight to the States, when his telephone rang. He was asked to please come back to Taiyuan. What prompted this change of heart was never made clear, but any uncertainty about the broader situation finally ended when Boss Wang issued an ultimatum: If Bonzi wasn't back by the Sunday night game against the Jilin Northeast Tigers, he was fired.

He was fired.

The Sunday night game against Jilin was a blowout loss. Pickett was not yet registered with the league, and the Brave Dragons played as if they had lost a limb. Throughout the Bonzi era, the offense had mostly consisted of passing the ball to Bonzi and watching him shoot. Now they were suddenly thrust back into the unknown: Who would shoot? How would they adjust? Could they adjust?

Not yet, at least. In the locker room, Boss Wang screeched for ninety minutes, reasserting his preeminence with Bonzi now gone. Weiss was again demoted to consultant, with Liu Tie now putatively in charge, though Boss Wang would be the real coach from here on. He screamed at Olumide and called him one of the five worst centers in the league—even though Olumide led the league in rebounding. "He yelled at him, saying, 'I'm paying you all this money and you're doing this and not doing that,'" Weiss said. "As hard as Olumide plays, he wants to be appreciated. Then you tell him he is not worth the money he is getting?"

Boss Wang concluded the meeting by ordering each player to sign a ball and carry it everywhere. "He wanted them to be married to the ball and learn how to handle it better," Weiss said a few days later, frustrated. "It's always got to be somebody's fault. It can't just be they had a bad night.

The Chinese players have been watching Bonzi for fourteen games and suddenly they have to go out and make their shots."

When the story broke of Bonzi's departure—"Wells Not Returning to Shanxi!" sports periodicals shouted—Chinese basketball commentators reacted with indignation, proclaiming good riddance, but also with introspection. A few people criticized the Brave Dragons for failing to hire enough interpreters to accommodate the team's large number of foreigners. Bonzi was isolated and lonely, they argued, and had not been able to explore and appreciate China. A poll on the CBA website found that 42 percent of respondents believed Bonzi left because the league was too low-level while another 42 percent said his moral character made his departure inevitable. The basketball editor of *Titan Sports,* a young journalist named Yang Yi, saw the Bonzi episode as a teaching moment in the development of Chinese basketball. Before Bonzi, the types of foreigners imported into the Chinese league fell into the same mold of high-scoring gunner. Bonzi had adapted to this role, Yang Yi argued, but it had not come naturally because he was accustomed to playing a prescribed role on a good NBA team. His teammates in China were not good enough to play with him. The league was not professional enough to accommodate and control someone of his talent and temperament.

"Bonzi is like a full dish of nutrients," Yang Yi argued. "The CBA is just not able to digest it right now." Whether Bonzi was a full dish of nutrients or just indigestible might be the open-ended epitaph of his basketball career. But his absence indisputably meant that the league's biggest draw was now gone and so was the spotlight that had followed the Brave Dragons. The young female reporters and bloggers disappeared from press row in Taiyuan, and the Brave Dragons largely disappeared from CCTV. Many of the Chinese players were relieved, though not Kobe. Bonzi had believed in him, had bucked him up, and now Bonzi was gone. Bonzi's departure also meant a premature end to www.MeandBonzi.com, though Garrison managed to post a few cultural insights before ending the blog.

"This story also taught me the importance of understanding each individual's different personality and temper when interacting with foreigners," Garrison wrote after relaying a tale of how Bonzi had once clashed with a teammate in the NBA. "Especially important is the culture gap between people. For example, our Chinese brothers all like hooking shoulders or climbing on each other's backs, and sometimes hit each other's butts. This is extremely taboo for black people."

Garrison saw the tale of Bonzi and Boss Wang as an ill-fated union.

They respected each other but neither could tolerate how the other infringed upon his personal authority; their conflict was rooted in tensions any Chinese would understand, the clash over power.

"There is a truth created in ancient times: The chancellor who wants to surpass the emperor often ends up losing both fortune and honor," Garrison wrote, "or even having his entire family exterminated."

Bonzi's family was actually in Muncie, which is where I assumed he was, too. I had tried in vain to call him and finally connected by email. His explanation of events would be my last contact with the greatest American to ever play in the Chinese league.

Jim,

Whats up buddy hope all is well I hate I'm not in China eating dragon testicule wit us guys. LOL anyway the reason Im not there is because the team never paid my salary and I asked them to wire to my acct before I came back and they were dragging there feet. Then they told me to come back and play for free Til they could pay me going against my better judgement. I agreed so they asked me to get on a last minute flight. I tried to explain to them that we had a blizzard in Indiana I couldn't make it to airport cause highways were closed til next day. They said if I don't make it back by gameday don't come back at all. If u don't believe me bout the blizzard check the Indiana weather report for those days. I'm really upset I couldn't finish the season for coach and O. Well I rambled enough it was nice and meeting and talking wit u Goodluck wit ur book.

Mr. Wells.

I do not know whether Bonzi truly wanted to return, but he was not lying about the weather on the day of his scheduled flight back to China. For the record, the state of Indiana experienced one of the heaviest snowstorms in its history in late January.

Little Sun got word from the general manager before he flew home to Taiwan for the New Year's break: Do not come back. You are cut.

Little Sun was almost relieved. Watching him during the season had become painful, not so much for his play on the court, which was inconsistent, but because it meant watching the steady disintegration of a nice young man. After his demotion, Liu Tie had softened his tirades, but his disdain for Little Sun had not changed. To him, Little Sun would always be a little Taiwanese guy, too short and too soft. China did not respect or indulge soft.

Little Sun collected his unpaid salary and bonuses and made a final visit to the World Trade to say goodbye. The foreigners had considered him a bridge to the Chinese guys, because of his broken English. He helped Olumide or Bonzi or Donta talk to their Chinese teammates to work out problems on the court. He was the one person who seemed to straddle both worlds, yet, if anything, he had been as perplexed by China as the other foreigners had. He had wanted to prove himself in China. He had wanted to become the first Taiwanese to play under an NBA coach. He had accomplished that, at least. When he landed in Taiwan, he sent an email to Weiss.

> Hello coach,
>
> I am in Taiwan now. I am really happy have you coaching the team during past half year.
>
> Especially it is my honor to meet a NBA coach and learn from you, not only the basketball but also the way to think about things.
>
> **You are the best coach I ever have!!**
>
> I am not sad about leaving the team, but I really miss Garison, you and Tracy. If you have time travelling to Taiwan, Please Do Come To See Me. I will be your tour guide, and also the translator (ha ha).

He sent me an email, too, and later, when I checked up on him, Little Sun was practicing hard in Taiwan, hoping to earn another chance at the CBA. He did not regret his time with the Brave Dragons, especially because of Weiss. He had decided what distinguished Weiss, as much as his tactical knowledge of the game, was his temperament. He was *xiuyang*, or accomplished. Sun was also still cherishing his finest moment of the season, from the opening game, when he stole the ball from the Chinese Olympian and made a basket. "I steal from a national team player," he said in his broken English. "He played for China in the Olympics. I steal his ball. Do you remember? I steal his ball and score. And we win the game. I could not sleep. Too excited!"

But Little Sun had been uncomfortable in China. He thought too many Chinese were arrogant, especially toward anyone from Taiwan, and he had been surprised at cultural differences between Chinese and Taiwanese, at what he considered the crudeness of some Chinese. Even so, he wanted to go back. He wanted to prove he could meet the challenge of China and was already scouting for a new team for the following season.

First, though, he had an obligation in Taiwan. From 1949 onward, every eligible Taiwanese male has been required to fulfill mandatory military service. This conscription system was evolving, as Taiwan was changing to an all-volunteer military, but Little Sun was required to enter basic training for at least a few months. He would learn to fire a rifle and also learn more about Taiwanese history. I had remembered how Liu Tie had berated him in practice about being soft and playing "Taiwan independence defense." When I spoke with Little Sun, I joked that now he really was playing Taiwan independence defense.

Little Sun laughed politely but waved away the thought. No, he said again, I don't care about politics. Basketball was life.

Tim Pickett would be the last American for the Brave Dragons that season. League rules permitted teams to change foreigners twice, and Pickett was the second change. Pickett also represented a return to a more familiar type in that he was flawed. Unlike Bonzi, who had played in the NBA and played at a high level, Pickett was another piece that hadn't quite fit into an NBA team, which meant he was like almost every other American in the Chinese league. Every one of them had talent, or size, but something was always missing. Sometimes the problem was between the ears; sometimes it was on the court, maybe a center like Olumide, who wasn't quite big enough or offensively polished enough to stay in the NBA. Weiss had once coached Jelani McCoy, the huge center now playing in Zhejiang, and considered him a real talent with a poor work ethic. Combine his talent and size with Olumide's hard work and you would have had a pretty solid NBA center.

Tim Pickett had never played in the NBA, and he was hungry to get there. The New Orleans Hornets had selected him from Florida State in the second round of the 2004 draft. He had been a tough defender with a deadly 3-point shot who had almost single-handedly engineered one of the great upsets in college basketball's greatest league, the Atlantic Coast Conference, against the dominant North Carolina Tar Heels. Florida State had been trailing at halftime by 24 points, when Pickett scored 22 of his 30 points in the second half, burying a string of 3-point bombs as Carolina collapsed. Pickett made First Team All-ACC and was seen as someone who could play in what he called "the league." But he was still an irregular piece; listed at 6'4", he was actually shorter, making him small for a shooting guard, yet he didn't have the skills of a point guard. At the Hornets' training camp, he was drowning and confused, uncertain when to pass or shoot, mystified by the different plays and sets. He scored 19 points in a preseason game against the Bulls and was fouled with time expired and the team trailing by one. He made the first. He missed the second. The Bulls won in overtime, and Pickett was cut the next day.

"I should have become more of a student of the game," Pickett would tell me. "But I realized that too late."

He spent twenty-two games in the NBA Development League, not playing especially well, still stung by getting cut from the Hornets. He felt the D-League was beneath him, and the pay was terrible. So he went to Europe the following season, first to France, later to Italy, where he played well but flunked a drug test for marijuana. He was expelled and embarrassed and returned determined to prove he was a good player and citizen. He later jumped to the same Bulgarian team as Donta Smith but he hated Bulgaria. His life was complicated; he had a fiancée and a daughter in Texas and another daughter in Italy, and he needed to keep playing ball. His soon-to-be brother-in-law, Mack Tuck, played in China for the Shandong team.

"He said, 'You gotta come to China. It's the next step to the league.' "

Pickett liked that teams played three times a week in China. He wanted to show he could be a winner, a star. He thought China might finally deliver him to the NBA.

"I came here to market myself," he told me. "That is my plan."

The Brave Dragons planned for him to score about 30 or more points a game and help the team make the playoffs. A successful season was still within reach, as was a playoff berth. Fifteen games remained, and Pickett had already impressed Weiss and the other coaches during workouts. He seemed comfortable working within an offense and getting his Chinese teammates involved. He was a little inscrutable but seemed friendly enough. A little breath of optimism seemed to blow through the team. Everyone assumed he would blend in better than Bonzi.

CHAPTER SEVENTEEN

CAST-OUTS

Leaving behind the cold, dry misery of Taiyuan, we stepped out of the Xiamen airport into the moist, enveloping air of the south China coast. It was February 12, but it could have been spring. My body felt like a dying plant unexpectedly sprinkled with water; corpuscles tingled and unclenched in the wet air. The skin breathed again. Tomorrow, the team was playing the Fujian Sturgeons. The players collected their baggage and boarded a chartered bus for the city of Jinjiang. I was taking a side trip, and a small, wiry man in a neat burgundy shirt and tan slacks was waving a sign with my name. He was a driver for the Yuanchi Rubber Sporting Goods Company, and we accelerated onto the highway through the green hills of Fujian to visit the factory that made 10,000 Spalding basketballs every day.

This part of Fujian was like northern California. We glided past a gated compound of tile-roofed Mediterranean-styled villas and then moved through an industrial zone, crossing the Ma River where, in the distance, I could see groaning orange machines lowering metal containers onto barges, yet another cog in the great Chinese export machine. We sliced through more humped, green hillsides, a few scarred by bulldozers, a handful sheared into quarries, and continued past a showroom for Infiniti, then a showroom for Ford, and finally the rising towers of another unfinished apartment complex, this one encircled by towering orange cranes. A highway sign in English and Chinese announced an exit for "Future Coast." We took it.

Fujian has always chased the future, though Fujianese were famous for going somewhere else to find it. Fujian was the locus of China's illegal human smuggling trade, where farmers or other idled workers paid smugglers known as snakeheads to transport them overseas for work. Illegal Fujianese migrants settled Chinatown in New York and continued seeding themselves around the world, despite the inevitable hazards. In 1993, the freighter *Golden Venture* ran aground near New York carrying 286 smuggled Chinese workers, most from Fujian. Ten people died. Then, in 2000, the bodies of fifty-eight Fujianese were discovered inside an airless tomato truck in England. Yet these periodic tragedies did little to deter migration. In 2004, smugglers posted fliers on one Fujianese island promising work and money in the new land of opportunity called Iraq. A handful of men jumped at the chance and were promptly kidnapped after crossing into the Iraqi war zone from Jordan. Their later release averted a diplomatic crisis with China.

The road to Future Coast soon delivered us into the countryside where we passed roadside clusters of three-story concrete houses, each in a different stage of construction. These houses were monuments to the Fujianese diaspora; when someone leaves for overseas work, he or she sends back remittances to family, often to build a house. When money arrives, the family pays for construction—maybe a new second or third floor—until the money runs out. The house exists in a state of suspended animation until the next wire transfer arrives from London or Vancouver or New York. These houses were far grander than those of the people who remained to farm or work in nearby factories and served the same purpose as the fliers circulated by snakeheads. Their message was to go.

We diverted off the road to Future Coast and climbed into the hills. This was where the factories were located, nearly all of them flat-roofed, tile-covered concrete buildings, one indistinguishable from the other, including the Yuanchi Rubber Sporting Goods Company. The factory manager, Alan Lin, greeted me in the factory courtyard. He was from Taiwan and his family owned the conglomerate that owned Yuanchi. His family had gotten into the rubber business in 1949, after fleeing the mainland following the Chinese civil war. They first produced rubber frogs that hopped, and later moved into sports balls after being contacted by Spalding. Spalding, maker of the official ball of the NBA, had already figured out that the future of manufacturing was in Asia.

When James Naismith invented basketball in 1891 as a tool of muscular Christianity, the commercial impulse inevitably followed his game. After all, someone had to make and sell the ball. Naismith had initially used a soccer ball, but within a few years, as basketball's popularity ensured its continued existence, he began looking for someone to make a ball specifically for his sport. He found A. G. Spalding.

Albert Goodwill Spalding was a baseball pitcher, eventually elected to the Baseball Hall of Fame, who opened a sporting goods store with his brother in 1876. His company not only manufactured sports equipment but invented it; he standardized the baseball, produced the first baseball gloves, manufactured the first football and the first volleyball, and, in 1894, made the first true basketball. It seems likely that the YMCA missionaries who brought the game to Tianjin arrived with a Spalding ball. Spalding did its manufacturing in the town of Chicopee, Massachusetts, not far from the YMCA's teaching college in Springfield. For almost nine decades, Spalding made basketballs and other inflatable balls in Chicopee before the rise of Asia upended the economics of manufacturing.

"There was always the issue of how to get lower costs," said Gary Gasperack, a longtime Spalding executive with extensive experience in Asia.

Spalding bounced between different corporate owners and ultimately became one of many examples of how companies that invented things in America could no longer afford to make them there. During the 1960s and 1970s, Spalding was owned by a conglomerate based in the Midwest that hewed to the era's prevailing business ethos that big corporations should diversify their portfolio of companies to protect against overdependence on one category.

In the early 1980s, Donaldson, Lufkin & Jenrette, the former investment bank, assessed Spalding, which was facing competition from other sporting goods manufacturers such as Wilson, MacGregor, and Rawlings, and recommended major changes. Manufacturing was becoming a race to find the lowest costs and that race could not be won in America. Lufkin advised that Spalding continue manufacturing products where they had technical expertise and patent protection, such as the company's line of golf balls, which were the first to use a hardened center rather than wound rubber. But other products needed to be outsourced overseas, almost always to Asia. Spalding had already outsourced some products, including cheap rubber balls, to Taiwan, India, and Pakistan, but now the company moved production of the high-end, laminated NBA game ball to a factory in South Korea.

"Korea had the necessary technical know-how," Gasperack said. "They knew how to work with leather."

While corporations like Spalding were chasing the lowest price from country to country, the rising affluence that resulted in East Asia was stirring political change. South Korea and Taiwan were still soft authoritarian states, but rising wealth brought rising expectations and emboldened democratic movements.

Except in China. China then was much like North Korea today: poor, desperate, and disconnected from the world until Deng opened the door in 1978. Western companies were initially cautious about entering China; businessmen in Hong Kong and Taiwan provided much of the early foreign investment. By 1992, after Deng had made his Southern Tour, Taiwanese companies had begun rushing into the mainland. Labor costs had been rising steadily in South Korea and Taiwan, and Spalding, among many companies, started complaining about rising production costs to manufacturing subcontractors like Yuanchi.

"We said to them that we are going to have to do something," Gasperack recalled. "You'll need to find an alternative. Prices are going up too high."

Alan Lin's family signed its first agreement with Spalding in 1973 to make cheap rubber balls. Yuanchi had been dividing its manufacturing between factories in Taiwan and Thailand until a fire destroyed the factory in Taiwan, leaving the company struggling to meet its orders. Deng's tour convinced the Lin family to get into China. Fujian was close to Taiwan, shared cultural and linguistic ties, and other Taiwanese companies were already opening factories there. Alan Lin's uncle toured the province and, helped by a Taiwanese friend already doing business in Fujian, secured the land where Yuanchi now made balls. The land was cheap, and the labor was the cheapest in East Asia.

Basketball had come to China to spread the word of God. The manufacturing of basketballs now came to China in search of the lowest price.

In the early 1990s, Alan Lin imagined his life involving something other than rubber balls. He left Taiwan and his family to study interior design at Michigan State University. He graduated and moved to New York, experiencing a very different world, before he ran into immigration problems and had to leave America for lack of a green card. He needed a job, and his father and two uncles were running the family conglomerate. He moved between different factories before being sent to Fujian to oversee Yuanchi.

Lin was a small man with styled, spiky black hair. He was wearing a trendy pair of red and black Puma running shoes, courtesy of the family's joint venture with Puma, and dressed in the athletic, casual chic popular in China. I had followed him into the administration building at the front of the factory complex to a second-floor conference room decorated with flow charts of the family's corporate structure. There were no power offices or lavish meeting rooms, no displays of corporate ego. Yuanchi was about delivering low prices and quality balls. Period.

Lin seemed happy to have company. He had lived in a bedroom down the hall from his accounting office for seven years, apart from his wife and daughter, and when I asked about any hardship, he smiled and shrugged. He flew home every five weeks, spent a week with the family, and then returned. Many of his workers were migrants from inland provinces and lived in the concrete dormitory near the administration building. They got free room and board, contingent on keeping their room clean, and earned, on average, about 1,000 yuan, or $150, a month, which was above the minimum wage.

Gary Gasperack had told me that the basic process of manufacturing a basketball had not changed much from the 1960s, which was why chasing cost became the priority. Profit margins were thin, and Lin said this factory did not make a profit the previous year because rubber prices, tied to oil, were very high. Moreover, the global recession hammered exports; Lin said sales in the United States dropped by about 15 percent. Some exporters had to close and Fujianese officials, desperate to keep factories open, sweetened a program to give tax rebates to exporters and also canceled plans to increase the local monthly minimum wage. The flicker of good news was that domestic sales were rising and that 10 million Spalding balls were sold in China the year before. The problem was that very few of those balls were actually Spalding balls.

"We found in the whole China market that if you buy ten Spalding basketballs, only one is made here," Lin said. "Nine are counterfeit. It is a very serious problem."

Yuanchi hired corporate spies to locate counterfeit factories and tried in vain to take legal action. "But afterward," he said, "they are still running." Local officials protect the counterfeit factories to protect tax revenues; sometimes the officials get a cut of the profits. Laminated leather balls were more expensive and easy to copy. A counterfeiter might reduce costs by 20 percent by using cheaper rubber and by not paying a licensing fee to companies like Spalding or Nike. Then the counterfeiters sold the

fake balls to retailers at lower prices than the real balls. A retailer know-
ingly kept a mix of real and fake balls and sold them for the same price.

"It is everywhere in China," Lin said.

We left the conference room and walked into the huge workrooms
where balls were made. Alan estimated that making a single rubber basketball took about twenty-nine minutes, a process that began in a large
workshop where blocks of yellow rubber were melted into thin sheets that
became the bladder of the ball. The ball's valve, though, was created in a
final workshop larger than a football field. The value was the brand. At
one end of the workshop, two women were bent over a long rectangular
glass table and carefully pressed pieces of gold-colored foil over the red
outline of the Spalding name to create the company's familiar red and
yellow logo, which would be applied to the ball.

"That's why we tell our customers that if you want to emboss your logo,
it will cost you more," said Alan. "It looks more expensive."

We then walked through a room surrounded by the totems of American sports. There were boxes and boxes of Spalding basketballs, of various models and embossments, but also boxes filled with Nike balls. One
box was filled with miniature black and yellow rubber Nike footballs.
Another overflowed with orange and white footballs embossed with the
familiar Longhorn logo of the University of Texas. Another had basketballs embossed with the word "Respect." Maybe the child of some illegal
Fujianese immigrant was playing with one in New York.

There also were balls embossed with the logo of the Houston Rockets,
stacks and stacks of them. Before Yao Ming went to the NBA in 2002,
Alan said the NBA struggled to sell branded balls in China. Few consumers knew the Spalding brand or connected it with anything desirable.
But once Yao started playing, and the NBA started appearing far more
frequently on CCTV5, Spalding's sales jumped sharply in the domestic
market. Counterfeiting was a major problem, but even fake Spalding balls
helped spread brand awareness with the buying public.

Yao Ming had stimulated an entire economy. No wonder the NBA was
so interested in having its own Chinese league. And no wonder China
was so eager to master the art not just of making basketballs, but of making basketball players.

The small man across the table in Jinjiang, where the Brave Dragons were
to play the Sturgeons, had a very long fingernail. He also had a flamboy-

ant Elvis hairdo and was grinning and leaning back in his chair, seemingly bemused by our meeting. In ancient times, a Qing nobleman might grow out the fingernail of his pinky to demonstrate refinement and advertise that his station placed him far above doing any manual labor. Now, like so many things, the long fingernail was mostly a symbol of money, if nouveaux money. I later learned that the foreigners on the Fujian Sturgeons called this man Longnail, and Longnail was the Sturgeons' Team Leader. He was once a party secretary in a small village outside Jinjiang who engineered a deal to sell village land to a local peasant. The peasant had started making zippers in a single room and wanted to build a factory. Outraged, and apparently cheated, the landless villagers tossed out Longnail, but the deal went through. The expropriated land was used for the first factory of what would become SBS, one of the world's largest zipper makers. The peasant, Shi Nengkeng, eventually bought the Sturgeons and created a job for Longnail, who was now a made man.

We were in a cinder block conference room in the underbelly of the Sturgeons' stadium. Tipoff was eight hours away, and we were discussing security. Weiss, Garrison, Wingtips, and I sat opposite the Sturgeons' coach, a police officer, Longnail, and an assistant manager. The game commissioner sat at the head of the table beside the referees.

"We will follow our normal principles," the game commissioner said, opening the meeting. "To be serious, to be fair, and to make the game go smoothly."

The morning security meeting was a ritual before every game in the Chinese Basketball Association. Attendance was mandatory for coaches. In Taiyuan, the meeting was conducted in the only heated space in the stadium, a large room with leather sofas dominated by a wall decorated by a floor-to-ceiling poster of a beach, with blue water, white sand, and swaying palm trees, If you posed for a photograph, you could convince someone that you had visited a tropical island rather than the coal capital of central China. To stay warm, Tracy often waited here before games. I called it the Hawaii Room.

When Bob Weiss attended his first security meeting in the Hawaii Room, he barely understood anything, other than the seriousness assigned to security in China. Everyone was grave. The game commissioner peppered various people with various questions. As the team's official representative, Wingtips nodded at appropriate moments. Police officers confirmed that there were enough police; only later, as the season wore on, did the meetings become fairly pro forma. Now, though, with the Brave Dragons and the Sturgeons fighting for playoff spots, the game commissioner spoke with a deep seriousness.

"This is a critical time in the season," the commissioner continued. "The rankings matter more and more, so the officials will take the game more seriously."

The referees nodded wordlessly. No words were needed. The game commissioner was talking about corruption without talking about it. Fujian held the sixth playoff position, while Shanxi had slipped into twelfth place. The Tim Pickett experience was not off to a good start. The Brave Dragons had not yet won a game with him. But the teams were bunched together and a winning streak could quickly reverse the rankings. With so much at stake, owners had been known to buy referees, or at least rent them for a night. Before the season, league officials instituted a new policy that required referees to always travel in groups. If they did anything by themselves—say, go have a cup of coffee—they were required to submit a form of explanation to the league. The thinking was that if they were never alone, they would never sneak away to accept a bribe from an owner, a logic that ignored the possibility that an owner might simply buy all the referees.

"The officials tonight are the best for this game," the game commissioner said, trying to instill confidence, describing the two men beside him as if they were some carefully calibrated chemical compound. "They are the best combination."

Then the game commissioner turned away from the refs to address the rest of the table. "If anything unexpected happens in the game, I hope everyone will handle it in the proper way," he said. He turned and looked directly at the police officer, who fidgeted in his chair. "Keep everything in order, especially the fans. Security has to be taken responsibility for.

"Seven-thirty tonight," the game commissioner said in conclusion. "Any questions?"

Garrison translated into Weiss's ear. He smiled.

"Meiyou," Weiss said in Chinese. I don't have any.

The table was tickled. The Sturgeons' coach was also an American, J. T. Prada, and his translator started laughing. Prada had coached here for four years, could not speak a word of Chinese, and had little interest in trying to learn any. Prada smiled as the Chinese men mocked him in a language he couldn't understand. He could not have cared less.

When Weiss and I met Prada before the security meeting, we made a little bet. I guessed Prada was a New Yorker. Weiss guessed New Jersey. He was all energy and wiseguy bluster. The answer was Cupertino, California. His parents had emigrated from Italy, first to South America, where Prada was born, and then to Cupertino, where his mother was a seamstress, his father was a janitor, and Prada picked lettuce with his five brothers. His parents divorced, and his mother raised the family. She had a winter dress and a summer dress. Her son learned to be tough.

"You come here as a foreigner and they beat on you to do things their way," Prada told me. "But if you don't fight that, you're done, you have no chance. The assistant coach will be Chinese and will start talking to the players, and then they won't listen to you."

Prada and I were having brunch at his hotel after the meeting. When I mentioned Boss Wang, he rolled his eyes. Once Boss Wang had hired a Korean coach, who prepared the team for weeks for the season opener against Fujian. Fujian won. Boss Wang fired the Korean after the game.

"Bob has got no chance," Prada said, taking a sip of soup.

Prada was wiry and intense. He ran every morning and seemed to barely eat. He had a few slices of cucumber and a piece of garlic bread on his plate. His narrow face was all sharp angles, his head shaved to the tiny nubs of his remaining black hair. Profane and funny, he had a habit of interrupting himself midway through telling a story—maybe about how he got fired from a job, or how he didn't realize that ass kissing was a prerequisite for coaching employment—and shaking his head with a wry smile as he told you how stupid he was. It was his rhetorical pump fake. Stupid he wasn't.

Prada considered himself the victim of an NBA system that would seem familiar, even logical, to many Chinese. He saw the NBA coaching fraternity less as a meritocracy than as a series of personal networks that sometimes contributed to the rise of talent and sometimes kept it from rising. The biggest network consists of former players who become coaches, and he could not be a member. He played at tiny Linfield College in Oregon and then moved up in coaching from high school to becoming an assistant at the University of California at Santa Barbara and, later, at Loyola Marymount. There, he worked under Paul Westhead, the former Los Angeles Lakers coach whose radical offensive philosophies would have appealed to Boss Wang. Visionary or madman, Westhead wanted his teams to play as fast as humanly possible. At one point, he ordered his players to shoot within three seconds of crossing half-court.

When Westhead left for the Denver Nuggets, Prada went with him. He was in a network.

It lasted a single year. He worked for Jerry Tarkanian when Tarkanian briefly coached the San Antonio Spurs. He worked for Jimmy Lynam in Philadelphia. But when they got fired, he got fired and eventually his network was dead. Nor was he likely to charm his way into a new one. "For me personally, I'm absolutely the worst at kissing ass and networking," he told me. He seemed to be offering this point as a character reference but also because it was true.

He went to Asia, spent a few years in Taiwan, and then ended up in Fujian. Every summer, he tried to reattach himself to an NBA team, and every fall he returned to Fujian. He had coached the Sturgeons for the previous four seasons, making the playoffs every year, his existence outside basketball almost monkish. He watched DVDs and got foot massages. His favorite place had installed a DVD player so he could watch footage of an opposing team while his feet were rubbed. "People are nice," he said. He had built a house in Colorado, where he lived four months of the year with his wife and their two children, ages six and five. The rest of the year he was in Fujian.

"It's life," he said, looking around the hotel restaurant. "You gotta pay the bills. Oh, I've really fucked my wife over."

He gestured toward the young waitresses. Maybe they were sixteen. They had bad haircuts and were trying not to stare at the two foreigners, and you could tell they were from the countryside. "In the rest of the world, this is just how it is," he said, pointing to a waitress as she refilled his water. "This lady here, she doesn't expect to have two cars, a home, and a bank account. Americans have this sense of entitlement. Well, I don't think the rest of the world thinks that way. These little waitresses will work seven days a week, twelve hours a day. To them, that is perfectly normal."

When he first arrived in Fujian, the team had practiced every day of the year, morning and evenings, with a single week off for Lunar New Year. The players took a three-hour midday nap, as was common in China. He immediately broke the cycle; he canceled the nap but also canceled the endless practices. His Chinese assistants and the general manager wanted him to practice for five hours daily but he refused. He restricted practice to a regimented ninety minutes to create a sense of urgency, efficiency, and purpose. Prada also did something unique; he designed his offense around his Chinese players because he thought it was the best way to play basketball in China and to keep his job. Without his interpreter, Prada could barely communicate, but he had learned all the cuss words in the Fujianese dialect. He could not order a beer in a restaurant, but he could tell his players to eat shit. They had reciprocated by learning to tell him to fuck off in English.

"What has really helped me out is my best local players are on my side," he said. "It doesn't matter if the American guys are on your side. There are ten of them and two of you. If you don't have the local guys, you have no chance of staying. The other coaches only run plays for American players. I don't. I try to use the team concept. And I think our Chinese players like that. It's human nature. No one wants to come down the court and just stand there."

He created a star out of his undersized point guard, Lu Xiaoming, who led the league in assists after his Chinese coaches had given up on him as too short. Prada believed the Chinese league was steadily progressing ("there are decent Americans who come over here and get their ass knocked"), but the legacy of bad coaching would take time to overcome. Chinese coaches rarely worked on more nuanced, technical aspects of the game, like helping out teammates on defense, Prada said. When I asked him where Chinese players excelled, he smiled and shook his head.

"Shooting," he said. "Chinese are great at copying shit. You give them a Rolex watch, they'll copy it, and make it better and cheaper. But they won't come up with the idea."

I asked about Shi Nengkeng, the owner. "I call him Boss," Prada said, grinning. "I don't know his name."

When Prada and Shi had a meeting, Shi spoke first. Then Prada spoke. The only ground rule established by the owner was that neither man interrupted the other. There was pressure, and when the team lost "it is like the world is coming to an end." But Shi had never attended a team meeting and never interfered. "I probably have the best situation in China," Prada said.

Yet Prada would have left tomorrow. He was curious about Weiss and seemed interested in making a possible attempt at networking. To him, Weiss embodied the NBA network, a former player and four-time head coach, a longtime assistant, a guy who had gotten breaks that he hadn't. "Most people like to hire people they know," he said. "That is absolutely normal." He smiled as he repeated what an unemployed coach once told him: "I'm just one phone call away from being happy."

"He's right," Prada said. "I'm still waiting."

He said he compartmentalized his emotions or otherwise he might go crazy, lying in bed, wondering what he was doing so far away from home and why an NBA team wouldn't give him another shot. "You go to other countries and see they are trying to survive day to day," he said. "Here you see families where the wife is here and the husband works in Beijing. Life is life. But you want to keep going forward."

I asked what he hoped for.

"My hope is that the kids need to eat. So I pay the bills."

The trip south had inspired the fashionista in Boss Wang. He was sitting in the front row of the bus in designer blue jeans, a cream-colored shirt, and a pair of large, tinted sunglasses. He appeared to have combed his hair. Not to be outdone, Garrison was in shades and tricked out in a tight white tank top under his black epauletted jacket. They were costars in a Chinese rendering of *Miami Vice*. It was two hours before tipoff, and the players clambered out of the bus into the locker room.

The arena was a centerpiece of the SBS zipper empire. Outside, billboards showed different Sturgeons players posed before images of half-opened zippers. Other billboards advertised SBS Olympic Spring, an enormous nearby residential community with a sales office across the stadium parking lot. The sales office was decorated with more SBS marketing posters, one with a zipper opening to reveal a line of mountains, another opening to reveal a flowing river. There were also schematic posters of SBS Olympic Spring with imaginary Americans frolicking on floats in the swimming pools. I asked the clerk if they expected lots of foreign buyers. It turned out the posters were made by a design team in the States. He showed me another poster populated by happy, imaginary Chinese.

The Sturgeons were another example of the irregular economic incentive structure of the Chinese league. The zipper king was a basketball nut but his team was also a handy tool for government relations. It might have made more sense to have been located in Xiamen or Fuzhou, the two biggest cities in Fujian Province, but the team was in Jinjiang because SBS was in Jinjiang. Jinjiang was a classic Chinese sweatshop city, with hundreds of factories making athletic shoes and other exports, yet despite this economic clout it lacked prestige or any national identity. Having a pro team gave face to the local officials, and local officials apparently gave the land for SBS Olympic Spring to the zipper king at a very cheap price.

The game was less than an hour away, and I found Weiss sitting on the sideline, appalled. Boss Wang had watched the NBA that morning and decided the Brave Dragons should run on every possession, driving to the basket every time or kicking out for a shot. No plays or offensive sets were needed. He had scrapped Olumide going to the foul line for the pick-and-roll. Just run and shoot. Somewhere Paul Westhead must have been smiling.

"It's insane," Weiss said, watching the players shoot layups. "You know, when you don't have any clothes on, and nobody is going to say anything, you always think you are right."

Olumide trotted by on the court and rolled his eyes. "I've *nayvuh* seen *thees* in my life," he shouted to me. "In my life."

At the opposite end of the court, Prada had taken his players into the locker room for a quick pregame meeting before they returned for final warm-ups. "This is American style," Weiss said. "He pulls his team in and they'll go talk about their strategies."

The Brave Dragons had no strategy. Longnail walked by, sunny as ever, resplendent in an orange shirt and a blue nylon jacket. "That's the guy who sold the village down the tubes," Weiss said, musing for a moment. "Everybody looks at the downside. He probably started the economic upturn of this area. And the village complained."

The game began with the desired dose of anarchy. Prada had prepared the Sturgeons to defend against the high pick-and-roll, but the Brave Dragons were not doing that or anything else. They were running wild. Kobe opened the game with a quick 3-point shot that completely missed the basket. The Chinese guards raced down the court and threw up wild shots at the basket, missing everything. But each time Olumide grabbed the rebound and scored an easy basket. Boss Wang was smiling on the bench.

Tim Pickett helped matters by scoring at will. He made a long 3-pointer and then banked in another. Fujian's point guard, Lu Xiaoming, made a 3, but the Sturgeons were struggling to make sense of this unrecognizable form of offense. Prada called a timeout, and the Fujian cheerleaders pranced onto the court and started thrusting their hips. They seemed comfortable with the task of wearing little clothing and conveying sexiness in public. Growing up in warm weather probably helped.

The game assumed a frenetic, methamphetimal rhythm. The Brave Dragons led 59–48 at halftime, and Tim Pickett had scored 31 points, if not necessarily winning the hearts of his teammates. At one point, when Duan Jiangpeng tossed the ball away, Pickett confronted him on the court. "What is wrong with you?" he screamed. He had not turned out to be the chemistry guy Weiss had hoped for. He had little patience with his teammates' mistakes and rarely passed. The Chinese players resented Bonzi but were awed by him. They already seemed to despise Pickett.

Yet he had played an incredible half. Before the game, Prada had predicted the Brave Dragons had little chance to make the playoffs. Their foreigners shot all the time, he said, yet weren't good enough to single-handedly win the game. Yet Pickett was doing just that. He had made seven 3-pointers and clearly unnerved the Fujianese fans. Cigarette smoke was pouring out of the lobbies and impressive nicotine clouds were hanging over the court. When the teams returned for the second half, Pickett started coughing and complained to a referee. The ref laughed.

The second half started and the Brave Dragons kept running and shooting. Pickett was navigating the smoke and made a long 3-pointer. Brave Dragons by 10. On the Sturgeons bench, Prada turned his head and said something. At the end of the bench, a large man with a flat-top unfolded his legs and stripped off his sweatsuit. He was built like a nose tackle with blocks of cement for calves. His name was Liu Yudong and he was the Chinese Michael Jordan. Or he once was. For years, Liu was Bayi's top star, carrying the Chinese flag during the 1992 and 1996 Olympics. Now he was almost in his forties and was playing out his career in his home of Fujian Province.

Prada had told me that Liu was still one of the finest shooters he had ever seen, but he didn't seem to be inserting him into the game for his shooting. On defense, Liu quickly hammered Olumide. Then he hammered him again. The Chinese Jordan soon had three fouls. But he was scoring, too. He pump-faked and got to the foul line. He buried a 3. The margin had narrowed to 74–71. The Brave Dragons were reluctant to guard him, almost deferential. At brunch, Prada had said that younger Chinese players rarely challenge the older, established veterans in practice, that doing so would be seen as a breach of etiquette. The Brave Dragons seemed to be carrying it over into the game. Prada knew exactly what he was doing. The third quarter ended with the Brave Dragons leading 81–79. The Chinese Jordan had contributed seven points.

The fourth quarter exposed the downside of just running rather than not running an offense. The Brave Dragons were exhausted. Pickett was starting to miss shots and growing frustrated. Liu Yudong went to the free throw line for two shots on a horrible call of a ghost foul. Wingtips walked down the sideline and complained to the game commissioner, who shooed him away. Prada had told me that the officiating was always skewed, especially for the road team. He had lost two playoff series in deciding games on the road. "They all take money on the side," he said. "We're probably the only team that doesn't pay them. You heard them saying in the meeting that we have the best three officials in the league. They say that in every game. You go on the road and you get screwed."

Fujian had now pushed ahead. They were playing a nice team game, spreading the ball around, with everyone scoring. Their point guard was dominating the perimeter, and refs were sprinkling a handful of friendly calls. It was 107–100, and the game seemed over. But then Olumide scored, and Pickett followed with a 3. With eleven seconds remaining, it was 107–105. Now Boss Wang and Wingtips approached the game commissioner. Boss Wang was furious, barking, his head shaking, until he was pulled away. There were still eleven seconds left. Fujian got another friendly call but their center missed both shots. Kobe grabbed the rebound and raced up the court. Pickett was waving for the ball, but Kobe sprinted toward the basket. Pickett was shouting, furious. But this was what Boss Wang said to do! Kobe crashed toward the goal. Foul. He was awarded two shots with one second left and the Brave Dragons down by two points.

Kobe stood at the line and took a breath. He bent his knees, lifted the ball, and released the shot. For a small moment there was a brief, expectant silence.

He missed. Then he missed again. He stood at the line, hands on hips, staring at the basket. The game was over.

Boss Wang stalked to the scorer's table, jabbing the air as he shouted at the game commissioner. The Fujianese fans started chanting for Boss Wang to shut up. The referees had hurried off the court. I could see Longnail. He had spent the game seated directly behind Prada. Now he was laughing. He walked to half-court and pointed to a nicely dressed man in the box seats. It was the zipper king, and he was smiling.

J. T. Prada joined us after the game at a Pizza Hut. He ordered juice. Weiss was having dinner, and the two men commiserated and were soon deep in coachspeak. Before the game, I had asked Prada if he especially wanted to win tonight, given all the hoopla about Weiss. "Oh, that doesn't really mean shit to me," he had said, convincingly. He knew Weiss was in an impossible situation and also knew Weiss might be a good person to get to know.

Weiss wanted to meet Prada, too. Because if J. T. Prada was angling to get back to the NBA, Bob Weiss had decided he wanted to stay in China. He was having a ball. Tracy loved it. She could even imagine returning to Taiyuan for the following season, though Weiss had a harder time imagining that. He was curious about other teams, other possibilities, and Prada knew people.

We walked outside to find Jinjiang vibrating in anticipation of Valentine's Day. Large booths were erected across from our hotel where couples could pay to shoot an arrow at Cupid's heart. Another booth had costumes for photographs. Our hotel, the Xingtai, had placed a large heart-shaped pink arch above the door to the lobby. Anyone without a date could go to the Xitai International Spa on the second floor. An advertisement in the elevator showed one masseuse in a belly dancer costume, posed in a bedroom atop a king-sized bed. Another showed a blond Russian woman lying in an empty bathtub in a yellow nightie, pulling a black stocking off her leg.

Weiss and Prada stopped on the street outside the Cupid booth. They exchanged telephone numbers and promised to keep in touch. A new network had been formed.

CHAPTER EIGHTEEN

THE PROMISED LAND

The experiment had not produced the expected result. Money had been spent to hire an NBA coach to serve as a change agent, a technology transfer to upgrade an inferior Chinese product, the Chinese player. Yet not long after this savior had arrived, the product had proved immutable, the transfer incompatible, not so much because of the raw materials—the actual players, who were flawed but seemed capable of change—but because of the system that produced the raw materials and the people who controlled the system. The court was the same, the ball was the same, the rules of the game were the same, but everything else was different. Even the rebels inside the system, including the very rich, very unpredictable, and very combustible man who instigated the experiment, held strong convictions about what could not and should not be changed. What had seemed to Boss Wang a logical idea—to try to copy the game as it was played on television by hiring the people on television—had foundered, in part, because changing how players played on the court meant changing how things were done off the court. What the rich man had really wanted was a result. He had wanted it immediately, which, as it happened, was not possible.

Yet one unexpected result of the failed experiment was that it had produced a better team anyway. This was an upside of starting at such a low base of performance and playing in a league where most teams didn't bother with experiments. The Brave Dragons, having won five games the previous season, were now very much in pursuit of the eighth and final playoff position. They had won 21 games and lost 21. Eight games remained in the season. Tim Pickett was not an avatar of team play, had little confidence in his teammates, and shot the ball even more than had Bonzi. This was partly out of frustration, since Pickett had never experienced a team like the Brave Dragons or an owner like Boss Wang, and his temperament was a poor match for the situation. Yet Pickett was averaging about 40 points a game, and while the Brave Dragons had not gotten better, they had not gotten appreciably worse.

Weiss was now mostly resigned to his predicament, if still frustrated at how the owner had dismantled a potentially top team. Weiss had decided that the benefits of being in China outweighed the frustrations presented by Boss Wang. Liu Tie was now acting as the head coach, though Boss Wang regarded him largely as a vassal. In one game, the owner had simply stepped into the huddle and begun barking orders. After a humiliating loss to Xinjiang, he screamed at the coaches and players for more than an hour, working himself into a frothy, blithering rage before suddenly announcing he would speak no more. "From now on, I'm not going to give my opinions or meddle," he told the players. "I'm not going to say anything. But for you coaches, you have to win five more games, or six."

The following day, he strode into the practice gym, stripped down to his underwear, slipped into his shorts and T-shirt, and summoned Liu Tie so that he could scream at him. Liu Tie spent the rest of the practice pacing the sideline, head down, pausing sometimes to rub a spot on the floor with his shoe. Boss Wang divided the players into two teams and installed an offense that called for the guards to throw the ball inside on every play, forcing the defense to collapse, so that the big men could kick it back out for open shots. "I think meddling has a different definition in China," Weiss said as he wandered at the periphery of practice. Weiss eventually stepped in, trying to organize something functional involving actual picks and movement off the ball out of Boss Wang's vision, while the boss pulled aside two players to show them how to lower their shoulder and ram into a defender. He was teaching them how to play linebacker.

The players existed in a state of deepening stupefaction. Pickett was especially bewildered. After practice, he had wandered over to the sideline and taken a seat. "I've never seen a team like this before," he said. "The owner says he is not going to speak anymore, but then he comes to practice the next day and speaks the whole time." Olumide had started counting down the days until the end of the season. Big Rus was no longer around to be stupefied. His foot never really recovered, and Boss Wang sent him back to Kazakhstan. Pan Jiang, the beleaguered point guard, appeared progressively more ashen, as if he were being drained of a pint of blood every day. He was suffering recurrent fevers. No one absorbed more verbal abuse from the owner than Pan, who had the impossible task of deciphering contradictory orders, of running a team when the instructions on how to run it changed every day. Even Garrison was on the injured reserve; his throat was sore from too much interpretation.

Yet winning always made things better, always provided the evanescent salve necessary for everyone to keep pushing ahead. If there had been a singular moment that provided validation, that demonstrated that the experiment might not be a complete failure, it had come the previous week during a rematch in Tianjin. In the fourth quarter, in a tight game, Pickett turned his ankle and crumpled to the floor. Now the team would have to win without him and prove they could win without any foreign scorer. Olumide was still on the floor, grabbing rebounds, but now the Chinese players had to prove they were more than props. Kobe scored on a drive and then Duan made two foul shots (Weiss had kept reminding him not to look at the floor). With Pickett icing his ankle on the bench, Duan scored again on a slicing drive, Pan hit two foul shots, and finally Little Ba, who had been getting better every game, hit a big 3-pointer. The Brave Dragons won, 107–95, with five players in double figures. When it ended, everyone raced to midcourt to celebrate, a little surprised at what they had managed to do. This, after all, was what the experiment was supposed to produce.

But now only eight games remained, and Boss Wang was right: The Brave Dragons needed to win five games, maybe six, to qualify for the playoffs. The margin was even tighter because no one expected them to win the next game. They were flying south again, this time to Guangdong Province, the engine of the Chinese economy and the place where experiments usually happened first. They would play the Guangdong Southern Tigers, the league's first-place team, which a few years before had produced China's second most famous player, Yi Jianlian, a forward in the NBA.

Unlike the Shanghai team, which had collapsed when Yao Ming departed, the Southern Tigers had gotten better when Yi left. They had won the previous year's championship and five of the last six.

Nature seemed to have disappeared. The car moved over the elevated highway above fields of factories: white tiles and gray concrete, followed by more concrete, and then distant smokestacks and, to the left, in the farther distance, the skyline of the provincial capital, Guangzhou. Dusk was falling. The smokestacks twinkled with tiny white lights. What we could see were the miles upon miles of unseen productive space, once green hills or farms, now filled with power plants and factories. Warehouses crouched at the edge of a canal. Barges were moving piles of dirt. The coast was not far away but the air smelled of chemicals and industry, not of the sea. The car kept moving, through a deceptive silence, at a deceptive elevation, since we could only see the buildings, not hear them, and what we saw were mostly rooftops, deliberately anonymous, one little different from another, rather than what these buildings were: hives. Inside were tens of thousands of workers doing thousands of small repetitive jobs to make millions of products: iPods, laptops, mobile phones, Christmas ornaments, cheap toys, fake paintings, T-shirts, basketballs, running shoes, screwdrivers, automobiles, love seats, coffee mugs. Even more than neighboring Fujian, this was where everything in the world was made.

The driver raced past an exit marked "Dongguan City," which, I mentioned, was our destination. He braked in the middle of the highway, shifted into reverse, and backed up, dodging, backward, the oncoming cars, which were determined to keep coming forward. We braked, dodged, backed up, braked, backed up, and dodged until we took the exit to Dongguan. We drove into the city, except the city didn't seem to recognize itself as one. It was a condensed version of what we'd already been seeing. It was crowded, with hotels and neon lights, with streets lined with dingy apartments and tiled office buildings, and still more streets, narrower ones behind gates that were lined with more factories. It was a formless incoherence, as if it had never intended to be a city, a social organism, but only a place for work and money. Which was what it was.

Dongguan was what happened in China when opportunism, profit, and desperation conflated at the edge of policy. For his great economic experiment, Deng Xiaoping had chosen Guangdong as a setting for several of his special economic zones. They would be petri dishes where droplets of market reforms and foreign investment could germinate without the risk of spilling out into the rest of the country. He wasn't looking for a contagion yet, just a lab experiment to see what happened when foreign ideas and foreign money were set loose again in China. Shenzhen, the most famous petri dish, the swamp turned megalopolis, was actually surrounded by a fence. Except fences were pointless, since the petri dishes had been created to culture money, and the thirst for money defies fences. Soon factories seemed to be spreading everywhere in Guangdong. Deng had ordered everyone to go make money. Who was willing to defy orders? Even before Shenzhen was formally established in 1979, a Hong Kong company had already opened a handbag factory in Dongguan, that city's first foreign factory. Unblessed and unrecognized, Dongguan would make the cheap stuff, the low-end products shunned by other cities, and would become China's fourth biggest export center. It would exploit and enrich. Millions of young people would flow out of the country-side, mostly teenage girls, to work in awful conditions for maybe $100 a month. Yet the sweatshop represented crude progress, a first step off the farm, where almost no one made $100 in a month or even four.

Dongguan was also a historical footnote: It was here, in 1839, that a Qing official, Lin Zexu, confronted the British and their debilitating opium trade. Lin appeared at a local harbor and ordered the incineration of 20,000 cases of opium. It was a defiant act by an imperial regime that had not yet realized it was already in irreversible decline. The British and Chinese engaged in the First Opium War, in which British war-ships routed the Chinese military in the waters of Guangdong, the Qing were forced to open the treaty ports to international trade and hand over Hong Kong to Britain. Later, when the Chinese realized that the world had lapped them, that the modern age was being forged with guns and machines, the Dongguan incident would be elevated to a historical mile-stone in China. It was considered the beginning of the country's century of humiliation and subjugation to foreign powers.

One hundred and seventy years later, Dongguan was now the sweat-shop that made the narcotic that had tilted an increasingly unbalanced global economy in China's favor—cheap everything.

The small metal plaque beside the guardhouse was engraved in English and Chinese: "Winnerway Basketball Club." In December 1987, a man named Chen Haitao founded the Guangdong Winnerway Group to capi-talize on the inconceivable boom spilling across the provincial coastline. First the company developed industrial parks, including the Winnerway Industrial Park that housed its headquarters. Winnerway (known in Mandarin as Hongyuan) would become Dongguan's first publicly listed company, on the Shenzhen exchange, and would later expand into pharmaceuticals. But property was the heart of the business, and, needing advertising, Winnerway decided to sponsor a soccer team bearing the company name. By the early 1990s, though, Winnerway decided that soccer wasn't the sport of China's future and basketball was. A dynasty was born.

I had arrived the morning of the game to meet the Winnerway general manager, Liu Hongjiang. The complex was less impressive than I had expected; a small, peach-colored dormitory, a narrow concrete courtyard and a small administrative building, right in the heart of Dongguan. The foreign players lived a short walk away in a hotel owned by Winnerway. But if the facilities were unremarkable, there were also small differences. Every player had his own apartment in the complex, and the covered garage was filled with luxury cars. I walked through a meeting room lined with trophies and team photographs as a secretary led me into the office where I would meet the general manager. At other appointments, etiquette called for a host to offer a cup of tea or a cup of heated water. At Winnerway, the secretary brought a can of Red Bull. On the wall above a conference table, a large, framed piece of calligraphy served as a mission statement: "If we combine our knowledge, and if we combine our strengths, we can all succeed." It was a Mandarin version of "There is no 'i' in team."

Liu Hongjiang arrived late, apologizing yet in a good mood. He was not expecting a close game that night. Liu had a shaved head and a pleasantly conspiratorial manner; as he talked, he leaned forward, elbows on knees, drawing closer, as if sharing a secret. He had been a sports journalist in Guangzhou, considered an expert on basketball, when the Winnerway owner cajoled him into running the team. He knew Winnerway had originally conceived the team for its corporate interests, as an advertising tool and also for government relations. Now, though, he told me, the team was evolving into something different, something organic and independent.

"We are the first and only professional basketball club in the CBA," he said. "We are different from the traditional way. We follow the management of private enterprise rather than following a government policy."

For all the mythology of China's economic renaissance and stories of men like Boss Wang who become multimillionaires, the China story is hardly a parable of capitalism as we know it. Private entrepreneurship exists in perpetual tension with the state, and those tensions seemed more starkly evident in a basketball league organized to be a commercial exercise, even when it actually was not one. Liu disagreed with even the most basic assumption that the CBA was a true professional league. He said league officials tried to copy the NBA, even as they maintained complete control of how the teams were allowed to do business.

Winnerway's changes started at the top. Chen Haitao once had a reputation for meddling much like Boss Wang, but as his sons had assumed more power in the company, the team had become less of a mere vanity project. Coaches and the front office usually made decisions about the team with less interference from the owners or corporate sponsors. More important, Winnerway was not at the mercy of sports bureaucrats, as were the Shanghai Sharks. Revenues came from ticket sales, sponsorship, and club-run businesses, including a store that sold T-shirts, jerseys, and other collectibles. Still, Liu chafed at not having control over advertising in his own arena.

The team's front office had also learned lessons during the NBA's recruiting of Yi Jianlian. Yi was a skilled small forward in a power forward's body and a potential marketing dream; Nike signed him when he was still a teenager and also signed a contract with the Winnerway team. The Milwaukee Bucks drafted Yi in 2007 with the sixth pick in the first round, and he ultimately signed a contract, after acrimonious negotiations between Winnerway, the NBA, and the Bucks. But the process provided an education for the team; the specialists and coaches who came to evaluate and tutor Yi also advised Winnerway on conditioning, weight training, and how best to prepare players. The advice was usually the same: The players are too tired because they practice too much, and they are too weak because the weight program is misguided. Liu said the team now spent $2 million a year to send players and coaches to train and practice in the United States, Europe, and Australia.

Liu thought the team's success validated their approach. Yet what frustrated him was the straitjacket presented by the league. Teams needed free agency, the ability to market their brand, to control sponsors inside their own arenas, and to sell more concessions and souvenirs. He agreed that the league needed to produce the best national team possible but thought the old model clearly wasn't doing that. Players were being wasted. Talent was not being properly developed.

"The NBA is a self-evolving league," he said. "The CBA is nothing at all. I disagree with the Chinese reporters who write that this is a professional league. This is not a professional league. The mind-set of the authorities must be thoroughly changed."

What most separated Winnerway from the rest of the league, however, was Chinese talent. They had more of it than any team in China. When I asked Liu how they got it, he placed his elbows on his knees, leaned forward, his face close to mine, and grinned.

Before the season, I had watched Winnerway in an exhibition tournament, which was sponsored by the Asian Basketball Association, and included teams from Hong Kong, South Korea, and Japan. I had finagled a seat on a VIP platform, not far from the commissioner of the Asian Basketball Association, Carl Ching. The ABA was the regional affiliate of FIBA, the global basketball body, which meant Ching was a powerful figure in Asian basketball. He also was reportedly one of the biggest crime syndicate kingpins in Hong Kong. He had denied these allegations but authorities in Australia and the United States had barred him from entering either country. When I first saw him, he was on the court before the game, a man in his sixties laughing and chucking set shots.

I was sitting with Gary Boyson, an international scout for the Los Angeles Lakers, who was scouting Winnerway. Many of the team's older stars were sitting out, so Boyson was taking notes on the teenagers who might one day become NBA prospects. Boyson was about 6'3", heavyset with thick legs and thick fingers, and was draped in a very large, very purple Lakers shirt. International scouting had existed for years, but now the NBA teams were especially eager to find players from China, given the commercial jackpot created by Yao Ming. Having a Chinese star meant having a piece of the Chinese market and also helped advance the NBA's ambitions in China. The previous season, Boyson had persuaded the Lakers to sign a raw Chinese player, Sun Yue, in the second round. (Sun never made it with the Lakers, though he became a starter on China's Olympic team.) When I followed Boyson through the bowels of the arena, the effect was of riding the wake of a visiting dignitary. Heads turned at the sight of a man with the power to catapult a kid out of south China onto an NBA court with Kobe Bryant.

During warm-ups, Boyson pointed out different players. There was Su Wei, 7'1", once considered a possible heir to Yao Ming. He was twenty. Another kid, Wang Zheng, was even bigger, maybe 7'2", and younger, barely seventeen. There were two point guards, Chen Jianghua and Liu Xiaoyu; a bruising eighteen-year-old power forward, Dong Hanlin; and a wiry, 6'9" small forward, Zhou Peng, not yet twenty. None of them started yet for Winnerway, except for the point guards, who shared the job, but they probably represented the heart of China's future Olympic teams.

As the players trotted through layups, I asked Boyson how many of them might be good enough in the future to play in the NBA.

"Maybe one," he guessed.

What about for a major college program in the United States?

"Every one of them," he answered more confidently. "These guys would win the NCAA." Then he reconsidered. "Don't say that. But they would make the Sweet Sixteen," the top sixteen teams in the annual National Collegiate Athletic Association tournament.

Winnerway's talent could be ascribed to the same forces that had once transformed Guangdong Province. Deng had unlocked China at a fortuitous demographic moment, with untold millions of young people idled, impoverished, and bored in the countryside. Deng began to let them loose, and the millions of migrants who poured out of the countryside to fill Guangdong's factories represented the competitive advantage that made China a manufacturing colossus. They were mostly literate and they mostly deferred to authority, meaning they were capable of learning to work on an assembly line and willing to do so for some of the lowest wages in the world.

Basketball, technically, remained under the old system. Once a kid was identified as a prospect, he was funneled into a sports school and his rights belonged to the provincial team. If a province lacked good players, a team had to get creative. When Winnerway first got organized in the early and mid-1990s, the team hired veteran players, including some recent retirees from the national team who were no longer affiliated with a sports bureau. But by 1998, the team realized it needed to develop talent of its own. It was under contract to draw players out of the sports systems in Guangdong and neighboring Guangxi Province, which had produced the team's current top star, Zhu Fangyu. But the local talent pool wasn't deep enough to match Winnerway's ambitions, so the team decided to do for itself what Gary Boyson did for the Lakers. The difference being that Winnerway was scouting kids as young as thirteen.

To find players meant outmaneuvering the sports system. Most kids in sports schools were required to sign a contract at a certain age that transferred their rights to the affiliated CBA team. But Winnerway began searching for kids *before* they signed the contract, or for kids who had opted out of the sports school system altogether. Winnerway now had players from at least nine Chinese provinces. Family members were often relocated to Dongguan and given a job in the company. The team also offered a correspondence program with two local universities so that players could work toward a degree. Perhaps the biggest enticement was that anyone playing for Winnerway was likely to get a shoe deal with Nike, Adidas, or the Chinese sportswear company Anta. Shoe companies, eager to find the next great Chinese star, were banking that he would be playing for Winnerway.

Liu Xiaoyu, the point guard, had actually recruited the team. Born in 1989, three months before the Tiananmen Square crackdown, Liu played in Changchun, the capital of Jilin Province. Jilin was an anomaly in that many of the best players attended regular high schools rather than government sports academies. A top student, fluent in English, Liu was recruited by the country's top two universities, Peking University and Tsinghua University, and also invited, at age fifteen, to join the junior team of the Shanghai Sharks. He spent two days in camp with the Sharks but returned to high school after feeling lonely and overwhelmed. Less than a year later, though, Liu contacted Winnerway and met with the same scout who had found Yi Jianlian.

"He said, 'Hey, Yi Jianlian. I found him, and now he's a superstar,'" Liu recalled. "Now he goes around saying, 'I found Yi Jianlian and Liu Xiaoyu.'"

Now Liu had a shoe deal with Nike and was one of the last two players cut from China's Olympic team. His parents had moved to Dongguan and he had bought them a BMW. The general manager, Liu Hongjiang, said Winnerway paid Chinese players some of the highest salaries in the league, ranging from $50,000 for a bench player to as much as $300,000 for one of the team's four Olympians. When it started investing so much in its Chinese players, Winnerway also began rethinking its approach to foreign imports. It stopped looking for Americans who would score 40 points a game and started looking for Americans who could tutor the team's younger Chinese players and fit into the team. It didn't want a hired gun scorer or a bad boy. Winnerway wanted a Good American.

For the past decade, they had found one in Jason Dixon.

Dixon was a star during his early years in Dongguan, a scorer and a rebounder, averaging more than 20 points and 12 rebounds a game, and the team depended on him the same way most Chinese teams still depend on their imports. His numbers mattered to him, because he played on one-year contracts, without any real job security other than a stat sheet that proved his value. But then, several years ago, the team's management told him they wanted to showcase Yi Jianlian, which meant that Dixon would become the team's designated rebounder and defender. The glory would go to the Chinese players.

Dixon was a little wistful about it all. At 6'9", thickly muscled with his hair braided into long black cornrows, Dixon was a formidable physical presence, if a quiet man. When the Chinese sports press lashed out at Bonzi and other Americans for shooting too much and passing too little, Dixon was often cited as the right kind of American, an import who knew his role and accepted it. Except Dixon was not actually very happy about it. "I don't like it," he admitted as we sat inside the Winnerway hotel. "I want to score."

Dixon was now the second-longest tenured player on the team, after Du Feng, the Olympian who was also an assistant coach. He set picks, guarded the other team's foreign big man, grabbed rebounds, and, when necessary, scored. He averaged about 15 points a game. When Bonzi was still playing and Winnerway needed more points inside, Dixon scored 32 points against Olumide, sending Boss Wang into a rage. But more often his role was to complement the Chinese stars on the court and tutor the young players in practice. His current project was the massive seventeen-year-old Wang Zheng, who Dixon thought had a chance at the NBA. "I'm telling you, Wang Zheng is going to be a beast!" he promised. "A beast!"

Dixon arrived in China in 1997, playing for the Fujian team before eventually joining Winnerway. He had always considered himself a "small-time player," having graduated from Jerry Falwell's Liberty University in 1995 and then playing in Turkey, Cyprus, Israel, and Argentina before arriving in China. The quality of play was best in Turkey, and he liked Israel "once you got over the fear of the bombs and all that stuff." But China became his career. He recalled that during the early days of the league, the team would travel to games on twenty-four-hour-long train trips.

"The hotels were so terrible," he said. "The beds were terrible. There were roaches."

He learned enough Mandarin to communicate with his teammates and began to understand why Chinese coaches often complained that

Chinese players were lazy. "They are overworked, so they are lazy," he said. "It's like people who work in factories here. Because they are so overworked, they do as little as possible because they know that no matter how hard they work, there is always something else waiting." Gradually, though, Winnerway changed as the team was more exposed to basketball outside China. He thought the head coach, Li Chunjiang, had improved dramatically after spending time in the United States with American coaches. The team's weight training also improved, and the Chinese players became stronger, which gave them confidence. Before, he said, "all we would do were squats and a couple of curls. And then they were smoking cigarettes."

He knew his reputation but questioned whether being the Good American brought any real reward. Dixon's wife and two children lived in Colorado, and he was gone much of the year while making a salary less than most foreigners. He was awed by Olumide's supposed $350,000 deal. Every season began with uncertainty as to whether the team would keep him. The previous season, the team had signed a new corporate sponsor, which wanted to dump Dixon and bring in a bigger center. Dixon wasn't certain he had a job, until the coaches overruled the sponsor and brought him back for the sake of team chemistry. He had held his own this season but the competition was improving.

"I noticed this year that no one was double-teaming me anymore," he said. "Then I realized everyone was seven feet tall and had played in the NBA."

Winnerway usually delayed hiring a second foreigner until midseason, when management had assessed the team's weaknesses. This year, they brought in Smush Parker, a former Lakers point guard, because the team's Chinese point guards were inexperienced and injured. Parker was probably the most talented player on the team but his minutes were restricted, except in the biggest games. His job was to help Winnerway win a championship and train the Chinese guards so they could help the team win championships in the future.

Dixon was not certain about next season, but he had had one recent ego boost that week. A Chinese reporter had approached him about a retrospective piece, having discovered that Dixon ranked among the Top Ten scorers and rebounders in the history of the Chinese league.

It seemed that a pretty good argument could be made that the Good American would belong in the Hall of Fame, if the league had one.

The score was 62–34 at halftime, in favor of Guangdong. They had 17 assists. The Brave Dragons had one. This was the first time this season when the outcome of the game was determined in the first five minutes, or perhaps before the tip. The previous night, Coach Liu had prepared the team by showing film of the *next* opponent, the neighboring Dongguan New Century Leopards. When Bonzi was around, he kept the score close against Guangdong until the final minutes, when he was exhausted. The players may have hated him, but he gave them confidence. Without him, they looked scared even before the opening tip. They kept peeking over their shoulders to look at the Guangdong team warm up: four Olympians, a former Laker, and the best young players in China.

I sat beside Tina, a nineteen-year-old editor for the website Netease. She covered the Guangdong team and made a point of showing me the young power forward, Dong Hanlin. "He's got a great body," she told me with a straight face. It took me a moment to understand that she meant just that: He's got a great body for basketball, like a prototype, and that maybe he could be the next Chinese star to make the NBA. This was the parlor game in Guangdong: Who would be next? When the injured point guard Chen Jianghua entered the game, Tina nodded. "He will be the Chinese Allen Iverson," she said, pausing to rethink her prediction. "Actually, his skills can't compare with Iverson's, so he'll have to try harder."

The Brave Dragons put up a better fight in the second half. This was a homecoming for the exiled Guangdongers, Joy and Little Ba, and they played well. The crowd cheered when Joy came into the game, and Little Ba and Wei put on a nice shooting display in the second half to draw the Brave Dragons closer, if never too close. Joy's girlfriend, whose English name was Michelle, was the head of the Guangdong's cheerleading team and—Tina told me—the most famous cheerleader in China. In a lopsided game, the crowd seemed most excited when Michelle trotted out with her girls at halftime and started grinding to an English-language techno-disco song that needed no translation: "I'll Lick Your Ice Cream, and You Can Lick My Lollipop."

The final score was 106–89, with Guangdong resting their starters for most of the second half. They could have won by 50, but I later learned that they pulled back out of respect for Weiss. Liu Hongjiang, the opposing general manager, was intrigued by the American coach and did not want to insult him.

The Brave Dragons now had seven games left. They could not afford to lose many more.

The following afternoon the Winnerway team gathered at their practice gym, a short drive from the team dormitory. The gym was a modernist glass and aluminum barn filled with natural light and surrounded by weeping willows and luxury high-rise apartments. I came on the bus with Liu Hongjiang and some of the younger players, but the stars arrived on their own. In the parking lot were a BMW, a couple of Audis, a Honda, a few Mercedes, and a Cadillac Escalade. I did not know of a single Chinese player on the Brave Dragons who owned a car.

Practice lasted precisely seventy-seven minutes, with every minute accounted for. I sat beside Liu Hongjiang and soon a handful of other men arrived. A man in a blue sweater and wire-rimmed glasses studiously watched the players run full-court fast break drills. He paced, head down, and occasionally checked the whiteboard where an assistant coach was keeping results for every player during timed shooting drills. "That's Liu Xiaoyu's father," the general manager said. A man in a zippered sweater standing by the door was the father of Wang Shipeng, one of the team's Olympians, while other fathers also trickled in. Liu Hongjiang was enthralled watching Smush Parker run the break; the previous night, Parker placed a perfect transition bounce pass into the hands of a player streaking toward the basket who then flushed a dunk over Olumide. It would have been a routine fast break in the NBA, but it was the first time I'd seen it all season in China.

"Our Chinese national team would be number four in the world if we had Smush Parker," Liu said, excited, if overly optimistic.

When I had asked him how long it would take for China to produce an NBA-quality point guard, he had replied ten or twenty years. Across the court, the small forward Zhu Fangyu was shooting 3-pointers in the timed drill. His form was perfect, the ball spinning tightly as it snapped through the net. He was the league's reigning most valuable player and he had toyed with the Brave Dragons, at one point laughing while he made an open layup. "I want Zhu to go play in Europe," Liu said. "His growth will be hampered if he stays here. He is well above other Chinese players."

Zhu fired another 3. The rotation was again perfect. Liu broke into a grin, unable to contain himself, proud of the talent assembled on this court. "This is the best of the best," he said.

Then he leaned over to me, and whispered in my ear. He wanted to know Weiss's salary.

"Is it a lot?" he asked.

"How much is a lot?" I answered, and Liu started laughing.

Winnerway was contemplating expanding its coaching staff. The head coach, Li Chunjiang, apprenticed in the United States and saw that NBA teams had position coaches and tactical coaches. Liu wondered if Weiss would be interested. I was not certain what to say but I offered that Weiss might be interested, that he had enjoyed Shanxi but that the team had issues. I mentioned that the owner was "unique."

Liu grinned and leaned in. His eyes widened and he spoke his first English word of the day to describe Boss Wang.

"Crazy!" he said, laughing.

Practice ended. The young point guard Liu Xiaoyu stopped over to say goodbye in his perfect English. Then he collected his father, and they drove off in their BMW.

The Brave Dragons left Guangdong Province defeated. Their next game, against the Dongguan New Century Leopards, was more evenly matched until the final quarter when Boss Wang, having pushed into the huddle to take over coaching duties, decided to remove Olumide and Pickett from a close game. The foreigners were baffled and angry, equating it to quitting, but Boss Wang saw it as lodging a protest, having watched Olumide get hammered all night and concluding that the refs were cheating and the game's outcome had already been decided.

As in many other things in China, the Leopards represented an attempt to copy a successful experiment, in this case the Winnerway team. The Leopards players lived in a lakefront luxury residential complex owned by the team's multimillionaire owner. They played in a new arena built by the owner, and their philosophy was grounded in developing future Chinese stars. Their 7'1" power forward, Zhang Kai, was already likened to Kevin Garnett, the great forward for the Boston Celtics. Their point guard, Meng Duo, had returned from a summer of strength training in Las Vegas with the muscular upper torso of an NBA guard. Just twenty, Meng also had "a very good body."

In the heartland of Chinese manufacturing, professional basketball teams were in the business of manufacturing players. Like the surrounding factories, they were still trying to manufacture for the American market or at least were trying to follow the American model. What had changed, or evolved, was the formula for doing it: better pay, better conditions, better management, and better training. There were flaws, and much to be learned, but change was happening in Guangdong, again. Outside, in the factories, the hives kept churning, but a new generation of teenagers coming off the farm now had higher expectations and lower tolerance for unending overtime and low pay. Economists were already predicting that China's moment as the world's lowest-cost manufacturer was coming to an end and that Guangdong, again, would have to become an experiment zone, another petri dish.

The airplane banked hard right as it turned sharply toward the Taiyuan airport. Out the window, the brown, desiccated ravines of Shanxi Province seemed as lifeless as the face of the moon. Winter showed no sign of abating. Six games were remaining, and the Liaoning Pan Pan Dinosaurs were the opponent tomorrow night. It would be an elimination game. The losing team would be out of the playoff chase.

On the bus back to the hotel Pickett sat alone, listening to music on his headset. He had already told me that he would never come back to this team, and it was hard to blame him. In Guangdong, he skipped a team video session to get a massage. He was a prisoner in the last two weeks of his sentence.

The bus exited onto Fuxi Road and we approached the mall with the Louis Vuitton store. Olumide leaned over, nodding toward Pickett, and whispered in my ear. "One of the Chinese players told me they may jump Tim," he said, eyes widening. He said they were fed up with his criticisms. They called him mini-Bonzi. "I've seen it happen before. They were giving me a warning."

I was stunned. It didn't seem possible. The bus passed the mall, and the gray tower of the World Trade came into view. Olumide was already thinking about next season, about who would need him and who would pay him. He said interpreters from six different teams were already calling him, gauging his interest. He was certain he didn't want to return to Taiyuan, though then he paused.

"Never say never," he said, laughing. "If they pay me $1 million, then I would suck it up."

He thought the Brave Dragons had almost no chance of making the playoffs. Bayi was also fighting for the last playoff spot, and Olumide said the refs always favored Bayi. Last season, the officiating was so bad that the league imported foreign referees for the final rounds of the playoffs. In China, this was how it worked. Corruption was part of the game.

CHAPTER NINETEEN

BLACK WHISTLES

What was transpiring was a theft in progress. Or at least an attempted theft, since the Brave Dragons seemed determined not to accept the victory the referees seemed equally determined to steal for them. This resistance might have been admirable were it a moral stand, but it was not that. It was plain incompetence. The game was now in the fourth quarter, with barely two minutes remaining, and the refs had sent three Liaoning starters to the bench with six fouls and had sent the Brave Dragons to the foul line more than sixty times. Some teams do not attempt sixty foul shots over the course of *three* games. This was a pistol-shooting contest where one competitor was getting twice as many chances. Yet the Brave Dragons had missed more than half of their free throws. So the refs had ejected Liaoning's biggest star. Yet the game was tied at 100.

Timeout. Ren Hongbing unleashed the Wave. It never got old. The crowd was loopy, leaping out of their seats. The referees were huddled on the sideline, plotting, presumably wondering what more they could possibly do. Everyone had warned that the refs might try to steer the outcome of that night's game. What was surprising was that they were trying to steer it to the Brave Dragons.

The morning had begun with a whiff of paranoia. On the way to the shootaround, Olumide spoke as if the wheels of some invisible piece of machinery were now beginning to turn. He spun various conspiracy theories, none of which involved a happy ending for the Brave Dragons. By this logic, the season had arrived at the moment when the league inevitably began acting like what it was: a system rigged to protect itself and its most important stakeholders, with no stakeholder presumed more important than Bayi. Just a phone call from a general in the People's Liberation Army and a whole cascade of dominoes could fall to clear a path for Bayi.

"The CBA decides who they want to make the playoffs," Olumide said, his eyes widening for effect, "and who they do not want to."

That games were sometimes fixed was obvious, if not necessarily proven. The Guangdong team was the league's template, as far as professionalization went, but also the object of occasional suspicions about gambling, such as when they lost badly earlier in the season to one of the league's worst teams. There was speculation that the private owner of the Dongguan New Century Leopards also secretly owned the Jilin team and had ordered Jilin's top foreign player to fall ill when the two teams met, which had helped Dongguan win the game and consolidate its playoff position. Prada had sworn the refs cheated all the time, but the motive was greed more than a skilled conspiracy, abetted by a failure of oversight, which was usually how corruption worked in society at large.

Every so often, Communist Party leaders launched an anticorruption campaign, and a high official might get taken down in the excitement. But few people interpreted these campaigns as genuine attempts to address the systemic corruption that pervaded so much of official and private life. It was either about public relations or political infighting; one political official or faction, having accrued enough leverage inside the party, was taking down a rival official or faction. When Shanghai's Communist Party secretary was defrocked in a salacious real estate and pension scandal, his real crime was bucking policies from Beijing. The arrest was a message intended for internal consumption within the Communist Party: Don't get too uppity. Corruption enraged ordinary citizens, yet their rage, unable to coalesce into anything broad-based or meaningful, usually dissipated into cynicism. Everyone knew the game was rigged and that the only people empowered to make changes were the people running the game, which meant the game wasn't likely to change. Many people simply played along, too. Cheating scandals erupted on national college entrance examinations. Fake receipts and fake diplomas were national industries, sold outside train stations or over the Internet. Cell phones buzzed with text message advertisements selling fake corporate records or fake visas to Canada. When President Hu Jintao ordered all 70 million Communist Party cadres to attend political education classes and write formal essays, a market quickly appeared online for prewritten essays.

Corruption presented a more complicated challenge to the Chinese Basketball Association. It was one thing to know that party officials or powerful real estate developers were stealing without having to witness the larceny. It was another to pay for a ticket to see it happen. A basketball game actually represented a rare social exercise in China where ordinary people could scream at authority figures such as referees and the game commissioner. Chinese soccer still had not recovered from the public revulsion over corruption scandals, and while basketball was now having its moment of popularity, if fans believed the games were all rigged, or that players weren't trying their best, then the essential aspect of the competition—that something real was at stake—would be lost.

This season, league officials had introduced an anticorruption policy titled the "Chinese Men's Basketball Industry Competition Law Punishment Guideline," which for the first time listed infractions and prescribed fines for wrongdoing. The league applauded itself for this newfound specificity, saying that it was reforming from "people rule" to the "rule of law." There were also new restrictions on smoking in arenas—this was working like a charm—and the self-babysitting policy for referees. "A minority of referees have a low ability to resist interference," *Titan Sports* had soberly reported. "After getting some 'advantage,' they give up their principles, and manipulation of games certainly exists." No longer, the league promised.

It all sounded nice. But no doubt those referees could find someone willing to sell them fake forms to turn in to the league office if they were still out drinking *baijiu* with general managers and taking envelopes of cash. No guideline addressed the broader corruption in basketball and elsewhere that was more about systemic favoritism than about bribing referees. No matter how fast the league or the country was changing, power had diffused far more slowly.

A few days before the game, I had lunch in Beijing with Boss Wang's son, Songyan, whose English name was King. The first time I met King, I had wondered about his choice for a name. It seemed a touch presumptuous. But he was merely using the English translation of his surname, Wang. King was the temperamental opposite of his father, forever friendly and reasonable, polished and proud of his correspondence degree in English from a school in California. We met at an Italian restaurant inside an expensive mall, and King arrived in his usual preppy attire. He traveled regularly for his different businesses but as the season wore on, he had started turning up on the bench beside his father during games. He had befriended Weiss and Tracy, joining them in Sanya for the Lunar New Year vacation. The clouds of anger that invariably darkened his father's face never seemed to touch King. And yet when I asked about the team's prospect for the playoffs, his mood turned sour.

"Not this year," he answered emphatically before catching my eye. "Too many complicated things in China."

He took a bite from his salad.

"Do you know the *hei shao*?" he asked. The black whistle.

I nodded. Fans had yelled it at a few games.

"When we played against Bayi in Ningbo, we only lost by two points. Ningbo is their hometown." He had counted five fouls called against the Brave Dragons in the final minutes. I had watched that game on television and noticed that Bayi was getting to the line but had not suspected corruption. I just thought their players were smarter about drawing fouls. But King was certain that the outcome was fixed and he wasn't alone. He had laughed when he saw someone on the Web had written that the refs should be called "Protect the Army Whistle."

King saw the cheating as part of the broader problem of the league clinging to control and power. Bayi represented the last stand of a system. The team was fighting with the Brave Dragons, the Pan Pan Dinosaurs, and a few other teams for the final playoff spot, so it was commonly assumed around the league that a general had made a call to the league office. With so many teams fighting for the spot, clearing the path would not be straightforward but no one seemed to doubt it was happening. That was the other part of having a rigged game; everyone always assumed the real game was hidden, even when sometimes it actually was not.

It would never be clear whether Boss Wang bought the refs, but if he did, he must have been wondering about his investment with three minutes left in the game.

The players returned from the timeout and Liaoning took a two-point lead. This inspired the referees to send Olumide to the line for six foul shots on the next three possessions. Miraculously, he made five of them. The odds of an asteroid strike had seemed greater, given the team's poor foul shooting, but those foul shots could have been enough to finally seal the game. With only five seconds remaining, the Brave Dragons led by three points. Except Liaoning's American import, Awvee Storey, who had played a fairly awful game, caught the ball cleanly, squared to the basket, and shot a lovely 3-pointer that snapped the net, tied the game, and sent the whole compromised mess into overtime.

The binding contract that had compelled the refs to aid and abet the Brave Dragons did not seem to extend beyond regulation. Overtime began with Olumide quickly being whistled for his sixth and final foul, as was Kobe. The game was at stake, and only then did the Brave Dragons seize it. With seconds remaining, Tim Pickett isolated his man, shook his shoulders, and then rose for the winning basket. It was a gorgeous shot and the crowd leaped out of their seats. The Brave Dragons had won, 118–117. Fans rushed onto the court to engulf Pickett and it wasn't even clear that everyone realized what they had really just witnessed.

Weiss had seen the game from the trenches and later was surprised when complaints arose about the officiating. He thought both teams got calls, but his view was in the minority. The postgame news conference began with an appearance by the Liaoning coach, who appeared to have been crying. His eyes were reddened and he left after making a short statement. The room overflowed with reporters, including several who covered the Pan Pan Dinosaurs, but no one asked the Liaoning coach any questions, much less the obvious one. When Weiss arrived, he looked exhausted. He began, almost out of habit, by praising the refs for controlling what was a rough, physical game. Toward the back of the room, a young reporter began frantically waving her hand. She was one of the Liaoning reporters and had already confronted the game commissioner about the 45 fouls called against her team. The commissioner had just shrugged.

Now she was seething, her voice cracking.

"You said the referees handled this game well," she began. "Do you think it was a fair game?"

Weiss waited for Garrison to translate the question.

"It's not my job to judge the referees going into the game and after the game," he said coolly.

The rest of the room wrote down his quote, presuming the subject had now been broached and deflected. But rising out of her seat, the young Liaoning reporter was trembling and shouted something in English. "I just don't think you guys are really honest!"

"Please speak in Chinese!" warned the news conference moderator, but the reporter had already stormed out of the room.

The game would become the scandal of the week in the CBA. What followed was a discussion of corruption without ever directly mentioning corruption. There were blaring Internet headlines about the travesty of a game with 79 fouls, as if the game were a road accident with a high fatality count. But any discussion of the conditions of the road, the highway patrol charged with overseeing the law, or the quality of the drivers was muted. The Liaoning team, last season's runner-up, was now eliminated from the playoffs. They were infuriated but could only vent their rage where it was inevitably vented in China: on the Internet.

"The basketball here is very dark," Zhang Qingpeng, the star guard who had been ejected, wrote on his blog. "The sky here was gray. When you come to the arena, you find the floor is black. And the basketball is different than in other places. It is dark and black."

His teammate Yang Ming, who had played the game with a broken nose, also wrote a note to his fans:

"This is the first time after so many years of playing basketball that I can only use one word: unbelievable. The only thing I can remember is whistle, whistle, whistle. My teammates kept going out of the game, one after another. The other team kept shooting free throws, one after another. But the whistles would not stop. I hope everybody can understand. This is something we could not control."

The next day at practice I asked Joy about the refs. He laughed.

"They were good for us," he said as he exercised his knee on a stationary bike. "They were bad for them."

Why?

"Home game," he said.

A win was a win. Five games remained, three on the road, two at home. Winning five would almost certainly secure the final playoff berth. Winning four might do it. From the outside, the season had been a success, and Taiyuan fans were thrilled with the team's progress. A television poll found that 90 percent of respondents thought the team had done very well. Even Boss Wang's boldest preseason goal had been tenth place. Now the team had a shot at the playoffs.

Yet the view from inside the team was of people being fed into a grinding machine. Winning a game fortified everyone temporarily, but winning was more often confusing than clarifying. What did it validate? The offense barely existed. Against the New Century Leopards, Pan had been so confused by the conflicting orders from Liu Tie and Boss Wang that at halftime he asked not to start the second half.

"When we win, everybody is happy, but I don't know how we are winning," Joy said as he grimaced and stretched his bad knee. "I can't understand. We are not playing well. We played badly last night. It must be because the foreign players are better."

Joy stepped off the bike and wrapped an elastic band around his knee. He blamed part of his gloomy mood on his injury. He had never been seriously hurt before and had hoped leaving Guangdong for Shanxi would allow him enough time on the court to achieve his dream of being chosen as an all-star. He was the most quietly indispensable Chinese player on the team, yet his injury had cost him a third of the season, and the erratic management of the team had left him disillusioned. The all-star team had just been announced, and the team's two selections were Olumide and Kobe, the latter selection a surprise to Weiss. He thought the league had at least forty Chinese players who were better. But Kobe played tough defense against foreign stars and was one of the rare Chinese players with an athletic game. Little Ba and Duan were selected to play in the rookie game, and Wei was picked for the 3-point contest. Having five players in the all-star events was considered a validation of the season. Weiss would be a judge at the dunk contest.

On the court, the junior team was running full-court layup drills. Three passes to cover the court, no dribbling, and then a layup.

"I can't learn anything at this club," Joy said before walking off to join the senior team for practice. "We have no teamwork. I don't know what I'm doing out there. I used to work really hard at practice, and I cared very much. But now my dream has died."

The season was nearly over, and Tracy was feeling a bit forlorn. China had disarmed her. Life seemed so vibrant, so strange and wonderful at the same time. On many of her walks, she carried her camera and marveled at what she saw through the viewfinder: a grinning shirtless man with a feathery white goatee practicing Kung Fu in the middle of a construction site; a man gabbing on his cell phone as he stood on the street beside his mule-drawn cart; a grinning workman slowly pedaling a bicycle with ten-foot bundles of used Styrofoam strapped in the back; two tiny, pink-cheeked children kissing on the lips. The soap opera of the team could be grinding and sometimes difficult emotionally, especially the situation with the owner, but the *experience* of China had overwhelmed her. It was like living in some crazily wonderful carnival. In Sanya, she had met a Chinese Elvis impersonator. In Urumqi, the team had been greeted by the staff at their hotel and presented with traditional skullcaps. She and Bob had bicycled atop the ancient wall in the city of Xi'an; outside Beijing, they had climbed up the Great Wall of China, and ridden down on a goofy tourist toboggan. In Guangdong Province, they walked through a forest of twenty-five-foot-tall bamboo. When her sister, Susan, visited, they toured the national panda research institute and hugged a four-year-old panda as he licked a spoon of honey. In the foothills of the Himalayas in Yunnan Province, they slept in a farmer's guesthouse beneath the jagged peak of Jade Snow Mountain.

Food had alternately amazed and appalled her. At seafood restaurants, you would select your meal from plastic bins filled with fish or eels or shrimp. Everything was still alive. At one place, Bob had pointed to a large sea bass; he and Tracy had taken their seats, when they heard the loud *thwack* of the chef clubbing the fish. At food markets, she saw bins of centipedes, scorpions, crickets, kidneys, testicles, and more. If she had failed at something, it was her impossible assigned task of liberating and returning to the wild every animal in the Middle Kingdom, what she jokingly called her "rescue list." Which partly explains why she brought a cage into the World Trade apartments. She had been wandering downtown, shopping, when she came to an outdoor market selling live chickens, turtles, and other animals intended for the pot. In one of the cages was a small, strange squirrel trapped somewhere in the mountains outside the city. Wildlife of any sort was a rarity in much of north China; Mao had once ordered a national campaign to eradicate pests, birds, rats, and other rodents, but the pressure now came from the encroachment of development or from trappers looking for something to eat or sell. The squirrel was gray with large pointy ears, a bushy tail, and silver hair that stood straight up on his head. Weiss thought he looked like the boxing promoter Don King.

Tracy had pitied the squirrel. He was a variety of flying squirrel, which, if left in the mountains, would have hopped from limb to limb, tree to tree, in search of food. The cage had altered his natural environment without altering his nature. He still wanted to move and glide, so he did flips inside the cage. Again and again, with the consistency of a metronome, he flipped. He flipped with an alarming frenzy. The cooking pot almost seemed a more charitable fate.

Tracy bought him with the idea of returning him to the mountains before she left China. In the interim, she placed his cage inside the enclosed terrace of their apartment, and he continued doing flips. It was a spectacle, first funny, and then almost exhausting to watch him flipping to the point of exhaustion, the cage rattling with a tiny thud each time his tiny squirrel feet stuck a landing. The repetition was hypnotic, if unsettling, since the flipping accomplished nothing, as if he were trying to escape a padded cell by slamming himself against the wall.

After a while, everyone started calling him Hoppy.

Boss Wang took the ball at the top of the key and the junior team obediently parted so that he could perform unimpeded his patented herky-jerky drive to the basket. The young players were making an almost comical effort to enable their owner to have a Jordanesque pickup game. He was being granted a demilitarized zone of about three feet between himself and his defender. So on the last jerk of his herky-jerky drive, Boss Wang dipped his shoulder, scored, and grinned.

"He's too good!" exulted his teammate, a league official named Hao Guohua.

It was not clear to me why Hao was sucking up. He was about sixty, maybe 5'7", and was responsible for overseeing China's national team. He and Boss Wang were working off their lunch in front of a small crowd, including me, at the practice gym. In a few hours, the Brave Dragons would play a vital game against the Shandong Lions, and I had arranged to talk to Boss Wang about it.

Three games now remained, and while the lines of dominoes had continued collapsing, they had created paths leading in unexpected directions. The universally accepted assumption that the league would place its unseen powers in the service of Bayi had not come to pass. Or if the league had tried, the conspiracy had not worked yet. Bayi was struggling. In fact, reliable word had now circulated that an anti-Bayi conspiracy had been initiated, a resistance movement of the embittered. In particular, the coach of a team whose playoff position was already assured decided to rest his top foreign players in a game against a team fighting for a playoff spot. This allowed the latter team to win the game, which also allowed it to edge ahead of Bayi in the standings. Cheating, apparently, was being democratized.

The Brave Dragons had not yet benefited, however. They celebrated their big win over the Pan Pan Dinosaurs by squandering an 18-point lead against their next opponent, the Jilin Northeast Tigers, and losing in a blowout. Jilin was helped because the same foreign star who had fallen inexplicably ill when the team lost earlier to the Dongguan New Century Leopards had now miraculously recovered and scored 66 points against the Brave Dragons. The loss almost ended any playoff hopes for the Brave Dragons, except that the team recovered with a win two days earlier. That was when the real miracle happened.

During the postgame news conference, Journalist Li and another reporter suddenly burst into the room shouting: "Bayi has lost! Bayi has lost!" No one could believe it. Not only had Bayi lost but so had Beijing and Shandong, the two other teams fighting for the last playoff spot. The Brave Dragons still trailed in the standings but could clinch a play-off spot by winning their last three games, assuming Bayi lost at least once. But, most of all, they had to win. One Brave Dragons loss meant they were out.

The pickup game was now over, and Boss Wang sat down and started changing into his street clothes. Hao was laughing and smoking a ciga-rette as he pulled on his long underwear, pants, and top, and palmed his hair into place. He shook hands with Boss Wang and left for the arena. The game started in less than two hours.

I asked Boss Wang about the Brave Dragons' chances. "Not good," he said solemnly, his hair wet with perspiration. "You saw what happened yesterday."

He was referring to practice the previous day. Everyone had been feel-ing pretty good, since the team had won the night before and gotten itself back into the playoff picture. A group of fans had come to the practice gym with a large banner to celebrate. They unfurled the banner on the court and posed beneath it with the team. No one seemed to notice as Boss Wang arrived at the opposite end of the gym. The fans left, and Liu Tie convened the players, talking about the game the night before and what the team had and had not done well. After about ten minutes, Boss Wang wandered across the court, hands in pockets, head down, and stopped at the edge of the huddle, listening, waiting. Finally, Coach Liu asked if he would like to speak.

Yes, Boss Wang said, he would. He started shouting at the coaches and the players, mocking Liu for focusing on offense, excoriating everyone else for losing their edge.

"You're talking about offense!" he shouted. "You're talking about defense! But none of that matters. Look at you! None of you are prepared to fight! None of you are ready!"

He worked himself into such a fury that his chest began to shake and his body trembled as he walked back to the seats on the opposite side of the court. The players seemed terrified and silently formed their stretching circle. Coach Liu approached the owner, but Boss Wang stood, stripped off his jacket, and took over practice. He grabbed Big Sun and showed him how to slam his body into a defender on a drive. This was supposed to be a light workout, a day before a critical game, but Boss Wang yelled at everyone to scrimmage and slash hard to the basket. He walked with his hips cocked, like a gunslinger, pushing players into position. Players were crashing into one another. Pickett tweaked his bad ankle. Little Ba got kicked in the knee.

Now, a day later and barely two hours before the game, Boss Wang had pulled on his knit shirt and checked his watch. He had not changed his opinion. "The players and the coaches are not ready," he told me. "They were taking pictures."

He paused, dripping with sweat. "Mentally, they have lost their spirit and their confidence. They don't have the will to fight."

The gym was empty and his voice rose against the silence. He was frustrated that the team lost the 18-point lead in the game against Jilin; it was a failing of character, evidence of a weakness he could not tolerate. He blamed Coach Liu. "After Bonzi left, Liu Tie took charge again," he said. "I think the team lost spirit and the coaches never got them back."

He stood up and started pulling on his trousers. Frustrations and suspicions spilled out of him. He was certain that the league was trying to thwart him, to somehow stop his team from making the playoffs. He was suspicious of Coach Liu. Boss Wang had distrusted other Chinese coaches, and now he wondered if Liu had an agenda, if he even truly wanted the team to qualify for the playoffs. They had already exceeded the goal of fourteenth place. Maybe he didn't want expectations set too high for next season? He had reinstated Liu Tie after Bonzi left, as a way to give him experience for next season, but the young coach had disappointed him.

"He's arrogant," said Boss Wang. "He doesn't listen. He resists too much.

"It's Chinese culture. American people are very straight. They just say what they are thinking. You can never tell what Chinese people are thinking. So you need to look at what they are doing."

We talked a few minutes about that night's game and then about Bonzi. I asked him which of the three Americans in his opinion best suited the team. He suddenly smiled. "Bonzi helped the most," he said. The problem was integrating him into the team. His level was too high and "some players couldn't understand his level. The rest of the players couldn't reach that point. That type of player has his own character. He knows how to help the team and you don't have to tell him. He doesn't want you to control him."

He turned and looked me directly in the eye and, unsolicited, addressed the festering sore of the season: when he hit Kobe. "We had different ways to help Zhang," he said. "I'm like his grandfather. Sometimes I kick him or punch him. But I'm trying to help him. Bonzi tried the American way. I tried the Chinese way.

"I could tell Bonzi really cared about the team," he said. "But my way is the Chinese way. He's my kid. By beating him, I'm trying to help him. To make that point."

We were done. It was 6 p.m., and he wanted to speak to the team before the game. He finished by telling me that Chinese culture was very complicated and that I would need to live here for ten years to understand it. He didn't seem impressed when I mentioned that I had already lived in China for six years. Chinese never say what they are thinking, he repeated. You need to see what they are doing.

Earlier that day, a rumor circulated among the Chinese players. Someone had seen Tim Pickett having a meal with the Shandong team. It was no secret that his brother-in-law, Mack Tuck, played for Shandong, but eating with the opposing team seemed unusual, if it were actually true, which maybe it was and maybe it wasn't.

When the team met for the usual morning shootaround, everyone was in a tetchy mood and still unsettled by Boss Wang's tirade the day before. The Chinese players staggered as much as they ran. Everyone looked exhausted and beaten down. Olumide wondered if the owner had an ulterior motive for his screaming. Maybe he didn't want the team to make the playoffs because it would save him money, since Olumide would get a $50,000 bonus.

Shandong used a zone defense, and Coach Liu spent a half hour trying to explain a play to free up a shooter on the wing for a 3-point shot. When Weiss made a suggestion, Liu called the team together, explained the suggestion in Chinese, describing it as "a good idea," and then instructed the team to keep doing it his way. Weiss was fuming as he and Garrison left for the security meeting in the Hawaii Room.

At the meeting, a league official introduced himself. He had been sent because this was an important game and the league did not want any problems. He warned the officials to call a fair game. He reminded the coaches not to do anything to discredit the league. And then he turned back to the referees to remind them that the league trusted them, but if only a single person lost that trust, then the reputation of the whole league would suffer.

Garrison interpreted the official's warning as an ominous sign. This was a home game. The refs were supposed to be in our corner. Now maybe they wouldn't be.

"Tonight," Ren Hongbing shouted into his microphone as the crowd started to scream, "is the last home game for Shanxi!"

The crowd was arriving late, as usual, and the cheerleaders on the court in their halter tops. They had brushed blue glitter onto their eyelashes and tossed their parkas onto the floor. Everyone rose for the national anthem and solemnly did not sing. Olumide loped over to the penalty box and high-fived his personal trainer, Ogoh. Pickett and Mack Tuck embraced near midcourt. Everyone was bumping shoulders. Tuck asked the referee for the ball. He wanted to feel it. He rubbed it in his palms, turning it in his fingers before flipping it back to the ref. Olumide walked to the midcourt circle opposite the Shandong center, Samaki Walker, the former Laker. They stared upward into the lights, crouched, eyes wide. The ref raised his thumb in the air and then held the ball above them for an instant. The arena was silent, expectant, and then the ref tossed the ball in the air and the two big men jumped after it.

Kobe had drawn Mack Tuck and swatted the ball out of bounds. Tuck had a temper, and Kobe was harassing him, getting under his skin. His confidence was soaring after his all-star selection and he slashed to the basket for a score. Tuck complained to a ref that Kobe was kicking him. A fan in a Brave Dragons jersey jumped up and yelled at Tuck in English: "Fuck you!"

The Brave Dragons were ferocious but sloppy. Pan turned the ball over. Big Sun turned it over. Samaki Walker pushed Shandong ahead with a few nice baskets. He was as calm and professional as everyone else was not. Kobe was stalking Mack Tuck, and Tuck was mouthing off, and the refs separated them as the crowd shouted at Tuck. The refs tried to bring Kobe and Tuck together to shake hands, but Tuck refused and started jawing at the fans behind the basket. The first quarter ended with Shandong leading 25–20.

Boss Wang was very wrong. They cared. They wanted to win. They just had to stop turning the ball over.

Shandong extended its lead to 34–29 in the second quarter and the Brave Dragons inserted Joy, Little Ba, and Duan into the game with Olumide and Pickett. Joy immediately changed the tenor of the game. He made a basket and followed it with a steal and assist to Duan. Pickett made a nice pass to Little Ba for another basket and the margin was now one point. Pickett started to find his shot, making two 3-pointers, thrusting out his chest and waving his arms. Brave Dragons led 41–39.

"Let's go!" Ren Hongbing shouted over the microphone.

Pickett was now guarding his brother-in-law. Every time Tuck touched the ball, the crowd was on him, shouting "Fuck you! Fuck you!" Tuck walked to the edge of the court and shouted back. Duan roared in for a breakaway but was hammered by Samaki Walker, who probably outweighed him by 100 pounds. Duan was splayed on the floor, rubbing his hip, as the crowd berated Walker and the Taiyuan press corps screamed in protest. Walker and Duan talked and shook hands. Now there were seconds remaining and the Brave Dragons raced to half-court and tossed up a prayer at the halftime buzzer. It went in. They led 50–46. Pickett topped all scorers with 24 points.

After halftime, Pickett came out of the locker room cold, missing his shots, and became more passive on offense. Shandong regained the lead, until Joy and Little Ba began hitting 3-pointers. Then came a moment that would help decide the Brave Dragons' season: Mack Tuck was bulling down the lane, raising the ball toward the basket, elbows extended, as Joy and Pickett converged to stop him. Pickett suddenly dropped to a knee, holding his head as if he had been struck. He was slowly shaking his head, cupping his skull in his hands, as he walked down the sideline to the bench. The Brave Dragons led 79–78 as the quarter ended.

The final quarter began with Duan making a 3-point play. But the spectacle was on the sideline. Pickett was sprawled on the floor, writhing in pain, holding an ice pack to his head. On the court, Joy stole the ball and dished to Olumide for an 84–80 lead as Ren Hongbing hit his soundboard for the Wave. The whole arena was rising and falling and shouting, and a minute later, Joy scored again.

"Ji Le!" screamed Ren Hongbing. *"Wo ai ni!"* Joy. I love you.

Shandong closed the gap to a point, 88–87. Weiss walked over to talk to Pickett, who was still on the floor beside the bench. Shandong was now pushing ahead. The Brave Dragons were sapped. They were turning the ball over and taking bad shots. Pickett slowly rose and the crowd began chanting his name. But he dropped to a knee and remained on the floor. Olumide made two foul shots to regain a one-point lead. Garrison walked over to Pickett, carrying a message from Boss Wang: Play and you'll get a double bonus for the game.

Five minutes and forty-seven seconds were remaining. Joy was fouled hard by Samaki Walker and made both free throws. Tie score, at 92. The crowd was jeering Shandong. A fan tossed a plastic bottle on the court. Pickett staggered to the scorer's table.

"Tim," shouted Ren Hongbing in English, as the crowd exploded. "I love you!"

Pickett was not himself. He moved in a daze, holding his head. Then he grabbed his tweaked ankle. He missed badly on a shot. Kobe got fouled hard, and the arena was boiling. More plastic bottles were tossed onto the floor.

"Please stop!" Ren Hongbing announced. "You are Shanxi people!"

Five minutes, twelve seconds left. The Brave Dragons led 94–92. Tuck had an awkward left-handed shot and had missed most of his 3-pointers, but now he made one to put Shandong ahead. Pickett could not respond. The crowd was chanting "Tim, Tim!" but he was staggering around as Shandong made another 3-pointer to lead 98–94. Weiss called a timeout. Little Ba checked in for Pickett, who took an ice pack and sat down on the floor near the bench. Boss Wang was pointing at him, furious, gesturing for him to return to the game.

Mack Tuck walked over to the Shanxi bench and confronted Boss Wang.

"Leave him alone!" Tuck screamed. "He's hurt. He would play if he could. You come in here and play! You come in here!"

One minute was remaining. Shandong led 101–96. Unthinkable news rippled across press row: Bayi had lost. The path for the Brave Dragons was almost cleared. Olumide was fouled and got two shots. He made both. The score was 101–98. Shandong called timeout with forty-nine seconds left. Coach Liu and Weiss were on the court together, talking to the players as Boss Wang remained on the bench, legs crossed. The coaches were calling for a press.

Shandong inbounded the ball and struggled to move it across midcourt in the required ten seconds. Mack Tuck picked up his dribble and was swarmed. He was trapped, with nowhere to go, but he had to hurry. And that was when the season was decided: Tuck took a step. Then another step. And then a third. No call! Weiss was shouting for a travel, but the whistle didn't come. Tuck tossed the ball down the court ahead of the defense for an easy layup. Shandong was now ahead 103–98. Thirty-six seconds were left.

Boss Wang walked down the sideline to the game commissioner. He was shouting at him, screaming, and the fans were screaming behind him. Then he drove his foot into the advertising board in front of the scorer's table. The sound was as sharp as a gunshot. The deluge followed: plastic water bottles, lighters, crumpled paper cups, even cell phones. Fans were screaming and throwing everything in their pockets.

The referees tried to keep the game going. Pickett, back in the game, missed a 3-pointer. More bottles banged onto the court. A Shandong player was fouled and went to the free throw line even as ball girls and ball boys were on the court with brooms, trying to sweep up the mess. More cups and bottles rained down.

"You are Shanxi people, right?" Ren Hongbing asked, desperately. "Please stop!"

But Boss Wang's signal had been clear. The game was fixed. The fans behind the basket in Brave Dragons jerseys were pelting cups on the floor as a chant filled the arena. *"Hei Shao! Hei Shao!"* Black whistle! Black whistle!

The Shandong coach pulled his players off the court. Police trotted onto the floor and formed a perimeter. Pickett was on bended knee. Ball girls were frantically pushing brooms over the court. Weiss was waving to the fans, gesturing for them to stop. Twenty-seven seconds remained and Shanxi trailed by only five. There was still a chance. But this was almost a riot. The Shandong player shot his foul shots as the ball girls kept sweeping. The deluge of plastic kept falling.

Now the refs wanted to run out the clock, so the game and the cleanup were under way at the same time. Tuck had to shove a ball boy out of his way as he ran down the floor. Tracy was sitting in the penalty box shielding a friend's child, trying not to get hit by any objects. There were maybe forty people on the court, not counting police, and finally the clock expired. Shandong won, 107–101.

The police began to move out the crowd. The arena was suddenly silent, except for the sound of cups and lighters hitting the court.

Trust is the essential intangible of any human experiment. Trust accrues from shared experience, mutual respect, and common purpose, and if it germinates, if it takes hold, it can create a reservoir of goodwill as strong as the foundation of a building. You give the benefit of the doubt to someone you trust if something goes wrong, if something seems a bit fishy. But someone you don't trust falls into a different category. You might think the worst of that person when something goes wrong, if something seems strange, even if you cannot prove it, even if it is not true. One thing Tim Pickett had never earned from his Chinese teammates, rightly or not, was trust.

The players trotted into the locker room after the buzzer sounded. Police were still on the court and had blocked off part of the hallway outside the locker rooms. The Shandong team was trying to leave the arena, but Shanxi fans had surrounded their bus, screaming and throwing things. Inside the locker room, the Brave Dragons were already furious when Boss Wang arrived in a rage and confronted Pickett, pointing at him and accusing him of throwing the game. A teammate shouted in his face, "Fuck you! You got paid!" Boss Wang kept shouting, and Pickett shouted back, furious that the team was turning on him.

"You guys can't even understand each other," Garrison said, intervening. "Let me translate."

But Boss Wang punched Garrison twice in the kidney and shouted for Pickett to leave. Big Sun started edging Pickett out of the room, when Olumide walked through the door and defused the situation by speaking to Big Sun.

"I told him not to touch him," Olumide would tell me the next day.

The foundation of the building had crumbled. Pickett and Olumide walked back to the pink sofas on the court. When Weiss returned from the news conference, he went to find them and took a seat beside Tracy on the team's empty bench. His eyes were red. Tracy was at the verge of tears.

Everyone wanted to leave, but they had to wait for the bus. The bus never left until Boss Wang finished screaming, and behind the closed door of the locker room, he was still screaming.

In the silence, the Shandong players walked onto the court. One player was piggybacking an injured teammate. They were sneaking out of the arena through a side entrance where a different bus was waiting.

"Call my translator!" Mack Tuck shouted to Pickett. "Am I gonna come to you or are you gonna come to me?"

"Tell them to bring the money!" Pickett yelled back, sarcastically.

Ten minutes passed. A few members of the cheerleading team had changed into street clothes and were sitting on the sideline. Then the sound of a door and Boss Wang strutted onto the court, shouting at Olumide and Pickett to return to the meeting. They walked back to the locker room with Weiss, but the meeting was over. The Chinese players were gone.

Boss Wang sat down beside a few of the cheerleaders. He was grinning, seemingly embarrassed, and then he started to laugh. Everyone laughed with him.

CHAPTER TWENTY

TENTH PLACE

The next morning, it seemed the season was over. The Brave Dragons had missed the playoffs, probably to the relief of CBA officials, who couldn't have relished the prospect of a nationally televised home game in Taiyuan, given the near riot of the previous night. The league levied a fine of 150,000 yuan, or about $22,000, the third fine of the season against the Shanxi team for fan infractions or owner misbehavior. Technically, a third fine represented a red line that, if crossed, could have meant expulsion from the CBA. Boss Wang and Zhang Beihai were summoned to the league office in Beijing to do their penance.

The next morning, Olumide was on the telephone at his desk in Little Nigeria, trying to finalize where next he would take his talents. He usually went to Puerto Rico, which amounted to detox after China, with fewer games, less pressure, and plenty of time to sit on the beach. "It *eees* like a vacation!" Olumide said. But agents had also contacted him about teams in Belgium, Israel, and a new option, Iran. An Israel-Iran bidding war seemed possible. He was open to either team. Now all he wanted was to get out of Taiyuan. He was still owed the final payment of his contract and he wasn't planning to do anything that might give cause for him not getting it. Practice was in a few hours.

"If they ask me to run 100 miles today," he said, "I'll run it."

Everyone awoke with a bitter aftertaste. The petri dish now seemed cracked into two pieces. The Chinese players had already built a circumstantial case against Tim Pickett. Most of them would tell me later, privately, that they believed Pickett had faked his injury. No one had any proof, but the players were still suspicious because Pickett had eaten with the Shandong players and because he had admitted that the Shandong translator offered him money not to play.

That was enough to convince them. Pickett was furious. Yes, he had eaten with the Shandong team, but only because he was supposed to eat with his brother-in-law, Mack Tuck. When he arrived to collect him, Tuck was already eating at the hotel with his teammates. He simply sat at Tuck's table. Yes, the Shandong translator had offered him a bribe not to play—but he said he refused. Losing had cost him money, he said, since Boss Wang had offered him a quadruple bonus for a win and since his contract would have paid him a bonus for making the playoffs.

"I just want to get my money and get out of here," Pickett told me later. "This place is crazy. I've never been in a place like this before."

Olumide now found himself in an unlikely position. Pickett had frustrated him as a teammate. He thought he was selfish, gunning too much and passing too little. During one game, Olumide had shouted toward the Shanxi bench: "He can't shoot all the time! We're all here! We're a team!" But if he resented Pickett on the court, he disliked the idea of ganging up on him off it. He thought Pickett was immature and had disrespected his Chinese teammates, but that they, in turn, were now too eager to make him a scapegoat. He thought they might try to gang up on him later, so he put out the word: Do not touch him. That would be enough.

"Five more days," he sighed as he gathered his shoes, ready to go down to catch the bus to practice, checking himself. "No, four more days."

The Chinese players were already circled around Coach Liu when Weiss, Olumide, and Pickett walked into the gym. A few players nodded at Olumide. No one acknowledged Pickett. "Last night, you had a great game," Liu Tie said, speaking softly. "We lost, but it was the best that you have executed. Although we lost, do not be sad or disappointed. We will take our victory."

Liu nodded to Weiss and asked if he wanted to say anything. Weiss did. He stood with his hands behind his back, speaking as Garrison translated. He told the players that he admired them for overcoming so much adversity. They had to adjust to three different leading scorers as well as four coaching changes between himself and Liu Tie. They had shown resilience and character and he told them to be proud of their effort. He then smiled and alluded to the owner's postgame tirades. "Liu Tie has the toughest coaching job in the world," he said. "Mine wasn't quite as bad because I didn't understand Chinese."

Everyone laughed.

Two games remained, one in Qingdao and the other in Hangzhou. Months earlier, Boss Wang had announced his goal for the season at Media Day: tenth place. In private, he had promised to pay the Chinese players bonuses worth 20 percent of their salaries if they finished tenth. Now, they still could, if they could win their last two games.

The team had won 24 games and lost 24. There was something to play for, after all.

The air smelled of the sea. A morning fog rolled over the city, shrouding the red-roofed buildings of the old German concession, but now the sun was shining down on Qingdao's No. 1 bathing beach. No. 1 was the city's most famous beach, a horseshoe of orange sand along the Yellow Sea where summer crowds easily reached 70,000 people on a narrow strip less than a third of a mile long. It was still chilly enough in mid-March that the crowds were small, and I found Weiss and Tracy in what might be described as the Muscle Beach section. Nearby on the sand were a few sets of dumbbells and barbells. Eight muscular guys in tiny bathing suits were standing in a circle, doing headers with a soccer ball. Their average age was probably fifty-five.

Garrison was down the beach, searching for shells to give his girlfriend, as Tracy and Bob were watching the middle-aged musclemen jab their heads at the soccer ball. The hangover from the Shandong loss had still not dissipated, and Tracy was especially melancholy. What had been the experience of a lifetime, a chance to dive into another culture, another world, had suddenly exposed how difficult it was to truly do that. Things seemed soured, as if a trust had been broken, or, worse, as if maybe it never had been truly earned. She didn't want to leave China with anyone doubting how much she loved the people she had met.

We bought soft drinks and sat on a bench near the barbells. Only gradually did we notice the man looking at us. He had thick salt-and-pepper hair, combed to the side, Western-style, and he kept staring at us, edging closer, until finally he was standing beside us. He was wearing a tiny, gold-colored bathing suit and was probably in his early sixties. I asked in Chinese if he were from Qingdao. Yes, he came to the beach every day, he answered, and then began speaking in very rough English. He was interested in philosophy and developing a moral outlook on life. Tracy wondered if he were a philosophy professor. I wondered if he were a member of the banned antigovernment spiritual sect, Falun Gong, secretly canvassing for new members.

We kept looking at the ocean. Ten minutes passed. We weren't certain quite what to do with him. He kept staring at us, smiling, yet quizzical. He was examining us more than befriending us. Finally, we noticed Garrison in the distance and found our excuse to leave. Tracy and Bob started walking, and I stayed behind to wish the man well.

"May I ask you one more question?" he asked, suddenly speaking in broken English. "Are you a wesp?"

"A what?"

"A wesp."

I cupped my ear and leaned toward him. He repeated the question, and I told him that there was no such thing in English as a wesp.

He seemed disappointed, so he spit out the letters one at a time. "W-A-S-P."

I had misunderstood. He slowly elaborated on his question. "Are you a white, Anglo-Saxon Protestant?" he asked.

"Yes, I am," I said.

He seemed immensely happy, as if he were a birder who after years of searching had finally spotted a very rare species. I mentioned that Germans had helped found Qingdao a century ago and wondered if he might have some German somewhere in his blood. He knew nothing about the Germans who had once built many of the yellow houses still ringing this beach. No, no, he answered. His mother came from the countryside, as did his father. They were just Chinese peasants. Nothing rare about them, he said. He thanked me and walked to the edge of the water. He lifted his arms into the sky, arched his head upward, and let the warm rays of the sun fall over him.

I caught up with Bob and Garrison, while Tracy slogged through the shallow water to join a couple throwing a stick to a golden retriever. I could see them nodding and laughing, somehow communicating despite being unable to communicate, and Tracy tossed the stick to the dog for half an hour before returning. The game was in a few hours, and we were about to leave, when we heard someone shout.

"Hey, Bao-bu Wee-Suh! Jia you, Shanxi!" Hey, Bob Weiss! Let's go, Shanxi!

Weiss turned to see a Taiyuan contingent running across the beach.

Red Guardian was in the lead, and Red Heroine was right behind him. Ren Hongbing was parking the bus. Forty-six fans had driven fifteen hours overnight for a game that supposedly no longer mattered. They were elated, laughing, pulling off their shoes to let the sand seep between their toes. This was the first time many of them had ever been to the beach or seen the ocean other than on television or in a photograph. Wang Hui, a doctor who walked with a cane and wore a team jersey, hobbled toward Weiss, hurriedly stabbing his walking stick into the sand, a huge smile on his face.

Everyone hugged and posed for photographs and laughed at the improbability of it all.

"How can we leave them?" Tracy asked.

Wingtips rose during the pregame meeting to deliver a message from Boss Wang to Tim Pickett. The owner wanted Pickett to know how much he personally liked and appreciated him. Pickett was a great player, the owner thought, and the team wanted him back for next season. Then Wingtips sat down.

"Amazing what he'll say to try to win one game," Weiss told me later.

Practicality was trumping enmity. Pickett was threatening to sit out, arguing that his head was still ringing. The distrust had softened a little. A teammate approached him at practice to apologize, but Pickett walked away. The owner and the general manager wanted to win the last two games, and not having the team's leading scorer would be a big handicap. Zhang Beihai had asked Weiss to persuade Pickett to play for the sake of the team. Weiss had discarded any pretense of a pep talk.

"Are you going to play?" he asked.

"I'm not sure," Pickett had answered.

"Well," Weiss said, "if you don't play, they may not pay you."

Pickett would play.

It would be one of the team's best performances. Five players scored in double figures, led by Pickett with 41 points. But the highlight was the Taiyuan crazies. The forty-six Taiyuan fans sat behind the basket with matching team scarves tied around their heads, Samurai-style. Ren Hongbing stood at the edge of the group, shouting out cheers, beating a small drum, and when the Brave Dragons started moving into a big lead, he even led the Taiyuan fans in the Wave.

When Bob Weiss coached in the NBA, a friend in the league had once offered him a little pep talk, a rationalization really, about overcoming the disappointment of losing a game in the final seconds. The friend said: What if you froze the game right before that deciding moment? How would the game then be remembered? If you felt good about how your team had played before that final shot, then shouldn't you also feel good about your team after that shot? No matter whether it went for or against you? The game itself, after all, is much more than one shot.

So now the game hung on the final shot. Ten seconds remained. If you had asked Bob Weiss at that moment about his team's performance, he would have felt pretty good. This was a game the Brave Dragons were supposed to lose badly. After their victory in Qingdao, they had traveled to the city of Hangzhou for their season-ending game. The Hangzhou team had already qualified for the playoffs and had whipped the Brave Dragons earlier in the season. Really, no one placed too much faith in Boss Wang giving out bonuses for finishing tenth. This was playing out the string. Yet the players came out with unexpected emotion. Hours before the game, Weiss had called a meeting that everyone assumed would be to review game film. Instead, Tracy had presented a twenty-minute slide show of the season after first reading a letter to the players. When they turned on the slide show, there was the season: photographs of every player and coach, including the departed Donta, Bonzi, and Big Rus. Zhang Beihai. Boss Wang. Trainer Yuan. The accountant. The ladies who swept the courts. The angry old guy who opened the gate. Even me.

"Your warmth, kindness, and love have filled each day with laughter and tears," Tracy had read aloud, before choking up and handing the letter to Garrison so he could finish translating it. "I will miss each of you so very much. Each of you, in your own special way, has given me a clear memory of China. You are not just an experience I have had, but are now a part of who I am."

Then just an hour before the game, Boss Wang rushed into the locker room. No one had known whether he was coming, and his sudden arrival apparently surprised the female general manager of the Hangzhou team. She hurriedly presented him with a gift of Longjing tea, wrapped in newspaper. He considered it an unconscionable affront.

"If she didn't know I was coming and had apologized for not having a gift, then that would have been fine," Boss Wang told me later. "But she thought that was a gift! That team looked down on us. They didn't think we were good and didn't take us seriously. I told our players that we had to fight. We had to beat them!"

Love or fury. Compassion or vengeance. How could anyone know which speech worked?

But while the Hangzhou team had not expected much of a contest, the Brave Dragons came out as if they were playing for first place. Little Ba and Duan streaked down the court, slashing to the basket. Olumide was a rebounding machine. The Brave Dragons fought to within a point and then had the ball with less than twenty seconds remaining. Liu Tie called a timeout to design a play for Pickett. The ball was inbounded to Pan, who dribbled at the top of the key, waiting for the play to develop. But the pass was never made to Pickett. Pan later said that the defender had blocked off Pickett, and maybe that was true, but it was certainly true that the game would not now rest in Pickett's hands.

Pan kept dribbling as the clock ticked down. He had seemed to wither as the season wore on. No one took more criticism than Pan; he needed to be Chris Paul or Steve Nash, but he wasn't. Yet when he judged his own game, he could be merciless, too. He needed to direct the team better. He needed to handle the ball better. He needed more confidence. Now, as his teammates moved around the court, he looked in vain for someone open. Thirteen seconds were left. At ten seconds, Pan made his move, down the side toward the basket. The defender pressed against him, but Pan kept going. Now he had jumped into the lane, into the banging bodies of the big men, having taken the game into his own hands. He leaned into his defender and then separated himself, tossing the ball one-handed toward the goal. Weiss and Coach Liu stared at the basket. The Brave Dragons rose off the bench. Boss Wang looked and waited. The ball clanged off the rim, bouncing along its edge. The big men stared up at the basket, positioning, jostling, waiting. The ball seemed to linger. Until it fell in.

When the buzzer sounded, the Brave Dragons screamed and shouted and piled onto a joyous scrum at midcourt. They celebrated as if they had won a championship.

Or maybe they celebrated because, finally, the season was over.

EPILOGUE

The Shanxi Brave Dragons finished the 2008–09 season in tenth place, with 26 wins and 24 losses, one of the most dramatic turnarounds in the history of the Chinese league. A few days after the season finale, more than a hundred hard-core Brave Dragons supporters filled a German-themed bar in downtown Taiyuan for Fan Appreciation Day. The Brave Dragons cheerleaders led a few cheers, and someone opened a few bottles of *baijiu*. Ren Hongbing blasted music and introduced Boss Wang as "the Mark Cuban of China," a comparison with the NBA's most controversial and mercurial owner that may or may not have been a compliment. Ren Hongbing's siblings Red Guardian and Red Heroine led the crowd in chants of "*Jia you! Jia you!*" Once the speeches began, Kobe thanked the fans for their support, Zhang Beihai proclaimed the season a major success, and Bob Weiss, now something of a folk hero in Taiyuan, offered a few words, too.

"I want to thank you as fans," Weiss began, as Garrison translated. "You are the wildest fans in the league. I know this because we have the most fines!" There was a silent moment as Garrison translated the joke and then the crowd laughed, if a little nervously. "Thank you for your support," Weiss concluded. "I saw you in many different cities. And you truly did help us when we played at home." Then he told another joke about how they helped by chucking lighters—but Garrison smoothed that one over in translation. There was more music, and enough *baijiu* flowing that a misty Pickett confided to me that he might come back next season if Olumide and Weiss came back, too. When the party finally broke up, Ren Hongbing played a techno rendition of the dance classic "Please Don't Go," and none of the players did. They loitered around the bus for about an hour as Boss Wang chewed out the general manager about something.

The following season Boss Wang broke up the nucleus of the team. Liu Tie left to coach a lower-division team in western China; he knew Boss Wang had soured on him and he also knew that he wanted to work for a different kind of owner. Liu Tie had started the year as a despot but had tasted humility. He and Weiss departed as friends, if not necessarily future coaching partners. Tim Pickett failed to catch on with an NBA team and became a high-scoring guard for another team in China. Olumide also returned to China, though not to the Brave Dragons. His old team decided he was big enough, after all. Olumide helped lead the Liaoning Pan Pan Dinosaurs back to the playoffs and also helped them deliver a few payback pastings to the Brave Dragons. He continued playing around the world, diving for loose balls and performing like a warrior for any team willing to pay his price. I can still hear him telling me how the Chinese system left players without *ohpe*. He never lost his.

Bonzi Wells was still in Muncie, hoping to make it back to the NBA, and also salvage his reputation. By 2011, Bonzi was coaching local teenagers and described himself as humbled to a hometown sports columnist. "Being humbled was the best thing for me," he promised. A few months later, his alma mater, Ball State University, inducted him into the school's Hall of Fame. Boss Wang's experiment with Bonzi initially persuaded the Brave Dragons to bring back the player Bonzi had replaced, Donta Smith. In Australia, Donta had led his team to a championship and been named most valuable player of the playoffs. He returned to Taiyuan, but he and Boss Wang soon clashed, and Donta moved to a different Chinese team. The Brave Dragons started the 2009–10 season with three wins and 10 losses and were again reduced to an inept afterthought when Boss Wang shook things up: He signed Stephon Marbury, a onetime NBA all-star who had bounced between different teams and experienced an especially turbulent tenure as a New York Knick. In his NBA career, Marbury had earned tens of millions of dollars while gradually devolving from a major star into a major head case. He had squabbled with coaches and posted some strange YouTube videos, including one in which he supposedly ate Vaseline. He was so unpopular with the Knicks that the New York *Daily News* described him as "the most reviled athlete in New York." Boss Wang was not deterred; he told reporters that Marbury's signing was "a reward to our fans." It could have been another Bonziesque mismatch, yet Marbury embraced Taiyuan, which embraced him back. Marbury's main purpose in China was to promote his Starbury line of basketball shoes; Boss Wang had apparently promised to help him crack the China market and hook him up with a local manufacturer. Yet Marbury played hard, didn't complain, and didn't hesitate to sign autographs or pose for photos with fans. Though the Brave Dragons finished the season with a losing record, Marbury described his Taiyuan experience as "nothing but love," and agreed to a three-year contract that would supposedly keep him in Taiyuan until 2013.

Instead, Marbury returned to Taiyuan and was summarily dumped without a contract by Boss Wang. Marbury was crestfallen, reportedly sobbing in his hotel room, though soon enough he signed with a new team in southern China and continued his pursuit of a global shoe empire. Money was reportedly an issue in dropping Marbury. By 2010, Boss Wang had fallen off the *Forbes* rich list in China, though it was hard to say if he had gotten appreciably poorer or if others had simply gotten richer. I last saw him at the practice gym a few days after the tenth-place-clinching win. He played a few games of pickup ball with the players—somehow managing to win every game—and then he stripped off his shirt, lines of sweat dripping down his chest, still relishing the comeuppance his team had delivered to the Hangzhou general manager and her shoddily wrapped gift.

"That team looked down on us," he said. "They didn't think we were good, and they didn't take us seriously. And I know they got to the referees. But we beat them. That game made me feel better about the whole season."

He paused and smiled. "I like revenge on people who disdain me and look down on me," he said.

We walked to the canteen, and Boss Wang bent over a bowl of noodles. He had barely eaten during the past four days. He almost never traveled with the team, and I imagined him racing frantically around China in his Mercedes, chasing his team, so possessed and focused that he would forget to eat. Earlier that season, I asked the basketball insider Xu Jicheng about Boss Wang, and Big Xu smiled. He knew the stories, as did almost everyone in the league, and knew how strange Boss Wang must seem to a foreigner (and to many Chinese), yet Big Xu considered him more a symptom of the moment. He was part of the first generation of Chinese that had tasted money and were able to use it to pursue their dreams, dreams often shaped by the West. He wanted to use modern methods,

Big Xu said, but he remained an old-school Chinese boss. He believed in toughness, in hard work, and that his word should be unchallenged, since it was his team. It was a generational thing, Big Xu thought. The next generation would be better.

The NBA still saw China as integral to the league's future but was beset by problems there and at home. In July 2011, the NBA locked out its players after the expiration of the league's collective bargaining agreement. Negotiators for the players' union and the owners hunkered down for a fight, and without anything to do, a few NBA stars decided to tour China. Paul Pierce of the Boston Celtics played a few exhibition games and was seen coughing on the court from the cigarette smoke. Other NBA stars like Carmelo Anthony and Chris Paul toyed with jumping to the CBA for the season, until CBA officials banned teams from signing any NBA players who had not been free agents before the lockout. This was a pity, because Boss Wang had reportedly offered a contract of $1.5 million per month to, yes, Kobe Bryant. Doctored photos of Bryant in a Brave Dragons uniform had circulated on the Internet. I can only imagine Kobe and Boss Wang playing one-on-one.

By November 2011, NBA owners and players finally cut a deal to end the lockout, salvaging most of the season. As for the NBA's ambitions in China, the league still continued to do a fine job of selling air. The NBA remained the most popular sports league in China, and continued to sell corporate marketing partnerships, television contracts, and jerseys. It still had perhaps the best model in professional sports for extracting money out of almost anything, even if the Great Recession made it harder to extract money from people who had less of it. But the NBA was facing other challenges in China. The once-grand vision of NBA Cities and hundreds of NBA stores never really materialized; fewer than a dozen NBA stores were opened, and not a single NBA City was built. The league's plan to manage a network of arenas across China also soured. It had stadiums in Beijing, Shanghai, and Guangzhou but no more. Nor did it have regular basketball games to put in those stadiums. The NBA's plans for a league in China were put on indefinite hold. Like the YMCA a century earlier, the NBA was learning its limits in China, or at least it should have been.

The CBA improved its financial position, partly because of Ma Guoli's ability to pull in more sponsors. The Guangdong team continued to dominate on the court. It won the championship after the 2009 season, followed by successive championships in 2010 and 2011. Bayi continued its steady decline and became a national embarrassment in August 2011 when the players got into an ugly brawl during a "goodwill" exhibition game against the visiting collegiate team from Georgetown. No one in the CBA would have been surprised that the fight was sparked, partly, by the fact that the officials appeared to be blatantly cheating on behalf of Bayi.

The biggest news in Chinese basketball was Yao Ming's retirement from the NBA in 2011. Only 30 years old, Yao could never overcome nagging injuries. If this placed him in the company of several other over-sized NBA centers who succumbed to injuries, Yao also was beaten down by years of endless practices and games in the Chinese system. He was truly a great basketball ambassador and his retirement signaled a new era in Chinese basketball, as more people began arguing that the old system needed to be changed. Yao himself may end up being part of the solution; the Shanghai Sharks, faced with ruin, had sold marketing rights and management control to Yao before his retirement. Yao hired an American coach for the Shanghai team, overhauled the roster, and the Sharks made the playoffs for two years running. The American coach needed a good interpreter, and the Sharks hired Garrison Guo, who skipped from Tai-yuan to Shanghai with glee. He had a new girlfriend who was now his fiancée. He was also the interpreter for China's national team.

Bob and Tracy Weiss did not return to Taiyuan. They spent the following season in Seattle, finally managing to sell their home. Bob was tickled that the buyer was a doctor originally from Taiwan. He was still feeling the tug of China when the Shandong Lions offered him their head coach job for the 2010–11 season. Weiss jumped at it, and he and Tracy spent the season in the eastern city of Jinan. Weiss's assistant turned out to be Mack Tuck, the brother-in-law of Tim Pickett and the villain of the crushing loss that had ended the Brave Dragons' playoff chances. Tuck turned out to be a great guy. The Lions were facing a rebuilding year, hav-ing lost several of their best players, and they started poorly. But slowly they improved, moving into playoff position behind a slick Chinese player named Sun Jie. His Chinese coaches had deplored Sun Jie as too rebel-lious, too American, but under Weiss he became one of the top scorers in the league. Then, with four games remaining in the season, Sun Jie went down with an injury, as did the team's top American player. The Lions lost all four games and slipped out of the playoffs.

Tracy finally managed to make good on her rescue list. She adopted a puppy in Jinan, a nine-month-old golden retriever named Bode, and took him back to Seattle. She and Bob have friends across China, including

Joe, who quietly left the Brave Dragons after their season and was now working, happily, as an interpreter for another team. Weiss was sixty-nine but didn't seem interested in retiring. He had feelers out for a possible assistant's position in the NBA, but he also thought he might keep coaching in China, assuming a team needed a former NBA coach who understood the place. When Weiss returned to Taiyuan as head coach of the Flaming Lions, he brought Boss Wang a nicely wrapped gift, a framed photograph of Boss Wang and his grandson. Weiss considered it a gesture of appreciation.

The Chinese owner seemed touched and had something for Weiss, too: an offer. He said Weiss was the only coach he could trust. He wondered if he would consider returning to the Brave Dragons.

Weiss listened, mildly flattered.

He said he was keeping his options open.

My final day with the Shanxi Brave Dragons came after the season-ending win against Hangzhou. I had finished my last talk with Boss Wang, and the players had left the practice facility for a short break. The gym was strangely empty, the orange dormitory silent. Outside, the wind was blowing and the air was still cold and the only sign of life was inside a small cage, left on the ground near the front gate.

It was Hoppy, the flying squirrel saved by Tracy. She had asked the team to release him back into the mountains. She wanted him to be free. But he was still in his cage, making one mad flip after another, his tiny feet sticking each landing, flipping and flipping and flipping, to the point of exhaustion.

ACKNOWLEDGMENTS

I can't recall precisely when Jon Kaufman suggested I write a book about Chinese basketball, or why I took the idea seriously. I'm not certain Jon ever did. Jon was the bureau chief in Beijing for *The Wall Street Journal*, who, while discussing book ideas with me one day, tossed out an unexpected one. "Why not basketball?" he asked. Jon soon returned to the United States but his idea stayed with me. When he later visited Beijing, I excitedly told him I had followed his advice. He paused for a moment, obviously having forgotten what advice I was thanking him for. And then he brightened and congratulated me, if also offering condolences, since I was far from done. So I begin the many thanks I owe many people by thanking Jon, a generous soul, who was there at the beginning, whether he remembers it or not.

I'm still astonished at how that conversation led to this book and am so grateful to the many, many people who helped me along the way. My agent, Amanda Urban, thought me neither deluded nor deranged when I arrived at her apartment in New York in the fall of 2008 and presented her with a 5,000-word proposal that I had started drafting during the flight from Beijing. She has been an unflagging advocate, and I'm immeasurably grateful. The folks at Knopf embraced my quirky idea and helped shape it with meticulous care. Jonathan Segal believed in this book and his careful editing saved me from myself more times than I care to admit; I couldn't have asked for better. Thanks also to Joey McGarvey.

I'm especially grateful to *The New York Times*, where I've worked for more than fourteen years and which continues to set the standard for the highest quality of journalism. Bill Keller gave me a leave to work on this book and then didn't fire me once I returned to my day job as a foreign correspondent while still juggling the final writing on the book. Susan Chira was a friend, advocate, supporter, and keenly incisive reader, as well as a terrific boss. In the *Times'* China bureaus, I learned invaluable insights from my friend and now boss, Joe Kahn. Chris Buckley was a terrific tutor on China and great fun to hit the road with. David Barboza, as good a friend as anyone could ask for, gave me wise, gentle advice after reading an early draft. Jake Hooker was a terrific traveling companion and sounding board.

I never could have covered China, or have come close to understanding it, without the help of my Chinese colleagues, especially Zhang Jing, Huang Yuanxi, Michael Zhao, Michael Anti, Zhao Yan, Chen Yang, and Du Bin. I also want to thank Keith Bradsher in Hong Kong, as well as Michael Wines and Sharon LaFraniere, who followed me in Beijing and fielded occasional requests for help after I had relocated to India. In India, I'm grateful for the goodwill and forebearance of Hari Kumar, Lydia Polgreen, Vikas Bajaj, Heather Timmons, and PJ Anthony. I'd also like to thank the staff of the Jawaharlal Nehru Memorial Museum & Library in New Delhi, where I spent many long weekends finishing the manuscript.

I began writing this book in China and initially lacked an office. Thanks to Lisa Minder-Wu and Wu Er Tao for providing me a perfect one on the outskirts of Beijing—a room attached to a greenhouse behind their restaurant, The Orchard. I lived in Beijing for six years and could not have undertaken this project without the support, advice, and encouragement of many friends and fellow journalists. Thanks to John Scales and Vivian Nazari; Tony Lee; Wang Tao and Louis Kuijs; Nicole and Malcolm Pruys; Charles Hutzler and Jen Schwerin; Mark Magnier and Karen Ma; Mimi Kuo-Deemer and Aaron Deemer; Phil Pan and Sarah Schafer; and Ching Ching Ni. Nathan and Kristi Belete were our adopted family in China (and India) and I owe them more than I can ever repay. Rebecca Blumenstein and Alan Paul were enthusiastic cheerleaders and great friends. Matt and Ellen Carberry are forces of nature. And I especially want to thank Stuart Schonberger and Carmen Dicinque for their friendship and support. Stuart, a China hand of nearly three decades, was a wise reader whose enthusiasm and skepticism helped me a great deal.

I also benefitted from the generosity of several China scholars and experts. David Shambaugh of George Washington University played college basketball in Beijing; his enthusiasm was contagious and his shrewd comments on the manuscript were invaluable. Susan Brownell, a leading

Western expert on Chinese sports, also gave me great advice and saved me from a few dumb errors. Zhao Xiaoyang at the Chinese Academy of Social Sciences helped me understand the role of the YMCA in China. Zhu Ying offered smart advice on CCTV. Wenfang Wang's research on the teaching of English in China was useful. Anne-Marie Brady was an enormous help in explaining Mao's early policies toward foreigners.

Jeanne Moore, a repository of China knowledge and a *Times* editor, gave me great advice and encouragement. Jing Jun, a fellow basketball nut as well as a leading scholar, made insightful comments on the draft. Michael Meyer, author of *The Last Days of Old Beijing,* offered sparkling advice and probably could have written this book better than I did. Michael Shapiro, McKay Jenkins, and Harvey Araton also were generous with their comments and time. Brook Larmer, author of *Operation Yao Ming,* represents the gold standard for Westerners writing about Chinese hoops; I drew upon his book for my chapter on Shanghai. Judy Polumbaum, a China scholar, also shared her terrific work with me on Chinese sports. And I also drew upon the work of Andrew D. Morris, author of *Marrow of the Nation: A History of Sport and Physical Culture in Republican China.* Arthur Kroeber helped me understand the Chinese steel industry. Sidney Rittenberg tutored me on Mao's use of foreign experts.

Special thanks also go to Joseph Torigian, Owen Fletcher, and Liz Peng for their great work translating the Chinese sports. Tyler Duffy was a big help on background research about Bonzi Wells. Thanks to Steven Shukow for drafting the book's China map.

Writing about Chinese basketball for me meant immersion in an altogether new and different ecosystem in China. It was more fun than I ever could have imagined. I benefitted from the insights of many helpful people, including Xu Jicheng, Zhang Weipeng, Yang Yi, Terry Rhoads, Chris Renner, Bruce O'Neil, Frank Sha, and others. I'm grateful to the folks at Li Ning, who offered insights into China's push to develop homegrown brands. Li Yuanwei, the recently retired commissioner of the CBA, granted me an interview, while other CBA officials also made time for me. Ma Guoli offered a unique perspective. I met with different team owners, Chinese journalists, interpreters, players, and others; to all of you, many, many thanks.

Most of all, I want to thank the Shanxi Brave Dragons. Wang Xingjiang, or Boss Wang, allowed me to be a part of the team and never hesitated to give me his unvarnished opinions. The coaches and players welcomed me and gave me shelter; at different times, I lived with Bob and Tracy Weiss, Olumide Oyedeji, and, for a few nights, I even managed to slip into the dorm for the Chinese players. Thank you all.

I was also fortunate to draw upon a lot of expert advice closer to home. I am from a family of journalists. My mother, Rosemary Roberts, taught me to write as a little boy, and I'm so grateful for the lifetime of love and support she has given me. My father, Jonathan Yardley, has been this book's most steadfast reader and biggest supporter. I could not have done it without him. My brother, Bill Yardley, offered me the best advice of anyone at a particularly dark hour in a long writing process: "Just quit," he said. It was the laugh I needed. I also want to thank my stepmother, the remarkable writer Marie Arana; and my mother-in-law, the remarkable editor Jennifer Blakebrough Raeburn. Much love and gratitude also goes to my stepfather, Don Boulton; to Barbara Livieratos and Vlad Marinich; and to my brothers-in-law, Cole and Alec Livieratos. Cole and Alec, I owe you each a street oyster.

Finally, I want to thank my wife, Theo, and my three children, Olivia, George, and Eddie. This book consumed three years of our lives, across three countries, and I am so grateful for your love, patience, and good humor. To Theo, I love you dearly. To Olivia, George, and Eddie, I promise to stop disappearing on weekends.

New Delhi, India
September 2011